Insufficient Funds

Insufficient Funds

Savings, Assets, Credit, and Banking Among Low-Income Households

Edited by Rebecca M. Blank and Michael S. Barr

The National Poverty Center Series on Poverty and Public Policy

Russell Sage Foundation

The Russell Sage Foundation

Library of Congress Cataloging-in-Publication Data

Insufficient funds : savings, assets, credit, and banking among low-income households / Rebecca M. Blank and Michael S. Barr, editors.
    p. cm.
  Includes bibliographical references and index.
  ISBN 978-0-87154-078-2
  1. Financial services—Case studies. 2. Low-income consumers—Case studies. 3. Finance, Personal—Case studies. 4. Households—Economic aspects—Case studies. I. Blank, Rebecca M. II. Barr, Michael S.
HG1601.I67 2009
332.1'7—dc22

                                                                                    2008046478

The paper used in this publication meets the minimum requirements of American National Standard for Information Sciences—Permanence of Paper for Printed Library Materials. ANSI Z39.48-1992.

Text design by Suzanne Nichols.

RUSSELL SAGE FOUNDATION
112 East 64th Street, New York, New York 10065
10 9 8 7 6 5 4 3 2 1

This book is dedicated to Ned Gramlich,
our friend and colleague, who fought tirelessly
on behalf of low-income households
and whose voice is present throughout these pages.

Contents

About the Authors

MICHAEL S. BARR is professor of law at the University of Michigan Law School.

REBECCA M. BLANK is Robert S. Kerr Senior Fellow at the Brookings Institution and a research associate at the National Bureau of Economic Research.

RAPHAEL W. BOSTIC is professor of economics and director of the Master of Real Estate Development Program at the University of Southern California.

DARYL COLLINS is senior associate at Bankable Frontier Associates in Boston.

KWAN OK LEE is a graduate student in policy, planning, and development at the University of Southern California.

RONALD J. MANN is professor of law at Columbia Law School.

JONATHAN MORDUCH is professor of public policy and economics at New York University's Wagner Graduate School of Public Service.

SENDHIL MULLAINATHAN is professor of economics at Harvard University.

UNA OKONKWO OSILI is associate professor of economics at Indiana University—Purdue University Indianapolis.

ANNA L. PAULSON is a senior financial economist at the Federal Reserve Bank of Chicago.

DANIEL SCHNEIDER is a graduate student in sociology at Princeton University.

JOHN KARL SCHOLZ is professor of economics at the University of Wisconsin, Madison, research associate at the National Bureau of Economic Research, and former director of the Institute for Research on Poverty.

About the Authors

ANANTH SESHADRI is chairperson and professor in the Department of Economics at the University of Wisconsin, Madison.

ELDAR SHAFIR is professor of psychology and public affairs at Princeton University.

MICHAEL SHERRADEN is Youngdahl Professor of Social Development and director of the Center for Social Development at Washington University in St. Louis.

PETER TUFANO is Sylvan C. Coleman Professor of Financial Management and senior associate dean at Harvard Business School.

Chapter 1

Savings, Assets, Credit, and Banking Among Low-Income Households: Introduction and Overview

Michael S. Barr and Rebecca M. Blank

Low-income individuals often lack access to the sort of financial services that middle-income families take for granted, such as checking accounts, bank loans, or easily utilized saving opportunities. High-cost financial services, barriers to saving, lack of insurance, and credit constraints increase the economic challenges faced by low-income families. The contributors to this volume analyze the financial constraints and choices of low-income families and describe the ways in which low-income families utilize financial services, through both formal and informal financial institutions. In these chapters, they also discuss policies that would spur the private sector to provide financial services that allow low-income families a better chance to achieve more stable economic lives.

Access to affordable financial services and opportunities to save and build assets are important to the lives of low-income families, who must deal with sometimes abrupt fluctuations in income that occur because of job changes, instability in hours worked, medical illnesses and emergencies, changes in family composition, and many other factors. If these families have limited access to savings, credit, or insurance, even small income fluctuations may create serious problems in their ability to pay rent, utilities, and other bills.

Unfortunately, access to mainstream financial institutions is often limited for low-income families. For many low-wage individuals, take-home pay is reduced by the high transaction costs they face when using financial services. Inadequate access to financial services may diminish the value of government income transfer programs such as the Earned Income Tax Credit (EITC) and increase the administrative costs for government and compliance costs for households in filing their tax returns and receiving refunds.

Limited access to mainstream financial services can also limit the ability of low-income families to build assets and save for the future. Savings are important because they help to smooth short-run income fluctuations. Savings can also provide capital for important long-term investment opportunities. For instance, middle- and upper-income families regularly use their savings to invest in educational opportunities, in the health of family members, in homeownership, and in pension funds for retirement.

Thinking cohesively about the financial service and wealth accumulation needs of low-income households is important because these areas are functionally related. Financial institutions can provide the necessary transactional services as well as the opportunities for saving and credit. Savings are needed to access credit, which can then assist with asset accumulation. Imprudent credit usage, however, can undermine asset-building and block access to future savings. As we shall see, some families that are even quite poor use credit and saving, although often through informal mechanisms.

The chapters in this volume provide greater understanding of these issues and present new evidence on assets, debt, and saving among low-income families. The volume includes chapters on financial services, credit card usage, and homeownership. Several chapters discuss the emerging literature in behavioral economics, which uses insights from psychology to understand saving, debt choices, and the financial behavior of low-income families. One chapter compares the financial behavior of poor families in the developing world and that of low-income families in the United States, while another chapter focuses on immigrants in the United States. Many of the chapters discuss policy changes that could address current problems.

This introductory chapter takes on four tasks. In the first section, we provide an overview of how low-income families manage their economic lives, highlighting key issues that are important in the choices that low-income families make in their use of financial services, saving, and credit. In the second section, we summarize the chapters in this volume, emphasizing their primary conclusions and contributions. We close that section by highlighting a few of the key themes that emerge across chapters.

The third section puts forth a single cohesive presentation of key policy options that would provide low-income individuals with better financial services and encourage better financial decisionmaking. Our view is that financial services policy for low-income households is ripe for reform. This section relies heavily on the policy discussions in later chapters but is not limited to those options; we emphasize the most promising new policies that would increase the financial stability and opportunities available to low-income families. In the final section, we discuss the research agenda, noting areas where academic research, data collection, and demonstration projects could enhance our understanding of the choices of low-income families and the effectiveness of different policy options designed to improve their financial lives.

The chapters in this volume were commissioned by the National Poverty Center at the University of Michigan, with funding from the Office of the Assistant Secretary for Planning and Evaluation within the U.S. Department of Health and Human Services. A grant from the Ford Foundation also provided important support for this project, including the conference held in October 2007 that launched this volume. We thank both of these funders for their generous support and insights on this project.

FINANCIAL SERVICES, SAVING, AND CREDIT USE AMONG LOW-INCOME HOUSEHOLDS

This section provides a brief overview of some of the financial service, saving, and credit issues that affect the financial choices faced by low-income households.

Financial Services

Low-income families are less likely to hold bank accounts and more likely to face high costs for transacting basic financial services through check-cashers and other alternative financial services providers (Barr 2004). High-cost financial services and inadequate access to bank accounts may undermine the widely shared societal goals of reducing poverty, moving families from welfare to work, and rewarding work through incentives such as the Earned Income Tax Credit.

Nearly 25 percent of low-income American families—those earning under $18,900 per year—are "unbanked," that is, they have neither a checking nor a savings account (Bucks, Kennickell, and Moore 2006). Even among moderate-income households earning between $18,900 and $33,900 per year, nearly 13 percent lack any bank account.

In lieu of bank-based transactions, saving, and credit products, low- and moderate-income households often rely on the more costly alternative financial services (AFS). AFS providers offer a wide range of services, including short-term loans, check-cashing, bill payment, tax preparation, and rent-to-own products, most often in low-income urban neighborhoods. AFS providers are the only source of basic financial services for many low-income persons, but those services come at a high price.

For example, while check-cashers offer essential services, the fees involved in converting paper checks into cash are high relative both to income and to analogous services available to middle- and upper-income families, such as check deposit into a bank account or electronic direct deposit. Check-cashing fees vary widely across the country and between types of checks, but they typically range from 1.5 percent to 3.5 percent of face value. The industry reports that it processes checks totaling more than $55 billion annually (Barr 2004).[1] Almost all of these checks are low-risk payroll (80 percent) or government-benefit (16 percent) checks (Bachelder and Ditzion 2000). While even payroll checks are not without some credit and fraud risk, average losses from "bad" checks at check-cashing firms are low and compare favorably with interbank rates (Barr 2004).

Surprisingly, it is not just the unbanked who use alternative financial services. Many low- and moderate-income families with bank accounts regularly rely on high-cost nonbank providers to conduct much of their financial business—such as cashing checks, buying money orders, or taking out payday loans (Barr, this volume; Rhine et al. 2001). We might think of these families as "underbanked."

The high costs of alternative financial services raise several concerns. First, the costs of these basic financial transactions reduce take-home pay. A worker earning minimum wage, working full-time, and making under $12,000 a year might pay $250 to $500 annually to cash payroll checks at a check-cashing outlet, in addition to fees for money orders, wire transfers, bill payments, and other common transactions (Bachelder and Ditzion 2000; Kennickell, Starr-McCluer, and Surette 2000). High fees for tax preparation and filing, check-cashing, and refund anticipation loans reduce the value of EITC payments by over 10 percent (Barr 2004; Berube et al. 2002). Bringing low- and moderate-income families into the banking system can help reduce these high transaction costs, substantially increasing the purchasing power of these families.

Second, without a bank account, low-income households face key barriers to saving. Promoting low-income household savings is critical to reducing reliance on high-cost, short-term credit, lowering the risk of financial dislocation resulting from job loss or injury, and improving prospects for longer-term asset-building through homeownership, skills development, and education.

Third, without a bank account, it is more difficult and more costly to establish credit or qualify for a loan. Holding a bank account is a significant predictor of whether an individual also holds mortgage loans, automobile loans, or certificates of deposit (Hogarth and O'Donnell 1999). Although there are many reasons why some low- and moderate-income households lack a bank account, the financial and nonpecuniary costs of account ownership are important in their decision to become and remain unbanked. Despite the need to understand how the decision-making process of low- and moderate-income households interacts with these external constraints, there is little research to inform us about how these households make decisions about bank account ownership or about the kinds of financial products that they would find attractive and in which they would participate.

We do know that checking accounts are ill suited to the needs of many low- and moderate-income households. Bank accounts are not structured to be low-cost and low-risk for low-income households. Financial institutions find low-balance accounts expensive (Barr 2004) and frequently require high minimum balances, credit checks to open accounts, high bounced check and overdraft fees, and long check-holding periods. Such accounts are not designed for the lives and finances of low- and moderate-income households that live paycheck to paycheck.

Some low- and moderate-income households have had a bank account in the past but were unable to manage their finances. Households that have had past problems with their accounts are listed in the Chex Systems, a private clearinghouse that most banks use to decide whether to open accounts for potential customers. Thus, not only does their own experience with high and unexpected fees as bank customers in the past keep some low-income households from opening an account, but they may also be formally barred from doing so by the Chex Systems. The minimum balance requirement on many checking accounts is another significant barrier for low-income households. Moreover, banks, unlike check-cashing outlets, sometimes hold checks for several days before crediting the deposit of funds; for low-income customers, this wait may not be practical.

These features of traditional bank accounts partially explain why many low- and moderate-income households are unbanked or underbanked. In addition, formal financial institutions are often less prevalent in low-income neighborhoods than alternative financial services providers (Temkin and Sawyer 2004). Still, for some households, non-economic factors, such as mistrust of financial institutions, may matter, and immigrant households often face documentation barriers to account ownership. Lack of financial education may also play a role in these choices.

Saving and Assets

Low-income families are less likely to hold significant savings or assets (Scholz and Seshadri, this volume). These families often find it difficult to save and plan financially for the future. Living paycheck to paycheck leaves them vulnerable to medical or job emergencies that may endanger their financial stability, and their lack of savings undermines their ability to invest in improving their skills, purchasing a home, or sending their children to college.

Just as many low-income households are effectively excluded from mainstream financial services, so too are these families largely excluded from society's mechanisms to encourage saving. These families often lack access to even basic institutional saving vehicles. Two-thirds of tax benefits for pensions go to the top 20 percent of Americans, while the bottom 60 percent receive only 12 percent of the tax benefit (Summers 2000). Most low-income workers either work for firms that have no savings plans or are not covered by such plans (Orszag and Greenstein 2005). As we mentioned previously, 22 percent of low-income households lack a bank account, a critical entry point for saving (Barr 2004). And given the low levels of assets among low-income households, most banks have historically not wanted these customers. Thus, saving among low-income households is depressed by the lack of sufficient income to afford saving and the lack of supply in savings products for the poor, coupled with the low rates of return offered to the poor given their low levels of wealth.

Yet evidence suggests that some low- and moderate-income households can and do save. For example, a high portion of low- and moderate-income workers participate in 401(k) plans if offered the chance to do so (Orszag and Greenstein 2005). In the 1990s, some 73 percent of federal employees earning $10,000 to $20,000 participated in the Thrift Savings Plan, as did 51 percent of those earning under $10,000 (U.S. Department of the Treasury 1998). About 30 percent of families in the bottom income quintile saved in 2000 (Aizcorbe, Kennickell, and Moore 2003). Automatic enrollment in employer-sponsored pension plans boosts participation and asset accumulation among low-income employees, as well as among African American and Hispanic employees (Choi et al. 2002; Madrian and Shea 2001). When welfare benefit asset limits are raised, low-income households may respond by saving more, although the empirical evidence is mixed (Hurst and Ziliak 2006;

Nam 2008; Sullivan 2006). This evidence provides some support for the notion that low-income households can save and that savings are shaped at least in part by the institutional mechanisms that encourage saving.

Low-income households may have different uses for their savings than middle-income and upper-income households. For example, Social Security covers a substantial share of low-income households' retirement needs, and it may be impractical to expect poor households to set aside more out of their current income for retirement. Yet there are many purposes for which low- and moderate-income households need savings, including housing acquisition and improvement, education, key life events, and emergencies. These households need easily accessible mechanisms through which to save and may need help in building up their savings. Many low-income households have been able to build up sufficient savings, for example, through homeownership. For some households, homeownership provides a means to build equity over time, as well as residential stability and economic security; for other households, the homeownership choice and the debt undertaken to purchase a home may be less beneficial, as Raphael Bostic and Kwan Ok Lee (this volume) make clear.

Low- and moderate-income households have lower savings and fewer assets to fall back on in an emergency. At the same time, these households have difficulty obtaining insurance for important life risks, including medical needs, divorce, and job loss. Insurance helps smooth consumption and protect asset accumulation while also preventing or minimizing cascading shocks. For example, an auto accident without insurance can lead to a job loss, which can have devastating consequences for family finances. Given insurance constraints, saving for precautionary reasons may be important for low-income households. At the same time, given income constraints, regular saving may put a heavy burden on consumption or contribute to high-cost borrowing for the poorest families. Government insurance programs might help by making it unnecessary for families to rely solely on self-insurance through savings.

Credit

Many low- and moderate-income households use an array of short-term and long-term credit products, provided by a range of institutions, both formal and informal. Alternative credit products include payday loans, tax refund anticipation loans, pawnshop loans, rent-to-own products, and secured credit cards. Some households use bank overdrafts regularly, at high cost, while others use credit cards, which often charge high interest rates and high fees. Some households have access to home mortgage and home equity loans, including loans from both prime and subprime lenders, as well as automobile loans and consumer loans backed by car titles. Again, these sources of credit for many low-income households are often costly. In addition, short-term credit products, such as payday loans, are structured in a way that makes it easy for households repeatedly to overborrow, and many subprime home mortgages are structured to disguise their true costs

(Barr 2004, 2005, 2007.) At the same time, credit access may provide an important insurance mechanism for low-income households facing emergencies and may provide an important means for smoothing consumption in the face of income volatility.

In our view, abstract debates about whether credit access is welfare-enhancing or welfare-reducing miss the point. Research on human failings in decisionmaking suggests that credit access through misleading products and inducements to over-borrow can be welfare-reducing (Barr, Mullainathan, and Shafir 2008), just as credit access through straightforward products can in principle be welfare-enhancing. Policy needs to focus on how to move the market toward provision of welfare-enhancing products and services. To that end, we explore several policy options in the final section of this chapter.

In sum, low- and moderate-income households are underinsured and financially underserved. They often lack savings, rely on expensive, short-term credit (formal or informal), and have limited access to formal financial services of the sort that many middle-class families take for granted. Only recently, and on a small scale, have some financial institutions begun to offer banking accounts and other services tailored to the needs of low-income households. Moreover, regulatory gaps often leave low-income families unprotected in credit transactions, and national saving policies focus heavily on the needs of middle- and upper-income Americans. As a result of these public- and private-sector financial service failures, low- and moderate-income households face barriers that can make it difficult for them to advance economically by effectively managing their financial lives. The chapters in this volume provide a better understanding of these problems and explore policy options to improve the situation.

THE RESULTS AND FINDINGS IN THIS VOLUME

The chapters in this volume range across a broad set of topics. They provide information on the use of financial institutions, savings, debt, and assets, based on the best data available. Some of the authors have tabulated information from existing data sets; others present results from original data newly collected from low-income communities. In interpreting their data, the authors compare their results against different theories about how low-income households make financial decisions and about the constraints they face. Finally, the authors relate their work to current policy debates, indicating the ways in which their evidence supports certain policy approaches.

Here we summarize the key results from these chapters in the order in which they appear in the volume. We start with three chapters that describe the financial lives of low-income households using national data sets, original survey data from a micro-study in metropolitan Detroit, and a comparison with financial diaries from low-income families in the developing world. We then turn to a chapter that utilizes behavioral economics to glean insights into these patterns. The final four chapters discuss public- and private-sector savings strategies, asset-building efforts, the costs and benefits of homeownership, and credit card usage among low-income families. The volume concludes with a chapter on the unique financial issues faced by immigrant families.

Summary of the Chapters

In chapter 2, John Karl Scholz and Ananth Seshadri present a portrait of the financial holdings of lower-income families. They introduce the two nationally representative data sets with significant wealth information, the Survey of Consumer Finances (SCF) and the Survey of Income and Program Participation (SIPP), and provide comparative information from both of these data sets throughout their chapter. Both data sets show a reasonably similar picture of asset holdings among lower-income households.

Net worth among families in the bottom quintile of the income distribution (that is, the poorest 20 percent of all households) has increased slowly. In 2004 (SCF data), 80 percent of bottom-quintile households reported positive net worth, compared to 71 percent in 1962, and the value of net worth among those who held it rose from about $74,000 to over $92,000 (in 2004 dollars). Both financial assets and stock holdings, two primary components of net worth, increased among lower-income families, while housing showed relatively little long-term trend. While assets grew, so too did debt. For example, credit card debt increased, although the share of lower-income households reporting serious credit problems, through 2004, was quite steady.

Scholz and Seshadri make a particularly valuable contribution in their chapter by using cohort analysis—tracing wealth holdings among specific age cohorts in the population as they age. In general, net worth grows within a cohort as it ages, and each cohort has done a little better than the last. Many of these gains, however, are concentrated among households headed by college-educated adults. It is striking how small the gains are over time among lower-income households, and particularly among African American households. The authors include a useful analysis and discussion of the research on why wealth among black families is so low.

Scholz and Seshadri conclude with a discussion of the question of how much lower-income households should save. They suggest that extensive savings among lower-income families may not be the best use of their money, given pressing needs for daily expenditures, and that government safety net and social insurance programs should be preserved and expanded to protect low-income families from serious economic shocks.

Chapter 3 by Michael Barr describes the use of financial services among lower-income families. This chapter is based on information from a unique data set collected by Barr in a survey of over one thousand low- and moderate-income families in the Detroit metropolitan area. These data provide detailed information on the financial services utilized by these families.

The results suggest that existing financial services, credit, and payment systems impose efficiency costs on lower-income households, increase their costs of credit, and reduce their opportunities to save. Like their higher-income counterparts, Barr argues, these lower-income Detroit households regularly conduct financial transactions, but the financial services system is not designed to serve them well. In his survey, about 30 percent of the adults were unbanked. A substantial share of these adults indicated that lower fees, less confusing fees, or more convenient bank hours and locations would make them more likely to open an account. Barr shows that households use a range of formal and informal mechanisms to meet their financial service needs. A surprisingly large share (65 percent) of those with bank accounts had also used money orders in the recent past, as had 77 percent of the unbanked. Money orders, pawnshops, and payday lenders appear to complement formal financial services for many of these households, who commented on their convenience and ease of use.

There was significant variation in saving patterns. About one-third of these families contributed to savings each month, while 42 percent said that they never saved. Savers were more likely to be employed and to have more education. Many of those who didn't save reported that they found it difficult to live on their current income. They were also more likely to have health expenses. When households faced a large expenditure need, they got help from family and friends, borrowed money, or spent down assets. Slightly less than 20 percent reported that they were in deep financial trouble.

After a detailed description of the financial lives of these families, Barr closes the chapter by discussing strategies to transform the financial services system to better serve low- and moderate-income households, including tax credits for banks that serve low-income customers and policies that make it easier for low-wage workers to utilize bank accounts and savings plans.

Chapter 4 by Daryl Collins and Jonathan Morduch complements Barr's chapter by providing a comparative perspective on the financial lives of the poor in another country. Collins and Morduch use detailed information on the finances of a sample of households in several South African areas. Because these families were interviewed once every two weeks for more than a year, these authors had much more information than is typically available from the usual cross-sectional survey of financial behavior. They argue that many families in this data set were at about the same income level as families in the bottom quintile of the U.S. population.

The households described in Collins and Morduch's chapter were active financial managers. Their gross cash flows over the year were often much larger than their net cash available at any point in time, a point that cross-sectional data fail to uncover. Like the lower-income populations that Barr describes, these families used both informal and formal financial instruments, not just because formal financial services were not available, but also because the informal arrangements were sometimes better suited to their household's cash flow needs. For instance, many families participated in "savings clubs" in which a group of people would contribute a set amount of money each month to a club "pot." Each month one member received the entire pot of money. This system provided a large amount of cash at a particular point in time, and social pressure to contribute one's appropriate share to these savings each month was strong.

Nonetheless, despite the availability of informal mechanisms such as these, Collins and Morduch note the need for better mechanisms to support savings and credit. In many cases, the savings mechanisms used by these households did not allow them to smooth over negative income shocks or to meet large cash demands (such as funeral or wedding expenses). Their need was less to invest in business (the aim of many micro-enterprise credit schemes) or to build long-term assets than to smooth consumption in the face of uneven income flows and to meet occasional spending needs that far exceeded their normal monthly income. Additional flexible credit and unstructured savings mechanisms would allow them to round out their financial portfolios to address these unmet needs.

While the previous two chapters provide a picture of financial decisionmaking among low-income families, Sendhil Mullainathan and Eldar Shafir use the tools of behavioral economics to develop a larger theoretical framework by which to think about savings and financial decisionmaking, especially among lower-income households. In chapter 5, they argue that low-income households exhibit the same fundamental biases and weaknesses in financial decisionmaking that are found among middle- and upper-income households, including being affected by context and situational factors and using simplified mental accounting techniques. Such human failings cause households to make easily predictable mistakes in utilizing financial services, in their saving behavior, and in their use of credit.

These insights suggest that the institutional contexts within which financial decisions are made may matter a great deal. These contexts shape behavior through the ways in which they offer choices. The authors argue that setting up the right institutional structure is particularly important for low-income families because they have little financial slack in their lives. Small mistakes in decisionmaking can cause much greater economic problems for them and their families than small mistakes do for higher-income families. For instance, a minor car accident requires mechanical work before the car can be used again; without a buffer stock of savings to make this bill affordable, the family has no functioning car, and the working adult in the family could experience job loss after being late for work for several days. Indeed, because small economic problems can have disastrous consequences, it may be entirely rational for lower-income families to engage in high-cost financial transactions, such as payday loans. It may be better to pay the costs of acquiring the short-term loan than to take on the problems that ensue without this small cash infusion.

Of course, such institutional contexts can be altered through private and public policies. Mullainathan and Shafir indicate a number of ways to make it easier to save and harder to undertake welfare-reducing transactions. For example, as in Barr (2004, 2007), the authors argue that the EITC should be directly deposited into households' bank accounts. They also argue for a range of savings policies that are automatic unless a person explicitly opts out of them. They suggest steps that the private sector could take to make it easier for low-income households to sign up for bank accounts, such as having a bank officer present at volunteer tax-filing sites. In short, the behavioral perspective in this chapter both explains the financial decisions of many low-income households and offers a framework by which to design policies to improve these decisions.

The remaining chapters focus on specific topics in financial decisionmaking. Peter Tufano and Daniel Schneider discuss policies to increase savings among the poor in chapter 6, which follows closely from the previous chapter, since Tufano and Schneider use behavioral economics to indicate why certain policy approaches are likely to be more successful in generating additional savings.

A goal of the Tufano and Schneider chapter is to develop a typology of savings policies. Hence, they discuss a range of policy approaches that have been tried, starting from coerced (mandated) savings plans such as Social Security. They discuss policies that make it hard to avoid saving, such as employer-sponsored savings plans that automatically enroll workers unless they opt out, and they discuss plans that make it easy to save, such as programs sponsored by tax preparation companies that encourage taxpayers to deposit a percentage of their refunds in savings accounts. Other policies bribe people to save through savings matches, such as those provided by individual development accounts (IDAs); create social mandates to save, such as the savings clubs discussed earlier; or make saving exciting, such as lottery-linked savings plans.

This chapter is particularly creative in thinking broadly about the problem of savings policy and about public and private strategies to improve savings outcomes, and it is particularly useful in describing some dimensions by which to judge the effectiveness of different approaches. Tufano and Schneider conclude that savings is hard work, particularly in a consumption-oriented society. Our retail and financial institutions are largely designed to make it easy to spend money, not to make it easy to save money. Some of the suggested policies in this chapter would alter that bias.

Michael Sherraden continues the focus on savings policy in chapter 7. Sherraden is less interested in short-term savings and more interested in long-term savings for the purpose of acquiring assets such as a home, a college education, or an adequate retirement nest egg. Over the past decade, a wide variety of communities have experimented with IDAs, and a number of these experiments have been evaluated by researchers. IDAs are matched-savings plans aimed at low-income households. Sherraden uses data from the American Dream Demonstration of IDAs to discuss the success of IDA efforts and to develop a broader theory about the policy components that are important to encourage asset development among lower-income households.

The most important message from the IDA experiments, claims Sherraden, is that the poor can save regularly if provided with greater incentives. About 52 percent of those enrolled in IDAs were "successful savers," meaning that they had net savings of $100 or more at a specific point after the beginning of the program. The most common use of IDA savings was to finance homeownership or home repair. The evidence suggests that while higher match rates did not induce higher savings, the "match cap"—the savings level beyond which matched dollars were no longer provided—did matter. Families in the IDA experiments seemed to take the match cap as a goal for their savings, so those facing higher match caps saved more. Financial education of up to ten hours also seemed to increase savings.

Sherraden notes many positive effects of IDAs but also indicates that the way in which they were operated by community nonprofit organizations (with relatively few savers at each site) made them quite costly. To be successful as a national policy, IDAs would have to be implemented in a different way. The IDA experiments do suggest that more than savings incentives are needed to encourage saving among the poor. Programs should facilitate savings (through such practices as direct deposit), set high expectations (through something like match caps), and help educate low-income households about financial decisionmaking and savings. The chapter ends with a discussion of national savings initiatives that might make sense for the United States to consider as a way to encourage greater asset accumulation among low-income families.

The biggest asset many families hold is their home. In chapter 8, Raphael Bostic and Kwan Ok Lee explore homeownership among lower-income families. They discuss the data on homeownership levels, noting a significant growth in homeownership over the past decade not in the first quintile of household income but in the second quintile, composed of lower-middle-income families. Much of this growth is related to the expanded availability of credit through subprime loans.

Bostic and Lee provide an informative discussion of the benefits of homeownership, such as decreased residential mobility and greater wealth accumulation through housing equity growth, and contrast this with the potential risks, including the potential for accumulating no wealth and becoming trapped in a deteriorating community. They note the ways in which some subprime mortgages increase so-called instrument risk—the risk associated with these particular mortgage instruments and their ballooning payment requirements. They conduct a series of simulations of the net value of homeownership to different types of families in different neighborhoods (that is, different initial housing prices), with different mortgage instruments and different levels of housing appreciation over time.

Their simulations support their cost-benefit analysis, suggesting that lower-income families who buy more expensive houses, make lower down payments, use higher-risk mortgage instruments, or invest in low-appreciation neighborhoods may easily lose money from homeownership. Furthermore, the authors note, foreclosure risk is concentrated in lower-income and heavily African American neighborhoods, and residents of these disadvantaged neighborhoods face particular risks to homeownership. Of course, families that do not face these problems may gain significant wealth from homeownership. This chapter ends with a discussion of the policy options available that would reduce the risk of homeownership and ease affordability burdens for low-income families.

While information on asset ownership is useful, it is equally important to know how debt burdens are changing. Ronald Mann focuses on credit card use and credit card debt in chapter 9. He opens the chapter by discussing the significant changes in the credit card market that have allowed credit card companies to expand credit to a larger number of lower-income (higher-risk) families by greatly increasing the fees paid by these families to access credit.

As a result, credit card usage and debt have risen over time. In 2004 one-third of all families in the first quintile of the income distribution (and one-half of all families in the second quintile) had credit card debt. Relative to their income, the magnitude of this debt was much greater than that held by higher-income families. Mann looks at the determinants of who acquires credit card debt. For lower- and moderate-income households, employment increases the use of credit cards to carry debt, and it is strongly correlated with other debt, such as mortgages and car loans. Mann interprets this as evidence that some persons are more "debt-prone" and willing to take the risks associated with higher debt levels. The chapter ends with a short discussion of the role of more stringent public requirements on credit card companies to provide greater disclosure of the actual interest rates embedded in credit cards that require up-front payments and multiple fees.

While the chapters in this book focus on lower-income families, there are particular groups among the low-income whose financial lives might be of special concern. For this reason, a number of chapters differentiate between families of different ages or families of different racial-ethnic backgrounds. One group of particular concern is immigrants, who may experience greater barriers to the use of formal financial services in the United States than others. In their examination in chapter 10 of the immigrant experience with financial services, Una Osili and Anna Paulson note the large wealth gap between immigrants and natives in the United States: the average immigrant family holds only one-fourth the wealth of the average family headed by a native-born adult. This wealth gap is much larger than the income gap between immigrant and native families.

Osili and Paulson use the SIPP data to explore these differences more closely, looking at both the probability of holding different types of financial assets and the amounts held. They find that the biggest difference is in the propensity to hold certain assets: immigrants are much less likely to hold checking or savings accounts, stocks, or IRA-Keogh plans. Although controlling for detailed demographic and economic characteristics of families significantly decreases the immigrant-native differences in wealth holdings, immigrants are still less likely to hold as much wealth as otherwise identical native-born families.

In exploring the reasons for these differences, the authors look at the greater priority that immigrants seem to place on homeownership, the trustworthiness of financial institutions in their home country, the likelihood that immigrants will send remittances home, and the integration of immigrants into the language and culture of the United States. The last effect is significant, while those who send remittances home are actually more likely to hold financial assets in the United States. The chapter ends with a discussion of ways to integrate immigrants more fully into formal financial institutions and increase their asset-holding in the United States.

Common Themes

Although the chapters in this volume focus on different aspects of the relationship of low-income households with formal financial services, they share a number of common themes. First and most important is the fact that low-income families are financial decisionmakers who need a range of financial services. Basic transactional services—receiving income, storing it, and paying bills—are less available and more expensive for low-income households. In addition, low-income households may have more acute needs for certain forms of finance. For example, less-skilled adults are more likely to face unemployment or involuntary part-time employment, and their incomes are more cyclical (Bania and Leete 2007; Hoynes 2000). Their need to smooth consumption may therefore be higher than it is among high-income households. This means that flexible credit or moderate levels of short-term savings may be quite important to the economic well-being of these families.

Second, lower-income families utilize both formal and informal means to manage their financial lives. Although low- and moderate-income U.S. households are less likely to hold checking or savings accounts than middle- and upper-income households, many such households do have bank accounts, and many low-income households, both banked and unbanked, also utilize a range of alternative financial services, such as check-cashers, payday lenders, and refund anticipation loan providers (Barr, this volume; Berube et al. 2002). This suggests that formal financial institutions are not fully meeting their needs. For instance, changes in banking have made low-fee bank accounts far less available in the past fifteen years. Many payday loan customers believe their loan is cheaper than the cost of returned check fees (Elliehausen and Lawrence 2001).

Third, lower-income families have substantially less wealth than high-income families. In itself, this is not surprising, since these families have less capacity to save and invest (Scholz and Sheshadri, this volume). But for some groups, particularly African Americans and immigrants, income differences alone do not explain these wealth differences; wealth holdings are lower even after accounting for income and demographic differences.

Fourth, the lower wealth holdings of low-income families have substantial implications for many aspects of their lives. Lower homeownership rates can mean greater residential relocation, which can in turn lead to greater instability in gaining access to schools, doctors, or family supports. The lack of short-term savings can lead to greater use of payday lenders for short-term loans and greater use of credit card debt. Lack of checking accounts can result in fees paid to check-cashing outlets or increased utilization of tax refund loans (Barr 2004). Use of these services increases the prices paid by lower-income families for financial services and makes saving even harder.

Fifth, when thinking of savings and the financial needs of lower-income households, we should consider their need for short-run economic flexibility, which savings and access to formal financial institutions can provide. By contrast, much of the recent policy discussion about saving among the poor has focused on long-run investment gains such as homeownership or future educational needs. While saving as a vehicle for long-term asset accumulation and investment is important, this is only half the story. The value of low levels of savings and low-cost credit to short-run economic flexibility and consumption smoothing is equally important. Indeed, for many low-income families the substantial dollars needed to ensure access to college or to stable economic retirement may be unattainable and can only happen if individual savings are supplemented by government assistance programs, such as Pell grants and Social Security.

POLICY DIRECTIONS

The chapters in this volume discuss a wide variety of policy initiatives that might improve the access of lower-income families to savings and financial institutions and help prevent serious problems with credit, such as falling into debt traps or losing one's home through foreclosure. In this section, we discuss some of the key policies that we think are important to consider and that emerge from the issues discussed in this book. We divide this discussion into two sections: the first is aimed at private-sector changes, and the second at public-sector changes.

Private-Sector Policies to Enhance the Financial Well-Being of Low-Income Families

Financial services firms, employers, and nonprofits all have important roles to play in better serving low-income families. Bank accounts tailored to the needs of lower-income families are likely to expand their use of formal financial services. Such accounts would have low fees and no minimum balance, and they would be debit card accounts that do not allow overdrafts or check-writing. These accounts would be lower-cost and lower-risk for both banks and households (Barr 2004). Banks in a wide variety of communities are beginning to offer a range of lower-cost accounts tailored to low-income households. In some cases, banks are working on larger community-wide efforts. For instance, the Bank on San Francisco project is trying to decrease the number of unbanked families in that city by at least 20 percent. Sheila Bair (2005) provides a number of examples of local credit unions or banks that offer short-term consumer loans explicitly designed to compete with payday lenders, for much lower fees than is found among AFS providers.

In addition to tailoring bank accounts to low-income families, financial institutions could increase their presence in low-income neighborhoods. AFS providers outnumber bank branches in many neighborhoods (Temkin and Sawyer 2004). Banks can develop innovative, low-cost means of increasing their presence, including such options as mobile banking and kiosks in stores. Government incentives for banks to serve lower-income customers with better products should help increase the presence of financial services in lower-income neighborhoods. In addition, the U.S. Treasury Department's CDFI Fund, which supports the activities of community development financial institutions (CDFIs), is a program that should continue to expand in communities (such as Native American reservations) where other formal financial services are not available.

Employers of low-wage workers also shape the financial choices that these workers make. Employers can encourage the use of direct deposit, and they can work with local banks to ensure that their workers have access to accounts structured to their needs. Employer-based savings schemes, with automatic savings provisions, can encourage saving, not simply for retirement but also for shorter-term or emergency needs.

Of course, private-sector policy changes will occur only if they benefit financial institutions or employers. The growing interest in providing better financial services to low-income populations has increased the number of institutions that are working to better serve these families. Where changes have been successful, it will be important to share information about promising practices and effective policies aimed at low-wage workers and low-income families.

Public-Sector Policies to Enhance the Financial Well-Being of Low-Income Families

The public sector has primary responsibility for making sure that low-income families escape economic disaster. Indeed, to the extent that publicly financed savings assistance plans or homeownership efforts help families achieve long-term economic stability, the public sector's safety-net expenditures to support people who face economic destitution and require help from public assistance programs should be reduced.

As previously discussed, a key role for the public sector is to work closely with the private sector, encouraging and incentivizing financial institutions to serve lower-income populations. A tax credit to financial institutions for offering low-cost electronic accounts for low-income persons could expand private-sector interest in serving these households (Barr 2004, 2007). The Internal Revenue Service (IRS) could be authorized to open up privately offered bank accounts for unbanked households receiving tax refunds as a way to decrease the use of refund loans, increase opportunities for saving, and lower administrative costs in the tax system (Barr 2007). States could use their electronic benefit transfer programs for cash welfare and other state-administered benefits to bring households into the banking system rather than simply treating these programs as income transfer mechanisms (Barr 2004).

Policies should also be pursued to encourage saving among low-income households. Making the Saver's Credit refundable would expand the opportunity for tax-advantaged retirement savings to low-income families (Gale, Iwry, and Orszag 2004); Congress could enact a new automatic IRA for a broad range of workers who have no access to pension plans at work (Iwry and John 2007); and new tax credits could be provided to banks and thrifts for setting up automatic savings plans for low-income households to meet their shorter-term savings needs (Barr 2007). Interest is growing in matched-savings plans by which government funds supplement savings by low-income households. A variety of people are also calling for government-provided savings accounts for children at birth, similar to the Child Trust Fund provided by the United Kingdom (Goldberg 2005).

The government also plays a key regulatory role. For example, improved disclosures might help consumers make better decisions about borrowing. There may be a need to require greater and more standardized disclosure of the financial implications of credit across both the mainstream and alternative financial sectors, including credit card fees, overdraft policies, and payday loans. Such cross-sector disclosures could improve the ability of consumers to comparison-shop across functionally similar credit products. Tailored disclosures regarding the consequences of certain borrower behaviors, such as making only the minimum payment on credit cards, might also help consumers make better choices (Barr 2007).

Moreover, we ought to consider how advances in behavioral economics, which have improved retirement savings outcomes, could be applied in the credit arena (Barr, Mullainathan, and Shafir 2008). While market forces in these two financial areas are quite different, the fundamental mistake that individuals make in not understanding the power of compound interest is strikingly similar. In the one case it leads to undersaving, and in the other to overborrowing. Congress could pursue opt-out strategies in the credit arena that would make it more difficult for households to make bad decisions with severe consequences. For example, credit card companies could be required to establish opt-out credit card repayment plans with the standard pay-down occurring over a reasonably short period of time (Barr 2007). As another example, Congress could require lenders to offer a standard set of home mortgages with straightforward terms; borrowers could opt out, but the opt-out rules would be "sticky," making it harder for lenders to encourage borrowers to take out loans not in their interest (Barr, Mullainathan, and Shafir 2008).

More broadly, as we write, the need to implement better protection for low- and moderate-income families who utilize subprime and alternative mortgages has become a national priority, and we expect national legislation in this area to occur in the near future. Such reforms should focus on tightening broker and lender licensing and regulation, trying harder to combat deceptive practices, making structural changes to reduce or eliminate conflicts of interest by mortgage providers, and implementing new oversight, supervision, and enforcement provisions regarding nonbank financial providers.

Homeownership assistance programs have long been supported by the federal government, and in our judgment they should continue, albeit in the context of better protections for borrowers from unscrupulous and misleading tactics by mortgage and real estate professionals. Rental assistance programs, by contrast, have in recent years lagged far behind the need. Low- and moderate-income households have been paying an increasing share of their income toward rent, and the federal government's Section 8 housing voucher program has never kept up with demand or met the promise of housing mobility embodied in its approach. As the nation recovers from the subprime mortgage fallout, we should be paying particular attention to the rental housing needs of families (Gramlich 2007).

The public sector assists low-income families in meeting their financial retirement needs, investing in education, covering major health expenditures, and, in some instances, meeting other needs that lower-wage workers cannot afford. These programs need to be preserved and strengthened. Long-term financial stability for Social Security is probably more important than improved savings plans for low-wage workers since 65 percent of retirees rely on Social Security for more than half of their current income (Mishel, Bernstein, and Allegretto 2005). Broadly available health insurance could prevent workers from incurring long-term debt or filing for bankruptcy when faced with a health crisis. Pell grants and other forms of educational subsidies can help low-income families educate their children beyond high school and give their children greater economic opportunities. Moreover, the government plays a central role in enhancing the take-home pay of low-wage workers through the Earned Income Tax Credit, which helps to lift millions of families out of poverty every year. The EITC has been effective and should be expanded, including for persons without children.

Finally, the public sector holds much of the responsibility for greater financial education for low-income families through public schools, regulatory disclosure requirements, and public subsidies to financial education programs. (The non-profit sector is also involved in these programs.) Evidence on the value of explicit financial education programs is admittedly mixed (Caskey 2006). There have been few entirely credible evaluations of financial education programs, however, so our knowledge about the best ways to provide financial education to lower-income families is limited at present. There is surely a role for financial education in high schools, for community-based short-term financial education programs for those who are motivated to attend, and for clearly understandable disclosure provisions aimed at those undertaking potentially high-cost financial transactions, such as credit card debt, payday loans, and mortgage lending.

THE RESEARCH AGENDA

This volume brings together the most recent research and data on the financial lives of lower-income families, but there is still much that we do not know. A variety of future research initiatives could greatly improve our understanding of the problems and possibilities facing lower-income families and give us better information about the effectiveness of different policies designed to increase savings and assets and reduce financial difficulties among low- and moderate-income families.

The U.S. data on wealth holdings and participation in financial services are extremely limited. Ongoing attention needs to be given to the coverage and reliability of data in both the Survey of Consumer Finances (SCF) and the Survey of Income and Program Participation (SIPP), our two primary sources of nationally representative wealth information. More detailed information about financial decisionmaking at the household level would be useful. The historical purpose of the SCF has been to collect information on wealth holdings; hence, it oversamples higher-income households. This survey could be expanded to provide more detail on the financial lives of lower-income households as well. The Federal Deposit Insurance Corporation (FDIC) will soon begin collecting baseline data on bank status from a nationally representative sample of low- and moderate-income households in collaboration with the U.S. Census Bureau. Such data collection efforts need to be supported and strengthened over time. In addition, it would be particularly useful to collect detailed household financial cash flow information in the United States from a sample of lower-income families, similar to the data collected by Daryl Collins (2003) in other countries. This would provide longitudinal data on how financial decisions are made over time.

The research on IDAs demonstrates how we can build knowledge about new policies designed to change the behavior or improve the economic well-being of lower-income families. A wide variety of financial services policies would benefit from seriously evaluated, random-assignment demonstration projects.

Many of these evaluations should be aimed at determining the most effective policy designs and best practices presented by a set of alternative program options:

- *Private-sector and community-based efforts to expand bank account usage within lower-income populations:* These evaluations should both measure the impact of policy efforts and look at the cost and implementation issues facing private-sector institutions that try to expand bank accounts for lower-income persons. We need both institutional best practice information and program design information.

- *Several types of savings enhancement programs:* These evaluations should include employer-based automatic opt-in and opt-out savings plans as well as public matched-savings opportunities.

- *Alternative regulatory and disclosure requirements on higher-risk financial actions:* Evaluations would focus on credit card loans, payday loans, and mortgage loans.

- *Alternative ways of providing effective financial education (not necessarily limited to lower-income families):* With systematic comparison of evaluations of such education efforts, which should be made by both community-based organizations and public-sector institutions, we could develop a portfolio of educational and disclosure policies that would clarify the risks and opportunities encountered by the persons making household financial decisions. Although much discussed, our knowledge of "what works" in financial education is woefully limited.

Other evaluations should test newer ideas about which we know even less in order to discover whether they might have significant impacts on financial behavior:

- The impact of *direct deposit employer programs* (potentially bundled with short financial education opportunities) on the use of financial services among lower-wage workers.

- The effectiveness of a few more innovative policy options such as *lottery-linked savings* (see chapter 6) and *Child Development Accounts* (see chapter 7).

Good research and good data make important contributions to the policy discussion around the financial lives of low- and moderate-income families. While we expect adults to make the best financial decisions possible for their family, it is clear that some families (both low- and high-income) have difficulty saving or using credit in ways that advance their welfare. Our financial institutions are not well designed to help low- and moderate-income families get access to financial services, savings, and credit products that meet their needs. If we want to demand financial responsibility from low- and moderate-income households, we have an obligation to ensure that they have access to the banking, credit, and savings institutions that are also available to higher-income families.

We thank Howard Lempel for his assistance in producing a final manuscript for publication.

NOTE

1. Most recent data available at Financial Services of America (FiSCA), "FiSCA Frequently Asked Questions, How Large Is the Financial Services Industry." Available at http://www.fisca.org/Content/NavigationMenu/AboutFISCA/FAQs/default.htm#how_large (accessed November 7, 2008).

REFERENCES

Aizcorbe, Ana M., Arthur B. Kennickell, and Kevin B. Moore. 2003. "Recent Changes in U.S. Family Finances: Evidence from the 1998 and 2001 Survey of Consumer Finances." *Federal Reserve Bulletin* 89(January): 1–32.

Bachelder, Ed, and Sam Ditzion. 2000. *Survey of Non-Bank Financial Institutions for the Department of the Treasury.* Boston: Dove Consulting.

Bair, Sheila. 2005. *Low-Cost Payday Loans: Opportunities and Obstacles.* Report by the Isenberg School of Management, University of Massachusetts at Amherst, to the Annie E. Casey Foundation. Baltimore: Annie E. Casey Foundation.

Bania, Neil, and Laura Leete. 2007. "Income Volatility and Food Insufficiency in U.S. Low-Income Households, 1992–2003." Discussion paper 1325-07. Madison: University of Wisconsin, Institute for Research on Poverty.

Barr, Michael S. 2004. "Banking the Poor." *Yale Journal on Regulation* 21(1): 121–237.

———. 2005. "Credit Where It Counts: The Community Reinvestment Act and Its Critics." *New York University Law Review* 80(2): 513–652.

———. 2007. "An Inclusive, Progressive National Savings and Financial Services Policy." *Harvard Law and Policy Review* 1(1): 161–84.

Barr, Michael S., Sendhil Mullainathan, and Eldar Shafir. 2008. "Behaviorally Informed Home Mortgage Credit Regulation." Working paper UCC08-12. Cambridge, Mass.: Harvard University, Joint Center for Housing Studies.

Berube, Alan, Anne Kim, Benjamin Forman, and Megan Burns. 2002. "The Price of Paying Taxes: How Tax Preparation and Refund Loan Fees Erode the Benefits of the EITC." Brookings Institution/Progressive Policy Institute, Center on Urban and Metropolitan Policy Survey Series (May). Available at: http://www.brookings.edu/es/urban/publications/berubekimeitc.pdf (accessed January 2009).

Bucks, Brian K., Arthur B. Kennickell, and Kevin B. Moore. 2006. "Recent Changes in U.S. Family Finances: Evidence from the 2001 and 2004 Survey of Consumer Finances." *Federal Reserve Bulletin* 92(February): A1–38.

Caskey, John P. 2006. "Can Personal Financial Management Education Promote Asset Accumulation by the Poor?" Policy brief 2006-PB-06. Terre Haute: Indiana State University, Networks Financial Institute.

Choi, James, David I. Laibson, Brigitte Madrian, and Andrew Metrick. 2002. "Defined Contribution Pensions: Plan Rules, Participant Decisions, and the Path of Least Resistance." In *Tax Policy and the Economy*, edited by James M. Poterba. Cambridge, Mass.: MIT Press.

Collins, Daryl. 2003. "Financial Instruments of the Poor: Initial Findings from the Financial Diaries Study." *Development Southern Africa* 22(5): 735–46.

Elliehausen, Gregory, and Edward C. Lawrence. 2001. "Payday Advance Credit in America: An Analysis of Customer Demand." Monograph 35. Washington, D.C.: Georgetown University, McDonough School of Business.

Gale, William G., J. Mark Iwry, and Peter R. Orszag. 2004. "The Saver's Credit: Issues and Options." *Tax Notes* 103(5): 597–612.

Goldberg, Fred. 2005. "The Universal Piggy Bank: Designing and Implementing a System of Savings Accounts for Children." In *Inclusion in the American Dream: Assets, Poverty, and Public Policy*, edited by Michael Sherraden. New York: Oxford University Press.

Gramlich, Edward M. 2007. *Subprime Mortgages: America's Latest Boom and Bust.* Washington, D.C.: Urban Institute Press.

Hogarth, Jeanne M., and Kevin A. O'Donnell. 1999. "Banking Relationships of Lower-Income Families and the Government Trend Toward Electronic Payment." *Federal Reserve Bulletin* 85(July): 459–73.

Hoynes, Hilary W. 2000. "The Employment, Earnings, and Income of Less-Skilled Workers over the Business Cycle." In *Finding Jobs: Work and Welfare Reform*, edited by David E. Card and Rebecca M. Blank. New York: Russell Sage Foundation.

Hurst, Erik, and James P. Ziliak. 2006. "Do Welfare Asset Limits Affect Household Savings? Evidence from Welfare Reform." *Journal of Human Resources* 40(1): 46–71.

Iwry, Mark, and David John. 2007. "Pursuing Universal Retirement Security Through Automatic IRAs." Working paper 2007-2. Washington, D.C.: Retirement Security Project.

Kennickell, Arthur B., Martha Starr-McCluer, and Brian J. Surette. 2000. "Recent Changes in U.S. Family Finances: Results from the 1998 Survey of Consumer Finances." *Federal Reserve Bulletin* 86(January): 1–29.

Madrian, Brigitte, and Dennis F. Shea. 2001. "The Power of Suggestion: Inertia in 401(k) Participation and Savings Behavior." *Quarterly Journal of Economics* 116(4):1149–87.

Mishel, Lawrence, Jared Bernstein, and Sylvia Allegretto. 2005. *The State of Working America: 2004–2005.* Ithaca, N.Y.: Cornell University Press.

Nam, Yunju. 2008. "Welfare Reform and Asset Accumulation: Asset Limit Changes, Financial Assets, and Vehicle Ownership." *Social Science Quarterly* 89(1): 133–54.

Orszag, Peter, and Robert Greenstein. 2005. "Toward Progressive Pensions: A Summary of the U.S. Pension System and Proposals for Reform." In *Inclusion in the American Dream: Assets, Poverty, and Public Policy*, edited by Michael Sherradan. New York: Oxford University Press.

Rhine, Sherrie L. W., Maude Toussaint-Comeau, Jeanne M. Hogarth, and William H. Greene. 2001. "The Role of Alternative Financial Service Providers in Serving LMI Neighborhoods." Paper presented to the Federal Reserve System Community Affairs Research Conference, "Changing Financial Markets and Community Development." Washington, D.C. (April 5–6).

Sullivan, James X. 2006. "Welfare Reform, Savings, and Vehicle Ownership: Do Asset Limits and Vehicle Exemptions Matter?" *Journal of Human Resources* 41(1): 72–105.

Summers, Lawrence H. 2000. "Remarks of Treasury Secretary Lawrence H. Summers at the Department of Labor Retirement Savings Education Campaign Fifth Anniversary Event." U.S. Department of the Treasury, Office of Public Affairs, press room release LS-785 (July 18). Available at: http://www.treas.gov/press/releases/ls785.htm (accessed January 2009).

Temkin, Kenneth, and Noah Sawyer. 2004. "Analysis of Alternative Financial Service Providers." Paper prepared for the Fannie Mae Foundation. Washington, D.C.: Urban Institute, Metropolitan Housing and Communities Policy Center.

U.S. Department of the Treasury. 1998. "TSP Participation and Contribution Rates." Internal document on file with Michael S. Barr.

Part I

The Financial Lives
of Low-Income Families

Chapter 2

The Assets and Liabilities
Held by Low-Income Families

John Karl Scholz and Ananth Seshadri

There are many reasons to be interested in the assets and liabilities held by American households. Net worth, the difference between assets and liabilities, can be used to maintain living standards when families are hit with adverse employment, income, or health shocks. These resources may provide the critical buffer that allows a poor family to fix a broken car and remain employed, find help in caring for a sick child, or move out of a dangerous neighborhood. Net worth may allow families to take advantage of investment opportunities, such as pursuing further education. Many families need to accumulate net worth outside of Social Security and employer-provided pensions to maintain living standards in retirement. Finally, wealth may expand opportunities: significant wealth almost surely provides political access for those who seek it, and wealth may also buy access to social networks that improve employment or the well-being of children.

The motives for wealth accumulation that are often the focus of attention for high-income households—namely, saving for retirement or sending children to college—may have less relevance for low- and moderate-income households. Social Security replaces a larger percentage of average lifetime earnings for low- and moderate-income households than it does for high-income households. Similarly, college financial aid, particularly through Pell grants, is targeted at children from low-income households. At the same time, low- and moderate-income households are generally much more susceptible to adverse economic shocks, such as unemployment or illness, than those with greater resources. Wealth may provide a crucial buffer that allows those facing economic shocks to keep a job or treat a problem before it has a major effect on the life course.

Over the past two decades, some striking changes have had important effects on low-income families. AFDC (Aid to Families with Dependent Children) was abolished. The broader safety net became more work-oriented. Rates of female labor force participation steadily increased, as did incarceration rates, particularly for men with low levels of education. The fraction of children living in a household with two married parents was 85 percent in 1970. By 2006 the corresponding figure was only 67 percent (Child Trends Data Bank 2007). Lastly, there have been widely noted changes (or perceptions of changes) in economic insecurity (see, for example, Gosselin 2004).

Financial markets changed as well. Equity market returns were strong, particularly in the 1990s. Mortgage access in low-income communities expanded as innovations in financial products, including so-called subprime mortgages, became available. A number of public policy initiatives were also taken to increase wealth and increase banking for low-income families. The Assets for Independence Act of 1998, for example, authorized the development of individual development account (IDA) demonstration programs. Efforts were made to extend banking services more broadly (see, for example, U.S. Senate Banking Committee 2002). The chapters in this volume discuss many other developments.

This chapter establishes a set of stylized facts about patterns of net worth held by low-income American families and individuals and discusses how these facts changed over time as the economy and financial markets changed (for a nice related contribution, see Carney and Gale 2001). The core of the chapter, given our interest in low-income families, is based on a series of appendix tables that show how major components of assets and liabilities evolved between 1962 and 2004 based on data from the Survey of Consumer Finances (SCF), which is widely viewed as the "gold standard" of wealth data for the United States. We start by examining net worth and presenting data on wealth holdings and patterns of wealth inequality from 1962 to 2004.

We also focus on homeownership, since housing remains by far the most important asset held in household portfolios, and on financial assets, the liquidity of which allows households to draw on them when confronted by adverse economic shocks. We provide information on credit card debt, bankruptcy, and access to credit, which are all measures of low-income families' access to credit markets and the vulnerabilities they may face. Our intention in this portion of the chapter is to establish a set of facts that provide a foundation for many of the other chapters in this volume.

We close with a discussion of three issues that have received somewhat less attention in research that focuses on the net worth and portfolios of low-income families. First, we look at wealth changes for specific cohorts in the economy. Many researchers try to make inferences about changes of wealth accumulation in the economy by looking at patterns over time in repeated cross-sectional data (see, for example, Wolff 2000). Focusing on cohorts gives a different, and arguably more accurate, description of how the wealth of typical families evolves.

Second, there is an extraordinary difference in wealth accumulation patterns between African American and white families. The difference is not simply that blacks have less wealth than whites, but that the underlying factors associated with wealth accumulation differ sharply between blacks and whites. These differences may provide clues about the factors influencing the wealth accumulation of low-income families.

Third, we close by offering some ideas about how to interpret the patterns of net worth shown here. A central question lurking below the surface in the literature is whether low-income families are behaving pathologically: is their saving behavior suboptimal, given their resources? The answer to this question has important implications for assessing the likely effects of policies targeted to the poor. We argue that low-income households, given the resources they command and institutions they face, are behaving in a manner consistent with their best interest. We close by briefly discussing the policy implications of this interpretation.

DATA ON NET WORTH

The analysis in this chapter relies primarily on the Survey of Consumer Finances (SCF) as well as its predecessor survey, the 1962 Survey of Financial Characteristics of Consumers. The 1962 survey was the first large-scale household wealth survey conducted in the United States (see Projector 1964). The SCF is a triennial survey of the balance sheet, pension, income, and other demographic characteristics of U.S. families that began in 1983. We exclude the 1986 survey because it was conducted by telephone rather than face to face and the data are suspected of being less accurate than data in the other surveys. The SCF is considered the gold standard of wealth data in part because it substantially oversamples very high-income households. The high-income supplement is critical in developing data on the aggregate amount of wealth held in the economy, as well as its distribution. But given the SCF's small sample sizes (typically around four thousand households), confidence intervals for typical sample statistics are large, particularly when data are broken down by race-ethnicity, education, and other factors of interest (for additional details on the SCF, see Bucks, Kennickell, and Moore 2006 and the papers cited therein).

All the appendix tables to this chapter were also reproduced with asset and liability data from the Survey of Income and Program Participation (SIPP), beginning in 1997. The SIPP data show patterns similar to those described here, so to save space we do not include them in our discussion.

It is not clear how we should best assess the quality of wealth data. A natural benchmark would be to compare wealth data to asset and liability categories in the household sector Flow of Funds accounts. It is difficult, however, to do this. For example, the household sector Flow of Funds accounts include nonprofit institutions, whose asset and liability holdings must be netted out when comparing data to households. More importantly, as Rochelle Antoniewicz (2000) emphasizes, the household sector Flow of Funds accounts are not a natural benchmark since it is computed as a residual from the other Flow of Funds sectors, so that errors elsewhere, unless they fully cancel out, will cause errors in the household sector account. Antoniewicz nevertheless provides a careful comparison of the SCFs from 1989 to 1998 to the relevant household sector Flow of Funds and finds that the two sources are "quite close" in 1989 and 1992 but move apart thereafter. It is not clear how the SCF should be adjusted, if some sort of adjustment is thought to be useful. Proportional adjustments implicitly assume that there is uniform percentage underreporting of the adjusted items. Nothing suggests that misreporting takes this pattern (for further discussion of these issues, see Kennickell 2001). Consequently, we present unadjusted tabulations from the SCF throughout the chapter.

Much of this chapter focuses on trends in holdings of assets and liabilities for various groups in the population. To discuss trends sensibly, dollar amounts need to be adjusted for inflation. We do this using the CPI-U, the consumer price index for urban consumers (who represent about 87 percent of the total U.S. population). The index is based on the expenditures of almost all residents of urban or metropolitan areas, including professionals, the self-employed, the poor, the unemployed, and retired persons as well as urban wage earners and clerical workers. The CPI-U series is collected by and available from the Bureau of Labor Statistics.[1]

Most of this chapter focuses on the assets and liabilities held by low-income families and individuals. But remarkable changes in the overall distribution of U.S. wealth, particularly over the past twenty years, form the backdrop for the discussion in the rest of the chapter.

These changes are analyzed by Thomas Piketty and Emmanuel Saez (2006), who find that in 2001 the top 10 percent of the income distribution had 42.6 percent of total income, up from 38.5 percent in 1989. The top 1 percent received 15.5 percent in 2001, up from 12.6 percent. Holdings of net worth—defined as housing assets less liabilities, business assets less liabilities, checking and saving accounts, stocks, bonds, mutual funds, retirement accounts, certificates of deposit, the cash value of whole life insurance, and other assets, less credit card debt and other liabilities (but, for our purposes, excluding defined benefit pension wealth, defined-contribution pension wealth held outside 401(k)s, Social Security wealth, consumer durables, and future earnings due to data limitations)—are far more concentrated. In 2001 the top 10 percent of the net worth distribution owned 69.6 percent of total net worth, up from 67.2 percent in 1989. The top 1 percent owned 32.4 percent of total net worth in 2001, up from 29.9 percent in 1989.

Figure 2.1 provides another perspective on the evolution of U.S. wealth inequality. Here we plot the ratio of net worth at a given percentile to the net worth of the median (or fiftieth percentile) household. In 1962 the seventy-fifth percentile had 2.7 times the net worth of the median household. The ninetieth percentile household had 6.1 times, the ninety-fifty percentile had 9.8 times, and the ninety-ninth percentile had 35.8 times the net worth of the median household.

Between 1962 and 2004 there was little change at the seventy-fifth percentile: the ratio rose to 3.5 from 2.7. But the ratios of net worth at high-net-worth percentiles to the median increased sharply. Households at the ninety-fifth percentile had 15.4 times the net worth of median household in 2004, compared to 9.8 times in 1962. Households at the ninety-ninth percentile had 67.2 times the net worth of the median, compared to 35.8 in 1962. These figures suggest that

FIGURE 2.1 / Net-Worth Ratios Relative to the Median, 1962 to 2004

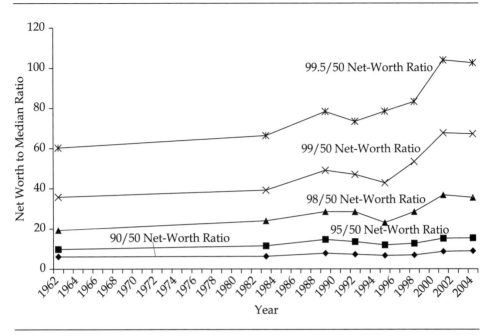

Source: Survey of Consumer Finances.

increases in wealth inequality over this period were driven by the extreme upper end of the wealth distribution.

THE ASSETS, LIABILITIES, AND FINANCIAL CHARACTERISTICS OF LOW-INCOME HOUSEHOLDS

A central objective of this chapter is to provide a comprehensive perspective on the portfolios of disadvantaged households and their evolution over time. For each of the measures we discuss, we present appendix tables showing the percentage of the population with positive amounts of the asset or liability, as well as mean and median amounts, conditional on having positive holdings. The information is also classified by income quintile, education, marital status, race-ethnicity, and age. Data are shown for eight waves of the SCF spanning forty years. We summarize selected trends through a series of figures. Our six measures are:

1. *Net worth,* the broadest measure of financial resources: Our definition of net worth is similar (and in some cases identical) to those used by other studies of wealth and wealth inequality. We think net worth is the single best measure of the financial well-being of households in the SCF.

2. *Financial assets,* which, for most years in our data include balances in checking and saving accounts, stocks, bonds, certificates of deposit, whole life policies, and selected other (uncommon) financial instruments: If needed, financial assets can be readily liquidated and hence provide the best measure of resources immediately available to address short-term emergencies.

3. *Stock holding and the value of equity:* With the spread of 401(k) plans and discount brokerages, equity ownership has become more common in the economy.

4. *Net equity in housing,* the most important asset in the typical household's portfolio: Homeownership remains an important aspiration for most American families.

5. *Credit card debt,* a proxy for financial vulnerability: Credit cards frequently carry high interest rates, and carrying balances on a credit card may indicate financial distress and a lack of financial sophistication.

6. The *value of the vehicles* held by the household: In most parts of the country, a car in good working condition is necessary to maintain solid employment.

Although we present trends for forty years, we must emphasize that there are likely to be differences in survey design that reduce the comparability of the 1962 and 1983 observations and the triennial SCFs that begin in 1989. The two earlier surveys nevertheless were state-of-the-art surveys in their day, and we think it is informative to see the very long-run trends. More weight, however, should be placed on data beginning in 1989, when the SCFs began to share a common structure and to be collected in a roughly consistent manner.

Before turning to measures of household well-being, we want to say a little about the classification variables we use in the appendix tables (and, to a lesser extent, our discussion in the text). Subpopulation classifiers are probably most useful when they identify a relatively consistent portion of the population. Income quintiles are ideal in this respect because, by definition, they identify equal fractions of the aggregate population. Educational attainment, at least in the long time period reflected in the data covered here, is probably the worst. Fifty-six percent of the population had less than a high school degree in the 1962 SCF. By 2004 only 16 percent had less than a high school degree. This difference implies that the "less than high school" category in the 2004 data is a far more disadvantaged group than the "less than high school" group in 1962. Even between 1983 and 2004, the fraction of the population with less than a high school degree fell to 16 percent from 29 percent. We have three additional qualifications for our classification variables. The "single parent" category in 1983 appears to have an unusually (and suspiciously) high number of people. We have not found any obvious mistakes in our code or in the data, but caution should be used in interpreting 1983 observations when data are broken out by marital status. Second, the 1962 SCF did not separately identify "Hispanic" households. Third, as described in the appendix to Bucks, Kennickell, and Moore (2006), the identification of Hispanic households has changed somewhat across recent years of the SCF.

FIGURE 2.2 / Positive Net Worth (Bars) and Median Net Worth (Lines)
for Lowest, Middle, and Highest Income Quintiles, 1962 to 2004

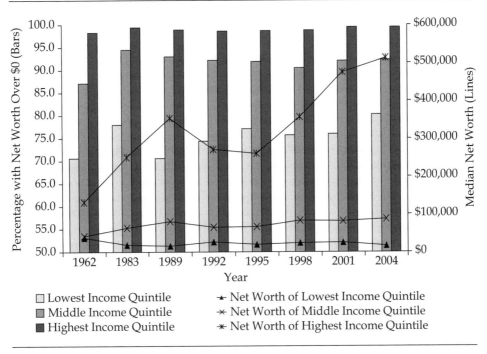

Source: Survey of Consumer Finances.

Net Worth

Figure 2.2 summarizes information in appendix tables 2A.1 and 2A.2. In the figure, we choose to look at three subgroups: households in the lowest income quintile (in the given year), the middle income quintile, and the highest income quintile. In the bars on the figure, read with the left-side axis, we plot the probability of holding positive amounts of net worth. Depending on the year in question, the bars show that between 20 and 30 percent of households with income in the bottom decile had negative or no net worth. Similar results hold for other disadvantaged groups, including those with less than a high school education, single parents, and black and Hispanic households. Fewer than 2 percent of households in the highest-net-worth quintile had negative or no net worth.

A number of factors can lead SCF households to have negative net worth, including being in a situation of near-bankruptcy, maintaining credit card balances with no assets though with steady income, or having poorly measured or misreported assets or liabilities. The probability of having negative net worth declines monotonically with household income, shows no strong trend over time in the SCF, is lower for those with exactly a high school degree than it is for those with less than a high school degree and those with more education, is higher for single parents, blacks, and Hispanics, and is much higher for households headed by a person under thirty.

The lines in figure 2.2, which should be read with the scaling on the right-side axis, show the median net worth for the lowest-, middle-, and highest-income-quintile households among those with positive net worth. We focus on median rather than mean values because the median reflects the holdings of typical families in the various groups. The lines in figure 2.2 reinforce the fact that the distribution of net worth is sharply skewed. Median net worth in 2004 was $17,000 for households in the bottom quintile, $87,000 for households in the middle income quintile, and $513,000 for households in the top. Since 1989, real net worth has been roughly stagnant for households in the bottom 60 percent of the income distribution. It increased by 45.1 percent for households in the top quintile, or 2.5 percent a year. (The growth rate since 1998 has been much faster.) Median net worth for other disadvantaged groups is similar, in both levels and trends.

Net worth for households in the lowest income decile is around 70 percent of annual income across years. Net worth for households in the middle three quintiles is between 130 and 240 percent of annual income (with a modest upward trend over time). Net worth is 250 to 360 percent of annual income for households in the top income quintile. These wealth-to-income percentages are consistent with the conclusion we would draw from the appendix tables: the net worth of disadvantaged groups in the population is low.

To summarize, a substantial portion of the population has zero or negative net worth. The likelihood of being in that situation is higher for young, nonwhite, single-parent, poorly educated, or low-income households or individuals than it is for others. These groups also tend to have lower levels of net worth even as a fraction of income. Moreover, median net worth has not increased, or has increased only modestly, across survey waves for these groups.

Financial Assets

Financial assets—a comprehensive set of liquid, easily marketable assets, including those in checking and saving accounts, certificates of deposit, mutual funds, and stocks and bonds—may be the measure of financial well-being that gets the most media attention and generates the most alarm: it is these assets that low- and moderate-income households can readily use to smooth consumption, invest in durables, or invest in human capital. This measure is summarized in figure 2.3 (and described in detail in appendix tables 2A.3 and 2A.4).

Financial assets are widely held, with at least 60 percent—and by 2004, 80 percent—of households in the lowest income quintile holding positive amounts. By 2004, 78 percent of those with less than a high school education, 86 percent of single parents, 85 percent of black households, and 80 percent of Hispanic households had positive financial assets. Since financial assets are the most easily acquired instruments in the formal financial system, these figures raise an immediate ques-

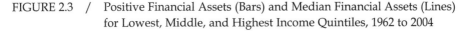

FIGURE 2.3   /   Positive Financial Assets (Bars) and Median Financial Assets (Lines) for Lowest, Middle, and Highest Income Quintiles, 1962 to 2004

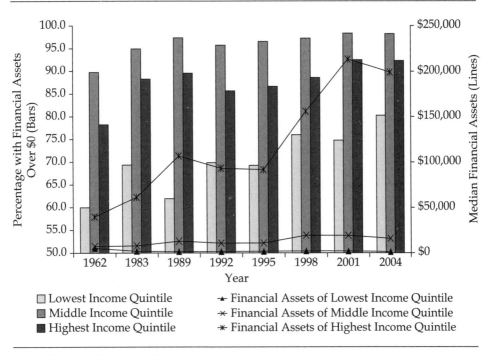

Source: Survey of Consumer Finances.

tion about the status of the remaining 14 to 22 percent of these subgroups—those with less than a high school education, single parents, black households, Hispanic households, or those in the lowest income quintile—who do not have positive financial assets.

The median amounts (again shown in lines, using the right-hand axis), conditional on having positive amounts, are even more striking. Even for those with some financial assets, the amounts held are negligible. Median holdings for the 80 percent of households in the bottom income quintile with positive amounts were $1,400 in 2004. This amount is lower than the peak amount ($2,318 in 1998), presumably reflecting the recession in the early part of the decade and slow subsequent economic growth. Financial assets of $1,400 provide a scant cushion against the negative economic shocks that may affect adults or children. Even financial asset holdings of $15,900 for families in the middle of the income distribution are a small fraction of average family income (median family income in 2004 was $43,129). Only in the top quintile of the income distribution has there been sharp growth in financial asset holdings. Later we discuss the implications of meager financial asset holdings across many disadvantaged subpopulations.

The Ownership Society

The term "ownership society" is sometimes used to describe the diffusion of equity ownership in American society. A colorful example is given in a magazine contribution by Grover Norquist, president of Americans for Tax Reform:

> In the old days, Democrat leader [Congressman Richard] Gephardt [D-Mo.] could say, "I am going to tax the rich and the big corporations and give everyone in the room a dollar." Then only a few shareholders—in 1980 it was less than 20 percent of households—owned stock directly, and they would cringe and hope they didn't get hit too hard. Everyone else was tempted to say, "Hey, this is great. I get a dollar. Let's play this game again." Now, however, 60 percent of the folks in the room are likely to say, "Hey, that is my retirement savings you are looting. Taxes on businesses are taxes on my 40l(k)." (see Norquist 2007)

Appendix table 2A.5 confirms that in 1983 fewer than 20 percent of Americans owned equity and that by 2004 this number exceeded 50 percent (though it was not 60 percent). But the ownership society is not deep. The median equity balance (including stocks, stock and half of blended mutual funds, 401(k)s, and managed assets if they included equity), conditional on having equity, was $32,500 in 2004, as seen in table 2A.6.

Equity holdings are also uncommon in groups with lower socioeconomic status. Twelve percent of households in the bottom income quintile, 28 percent of single parents, 26 percent of black households, and 22 percent of Hispanic households own equity, either directly or through a mutual fund or employer-provided pension.

Net Housing Equity

The conditional medians (and means) for net housing equity (the value of the house less outstanding housing debt) are much less dispersed than the corresponding figures for net worth, financial assets, and equity. These are shown in appendix tables 2A.7 and 2A.8. As shown by the lines in figure 2.4 (with scaling on the right-hand axis), net housing equity, conditional on a positive amount, was $57,000 for households in the bottom income quintile in 2004, and $168,000 for households in the highest income quintile. These amounts have been fairly consistent over time.

There is sharp variation across income quintiles and other subpopulations in the percentage of the population with net housing equity (shown in the bars in figure 2.4, with the scaling on the left-hand axis). In 1962, 40 percent of households in the bottom income quintile had positive net housing equity. This is the same percentage of households with net housing equity in 2004. It is striking that homeownership has not increased in the bottom quintile of the income distribution over the last forty-two years. Homeownership rates increased from 52 percent (in 1962) to 70 percent in 2004 for households in the middle income quintile, and from 78 percent to 92 percent for

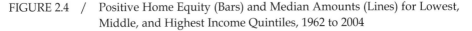

FIGURE 2.4 / Positive Home Equity (Bars) and Median Amounts (Lines) for Lowest, Middle, and Highest Income Quintiles, 1962 to 2004

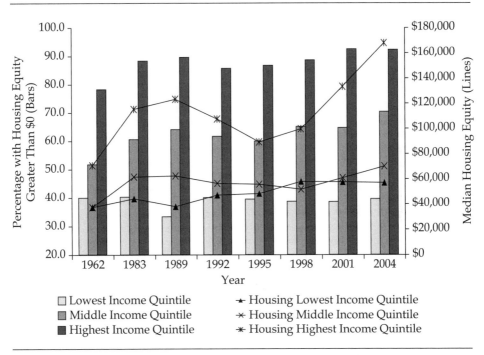

Source: Survey of Consumer Finances.

households in the top income quintile. Single parents and black households saw modest 9- and 7-percentage-point increases in homeownership rates, respectively, starting from low bases of 43 percent and 38 percent, between 1962 and 2004.

Raphael Bostic and Kwan Ok Lee (this volume) provide a much more complete discussion of housing and low-income communities.

Credit Card Debt and Vehicle Wealth

To conserve space we only summarize some of the results on credit card debt and vehicle equity. See Ronald J. Mann (this volume) for a thorough discussion of credit cards and low-income families and individuals. The expansion of credit access to low-income families is apparent in appendix table 2A.9. The percentage of households in the bottom income quintile with positive credit card balances increased to 30 percent in 2004 from 16 percent in 1989. (Recall that the SCFs are most comparable from 1989 on.) The existence of positive credit card balances has no time trend in the top 60 percent of the income distribution. Credit balances are also more prevalent for black and single-parent households over time. Given median financial assets of $1,400 among those in the lowest income quintile, it is particularly striking that the median credit card balance (for those who have positive credit card balances) is $1,000, as seen in table 2A.10. Clearly, households with low levels of financial assets and large credit card balances are financially vulnerable.

An automobile in good working order is an indispensable life accessory for many households. Appendix table 2A.11 makes it clear that cars are not universally held assets: more than 35 percent of households in the bottom quintile of the income distribution do not have a car (or if they have a car, the value is $0 or less). The corresponding figures for population percentages without cars are 22 percent for single parents and 30 percent for black households. For all groups, the trends in car ownership are increasing. The median (and mean) values, conditional on having a car, are seen in table 2A.12 to be increasing with economic resources, but not sharply so.

Further Measures of Financial Health: Bankruptcy, Credit Market Access, and Pension Coverage

One factor correlated with financial vulnerability may be the declaration of bankruptcy. In 1998, 2001, and 2004, the SCF asked households: "Have you (or your husband/wife/partner) ever filed for bankruptcy?" Responses are given in table 2.1. By 2004, 11 percent of the total U.S. population had declared bankruptcy. Interestingly, bankruptcy seems to be more of a middle-income phenomenon—rates were lowest in the bottom quintile (8.9 percent) and top quintile (6.0 percent) of the income distribution. Although rates are low for households in the bottom income quintile, they are high (around 16.5 percent) for single-parent and black households. (Rates are relatively low, 7.3 percent, for Hispanic households.) Bankruptcy rates increased between 1998 and 2004 across most subpopulations.

Since 1983, the SCF has posed the following series of three questions: (1) "In the past five years [in 1983 it was 'the past few years'], has a particular lender or creditor turned down any request you made for credit, or not given you as much credit as you applied for?" (2) "Was there any time in the past five years that you thought of applying for credit at a particular place, but changed your mind because you thought you might be turned down?" (3) "Were you later able to obtain the full amount you requested by reapplying to the same institution or by applying elsewhere?" We code someone as having problems getting access to credit as someone who was turned down for credit or discouraged from borrowing and who did not subsequently receive the amount of credit they were looking for. The question, of course, is not perfect, since we do not know, for example, how much credit a household hoped to receive and whether this desired amount was consistent with the household's ability to repay the loan. Nevertheless, we think the question is informative about potential problems with credit access in the economy. Table 2.2 tabulates the credit access question for subpopulations in the SCF data.

One out of every five American households has credit access problems, as defined here, and this percentage has stayed fairly steady over time. It is not clear what we should expect in time-series trends for this proxy variable. On the one hand, as shown in appendix table 2A.9, the fraction of low-income households

TABLE 2.1 / Population Groups That Declared Bankruptcy, 1998, 2001, 2004

	1998	2001	2004
Full sample	8.5%	10.0%	11.1%
Income quintile			
Lowest quintile	6.4	7.1	8.9
Second quintile	9.2	12.5	13.8
Middle quintile	11.6	13.4	15.3
Fourth quintile	10.8	10.9	11.3
Highest quintile	4.8	5.8	6.0
Education			
Less than high school	7.4	9.1	10.0
High school	10.8	12.4	13.5
More than high school	7.6	8.9	10.1
Marital status			
Single parent	14.2	14.4	16.7
Married	8.7	10.3	10.0
Single, childless	6.1	7.6	11.0
Race-ethnicity			
White and other	8.6	9.4	10.6
Black	10.5	10.3	16.3
Hispanic	4.4	15.8	7.3
Age			
Under thirty	4.7	4.0	2.8
Thirty to sixty-four	11.1	13.6	14.1
Sixty-five or older	3.0	2.8	7.1

Source: Survey of Consumer Finances and authors' calculations.

gaining access to credit cards has increased over time. Increasing credit access might imply that we would see fewer households with access problems. On the other hand, expansion of credit may encourage more marginally creditworthy borrowers to seek credit, leading to more frequent indications of credit access problems. To the extent that these tendencies exist, they appear to largely offset one another. Twenty-five percent of households in the bottom income quintile have credit access problems, and more than one-third of single-parent households and black households have credit access problems.

The last measure of financial well-being that we examine is a question posed in the SCF beginning in 1989 about whether a household has ever, in the current or past job, been covered by an employer-provided pension. Table 2.3 shows that 57 percent of households have been covered by pensions since 1989, and this percentage has remained steady over time. Not surprisingly, however, the probabilities increase with household resources. Only 20 percent of households in the lowest income quintile are covered by pensions. Forty-two percent of single parents and

TABLE 2.2 / Population Groups with Problems Getting Access to Credit, 1983 to 2004

	1983	1989	1992	1995	1998	2001	2004
Full sample	16.9%	17.1%	20.1%	20.4%	19.4%	19.3%	20.1%
Income quintile							
Lowest quintile	24.5	21.0	25.9	28.3	25.5	25.7	25.3
Second quintile	21.0	25.2	22.9	23.9	24.9	27.0	29.9
Middle quintile	20.6	16.0	22.9	22.8	21.8	20.9	22.8
Fourth quintile	11.6	14.5	17.7	17.4	15.8	14.8	15.0
Highest quintile	6.6	7.8	10.5	9.1	8.7	7.3	7.3
Education							
Less than high school	15.2	17.5	20.8	24.5	24.3	24.4	26.7
High school	18.4	19.3	22.1	20.3	20.8	21.9	22.3
More than high school	16.9	15.4	18.7	18.7	16.8	16.0	17.0
Marital status							
Single parent	21.9	26.8	40.8	35.9	35.0	36.2	38.2
Married	13.0	15.8	17.7	17.6	17.4	16.7	17.2
Single, childless	24.4	16.2	17.3	19.6	17.5	18.0	18.3
Race-ethnicity							
White and other	14.0	14.2	16.5	16.5	15.8	15.3	15.8
Black	33.5	26.6	33.5	40.6	36.9	35.6	37.9
Hispanic	23.9	31.2	36.1	30.3	31.6	31.7	29.2
Age							
Under thirty	34.3	28.9	33.1	36.4	37.2	39.6	34.8
Thirty to sixty-four	15.2	18.4	22.4	21.7	20.9	19.7	22.1
Sixty-five or older	4.4	4.6	5.3	6.0	3.5	4.8	4.4

Source: Survey of Consumer Finances and authors' calculations.

half of black households have pension entitlements. Pension coverage has been fairly steady over time. Households without pension entitlements and low levels of private net worth generally rely on Social Security in retirement. As reported in Scholz, Seshadri, and Khitatrakun (2006), Social Security replacement rates in 1993, as measured by an average of the last five years of earnings prior to retirement, were 41.7 percent for married couples without a high school degree and 28.2 percent for married couples with a college degree.

THE WEALTH ACCUMULATION OF HOUSEHOLD COHORTS

This section presents a novel analysis of how the wealth of cohorts of households evolved between 1962 and 2004. Typical analyses of wealth accumulation— including the analysis up to this point in the chapter—look at statistics about the

TABLE 2.3   /   SCF Households with Any Pension Coverage

	1989	1992	1995	1998	2001	2004
Full sample	56.3%	56.2%	56.9%	56.9%	57.1%	57.5%
Income quintile						
Lowest quintile	24.0	20.1	20.6	22.7	20.8	19.6
Second quintile	42.9	46.4	45.6	45.2	47.0	46.9
Middle quintile	65.1	63.3	63.8	63.0	63.1	65.8
Fourth quintile	75.5	75.1	75.1	78.1	77.8	75.7
Highest quintile	79.4	79.4	81.1	78.6	78.4	80.1
Education						
Less than high school	44.3	37.1	37.2	37.5	34.7	34.2
High school	53.0	52.6	55.8	53.8	53.4	55.8
More than high school	65.9	66.4	65.6	65.9	67.0	65.2
Marital status						
Single parent	36.9	42.7	40.4	38.4	41.4	42.1
Married	67.8	66.8	65.2	65.2	66.0	65.3
Single, childless	41.8	41.6	47.3	47.9	44.4	48.5
Race-ethnicity						
White and other	61.4	59.7	59.1	60.7	59.9	61.6
Black	38.9	47.1	48.2	46.0	50.2	49.9
Hispanic	34.5	34.7	45.4	32.3	40.6	34.8
Age						
Under thirty	29.7	36.8	41.2	33.4	35.3	32.7
Thirty to sixty-four	64.3	63.0	63.7	64.1	64.1	62.2
Sixty-five or older	53.2	49.0	47.4	50.4	49.7	58.7

Source: Survey of Consumer Finances and authors' calculations.

evolution of mean or median wealth held by the population, sometimes broken out by subgroups. The discussion of these trends often includes statements that the financial well-being of representative families has increased (or decreased) relative to other populations. But these analyses miss the fact that the median household in one year is quite unlikely to be the median in another, if for no other reason than that people age, and as they do they typically accumulate wealth, at least into retirement.

With repeated cross-sectional data, as we have with the SCF, we can follow the financial fortunes of cohorts of households over time and look at how their experiences differ from other household cohorts. Focusing on cohorts provides a different and arguably more informative analysis of the evolution of resources for typical American families over time.

In figure 2.5, we show the evolution of wealth for two age groups: households with a head between the ages of twenty-five and thirty-nine and households with a head between forty and fifty-four. In the SCF, the head is arbitrarily chosen to

FIGURE 2.5 / Median Net Worth of Household Cohorts, Full Population
(2004 Dollars)

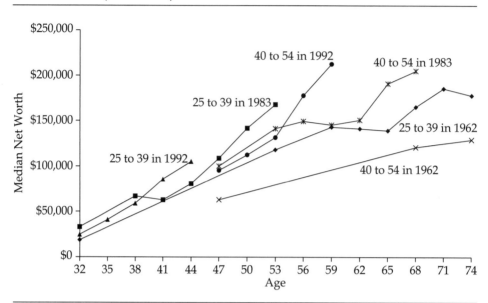

Source: Survey of Consumer Finances.

be the male in households with both a male and a female adult; it is the oldest adult in households with two adults of the same sex. Spanning four decades, our wealth data allow us to plot the evolution of median net worth for three cohorts of twenty-five- to thirty-nine-year-olds: those who were in this age group in 1962, those who were in this age group in 1983, and those who were in this age group in 1992. We also plot the evolution of median net worth for three older cohorts: those who were between the ages of forty and fifty-four in 1962, 1983, and 1992.

The age bands we use are broad owing to sample size considerations (particularly in subsequent figures, where we disaggregate by education and race-ethnicity). In figures 2.5 through 2.9, we plot the median net worth for the middle age in the given age band. (For example, households with a head age forty to fifty-four are plotted as if they were forty-seven years old.) The figures show the evolution of median net worth for the *same sets of households over time,* since we know that the heads of households who were twenty-five to thirty-nine in 1962 will be forty-six to sixty in 1983, fifty-two to sixty-six in 1989, and so on, until their final observation as sixty-seven- to eighty-one-year-olds in 2004 (aside from mortality, immigration and emigration, and changes in household composition). We follow the other cohorts similarly. Obviously, we observe fewer years for cohorts that begin in 1983 (who are followed to 2004) and 1992 (who are also followed to 2004) than we do for the cohorts that we first observe in 1962. Because mortality rates grow appreciably higher for household

FIGURE 2.6 / Median Net Worth of Household Cohorts with a College Degree
(2004 Dollars)

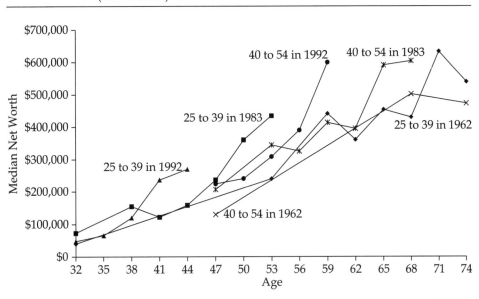

Source: Survey of Consumer Finances.

heads in their midseventies, we truncate the ages shown in the figures at age seventy-four.

There are three noteworthy aspects of figure 2.5. First, the forty- to fifty-four-year-old cohort in 1962 (the line marked by "x" in the lower right portion of the figure) had significantly lower net worth than the other cohorts. Individuals in this cohort were children or young adults during the Depression and young adults during World War II. Opportunities for human capital acquisition and wealth accumulation were more limited for this cohort than they were for subsequent cohorts. Second, median net worth grows steadily for each cohort. The patterns shown here are difficult to reconcile with assertions that living standards for typical Americans are declining. Third, each successive cohort ends up with somewhat more wealth after the last period of observation (in 2004) than the cohort before it. To see this, at each of the six endpoints for the cohort, the highest marker is for the youngest cohort examined (read straight down, which holds age constant). This suggests that net worth (in levels) is growing across cohorts.

Figures 2.6 and 2.7 repeat the same analyses, splitting the samples into households whose heads have a college degree (figure 2.6) and households whose heads do not (figure 2.7). The highest median net worth of the college sample is $633,311, while the highest for the noncollege sample is $137,800. Given the widely differing levels and growth rates of the two groups, we use different scales for the Y-axis of the two figures.

FIGURE 2.7 / Median Net Worth of Household Cohorts Without a College Degree
(2004 Dollars)

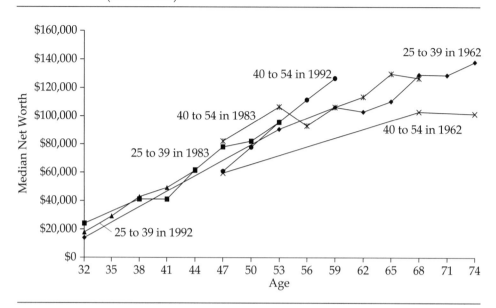

Source: Survey of Consumer Finances.

The breakouts by education suggest that the disadvantage faced by the cohort that was age forty-five to fifty-four in 1962 (those who were children and young adults in the Depression and entered the labor market during World War II) is largely confined to those without a college degree. While college graduates in the Depression cohort started with less net worth than later college graduate cohorts, they reached retirement with similar amounts of net worth.

Significant accumulation occurs in both figures 2.6 (for households with a college degree) and 2.7 (for households without a college degree) as households age, though households without a college degree start from a very low base. We also find it striking how similar median net worth is across cohorts at a given age. While the evidence is suggestive, if households are making severe, systematic mistakes in retirement planning, the mistakes appear to be happening consistently across cohorts. This interpretation is consistent with the evidence in Scholz, Seshadri, and Khitatrakun (2006) suggesting that American households in the original Health and Retirement Study (HRS) cohort—households with heads born between 1931 and 1941—are preparing optimally for retirement, in the sense that they are maximizing the discounted value of lifetime utility, given their lifetime resources. We elaborate on this idea in the final section.

It is also striking that the very strong economic and stock market performance between 1998 and 2004 is evident only in figure 2.6, which is restricted to those with a college degree. The upticks in 2001 and 2004 are not solely or

FIGURE 2.8 / Median Net Worth of White Household Cohorts (in 2004 Dollars)

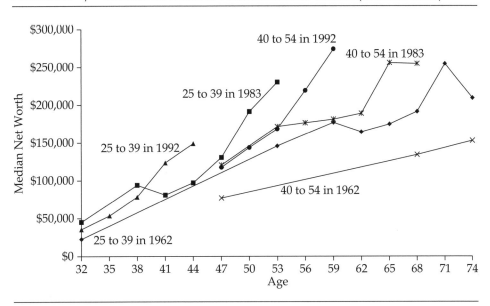

Source: Survey of Consumer Finances.

primarily a stock market phenomenon. Consider, for example, the cohort that was twenty-five to thirty-nine in 1962. In 1998 their median housing equity was $108,500, and their stock market wealth (stocks, stock mutual funds, and defined-contribution pensions) was $75,950. In 2001 these assets had grown to $160,000 and $119,000. Similar patterns hold (and more dramatically) for the young cohort (twenty-five to thirty-nine) defined in 1983 and 1992. The typical American's balance sheet is still tied more closely to housing markets than stock markets.

Figures 2.8 and 2.9 present the evolution of cohort net worth for whites and all other racial and ethnic groups. (Black and Hispanic households are combined, owing to small sample sizes.) Figure 2.8 (for whites) shows the patterns described previously. The Depression cohort has significantly lower levels of net worth than other cohorts. There is a steady increase in net worth over the life cycle. Median net worth appears to be growing strongly over time.

The patterns for nonwhites shown in figure 2.9 make vivid the enormous economic disadvantage faced by black and Hispanic households. Median net worth across cohorts is extremely low—in many cases less than half the amounts shown in figure 2.7 for cohorts with less than a college degree. Moreover, there is very little increase in net worth over time for the twenty-five- to thirty-nine-year-old cohorts in particular. The only (slightly) heartening result is that for the older cohorts (age forty to fifty-four), starting net worth appears to be increasing with each cohort. But the levels are still strikingly low.

FIGURE 2.9 / Median Net Worth of Nonwhite Household Cohorts (in 2004 Dollars)

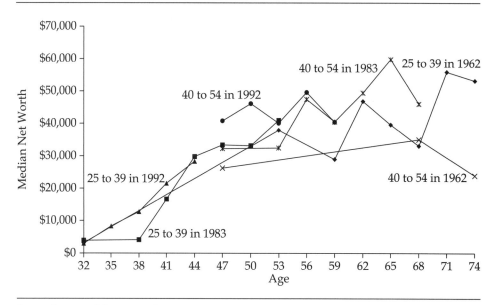

Source: Survey of Consumer Finances.

BLACK-WHITE DIFFERENCES IN WEALTH ACCUMULATION

The cohort differences in white-black median wealth shown in figures 2.8 and 2.9 are striking. A natural reaction might be to wonder whether black families have lower net worth than white families because their income is lower. This is not the sole explanation, however, since even when black and white families with similar incomes are compared, black families accumulate less wealth. A near-universal finding of studies that seek to explain differences in the wealth held by black and white families is that considerably more of the wealth gap can be "explained" if the regression coefficients estimated on a sample of white households are used to predict wealth for black households than if the regression coefficients estimated on a sample of black households are used to predict wealth for white households. This discrepancy is unsatisfying, since there is no a priori reason to prefer one approach to the other.

We briefly discuss the factors that affect wealth accumulation across groups as a way to highlight many of the broader behavioral mechanisms affecting wealth accumulation. Our discussion draws on the work of John Karl Scholz and Kara Levine (2004), who have surveyed the academic work on black-white wealth differences.

The first observation is that blacks have systematically less income than whites. If wealth is a convex function of income (if wealth increases with income at an increasing rate), the predicted wealth function using only the low end of the income distribution will be flatter—there will appear to be a weaker relationship between income and wealth—than we would observe when using households throughout the income distribution. Recent papers (see, for example, Altonji and Doraszelski 2005) are sensitive to this consideration. It does not appear to be the explanation for black-white wealth differences.

Second, as Charles and Hurst (2002) show, 42 percent of white households in the Panel Study of Income Dynamics (PSID) get help from their family in making a down payment on a home. Fewer than 10 percent of black families get such help. This specific example suggests that there may be racial differences in the likelihood (or ability) of parents helping children make high-return investments. Differences in intrafamily transfers appear to play some role. There is conflicting evidence, however, on the importance of inheritances. Our best guess is that they play a modest role in understanding black-white wealth gaps at the median of the population.

Third, family background would appear to be another factor useful in explaining black-white wealth differences. Joseph Altonji and Ulrich Doraszelski (2005) address the role of family background in a clever way. They compare the degree to which the black-white wealth gap can be explained by standard models incorporating a rich set of demographic characteristics and income, with the degree to which the black-white wealth gap can be explained by the same models augmented with family-specific fixed effects. The effect of family background on wealth should not differ for siblings; that is, it should be "fixed" within a given family. Altonji and Doraszelski conclude that family background does not play an important role in understanding black-white wealth gaps, but their conclusion is not universally held. The results in Charles and Hurst (2003), for example, suggest that saving preferences are inherited, though perhaps not uniformly across children, so that family background could affect wealth beyond direct financial transfers.

Fourth, consumption patterns may differ for blacks and whites. There is no solid evidence on racial differences in saving rates. Francine Blau and John Graham (1990) argue that blacks' higher unemployment rates (and transitory income) result in their holding assets in a more liquid form, particularly at lower levels of income and wealth. There is also suggestive (but hardly definitive) evidence from the SCF that households may have systematically different preferences for risk, even after conditioning on observable characteristics, and that these preferences may be related to wealth. Perhaps the most striking related evidence comes from Kerwin Charles, Erik Hurst, and Nikolai Roussanov (2007), who show that blacks consume a greater share of their income in highly visible "conspicuous consumption" (clothing, jewelry, automobiles) than whites. Their evidence is only suggestive, but they conclude that at least some of this greater level of visible consumption may be financed by less saving. More work needs to be done, however, to assess the quantitative importance of this explanation.

Fifth, the strong correlations between health and wealth and between race and health suggest that differences in health status may have an important influence on wealth inequality. These relationships clearly need to be better understood, but the task will be difficult. A central impediment to making further progress is identifying plausible exogenous variation in health that can inform evidence on the direction of causality in the relationship between health and wealth.

Sixth, there is little evidence that blacks and whites get different rates of return on specific portfolio investments, though Altonji and Doraszelski (2005) point to rate-of-return differences (as well as black-white differences in saving rates) as the most likely explanations of the black-white wealth gap. Blacks indeed have a greater share of their household net worth invested in housing, so differences in housing and equity market returns may play some role in understanding wealth gaps. Also, the existing evidence, though somewhat sparse, suggests that the effects of antipoverty program asset tests are not large and that only a small percentage of the population is affected. In the absence of more evidence, we conclude that public assistance programs do not contribute significantly to racial wealth inequality.

Seventh, discrimination against black households in financial markets, such as red-lining or mortgage discrimination, may contribute to racial differences in wealth accumulation (for literature reviews, see Barr 2005; Ross and Yinger 2002).

Interesting work is being done that will help us better understand these differences, but more needs to be learned about racial differences in wealth accumulation if we are to design policies that will more effectively address the disparities.

AN INTERPRETATION OF THESE RESULTS

This chapter documents the fact that the typical household in the bottom quintile of the income distribution, the median single-parent household, the median black household, and the median Hispanic household have very low levels of financial assets.

It is natural then to ask what this implies about public policy targeted to disadvantaged populations. The answer depends importantly, we believe, on one's views about the decisionmaking of low-income households. Reasonable people can certainly differ in their views, and any informed view requires an assessment of complex behavior based on limited information. With these qualifications, however, we think the evidence is consistent with the view that low-income households behave in a manner broadly consistent with rational, forward-looking financial decisionmaking. Two primary pieces of evidence support this viewpoint.

First, in Scholz, Seshadri, and Khitatrakun (2006), we examine the degree to which households born between 1931 and 1941 are "optimally" accumulating wealth. Scholz and Seshadri (2008) extend these results to a representative sample of American households born before 1954. In these papers, we build a stochastic life-cycle model that captures the key features of a household's consumption decisions. Our model incorporates many behavioral features shown by prior work to affect consumption, including precautionary saving in the presence of uncertain earnings. In addition to earnings uncertainty, households face uncertainty about longevity and end-of-life medical shocks. Families can draw on income- and asset-tested public transfers, the rules of which vary realistically over time and by household size. We also incorporate a stylized, time-varying progressive income tax that reflects the evolution of average effective federal income tax rates over the period spanned by our data. Households in the model form realistic expectations about earnings; about Social Security benefits, which depend on lifetime earnings;

and about pension benefits, which depend on earnings in the final year of work. We incorporate detailed data from the Health and Retirement Study on family structure and age of retirement (treating both as exogenous and known from the beginning of working life) in calculating optimal life-cycle consumption profiles.

Our approach has other distinctive features. Most important, we calculate household-specific optimal wealth targets using data from the HRS. A crucial input to our behavioral model is forty-one years of information on earnings realizations drawn from restricted-access Social Security earnings records. The timing of earnings shocks can cause optimal wealth to vary substantially, even for households with identical preferences, demographic characteristics, and lifetime income. Hence, it is essential for life-cycle models of wealth accumulation to incorporate earnings realizations, at least to the extent that model implications are compared to actual behavior.

In Scholz, Seshadri, and Khitatrakun (2006), we find that over 80 percent of HRS households have accumulated more wealth than their optimal targets in 1992. In Scholz and Seshadri (2008), we find that more than 90 percent of households (with a broader range of ages) have accumulated more wealth than their optimal targets in 2004. These targets indicate the amounts of private saving that households should have acquired at the time we observe them in the data, given their life-cycle planning problem and Social Security and defined-benefit pension expectations and realizations. For those who do not meet their targets, the magnitudes of the deficits are typically small. Importantly for readers of this chapter, the likelihood of undersaving varies little with lifetime income, so households with low lifetime income are only somewhat (in the more recent work) more likely to have accumulated too little wealth than households with high lifetime income. We emphasize that our study is not only about "saving for retirement." Households in the model have uncertain future earnings, so the wealth targets incorporate precautionary motives that arise from earnings volatility.

The cross-sectional distribution of net worth matches closely the predictions of our life-cycle model. We also show that our model matches patterns of observed wealth holdings far better than models that emphasize simpleminded rules of thumb. This evidence suggests that the life-cycle model, in which rational, forward-looking households make consumption decisions to equate the discounted marginal utility of consumption over time, is a very good way to understand household consumption decisions.

The second piece of evidence comes from figures 2.5 through 2.9. As noted earlier, we find it striking how closely distributed median net worth is across cohorts at a given age. If households are making severe, systematic mistakes in retirement planning, the mistakes appear to be happening consistently across cohorts. We think it is unlikely that major life-cycle planning mistakes would be made across generations, though we note that major social insurance programs for the elderly have become more generous in recent decades. Parents, who care about their children, would presumably advise their children about financial planning decisions that could significantly decrease their well-being. Even if communication does not occur within the family, if older generations of households were making significant financial planning mistakes, surely popular media outlets would be calling attention to such problems. But strikingly few journalistic pieces make this argument. Indeed, as noted in Scholz and Seshadri (2008), only 9 percent of retired households born before 1954 find retirement "not at all satisfying," and only 19 percent find their living standards worse in retirement than they were prior to retirement.

How can the low levels of financial assets held by households in the bottom quintile of the income distribution, by single parents, and by black and Hispanic households be consistent with these households doing the best they can, given the circumstances and constraints they face? There are two central considerations. First, fertility rates typically decrease with household income, if for no other reason than that the opportunity cost of the time it takes to raise children increases with income. Children consume significant resources, so families with more children may have less wealth than otherwise identical families with fewer children. Second, the adults in families with more children get used to consuming fewer resources than the adults in otherwise identical households with fewer children. Thus, the adults in families with more children may need to accumulate fewer resources to support consumption in retirement than otherwise identical adults in families with fewer children. This observation, along with the fact that the Social Security system is sharply progressive in lifetime income—replacement rates (when measured against average lifetime earnings) for low-income families can exceed 50 percent—results in the optimal saving rate for many low-income families being effectively zero.

We emphasize that our view that people are doing the best they can is not intended to imply that we think the state of affairs is desirable—we would like poor households to have greater resources. But how should wealth-related policy best assist poor families? We have argued that low or zero net worth may be optimal for many low- and moderate-income families at particular points in time. Indeed, the presence of public safety net programs recognizes that some families need all their resources (and some public assistance) at points in their lives.

The logic of the budget constraint implies that less consumption is needed if households are to accumulate greater wealth, holding income constant. We fear that policies that encourage poor families with children to consume even less than they already do may be counterproductive to the well-being of those families. One of the most compelling rationales for *social* insurance programs is that it is inefficient for individuals to self-insure against, for example, longevity risk (or unemployment, or workplace injuries). By pooling risks, individual households can collectively finance the insurance pool and have higher consumption (and hence well-being) than they would if they had to set aside resources to cover adverse shocks individually. In the event of a bad shock, they can draw on the social insurance mechanism. The same intuition is likely to apply to the consumption-smoothing needs of disadvantaged populations. We are skeptical that it is efficient for disadvantaged households to self-insure for possible adverse economic events by depressing already low consumption levels. Instead, well-being is likely to be enhanced by strengthening social insurance mechanisms. Similarly, given that the public resources available to support programs targeting low-income households are scarce, cost-effective efforts to enhance consumption or human capital are more attractive to us than wealth-building initiatives.

As the chapters in this volume make clear, there may be important opportunities to improve household well-being by disseminating cost-effective approaches to improving financial education, providing greater access to financial services, and promulgating harsh restrictions on predatory lending practices.

We thank Michael Barr and Becky Blank for their guidance, Ben Cowan for outstanding assistance, Jeff Liebman and conference participants for their comments, and Karen Pence for her insights on the Survey of Consumer Finances. We also thank Arthur Kennickell and his colleagues at the Board of Governors of the Federal Reserve for their extraordinary work in developing, conducting, and analyzing the SCFs, and Kevin Moore and Chris Carroll for generously sharing their net worth definitions for the 1962 Survey of Financial Characteristics of Consumers.

APPENDIX

TABLE 2A.1 / Population with Positive Net Worth, 1962 to 2004

	1962	1983	1989	1992	1995	1998	2001	2004
Full sample	86.7%	92.1%	88.4%	89.8%	90.4%	89.6%	90.4%	91.0%
Income quintile								
Lowest quintile	70.6	78.0	70.6	74.4	77.1	75.7	76.0	80.3
Second quintile	82.2	90.0	88.0	90.5	88.5	88.3	88.7	87.9
Middle quintile	87.1	94.5	93.0	92.2	91.9	90.5	92.1	92.3
Fourth quintile	95.4	98.5	94.1	94.7	96.5	95.9	96.5	95.4
Highest quintile	98.3	99.4	98.9	98.6	98.7	98.8	99.5	99.5
Education								
Less than high school	83.2	87.3	82.9	83.2	84.1	82.8	82.2	86.1
High school	90.8	94.7	88.0	89.8	91.4	92.0	91.3	93.7
More than high school	91.4	93.5	92.1	92.5	92.4	90.7	92.8	91.1
Marital status								
Single parent	70.1	86.0	73.8	77.3	77.2	80.9	76.6	82.3
Married	89.6	96.2	93.9	93.3	94.4	93.2	94.7	94.7
Single, childless	82.3	85.2	83.4	87.8	87.8	85.9	87.0	87.5
Race-ethnicity								
White and other	89.0	95.1	93.2	92.7	92.8	92.2	93.3	93.3
Black	65.8	77.8	68.4	80.0	79.2	78.8	78.7	80.2
Hispanic	—	73.3	73.3	74.9	81.9	77.9	81.4	88.6
Age								
Under thirty	67.3	82.3	77.5	73.3	78.2	72.0	73.8	74.9
Thirty to sixty-four	89.1	94.5	89.0	91.3	91.1	91.2	92.2	92.3
Sixty-five or older	91.1	94.3	95.1	96.2	96.4	96.0	95.8	97.5

Source: Survey of Consumer Finances.

TABLE 2A.2 / Mean and Median Net Worth, Conditional on Having Positive Amounts, 1962 to 2004 (2004 Dollars)

	1952	1983	1989	1992	1995	1998	2001	2004
Means								
Full sample	164,531	250,822	326,722	280,868	292,649	366,975	469,293	493,205
Income quintile								
Lowest quintile	67,193	61,140	57,381	63,918	75,568	79,739	75,861	92,359
Second quintile	74,167	92,414	124,695	97,215	113,116	130,161	144,017	142,066
Middle quintile	92,650	114,840	173,098	156,000	138,509	162,504	198,156	214,667
Fourth quintile	118,101	166,451	229,993	197,953	210,990	249,160	329,939	356,835
Highest quintile	418,987	756,494	969,134	828,987	861,537	1,119,857	1,502,622	1,527,850
Education								
Less than high school	113,601	111,889	142,251	110,467	120,696	112,432	137,359	158,497
High school	128,850	171,167	207,186	171,793	186,906	204,946	218,318	215,753
More than high school	320,045	404,000	505,728	408,039	419,180	548,112	711,894	735,634
Marital status								
Single parent	74,984	147,499	130,505	95,104	119,644	148,463	133,916	160,358
Married	178,363	317,469	424,426	366,627	372,196	475,274	608,668	651,423
Single, childless	138,700	115,166	181,228	172,048	185,137	218,847	265,083	287,937
Race-ethnicity								
White and other	174,728	279,719	373,350	321,006	333,924	420,306	551,177	585,686
Black	35,858	71,206	91,278	88,056	74,269	88,010	98,822	134,545
Hispanic	—	67,888	93,154	102,165	95,838	126,961	124,760	157,192
Age								
Under thirty	36,447	45,356	79,852	51,784	52,188	55,765	91,575	68,390
Thirty to sixty-four	167,381	267,811	342,251	293,779	300,672	382,911	475,659	518,980
Sixty-five or older	217,953	378,833	434,760	358,135	397,352	473,208	638,990	624,476

Median amounts							
Full sample	60,523	79,467	96,141	83,719	87,013	104,683	115,633	119,900
Income quintile								
Lowest quintile	37,348	18,494	15,843	26,443	19,832	23,873	25,066	17,000
Second quintile	34,183	40,244	56,304	51,702	57,451	59,532	54,931	52,300
Middle quintile	41,933	63,490	80,404	65,220	66,412	82,861	81,490	87,200
Fourth quintile	67,141	93,600	116,478	106,947	99,767	136,518	167,429	167,990
Highest quintile	131,611	250,054	353,426	270,492	259,614	356,534	474,970	512,800
Education								
Less than high school	53,011	52,080	61,591	43,085	49,047	48,650	52,265	41,460
High school	63,325	71,805	82,720	63,685	81,919	77,530	77,971	81,000
More than high school	75,322	120,471	154,014	125,888	113,166	149,718	193,273	197,500
Marital status								
Single parent	26,921	58,034	30,955	28,948	36,925	33,202	35,039	36,920
Married	65,771	102,833	139,207	118,887	111,171	140,620	169,701	171,482
Single, childless	48,739	22,488	49,480	54,125	58,653	70,727	73,971	77,000
Race-ethnicity								
White and other	66,690	91,262	121,414	102,542	102,817	124,836	151,035	155,000
Black	12,910	24,879	34,657	37,767	33,739	28,972	37,119	34,700
Hispanic	—	28,580	23,917	30,161	32,847	31,464	28,586	35,300
Age								
Under thirty	8,963	13,940	15,188	15,214	17,911	14,139	17,119	15,700
Thirty to sixty-four	67,816	95,901	116,204	91,690	91,227	106,966	125,105	129,250
Sixty-five or older	69,011	114,201	129,488	131,543	130,357	166,417	191,588	184,700

Source: Survey of Consumer Finances.

TABLE 2A.3 / Population with Positive Financial Assets, 1962 to 2004

	1962	1983	1989	1992	1995	1998	2001	2004
Full sample	85.0%	89.6%	88.5%	90.3%	90.7%	92.8%	93.1%	93.8%
Income quintile								
Lowest quintile	60.0	69.4	62.0	69.9	69.3	76.0	74.8	80.3
Second quintile	79.7	85.4	88.3	88.9	90.4	93.0	93.2	91.7
Middle quintile	89.8	95.0	97.4	95.8	96.6	97.3	98.4	98.3
Fourth quintile	97.1	98.6	98.6	99.4	98.2	99.1	99.7	99.1
Highest quintile	98.3	99.8	99.8	99.4	100.0	99.9	99.7	99.9
Education								
Less than high school	79.2	76.9	74.2	73.2	76.0	77.6	78.4	78.4
High school	91.9	93.2	88.3	90.5	90.2	93.7	92.9	93.4
More than high school	92.7	96.1	97.3	97.5	97.0	97.8	98.3	98.6
Marital status								
Single parent	62.2	80.3	72.1	75.9	76.2	82.5	81.1	86.2
Married	88.6	93.7	94.0	94.1	94.5	95.4	95.7	95.8
Single, childless	79.8	88.7	84.0	88.5	89.1	91.5	92.2	93.2
Race-ethnicity								
White and other	87.7	94.1	94.8	95.0	94.5	96.0	96.3	97.0
Black	57.7	67.7	62.5	77.2	73.4	80.4	83.7	85.3
Hispanic	—	63.9	67.7	62.3	75.5	76.9	76.0	79.5
Age								
Under thirty	81.0	85.7	84.2	84.0	84.9	85.9	87.4	90.4
Thirty to sixty-four	86.1	90.9	88.6	91.3	91.2	93.8	93.7	93.5
Sixty-five or older	83.6	89.3	91.5	91.4	93.0	93.9	94.8	97.0

Source: Survey of Consumer Finances.

TABLE 2A.4 / Mean and Median Financial Assets, Conditional on Positive Amounts, 1962 to 2004 (2004 Dollars)

	1962	1983	1989	1992	1995	1998	2001	2004
Mean								
Full sample	72,145	85,581	113,653	103,425	121,139	166,703	217,303	200,298
Income quintile								
Lowest quintile	28,484	10,319	19,207	15,524	19,841	24,583	26,062	23,061
Second quintile	21,348	22,102	33,770	30,525	39,702	49,019	48,895	42,797
Middle quintile	32,434	30,550	49,534	51,179	49,937	60,468	87,138	74,076
Fourth quintile	40,731	47,194	79,895	67,188	84,611	111,174	158,101	145,497
Highest quintile	207,402	282,614	349,721	324,616	375,984	552,736	734,466	671,451
Education								
Less than high school	39,380	32,816	39,984	34,594	38,656	34,987	47,953	43,216
High school	47,619	44,730	62,356	58,314	65,368	81,164	83,067	80,206
More than high school	169,028	145,389	179,754	149,943	178,653	252,685	336,453	296,582
Marital status								
Single parent	29,543	57,358	38,079	35,153	44,551	70,066	54,747	51,372
Married	72,721	105,592	145,280	130,801	150,664	212,738	281,150	269,352
Single, childless	77,915	41,008	70,170	70,871	85,719	107,335	133,702	118,525
Race-ethnicity								
White and other	77,613	95,751	129,550	118,504	137,106	190,297	255,778	240,197
Black	8,767	14,086	25,175	24,039	28,436	45,030	43,695	41,773
Hispanic	—	10,908	24,684	25,736	36,558	47,516	46,544	43,654
Age								
Under thirty	14,181	12,018	24,010	14,394	19,789	19,459	39,660	18,924
Thirty to sixty-four	69,482	80,253	106,716	102,559	115,783	170,502	218,195	205,560
Sixty-five or older	119,904	174,163	194,984	158,803	196,717	242,921	320,818	291,689

(Table continues on p. 54.)

TABLE 2A.4 / Continued

	1962	1983	1989	1992	1995	1998	2001	2004
Median amounts								
Full sample	12,510	12,021	17,214	15,282	17,601	25,612	29,865	23,000
Income quintile								
Lowest quintile	5,248	2,156	1,600	1,618	1,785	2,318	2,133	1,400
Second quintile	5,567	6,828	6,413	5,790	7,437	8,170	8,533	4,970
Middle quintile	7,462	7,966	13,101	10,812	11,032	19,354	19,199	15,900
Fourth quintile	13,454	15,121	22,851	22,216	26,017	41,593	60,265	49,480
Highest quintile	39,707	61,448	106,789	93,306	91,723	156,068	213,112	199,000
Education								
Less than high school	9,601	5,906	6,094	3,905	4,834	5,794	5,333	2,580
High school	12,541	9,946	12,187	10,381	12,581	16,109	14,869	12,840
More than high school	23,212	20,862	28,335	28,342	28,942	44,617	60,478	48,020
Marital status								
Single parent	4,760	8,034	4,860	3,770	4,710	6,142	7,520	3,280
Married	12,516	16,438	24,679	24,101	26,030	37,664	46,985	39,500
Single, childless	14,111	5,766	10,511	10,381	11,032	15,147	16,138	12,800
Race-ethnicity								
White and other	13,292	14,659	22,866	19,792	21,691	33,782	39,999	35,000
Black	2,615	2,955	2,742	3,905	5,330	6,409	8,426	3,580
Hispanic	—	3,604	2,742	2,693	4,871	3,651	4,480	4,570
Age								
Under thirty	1,876	2,822	3,504	2,801	4,462	3,593	4,149	3,100
Thirty to sixty-four	14,443	14,704	20,231	18,257	20,328	30,943	37,087	31,300
Sixty-five or older	18,765	26,837	35,221	32,448	28,632	46,124	46,825	38,100

Source: Survey of Consumer Finances.

TABLE 2A.5 / Population with Positive Equity, 1962 to 2004

	1962	1983	1989	1992	1995	1998	2001	2004
Full sample	17.2%	19.1%	31.7%	36.7%	40.4%	48.6%	52.2%	50.2%
Income quintile								
Lowest quintile	7.4	4.2	3.7	8.0	6.4	10.8	13.0	11.7
Second quintile	7.2	10.5	16.0	20.3	26.0	31.3	34.7	30.0
Middle quintile	13.4	15.8	31.6	35.1	41.5	50.8	54.1	51.9
Fourth quintile	20.7	22.9	43.7	51.2	54.3	69.3	74.5	69.8
Highest quintile	37.4	42.0	68.2	71.9	75.0	84.0	87.4	88.2
Education								
Less than high school	10.3	6.6	10.2	11.8	15.6	18.6	19.7	15.7
High school	20.3	17.0	26.9	29.4	33.7	42.6	43.7	41.8
More than high school	31.8	29.6	48.0	51.5	54.5	63.2	68.4	64.6
Marital status								
Single parent	7.4	12.0	16.1	19.9	24.3	30.4	29.8	28.2
Married	18.9	22.2	39.5	44.9	48.3	57.5	61.6	60.0
Single, childless	14.6	18.1	22.7	27.5	31.2	38.2	41.3	40.1
Race-ethnicity								
White and other	19.0	21.9	37.2	42.0	44.6	54.0	57.7	57.7
Black	1.5	6.0	10.5	18.0	20.0	28.7	33.2	26.4
Hispanic	—	1.0	12.1	11.8	24.9	21.0	29.4	22.0
Age								
Under thirty	9.2	11.4	18.4	23.6	32.7	33.2	43.2	34.3
Thirty to sixty-four	18.9	20.7	37.0	42.6	45.1	56.0	58.7	56.5
Sixty-five or older	16.5	21.8	26.5	28.1	31.4	36.1	37.9	40.7

Source: Survey of Consumer Finances.

TABLE 2A.6 / Mean and Median Equity, Conditional on Positive Amounts, 1962 to 2004 (2004 Dollars)

	1962	1983	1989	1992	1995	1998	2001	2004
Mean								
Full sample	123,668	110,381	91,079	85,402	112,757	172,206	219,140	191,675
Income quintile								
Lowest quintile	78,102	11,853	39,952	18,861	32,607	39,563	59,022	50,408
Second quintile	47,203	16,842	21,537	21,389	41,040	42,785	48,967	40,670
Middle quintile	46,725	18,082	26,681	28,576	33,364	45,078	77,684	61,313
Fourth quintile	23,019	25,779	40,820	37,435	56,595	73,784	110,925	86,538
Highest quintile	230,886	224,151	173,264	174,242	231,589	396,739	504,757	423,809
Education								
Less than high school	87,428	40,417	40,349	25,929	35,751	41,058	57,711	42,330
High school	62,638	53,078	38,468	44,666	55,120	84,200	81,866	68,497
More than high school	193,946	146,087	118,064	104,847	143,156	220,643	285,194	244,186
Marital status								
Single parent	63,423	90,251	37,236	24,917	38,600	105,023	50,804	68,625
Married	119,298	128,217	103,665	93,715	126,071	194,919	251,388	227,927
Single, childless	146,950	40,922	63,507	76,028	95,391	126,681	165,836	121,651
Race-ethnicity								
White and other	126,993	115,030	96,769	91,162	122,339	186,877	244,477	209,892
Black	12,472	5,991	23,439	28,119	20,586	35,756	44,637	44,129
Hispanic	—	9,413	12,129	16,395	32,604	58,096	49,070	52,492
Age								
Under thirty	41,437	11,453	29,234	10,338	14,531	21,787	42,354	18,985
Thirty to sixty-four	86,814	85,876	77,881	80,995	103,771	159,976	200,195	183,064
Sixty-five or older	308,884	236,249	176,725	145,458	216,918	319,524	440,671	320,767

Median amounts								
Full sample	8,945	7,617	13,710	14,676	17,973	28,972	37,332	32,500
Income quintile								
Lowest quintile	21,023	3,630	21,327	8,886	4,338	5,794	8,320	8,000
Second quintile	11,140	6,638	9,140	5,116	8,057	11,010	8,533	10,000
Middle quintile	3,127	5,713	7,617	6,732	7,437	14,023	15,999	15,000
Fourth quintile	5,042	4,116	9,140	10,973	16,114	21,440	31,466	27,000
Highest quintile	20,523	18,966	35,419	37,699	45,862	92,132	131,195	110,000
Education								
Less than high school	4,941	6,638	12,187	6,732	6,817	11,589	9,600	9,000
High school	6,593	5,690	11,425	8,078	12,395	18,542	18,133	18,000
More than high school	15,481	9,483	15,234	18,850	24,170	38,719	53,331	46,800
Marital status								
Single parent	7,506	7,586	6,094	5,924	7,437	14,718	8,746	9,600
Married	6,593	9,483	15,234	16,157	21,072	35,028	46,729	40,000
Single, childless	28,116	4,741	12,187	13,464	13,635	20,860	26,666	27,600
Race-ethnicity								
White and other	9,382	8,535	15,234	15,484	19,832	34,014	43,732	39,000
Black	1,876	1,138	6,094	8,078	5,578	8,112	9,706	11,000
Hispanic	—	9,413	1,523	5,857	6,321	10,430	8,213	9,400
Age								
Under thirty	3,615	1,897	3,047	3,097	4,710	5,215	4,160	4,700
Thirty to sixty-four	7,900	7,586	13,710	15,484	18,679	30,131	38,399	32,500
Sixty-five or older	32,413	22,759	38,085	28,274	34,086	64,898	140,795	75,800

Source: Survey of Consumer Finances.

TABLE 2A.7 / Population with Positive Housing Wealth

	1962	1983	1989	1992	1995	1998	2001	2004
Full sample	56.2%	63.1%	62.7%	63.0%	63.2%	64.3%	66.3%	68.0%
Income quintile								
Lowest quintile	40.0	40.3	33.4	40.1	39.5	38.7	38.6	39.6
Second quintile	42.8	51.5	55.3	56.9	55.3	54.8	56.3	56.3
Middle quintile	51.8	60.6	64.1	61.7	60.0	65.1	64.7	70.4
Fourth quintile	67.9	74.9	75.2	73.1	75.7	76.6	81.0	82.1
Highest quintile	78.3	88.3	89.6	85.7	86.7	88.6	92.5	92.3
Education								
Less than high school	55.4	61.3	59.9	57.2	58.0	53.8	56.1	56.5
High school	57.8	64.7	59.4	61.8	64.1	63.8	64.0	65.4
More than high school	56.4	63.2	66.8	66.2	64.8	68.5	71.1	72.8
Marital status								
Single parent	42.6	51.3	41.1	44.0	45.0	45.2	44.5	51.9
Married	62.8	75.3	77.5	74.1	73.6	75.9	77.5	78.5
Single, childless	40.3	32.1	42.7	49.5	50.1	49.2	51.0	54.4
Race-ethnicity								
White and other	57.6	67.4	68.6	67.4	67.4	70.0	72.4	73.7
Black	38.0	44.0	40.5	48.5	45.0	38.9	40.9	45.3
Hispanic	—	31.6	40.2	41.4	44.4	42.5	46.5	54.1
Age								
Under thirty	26.5	29.8	27.1	24.4	27.9	26.3	28.3	29.4
Thirty to sixty-four	60.3	70.0	67.9	66.3	66.7	67.5	70.1	71.1
Sixty-five or older	60.8	75.1	74.4	78.3	76.0	79.2	79.0	83.2

Source: Survey of Consumer Finances.

TABLE 2A.8 / Mean and Median Net Housing Wealth, Conditional on Positive Amounts, 1962 to 2004 (2004 Dollars)

	1962	1983	1989	1992	1995	1998	2001	2004
Mean								
Full sample	60,869	102,871	121,602	101,349	94,032	105,165	131,721	163,715
Income quintile								
Lowest quintile	45,105	59,227	56,337	63,703	63,014	72,197	70,735	85,021
Second quintile	51,240	77,119	87,056	73,868	76,605	82,995	96,409	99,215
Middle quintile	47,612	77,856	97,738	81,692	78,489	80,270	87,992	116,000
Fourth quintile	55,881	88,077	99,891	86,462	80,413	88,289	111,219	136,371
Highest quintile	87,337	167,561	207,059	166,235	143,368	167,420	232,783	299,000
Education								
Less than high school	53,424	73,731	80,181	67,478	68,970	71,818	80,287	111,930
High school	59,434	87,124	99,865	79,232	78,677	87,199	90,951	106,458
More than high school	81,158	135,146	157,312	125,914	112,287	124,552	166,736	202,553

TABLE 2A.8 / *Continued*

	1962	1983	1989	1992	1995	1998	2001	2004
Marital status								
Single parent	48,242	85,806	89,928	75,396	76,447	75,793	74,134	83,381
Married	60,523	109,951	127,747	108,099	99,450	114,767	145,796	183,250
Single childless	65,478	80,448	111,525	91,034	84,687	86,856	106,387	140,052
Race-ethnicity								
White and other	63,328	107,445	129,247	108,431	99,655	110,848	142,865	178,095
Black	32,731	58,495	70,819	58,022	54,292	54,971	55,276	82,242
Hispanic	—	98,091	74,771	64,921	61,919	76,489	69,623	100,441
Age								
Under thirty	32,241	40,160	46,724	40,883	31,321	39,218	43,490	45,391
Thirty to sixty-four	61,032	107,167	123,837	97,596	89,028	97,194	124,204	160,254
Sixty-five or older	68,644	115,447	136,070	122,710	121,825	139,925	172,860	199,361
Median amounts								
Full sample	48,163	74,809	76,169	64,627	61,975	69,534	77,864	90,000
Income quintile								
Lowest quintile	37,530	44,293	38,085	47,124	48,341	57,945	57,598	57,000
Second quintile	42,534	65,451	67,197	53,856	61,975	63,739	60,798	68,000
Middle quintile	37,530	61,707	62,459	56,549	55,778	51,745	60,798	70,000
Fourth quintile	46,912	71,306	71,599	58,972	57,017	61,421	70,398	89,000
Highest quintile	70,812	115,508	123,394	107,712	89,244	99,665	133,329	168,000
Education								
Less than high school	43,785	56,898	60,935	49,817	49,580	57,945	58,665	60,000
High school	56,295	70,174	68,552	54,529	57,017	61,421	63,998	70,000
More than high school	61,724	94,829	99,020	79,438	73,131	75,328	93,863	110,000
Marital status								
Single parent	37,530	66,381	65,506	51,163	50,820	42,879	45,865	45,000
Married	46,912	77,147	77,693	65,974	64,454	71,852	85,330	100,000
Single, childless	55,188	54,007	68,552	67,320	61,975	63,739	70,504	85,000
Race-ethnicity								
White and other	50,040	75,863	83,786	70,013	68,173	71,852	85,330	97,000
Black	23,143	41,355	45,702	43,085	37,185	37,085	38,399	47,000
Hispanic	—	79,657	38,085	42,412	49,580	49,833	50,132	60,000
Age								
Under thirty	13,761	31,038	25,898	20,196	22,311	18,542	23,466	24,000
Thirty to sixty-four	49,571	78,818	79,216	60,588	57,017	61,421	69,331	82,000
Sixty-five or older	53,167	75,863	77,693	87,516	95,442	93,871	106,663	120,000

Source: Survey of Consumer Finances.

TABLE 2A.9 / Population with Positive Credit Card Debt, 1962 to 2004

	1962	1983	1989	1992	1995	1998	2001	2004
Full sample	0.0%	37.0%	39.6%	43.8%	47.4%	43.9%	44.3%	46.3%
Income quintile								
Lowest quintile	0.0	12.3	15.9	24.8	26.5	24.9	30.2	29.3
Second quintile	0.0	26.1	30.3	42.6	44.2	41.0	44.4	42.6
Middle quintile	0.0	45.0	50.0	52.1	52.7	50.2	53.0	55.3
Fourth quintile	0.0	53.6	56.7	55.9	60.4	57.7	53.0	56.1
Highest quintile	0.0	48.3	48.9	45.3	54.1	47.5	40.7	48.1
Education								
Less than high school	0.0	21.4	24.2	29.9	32.6	29.4	29.3	29.7
High school	0.0	41.0	41.1	45.7	51.1	43.5	47.8	49.3
More than high school	0.0	45.3	47.7	48.6	51.3	49.6	47.5	49.5
Marital status								
Single parent	0.0	27.7	35.3	43.5	44.3	37.7	47.7	48.5
Married	0.0	43.1	46.8	49.5	53.0	49.9	46.6	50.1
Single, childless	0.0	27.8	27.5	33.6	37.8	34.8	38.0	38.0
Race-ethnicity								
White and other	0.0	37.9	41.2	44.0	46.9	44.2	43.2	46.0
Black	0.0	32.9	33.0	44.5	46.8	40.8	50.9	46.1
Hispanic	—	32.8	34.3	40.4	56.5	46.0	44.1	49.0
Age								
Under thirty	0.0	33.7	41.6	49.8	51.4	49.7	48.0	46.4
Thirty to sixty-four	0.0	45.5	45.8	48.2	54.3	50.4	50.0	52.2
Sixty-five or older	0.0	13.7	20.0	27.2	24.9	20.5	24.2	27.8

Source: Survey of Consumer Finances.

TABLE 2A.10 / Mean and Median Credit Card Debt, Conditional on Positive Amounts, 1983 to 2004 (2004 Dollars)

	1983	1989	1992	1995	1998	2001	2004
Mean							
Full sample	1,644	2,877	3,116	3,709	4,780	4,415	5,132
Income quintile							
Lowest quintile	994	937	1,698	2,510	2,890	2,217	2,691
Second quintile	1,087	1,857	2,215	2,879	3,252	2,966	3,811
Middle quintile	1,402	2,494	2,547	3,397	4,974	3,927	5,161
Fourth quintile	1,706	2,948	3,811	3,482	5,286	5,345	5,552
Highest quintile	2,267	4,551	4,660	5,576	6,351	7,251	7,304
Education							
Less than high school	1,348	1,918	2,188	2,615	3,072	2,328	3,600
High school	1,384	2,610	2,567	3,062	4,050	3,883	4,495
More than high school	1,920	3,328	3,662	4,381	5,524	5,168	5,734

TABLE 2A.10 / *Continued*

	1983	1989	1992	1995	1998	2001	2004
Marital status							
Single parent	1,205	2,094	2,786	3,038	3,811	3,317	4,257
Married	1,809	3,001	3,432	4,086	5,316	4,785	5,725
Single, childless	1,331	2,838	2,415	2,984	3,697	4,003	4,072
Race-ethnicity							
White and other	1,556	2,839	3,238	3,997	5,173	4,690	5,620
Black	2,080	3,215	2,337	2,562	2,870	3,225	3,324
Hispanic	2,419	2,797	3,157	2,414	3,358	4,005	3,811
Age							
Under thirty	1,296	2,439	2,569	3,061	3,237	3,447	2,975
Thirty to sixty-four	1,788	3,150	3,421	4,117	5,207	4,647	5,571
Sixty-five or older	1,000	1,735	2,200	1,981	4,047	4,182	4,865
Median amounts							
Full sample	948	1,371	1,346	1,847	1,970	2,027	2,150
Income quintile							
Lowest quintile	664	533	741	868	1,101	1,067	1,000
Second quintile	749	990	1,144	1,611	1,565	1,280	1,800
Middle quintile	759	1,219	1,252	1,859	2,271	2,133	2,100
Fourth quintile	998	1,523	2,020	1,934	2,665	2,613	3,000
Highest quintile	1,517	3,047	2,383	2,727	2,781	3,200	3,000
Education							
Less than high school	759	1,066	942	1,240	1,367	960	1,100
High school	802	1,371	1,346	1,487	1,622	1,920	2,000
More than high school	1,138	1,523	1,548	2,169	2,318	2,453	2,500
Marital status							
Single parent	759	1,219	1,481	1,860	1,622	1,824	2,080
Married	1,000	1,523	1,521	1,958	2,318	2,240	2,400
Single, childless	759	1,051	1,077	1,240	1,738	1,419	1,850
Race-ethnicity							
White and other	910	1,386	1,346	1,859	2,318	2,133	2,500
Black	1,146	914	969	1,240	1,043	1,547	1,330
Hispanic	1,612	1,676	2,289	1,735	1,391	1,728	1,780
Age							
Under thirty	759	1,219	1,306	1,425	1,507	1,600	1,330
Thirty to sixty-four	1,043	1,523	1,535	2,219	2,318	2,240	2,500
Sixty-five or older	379	777	916	781	1,159	960	1,770

Source: Survey of Consumer Finances.

TABLE 2A.11 / Population with Positive Vehicle Wealth, 1962 to 2004

	1962	1983	1989	1992	1995	1998	2001	2004
Full sample	73.9%	84.4%	83.7%	86.3%	84.2%	82.7%	84.7%	86.3%
Income quintile								
Lowest quintile	30.9	52.6	52.6	58.5	59.4	59.6	56.7	64.9
Second quintile	68.9	82.5	84.1	87.3	86.2	82.4	86.8	85.4
Middle quintile	83.3	93.5	94.0	94.2	91.0	89.4	91.7	91.4
Fourth quintile	92.3	96.6	95.8	96.3	92.8	92.9	95.1	95.4
Highest quintile	94.1	96.8	96.0	97.6	92.9	91.5	93.9	94.5
Education								
Less than high school	66.6	72.5	70.6	71.8	71.7	71.4	68.3	71.9
High school	85.9	88.1	84.8	86.0	87.0	84.6	86.8	87.5
More than high school	80.3	90.0	90.8	92.5	87.6	85.9	89.2	89.8
Marital status								
Single parent	51.7	67.6	61.7	67.4	69.9	67.0	72.1	77.5
Married	88.1	94.9	96.5	95.8	92.2	91.4	92.6	93.1
Single, childless	38.2	69.1	67.4	75.4	74.2	71.9	72.9	76.5
Race-ethnicity								
White and other	77.2	88.6	88.8	90.4	87.9	87.1	88.6	89.8
Black	48.0	61.5	56.4	67.8	63.1	59.7	68.5	69.5
Hispanic	—	67.6	76.7	73.6	79.5	71.1	73.0	81.2
Age								
Under thirty	81.7	81.1	79.2	81.2	81.6	76.4	75.2	80.5
Thirty to sixty-four	80.4	89.4	87.7	89.4	87.0	86.0	89.0	88.5
Sixty-five or older	44.9	71.9	75.2	80.3	77.8	76.9	77.6	82.9

Source: Survey of Consumer Finances.

TABLE 2A.12 / Mean and Median Vehicle Equity, Conditional on Positive Amounts, 1962 to 2004 (2004 Dollars)

	1962	1983	1989	1992	1995	1998	2001	2004
Mean								
Full sample	8,035	10,629	14,988	13,289	16,495	17,611	19,578	20,132
Income quintile								
Lowest quintile	3,384	4,770	6,156	5,701	6,904	7,398	8,471	7,920
Second quintile	4,226	6,567	8,360	7,839	9,849	10,414	12,050	11,018
Middle quintile	6,246	8,182	11,840	10,752	13,880	14,330	16,034	15,927
Fourth quintile	8,799	11,718	16,794	14,943	19,329	19,443	22,234	24,046
Highest quintile	13,193	18,557	27,773	24,098	28,782	32,704	34,994	37,104
Education								
Less than high school	6,415	7,545	9,938	8,847	11,617	11,921	13,665	12,870
High school	8,774	10,122	15,390	11,403	16,326	15,140	17,180	18,033
More than high school	10,665	12,780	17,080	15,782	18,216	20,775	22,478	22,905

TABLE 2A.12 / *Continued*

	1962	1983	1989	1992	1995	1998	2001	2004
Marital status								
Single parent	6,378	7,444	8,643	8,479	9,472	9,902	11,980	11,111
Married	8,396	12,307	18,045	16,094	19,914	21,659	23,674	25,495
Single, childless	6,161	6,336	8,804	8,288	10,778	10,431	11,524	11,185
Race-ethnicity								
White and other	8,136	10,884	15,919	14,029	17,368	18,680	20,751	21,581
Black	6,277	8,953	10,745	9,851	11,202	10,913	14,016	12,822
Hispanic	—	8,373	9,317	9,017	12,072	12,260	14,011	15,944
Age								
Under thirty	6,570	7,700	10,479	9,559	13,336	11,844	14,050	13,169
Thirty to sixty-four	8,664	12,095	16,848	14,796	17,971	19,388	21,140	22,412
Sixty-five or older	5,718	8,241	12,205	10,873	13,825	15,353	17,519	16,896
Median amounts								
Full sample	6,255	7,776	10,664	9,156	12,271	12,748	14,506	14,000
Income quintile								
Lowest quintile	1,564	2,754	3,047	3,501	4,710	4,867	5,653	4,500
Second quintile	3,127	4,918	6,094	5,655	7,809	7,533	9,173	8,100
Middle quintile	4,691	6,685	9,140	8,280	11,527	11,241	13,866	13,100
Fourth quintile	7,475	9,557	13,710	12,522	16,114	16,225	19,199	20,000
Highest quintile	11,259	14,177	20,413	18,042	24,294	24,569	27,306	29,200
Education								
Less than high school	4,378	5,168	6,094	5,386	8,057	7,417	9,386	8,400
High school	7,350	7,804	10,664	8,348	12,519	11,473	13,173	12,300
More than high school	8,131	9,318	12,187	11,175	13,635	15,066	16,853	17,000
Marital status								
Single parent	4,691	4,931	6,094	5,386	7,313	7,069	8,640	7,700
Married	6,255	9,407	13,710	11,848	16,114	16,340	18,559	19,700
Single, childless	4,222	5,121	6,094	5,251	7,933	7,069	8,213	7,700
Race-ethnicity								
White and other	6,255	7,918	11,425	9,694	13,263	13,710	15,679	15,700
Black	4,160	5,737	7,617	6,463	8,800	8,344	10,666	8,300
Hispanic	—	6,496	6,094	5,655	9,048	8,344	10,026	9,800
Age								
Under thirty	5,004	6,354	7,617	7,136	10,288	8,692	10,666	11,000
Thirty to sixty-four	6,411	8,867	12,187	10,637	13,635	13,907	15,999	16,800
Sixty-five or older	3,127	5,233	7,617	6,328	9,048	10,198	12,800	10,200

Source: Survey of Consumer Finances.

NOTE

1. See Bureau of Labor Statistics, "Consumer Price Index," available at: http://www.bls.gov/cpi.

REFERENCES

Altonji, Joseph G., and Ulrich Doraszelski. 2005. "The Role of Permanent Income and Demographics in Black-White Differences in Wealth." *Journal of Human Resources* 40(1): 1–30.

Antoniewicz, Rochelle L. 2000. "A Comparison of the Household Sector from the Flow of Funds Accounts and the Survey of Consumer Finances." Unpublished paper, Board of Governors of the Federal Reserve (October).

Barr, Michael S. 2005. "Credit Where It Counts." *New York University Law Review* 80(2): 101–233.

Blau, Francine D., and John W. Graham. 1990. "Black-White Differences in Wealth and Asset Composition." *Quarterly Journal of Economics* 105(2): 321–39.

Bucks, Brian K., Arthur Kennickell, and Kevin B. Moore. 2006. "Recent Changes in U.S. Family Finances: Evidence from the 2001 and 2004 Survey of Consumer Finances." *Federal Reserve Bulletin*. Available at: http://www.federalreserve.gov/PUBS/oss/oss2/2004/bull0206.pdf (accessed September 9, 2008).

Carney, Stacie, and William G. Gale. 2001. "Asset Accumulation Among Low-Income Households." In *Assets for the Poor*, edited by Thomas M. Shapiro and Edward N. Wolff. New York: Russell Sage Foundation.

Charles, Kerwin Kofi, and Erik Hurst. 2002. "The Transition to Homeownership and the Black-White Wealth Gap." *Review of Economics and Statistics* 84(2): 281–97.

———. 2003. "The Correlation of Wealth Across Generations." *Journal of Political Economy* 111(6): 1155–82.

Charles, Kerwin Kofi, Erik Hurst, and Nikolai Roussanov. 2007. "Conspicuous Consumption and Race." Available at: http://faculty.chicagogsb.edu/erik.hurst/research/race_consumption_qje_submission.pdf (accessed September 9, 2008).

Child Trends Data Bank. 2007. "Family Structure." Available at: http://www.childtrends databank.org/indicators/59FamilyStructure.cfm (accessed September 1, 2007).

Gosselin, Peter. 2004. "The New Deal" (series). *Los Angeles Times*, October 10 to December 30. Available at: http://www.latimes.com/business/la-newdeal-cover,0,6544446.special (accessed January 21, 2009).

Kennickell, Arthur B. 2001. "An Examination of Changes in the Distribution of Wealth from 1989 to 1998: Evidence from the Surveys of Consumer Finances." Unpublished paper, Board of Governors of the Federal Reserve (March 29).

Norquist, Grover. 2007. "America's Tax Policy." *The New Republic* online debate, part 7, posted September 13, 2007. Available at: http://www.tnr.com/doc.mhtml?i=w070910&s=chaitnorquistVII091307 (accessed September 13, 2007).

Piketty, Thomas, and Emmanuel Saez. 2006. "The Evolution of Top Incomes: A Historical and International Perspective." *American Economic Review: Papers and Proceedings* 96(2): 200–205.

Projector, Dorothy S. 1964. "Summary Description of 1962 Survey Results: Survey of Financial Characteristics of Consumers." *Federal Reserve Bulletin* 51(March): 285–93.

Ross, Stephen L., and John Yinger. 2002. *The Color of Credit: Mortgage Discrimination, Research Methodology, and Fair-Lending Enforcement.* Cambridge, Mass.: MIT Press.

Scholz, John Karl, and Kara Levine. 2004. "U.S. Black-White Wealth Inequality: A Survey." In *Social Inequality,* edited by Kathryn Neckerman. New York: Russell Sage Foundation.

Scholz, John Karl, and Ananth Seshadri. 2008. "Are All Americans Saving 'Optimally' for Retirement?" Unpublished paper (August). Available at: http://www.ssc.wisc.edu/~scholz/Research/Are_All_Americans_v2.pdf (accessed September 10, 2008).

Scholz, John Karl, Ananth Seshadri, and Surachai Khitatrakun. 2006. "Are Americans Saving 'Optimally' for Retirement?" *Journal of Political Economy* 114(4): 607–43.

U.S. Senate Banking Committee. 2002. "Bringing More Unbanked Americans into the Financial Mainstream" (hearings). Available at: http://banking.senate.gov/02_05hrg/050202 (accessed November 17, 2008).

Wolff, Edward N. 2000. "Recent Trends in Wealth Ownership, 1983–1998." Working paper 300 (April). Annandale-on-Hudson, N.Y.: Jerome Levy Economics Institute. Available at: http://www.levy.org/pubs/wp300.pdf (accessed September 9, 2008).

Chapter 3

Financial Services, Saving, and Borrowing Among Low- and Moderate-Income Households: Evidence from the Detroit Area Household Financial Services Survey

Michael S. Barr

This chapter presents new empirical evidence documenting the financial services behavior and attitudes of low- and moderate-income (LMI) households. The Detroit Area Household Financial Services (DAHFS) survey uses a random, stratified sample to explore the full range of financial services used by LMI households, together with systematic measures of household preference parameters, demographic characteristics, and households' balance sheets. Results from over one thousand interviews in the DAHFS study suggest that the structure of the financial services, credit, and payments systems in the formal and informal sectors imposes significant costs on LMI households.

Within the severe income constraints they face, LMI households seek to use both formal and informal mechanisms available to them to manage their financial lives. Like their higher-income counterparts, LMI households regularly conduct financial transactions: they convert income to a fungible medium, make payments, save, borrow, seek insurance, and engage in necessary financial and economic decisionmaking. Yet the formal financial services system is not designed to serve them well.

The line between the formal and informal financial services systems used by LMI households is not impermeable. Contrary to popular belief, being unbanked is not necessarily a fixed state. Approximately 70 percent of the unbanked previously had a bank account, and more than 10 percent of banked households were recently unbanked. While the unbanked are much more likely to turn to alternative financial services (AFS) providers, such as check-cashers, than banked households, even banked individuals often use some AFS providers that operate outside the formal banking system. In fact, one type of alternative credit provider, the payday lender, exclusively serves banked individuals.

The financial services choices facing households are complicated; these choices not only involve trade-offs among functionality, convenience, and cost but also require cost comparisons across highly differentiated products in both the AFS and formal sectors. AFS transactions are often described as convenient but high-cost; at the same time, bank accounts are also perceived as high-cost and not usually well structured to serve LMI households. For example, over half of banked LMI households reported paying minimum balance, overdraft, or insufficient funds fees in the previous year. The financial services mismatch between the needs of LMI households and the products and services offered to them largely forces these households to choose among the high-fee, ill-structured products offered by both banking and AFS institutions. These constrained choices reduce take-home pay, making it harder to save and more expensive to borrow.

This chapter begins by briefly describing the financial services marketplace for low- and moderate-income households based on prior research. The following section describes the source of the new data for the chapter regarding the financial services behaviors and attitudes of LMI households. Next is an analysis of the mix of banking and alternative financial services used by banked and unbanked households, the reasons why LMI households use these services, and the trade-offs involved in their usage decisions. The chapter then turns to the savings patterns, attitudes, and decisionmaking of LMI households. The chapter concludes by suggesting directions for financial services and savings policy.

THE FINANCIAL SERVICES MARKETPLACE FOR LMI HOUSEHOLDS

The formal financial services system does not serve LMI households well. Although the overwhelming majority of low- and moderate-income households have and use bank accounts, both these households and their unbanked counterparts often face high costs for transacting basic financial services, significant barriers to saving, and more expensive forms of credit (Barr 2004; Barr and Blank, this volume). High cost and inadequate financial services reduce take-home pay and increase the costs of administration and compliance for essential governmental programs, including Social Security, the Earned Income Tax Credit (EITC), and income transfer and welfare-to-work programs administered by states. In addition, high cost and inadequate financial services diminish the opportunities for LMI households to save readily. Saving is critical for LMI households, in part because LMI households are vulnerable to income shocks, medical emergencies, and even car repairs that can upset their fragile financial stability. Moreover, the lack of bank account ownership and savings increases the cost of credit for these households, reduces their opportunities for stable homeownership through sound credit choices, and diminishes their ability to save or borrow to invest in their own human capital and that of their children.

Nationally, nearly 25 percent of low-income American families—those earning under $18,900 per year—are unbanked (Bucks, Kennickell, and Moore 2006). Even among moderate-income households earning between $18,900 and $33,900 per year, nearly 13 percent lack any bank account (Bucks, Kennickell, and Moore 2006).

These households lack the basic mechanisms provided by our formal financial system for the receipt of income, the store of its value, and the payment of bills. They also lack ready opportunities for saving in interest-bearing accounts as well as the ease of direct deposit and automatic savings plans that can significantly increase the level and rate of savings over time.

These unbanked households do not, however, escape the need to use financial services. Rather, they piece together strategies to use AFS providers and informal mechanisms to achieve their financial needs. In doing so, they often seek to optimize their financial behavior within external constraints that impose serious financial costs. For example, while check-cashers offer essential services, the fees involved in converting paper checks into cash are high relative both to income and to analogous services that middle- and upper-income families use, such as depositing a check into a bank account or using electronic direct deposit (Barr 2004). Pawnshops, check-cashers, rent-to-own stores, tax refund lenders, and other AFS providers are often the dominant means for LMI households to access financial services in their neighborhoods, but those services come at a high cost.

Beyond the unbanked, moreover, many additional low- and moderate-income families have bank accounts but also rely on high-cost AFS providers to conduct much of their financial business—such as cashing checks, buying money orders, paying bills, or taking out payday loans. We might think of these families as "underbanked," in the sense that formal financial institutions are not offering them the products and services they need in their daily lives, even though they have bank accounts. Far too little attention has been paid to the ways in which even "banked" LMI households are ill served by the financial system.

Despite the importance of financial services to the lives of LMI households, little scholarly attention was paid to the topic until the pathbreaking work of John Caskey (1994). Caskey showed that careful attention to the financial behaviors and attitudes of LMI households could yield a more nuanced understanding of the choices facing them. Existing national data sources that focus on wealth holdings, such as the Survey of Consumer Finances (SCF), are geared toward the wealth holdings of middle- and upper-income households and oversample wealthy households; the SCF collects limited data on financial services or transactions, particularly those services geared toward LMI households. Surveys that include large numbers of low-income households, such as the Survey of Income and Program Participation (SIPP), are not focused on financial services (Scholz and Sheshadri, this volume). At the Office of the Comptroller of the Currency (OCC), which supervises national banks, Constance Dunham and her colleagues (Dunham 2001; Dunham, Scheuren, and Willson 1998) broke new ground when they implemented the first random, stratified survey geared toward understanding the financial behaviors of LMI households in two communities. Shorebank, a leading community development bank, implemented a second such study (Seidman, Hababou, and Kramer 2005). Both studies, however, were constrained in the data that they collected regarding income, asset, and debt levels, employment, the broad range of financial services usage patterns across transactional services, credit, insurance, and savings, and the attitudes and preferences of LMI households.

To explore the range of financial services needs, behaviors, and attitudes of LMI households, as well as the constraints they face, collecting additional field data was imperative. LMI households operate in the context of severe constraints on income and wealth and a limited supply of financial services. Understanding the costs of different financial services choices, the nature of the products and services offered to LMI households, the framework within which LMI households make their financial decisions, and the preferences and attitudes of LMI households can help us understand better both why households are unbanked and whether and how to alter that status. Although there are many reasons for the lack of bank account ownership among LMI households, their preferences interact with the financial and nonpecuniary costs of account ownership in their decisions to become and remain unbanked. Uncovering the trade-offs households are willing to make between the costs and benefits of bank account ownership is paramount to ascertaining how to integrate the unbanked into the financial mainstream. In addition, households' preferences determine whether varying account features will induce more of them to own bank accounts. Despite the need to understand the role of preferences, there is little research to inform us of households' preferences for bank account ownership, as well as the kinds of products they would find attractive enough to induce them to open some type of bank account, if banks were willing to offer such accounts to them.

As currently structured, the financial services system does not work for LMI households. Many LMI households find that checking accounts are ill suited to their needs, and for many financial institutions checking accounts are expensive to offer for low-balance accounts (Barr 2004). Living paycheck to paycheck, LMI households face a significant risk of overdrafting their checking accounts and paying high fees. Many LMI households have had a bank account in the past but were unable to manage their finances to avoid overdrafts or insufficient funds fees, or they were unwilling to pay high fees. Minimum balance requirements may also be a significant barrier for low-income households. By contrast, if banks could be encouraged to offer low-cost, electronically based bank accounts and payment cards, without the costly attributes of the checking system, these types of accounts in principle might provide a more efficient and effective means of serving the financial services needs of LMI households, if such households would use them. No previous empirical study, however, has asked LMI households about their preferences for these types of products and services.

DESCRIPTION OF SURVEY, SAMPLING, AND DATA

The Detroit Area Household Financial Services study, conducted with the University of Michigan's Survey Research Center (SRC), was designed to advance our understanding of the financial services attitudes and behaviors of LMI households. The data for this chapter are from a survey that Jane Dokko and I designed. The survey focuses on LMI individuals' experiences with formal and informal financial institutions, in addition to their socioeconomic characteristics. Because there is no such comprehensive survey about the financial services experiences and attitudes of low- and moderate-income households, the questionnaire required extensive development, pretesting, and validation. There were numerous challenges in tailoring a survey for LMI households. We built on the work of the OCC and Shorebank, whose surveys, described earlier, are more limited regarding low-income households' banking status. We also used the Survey of Consumer Finance (SCF), the Panel Study on Income Dynamics (PSID), and the Health and Retirement Study (HRS); these surveys are not focused on low-income households and are not tailored to their experiences. We adapted questions for LMI households, developed a wide range of new questions to cover the broad range of financial services of interest, and vetted the survey instrument with our advisory board and a wide range of outside experts in financial services, low-income communities, survey methodology, psychology, sociology, economics, and related disciplines, as well as with practitioners.

SRC's Survey Methods Group provided invaluable assistance in working with us on question wording and ordering. We also conducted extensive pretesting on a representative subsample of LMI households to validate our methodology and instrument. Moreover, we were concerned about the overall literacy level and the ability of LMI households to provide reliable responses to seemingly difficult questions about financial behavior and individual preference parameters. To address these concerns, we conducted cognitive interviews regarding the most difficult questions and modified the instrument based on how these subjects processed the questions. The final survey was programmed for computer-assisted, in-person interviewing, and then the programmed survey was tested again multiple times.

In addition to standard survey methodology, we employed a conjoint, choice-based test of consumer preference. In this survey, we asked LMI households to choose from among sets of hypothetical purchase cards with varying features and prices. We analyzed these data using a hierarchical discrete-choice model and investigated consumers' preferences for alternative payment card designs. The conjoint analysis focused on a payment card intended to facilitate the receipt of income, storage of value, and payment of bills. We chose this type of account for two reasons. First, as noted earlier, electronically based bank accounts and payment cards can be offered by financial institutions, payment card providers, employers, and government agencies at lower cost and lower risk to LMI households, as compared to checking accounts. But little is known about whether such products provide sufficient utility to LMI households to generate scale. Second, given the inefficiencies in the payments system from an overreliance on paper checks, which impose costs on the national economy, we felt that exploring the potential take-up of a payment card would be useful for policy. Increasing the efficiency in the payments system for the poor could have modest positive effects on the economy as a whole. Because of positive network externalities, funds spent converting the poor to electronic payment might speed conversion to electronic payments more generally.

After a year's work on sample design and survey development, we were in the field interviewing households from July 2005 through March 2006. In addition to SRC's regular oversight of our field staff, the SRC's Survey Design Group aided in monitoring and, as necessary, adjusting our field strategy. The final survey instrument was seventy-six minutes in length on average and required nearly nine hours of interviewer effort for each completed interview. All interviews were conducted in person, usually in the home of the respondent. Occasionally, interviews were conducted at the respondent's place of work, in the respondent's automobile, or at another location.

Our sample consists of 1,003 completed interviews, with a response rate of 65 percent. The sample members were selected to form a stratified random sample of the Detroit metropolitan area (Wayne, Oakland, and Macomb Counties). We drew sample members from census tracts with median incomes of 0 to 60 percent (low), 61 to 80 percent (moderate), and 81 to 120 percent (middle) of the Detroit area's median income of $49,057. The sample frame includes more census tracts from the LMI strata than the middle one. Hence, sample members are more likely to be drawn from the low- and moderate-income strata. Stratum definitions do not, however, require that the income levels of the sample members fall within these ranges. For purposes of this chapter, data are restricted to households living in LMI census tracts and are weighed to represent these LMI communities.[1]

Overall, the demographic characteristics of our sample reflect the average characteristics of LMI households in the Detroit metropolitan area as reported by the census, although a significantly higher percentage of our sample is female compared to census data for the Detroit area (see table 3.1). Our sample is socioeconomically disadvantaged relative to the average American household. The sample is more than two-thirds African American and nearly two-thirds female. Only 20 percent of respondents are currently married, and 46 percent have never been married. Nearly 30 percent have less than a high school diploma, but 47 percent have some education beyond high school. Although most of the respondents are of working age, only 54 percent were employed at the time of interview. The median household income of the sample is $20,000, which is much lower than the Detroit metropolitan area's median income of $49,057 and the national median of $44,684. Thirty-three percent of these households live below the poverty line. The modal respondent to the survey is an African American working-age woman, without children, who has lived in the Detroit area for a long time. Her income from work is low and close to the federal poverty line, and she is likely to receive some public assistance.

UNBANKED HOUSEHOLD FINANCIAL BEHAVIORS AND PREFERENCES IN BANKING SERVICES

Although most LMI individuals had bank accounts, a significant portion did not. Twenty-nine percent of individuals in our sample did not have a bank account. Some of these individuals lived in households in which another adult had an account that may sometimes have been available to meet the needs of the unbanked individual in the household. Although 29 percent of individuals in our sample were unbanked, nearly one-fifth of unbanked respondents lived with

TABLE 3.1 / Characteristics of Sample Members, by Banked Status

	Census	All	Banked	Unbanked
Black	70.5%	69.1%	65.3%	78.3%
White	21.8	20.4	23.1	13.6
Arab	NA	1.9	2.0	1.5
Other	7.7	8.6	9.5	6.5
Female	52.3	64.3	64.5	63.6
		(1.6)	(2.3)	(3.4)
Less than high school diploma	35.8	29.6	26.6	37.1
High school diploma or GED	31.0	23.0	19.1	32.7
More than high school diploma	33.2	47.4	54.3	30.2
Employed at interview	44.5[a]	54.3	59.3	41.9
Unemployed at interview	8.2	5.8	3.9	10.7
Not in labor force at interview	47.0	39.9	36.8	47.5
Age	NA	43.5	44.9	40.0
		(1.0)	(1.1)	(1.2)
Born in the United States	92.7	92.1	90.5	95.9
		(1.9)	(2.4)	(1.4)
Single or never married	44.1	45.6	37.7	65.1
Married and living with spouse	24.5	19.7	24.0	9.1
Living with partner		4.1	3.7	5.0
Separated, widowed, or divorced	31.3	30.6	34.6	20.9
Households with no children	NA	67.2	70.6	58.9
		(2.2)	(2.5)	(4.3)
Total household monthly income	NA	$ 2,248	$ 2,703	$ 1,156
		(334)	(439)	(399)
Annual household income in 2004	NA	28,435	33,224	17,078
		(2,118)	(2,573)	(1,467)

TABLE 3.1 / *Continued*

	Census	All	Banked	Unbanked
Median household income in 2004	$ 24,146	$ 20,000	$ 25,000	10,000
Below the poverty line	31.5%	33.2%	26.2%	50.5%
		(2.4)	(2.5)	(3.9)
Sample size	626[b]	938	668	270

Source: Detroit Area Household Financial Services study.
Notes: Standard errors are in parentheses. "Not in labor force" includes respondents who said they were retired, homemakers, students, those who did not have the required documentation, and those who chose not to work. "Unemployed" is the percentage of people currently unemployed who are in the labor market. Poverty guidelines come from U.S. Department of Health and Human Services (2004).
[a]Based on the civilian employment rate.
[b]The sample in column 1 consists of census tracts in the Detroit metropolitan area (Wayne, Oakland, and Macomb Counties) with median income under $36,073 (80 percent of the Detroit metropolitan area's median $49,051).

another adult with a bank account, leaving 23 percent of all households in the DAHFS sample unbanked. This sample proportion is consistent with the estimates of previous large-scale surveys of the low- and moderate-income population that 20 to 30 percent of households and 28 to 37 percent of individuals are unbanked (Aizcorbe, Kennickell, and Moore 2003; Dunham, Scheuren, and Willson 1998; Seidman, Hababou, and Kramer 2005). Evidence from the nationally representative Survey of Consumer Finances suggests that the number is close to 10 percent of the overall population (Bucks, Kennickell, and Moore 2006).

The unbanked subpopulation of our sample differs from the banked population in several observable ways (see table 3.1). The unbanked group is younger, is predominantly African American, and has relatively less education than the banked. The unbanked are much more likely to be unemployed and much more likely to live below the poverty line. Only 42 percent of the unbanked are employed, and 50 percent of the unbanked live in poverty. The unbanked are economically more isolated and have worse job prospects than those with bank accounts.

Being unbanked is not a permanent state (see table 3.2). Of the subsample of unbanked respondents, 70 percent had previously had a bank account, and 66 percent of these individuals had had an account within the last five years. Among those who formerly had a bank account, 70 percent had chosen to close the account themselves, citing moving, worrying about bouncing checks, or excessive fees as their reasons for closing the account. The remaining formerly banked, 30 percent, reported that their bank had closed their account. In the majority of cases in which the bank had closed an account, the primary reason was bounced checks and overdrafts.

Not only were the bulk of the unbanked formerly bank account holders, but the reverse was sometimes true as well: many banked households had previously been involuntarily unbanked. Despite currently being banked, 12 percent of bank

TABLE 3.2   /   Transitions Into and Out of Banking

	All	Banked	Unbanked
Respondent has bank account	71%	100%	0%
Household has bank account	77	100	20
Previously had bank account	91.5	100	70.3
Chose to close account		54.6	70.3
Worried about bouncing checks		4.2	14.2
Moved		—	13.0
Minimum fees too high		21.0	11.5
Convenience of a different bank		27.4	
Bank closed account		12.3	29.9
Bounced checks		51.3	55.2
Low balance or inactive		63.4	29.2
Fraud		7.2	9.5
Grew up with banked adults in home	72.2	72.9	70.7
Has shopped around for bank accounts[a]	36.1	37.3	33.2
Wants to open bank account in next year	—	—	75.1
Denied when tried to open account	—	—	16.9
Income volatility previous twelve months			
Gone up	24.0	27.5	15.3
Gone down	17.0	15.1	21.4
Up and down a little	23.0	22.3	25.0
Up and down a lot	7.0	5.1	11.6
Stayed the same	29.1	30.0	26.7
Lost job in last twelve months	22.9	18.9	32.8
Sample size	938	668	270

Source: Detroit Area Household Financial Services study.
Note: Standard errors are in parentheses.
[a]Banked respondents were asked if they shopped around before getting their current account; unbanked respondents were asked if they shopped around to look into getting an account.

account holders had previously had a bank account closed by their bank. Nearly two-thirds of those whose previous account had been closed said that their account was closed by the bank because they had a low balance or an inactive account (63 percent) or bounced checks or overdrafts (51 percent). Despite having previously been unbanked because a bank closed their account, these households were able to transition back into the banking system. In addition to those who had had their accounts involuntarily closed, a large portion of the banked had previously closed a different account. Nearly 55 percent of the banked subpopulation had closed a previous bank account, most commonly because of the convenience of another bank (27 percent) or a desire to reduce excessive fees (21 percent). Unbanked status does not appear to be a permanent state or tightly linked to

FIGURE 3.1 / The Top Reasons Given by the Unbanked For Why They Were Unbanked

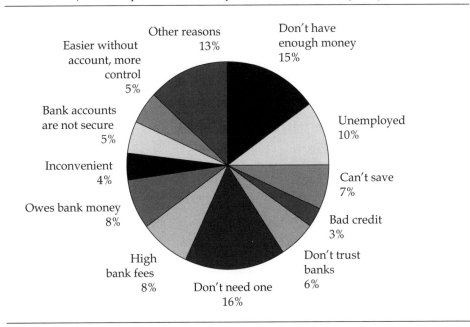

Source: Detroit Area Household Financial Services study.

demographics or attitudes; rather, some unbanked LMI individuals make transitions into and out of being banked.

Moreover, the unbanked reported that they would prefer to be banked. There was significant interest among the unbanked population in entering the mainstream financial services sector. Of the unbanked respondents, 75 percent said that they would like to open a bank account in the next year, and 33 percent said that they had recently looked into getting a bank account. However, 17 percent reported that a bank had denied their application to open a bank account when they sought to open one, reflecting continued constraints on account opening.

Unbanked individuals reported a variety of reasons for why they were unbanked (see figure 3.1). About two-thirds cited primarily financial reasons for their current status. These financial reasons were described in different ways, but we can analyze them as relating to the low income and asset levels of the household in relation to high bank fees or other bank requirements. For example, 15 percent reported that they did not have enough money, 10 percent reported that they were unemployed, 16 percent reported that they did not need a bank account, and 8 percent cited high bank fees. Nonfinancial reasons included not trusting banks (6 percent), inconvenience (4 percent), the belief that bank accounts are not secure (5 percent), and the belief that one can have more control over one's finances or conduct transactions more easily without an account (5 percent).

FIGURE 3.2 / Desired Account Changes Cited by the Unbanked That Would Induce Them to Open a Bank Account

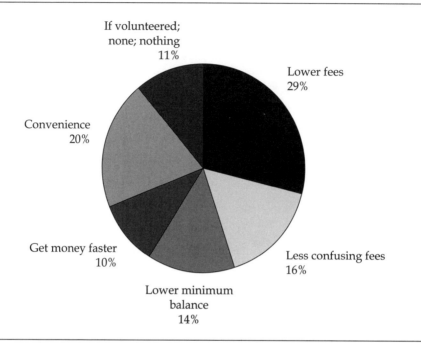

Source: Detroit Area Household Financial Services study.

To assess which barriers to account opening were most important to the unbanked, interviewers asked them what improved feature of a bank account would make them most likely to open an account (see the distribution of responses in figure 3.2). For 29 percent of the sample, lower fees were perceived as the primary facilitator to opening an account, while 20 percent considered more convenient bank hours and locations the most important reason why they might open an account with a particular bank. Respondents cited less confusing fees (16 percent), lower minimum balances (14 percent), and the ability to get money faster (10 percent) as the other main obstacles they would like to see removed. More than 10 percent stated that none of these changes in bank account features would encourage them to open an account.

HOUSEHOLD PREFERENCES FOR ELECTRONIC BANKING AND PAYMENT CARDS

To further examine these preferences, we included a discrete-choice method to predict consumer interest in payment cards as a function of the features that the card offers the consumer. We explored the potential use of debit cards, prepaid debit cards, and payroll cards by low-income households, including the individuals without bank accounts. Such payment cards may be a means of providing financial services to LMI households that is less expensive and not as risky as traditional checking accounts and that may thus be attractive to both banks and LMI households. In particular, debit cards can be designed to avoid overdrafts, lowering the risks and costs of the checking account. Debit cards also have lower cost structures than checking accounts and so can be offered at lower prices.

Discrete-choice analysis is a statistical method of identifying the structure of consumer preferences for a product with many attributes (Green and Srinivasan 1978; Luce and Tukey 1964). Based on individuals' responses to a series of questions about the characteristics of a payment card they would like, it is possible to uncover several aspects of their decisionmaking process. The analysis decomposes products and services into discrete components and then methodically varies the product configurations while measuring consumers' responses to the changes. The variation in the attributes follows an orthogonal design that exhibits no inter-attribute correlations across the questions. This approach enables us to identify the effect of each attribute on the decisions of individuals in choosing a payment card. We use the Sawtooth software program to both design the questionnaire and analyze the results.

Our main findings, reported in Barr, Bacheldor, and Dokko (2007), are twofold. First, we report that many households without bank accounts expressed a desire to open one. In particular, the most attractive payment card achieved a hypothetical "take" rate of 60 percent among unbanked LMI households and only slightly less than that rate among banked LMI households (results not shown). In light of the general patterns of account ownership among LMI households, we believe that this finding suggests that there is a sizable opportunity for commercial banks to offer products that would be meaningful to LMI households. Our second finding pertains to the particular types of payment cards that banks may offer to LMI households. We find that the two most important features influencing individuals' decisions to pick a particular payment card were monthly cost and the availability of federal consumer protection with respect to the account (see figure 3.3), although there was significant heterogeneity in preferences among LMI households. We hope that our analysis will be informative to commercial banking institutions, payment card providers, employers, and government agencies regarding how to design accounts and payment cards to bring LMI households into the financial mainstream.

BANKED AND UNBANKED HOUSEHOLD BEHAVIOR: INCOME RECEIPT AND BILL PAYMENT

Despite the general characterization of LMI households as operating in a cash economy, these households usually receive their income through other means (see table 3.3). During the month prior to the interview, 54 percent of the sample received a check, 21 percent received cash, and 22 percent received government cash benefits through a Bridge Card, Michigan's electronic benefits transfer program that uses a prepaid debit card. Another 5 percent received income from an

FIGURE 3.3 / Relative Importance of Attributes on Choice of Product

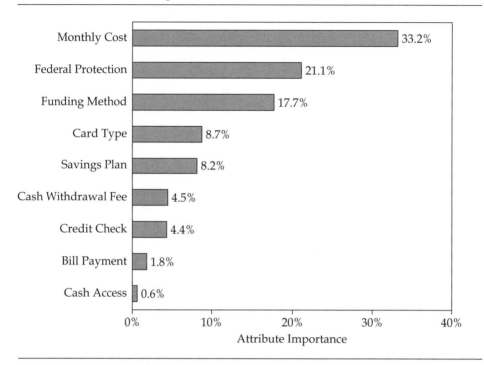

Source: Detroit Area Household Financial Services study.

electronic transfer to a place that was not a bank (for example, a check-cashing outlet), while only 1 percent had a payroll card from their employer.

Both banked and unbanked households used a mix of banking and AFS providers to meet their transactional needs to receive their income and pay their bills. Unbanked households were more likely to use AFS providers than banked households, but they still relied significantly on banking services. Despite their lack of ready ability to cash checks at a bank, and as a function of their inability to receive direct deposit, unbanked households were *more* likely than banked households to be paid by check: nearly 64 percent of unbanked households reported receiving income by check. Unbanked households were also, understandably, more likely than banked households to be paid in cash: nearly 30 percent were paid that way. Given their lower incomes and greater reliance on government support programs, unbanked households were also much more likely to receive income or food stamps through the Bridge Card: more than 40 percent received funds this way.

Unbanked households used a variety of formal and informal means to convert the income they received by check into usable form. The dominant check-cashing strategy used by unbanked households was to go to a bank. Over 83 percent of unbanked households cashed checks at a bank—most often the bank that had issued the check. The next most common place where the unbanked cashed checks was

TABLE 3.3 / Transactional Services: Income Receipt, Check-Cashing, and Bill Payment

	All	Banked	Unbanked
How income is received			
Direct deposit		62.9%	–
Check	54.3%	50.5	63.6%
Cash	20.7	17.1	29.5
Payroll card	1.2	0.8	2.2
Bridge Card	21.6	14.0	40.5
Check-casher	5.0	5.9	2.7
Other	4.3	4.1	4.8
Number of checks cashed	2.56	2.83	2.06
in last month[a]	(.35)	(.51)	(.11)
Check-cashing method[b]			
At a bank	93.4	96.1	83.1
Mean (conditional)	2.5	2.7	1.8
	(.11)	(.12)	(.16)
At a check-casher	21.4	16.3	30.7
Mean (conditional)	2.2	2.0	2.3
	(.15)	(.22)	(.23)
At workplace	5.2	5.1	5.5
Mean (conditional)	2.5	2.4	2.6
	(.39)	(.52)	(.64)
Signed over to family or friend	8.5	4.6	15.4
Mean (conditional)	1.5	1.7	1.4
	(.25)	(.35)	(.22)
At supermarket or store	33.3	20.7	55.7
Mean (conditional)	2.11	1.93	2.24
	(.13)	(.18)	(.18)
Bill payment method[c]			
Personal check	—	62.1	—
Automated payment	—	32.3	—
Online payment	—	21.9	—
Over phone (with credit, charge, or debit card)	—	41.3	—
In cash	42.1	37.8	52.8
Money order	52.1	47.6	63.2
Payment center	36.6	33.2	45.2
Prepaid debit card	5.6	6.2	4.1
Purchased money order	68.3	64.8	77.1
Does landlord accept personal checks?[d]	54.6	64.9	38.4
Sample size	938	668	270

Source: Detroit Area Household Financial Services study.
Note: Standard errors are in parentheses.
[a]Conditional on receiving income by check.
[b]Conditional on having cashed at least one check in the month prior to interview: n(all) = 404; n(banked) = 265; n(unbanked) = 139.
[c]Personal check, automated payment, online payment, and paying by phone were questions asked only of banked respondents.
[d]Asked only of renters.

grocery and other stores: 56 percent of unbanked households reported such a strategy. More than 30 percent of unbanked households used check-cashers. Another mechanism deployed by over 15 percent of the unbanked was to sign over their check to a family member or friend.

In paying bills, unbanked households cannot use personal checks, automatic payment through a bank, online payment using a credit card, or payment over the phone with a credit card. Instead of such services, 63 percent of unbanked households used money orders, 53 percent paid in cash, and 45 percent visited a payment center in person. Usage of each of these AFS bill payment services was about 15 percentage points higher for the unbanked than for the banked. Interestingly, use of AFS bill payment by the unbanked may also be related to whether mainstream bill payment would be accepted in their community. For example, only 38 percent of unbanked renters stated that their landlords would accept personal checks for payment of rent, while nearly two-thirds of banked renters stated that their landlords would accept personal checks. Future research might help to untangle the relationship between the payment options preferred by renting households and those accepted by landlords.

Banked respondents used a variety of services offered by their banks, as well as a range of AFS providers (see table 3.3). Among banked LMI households, there was a strong usage of mainstream financial products. For example, 63 percent of the banked received their income through direct deposit, a higher percentage than reported for the U.S. population as a whole. During the twelve months prior to the interview, banks played an important role in facilitating bill payments. Among the banked, 62 percent paid bills by check, and 41 percent used a credit or debit card over the phone. Thirty-two percent used automated bill payment, and 22 percent paid their bills online, most likely by allowing the recipient to access their bank accounts electronically.

Despite their access to checks and automated payment systems, the banked were also likely to use AFS providers for their financial transactions. A surprisingly large fraction of the banked population, 65 percent, purchased a money order, and 48 percent used a money order to pay a bill. Moreover, 14 percent reported that they purchased a money order from a bank—in effect purchasing an alternative payment mechanism through a mainstream financial provider. In addition, 38 percent of banked households paid a bill in cash, and one-third visited a payment center in person to pay bills. Despite having access to a bank account, 6 percent of the banked also paid bills using a prepaid debit card, which can be purchased without the need for a bank account. Although the overwhelmingly dominant check-cashing strategy for banked households was to use a bank, more than 16 percent of the banked population used a check-casher, and 21 percent cashed a check at a supermarket or other store.

FINANCIAL HARDSHIPS AMONG LMI HOUSEHOLDS

LMI households face serious obstacles to financial and physical well-being (table 3.4). Overall, 27 percent of the sample felt that it was "very difficult" to live

TABLE 3.4 / Hardships Facing Respondents in the Last Twelve Months

Hardship Experienced	All	Banked	Unbanked
In poor health	7.9%	6.7%	11.0%
Very difficult to live on household income	27.3	23.1	37.7
Major illness or medical expense	26.9	26.1	28.8
Evicted	5.9	4.1	10.5
Utility shut off	10.0	7.5	16.2
Phone disconnected	18.3	13.9	29.4
Filed for bankruptcy	3.9	3.9	4.1
Did not have enough food	16.8	13.1	25.9
Lacked health insurance	20.1	15.0	32.9
How respondents managed when expenses exceeded income			
Ask family and friends for help	53.0	50.7	56.7
Spend down assets	24.6	32.6	11.4
Borrow from the bank or use credit card	14.6	21.3	3.6
Sample size	938	668	270

Source: Detroit Area Household Financial Services study.

on their household's income. In addition, 27 percent had had a major illness or paid a significant medical expense in the last twelve months. Moreover, 6 percent of the respondents had been evicted, 10 percent had had a utility shut off, 18 percent had had their phone disconnected, 17 percent had experienced not having enough food to eat, and 4 percent had filed for bankruptcy, a rate far above the national average. About 90 percent of LMI households had experienced at least one of these hardships in the prior year.

The unbanked, who generally have lower incomes and hold lower levels of assets than the banked, are characterized by a much greater likelihood of facing financial hardships. Nearly 38 percent of the unbanked said that it was very difficult to live on the household's current income, compared to 23 percent of those with bank accounts. The unbanked were nearly three times more likely than the banked sample to have been evicted, and twice as likely to have not had enough food to eat or to have had a phone connection or utility shut off. The banked and unbanked were equally likely to have had a major illness or to have suffered a significant medical expense in the last twelve months. However, the unbanked were much more likely to classify themselves as being in poor health; this could be the result of the two groups having different subjective self-classification scales or different views of what a "significant medical expense" entails. In any event, the unbanked considered themselves to be much less healthy than the banked population.

FINANCIAL SERVICES AND SAVINGS

LMI households exhibit considerable diversity in their savings behaviors (table 3.5). Given financial hardships, ongoing needs, and low income, saving is difficult for many LMI households. Moreover, many LMI households lack access to ready mechanisms that enable saving, such as bank accounts with direct deposit and automatic savings plans or retirement plans at work. Nonetheless, more than half of LMI households in the sample contributed to savings in the year before the survey. Banked households were nearly twice as likely to have added to savings as unbanked households. Households also varied in the regularity of their saving. About 20 percent of respondents contributed to financial savings at least every month. A larger portion of respondents never contributed to savings (46 percent), while 11 percent contributed once or twice a year. In the year prior to the survey, the mean contribution to savings (among those who saved) was $2,474, and the median contribution was $1,000.

Households deploy different methods of saving, using both formal and informal mechanisms. For example, nearly half of households in the sample saved through savings accounts and more than one-third through retirement vehicles, while 15 percent saved through holding jewelry, electronics, appliances, or cash. Moreover, as reported in Barr and Dokko (2007), 75 percent of LMI households that file tax returns wanted to over-withhold their income. We suggest that over-withholding is related to dynamic inconsistency and that wanting to use the withholding system, with its built-in capacity to generate illiquid savings, is a precommitment device against overconsumption. In addition, more than half of LMI tax filers reported that they saved some or all of their tax refund, suggesting that tax filing is an important savings opportunity for LMI households.

Households tended to express "pro-savings" attitudes. About 67 percent of respondents strongly agreed that it is hard to save because most of their money goes toward basic necessities, such as food, rent, and housing. When asked if it was hard to resist the temptation to spend money, 41 percent "strongly agreed," and only 8 percent strongly agreed that saving money is "not worth it." Bank account ownership may help some LMI households save. For those who had a bank account, 85.1 percent believed that it helped them to save. Among those who were unbanked, 37 percent strongly agreed that an account would help them to save, and 30 percent somewhat agreed.

"Savers" are in some ways different from those who do not save (table 3.6). Savers tend to be more educated and more likely to be currently employed. Strikingly, however, there were no significant differences between African Americans, whites, and other races or ethnicities when looking at savers and nonsavers. Bank account ownership is an important factor that may distinguish savers from nonsavers. About 83 percent of savers had bank accounts, while 58 percent of nonsavers had an account. A poor credit history, surprisingly, was not related to savings behaviors (results not shown).

TABLE 3.5 / Savings

	All	Banked	Unbanked
Savings horizon[a]			
This year	47.6%	47.8%	46.3%
Next year	33.9	33.7	34.8
In five years	17.4	17.9	14.9
In ten years	7.3	7.3	7.1
In more than ten years	14.2	14.9	10.8
Faces major expense for which unable to save	37.0	36.7	37.7
Feels in deep financial trouble	18.4	14.6	28.0
Saving is not "worth it"			
Agree	16.4	16.6	16.4
Disagree	83.4	83.3	83.6
Hard to save because money goes to necessities			
Agree	85.1	81.7	93.5
Disagree	14.6	17.9	6.5
Hard to save because hard to resist spending			
Agree	64.9	61.3	73.8
Disagree	34.6	38.3	25.6
Frequency of saving			
Contributed in past year	54.1	62.7	32.8
More than once a month	10.4	12.8	4.5
Every month	19.2	23.2	9.4
Most months	4.0	4.0	4.0
About half of months	3.7	4.6	1.7
A few months	5.5	6.3	3.7
Once or twice	11.3	12.0	9.5
Never	45.9	37.3	67.2
Amount contributed to savings	$2,474	$2,825	$949
	(385)	(447)	(202)
	$1,000	$1,000	$300
Asset holdings			
Savings account	49.2%	67.8%	0.0%
Retirement savings	48.2	51.1	34.9
Life insurance	30.3	35.7	16.9
Money market funds	17.0	22.9	2.4
Jewelry, electronics	15.3	14.9	16.5
Car	73.0	79.6	56.5
Home	45.4	53.4	25.7

(Table continues on p. 84.)

TABLE 3.5 / *Continued*

	All	Banked	Unbanked
Reasons to save			
To feel financially secure	78.2	79.1	74.3
Emergency or medical costs	69.9	68.7	75.8
Unanticipated job loss	50.9	48.1	64.3
Special events	52.8	49.3	69.2
Home improvements	49.3	49.1	50.3
Furniture or appliances	33.5	30.7	46.9
Education or training	39.5	37.0	51.3
Invest in business	16.4	16.0	18.5
Retirement	48.2	51.1	34.9
Over-withholds to save	75.3	77.1	69.5
Saves some or all of tax refund	50.2	53.2	40.1
Agrees account helps or would help respondent save	—	81.5	67.4
Sample size	938	668	270

Source: Detroit Area Household Financial Services study.
Note: Standard errors are in parentheses.
[a]Asked only of respondents who had saved in the past twelve months. Respondents could give multiple responses.

TABLE 3.6 / Characteristics of Savers

	All	Savers	Nonsavers
Black	69.1%	68.7%	70.5%
White	20.4	21.2	18.8
Arab	1.9	1.2	2.7
Other	8.6	8.9	8.0
Less than high school diploma	29.6	19.5	40.9
High school diploma or GED	23.0	20.2	26.8
Greater than high school diploma	47.4	60.3	32.3
Employed at interview	54.3	65.6	41.0
Unemployed at interview	5.8	3.1	9.1
Not in labor force at interview	39.9	31.3	49.9
Banked status	71.3	82.6	57.9
Below the poverty line	33.2	23.6	44.5
	(2.4)	(2.6)	(2.8)
Sample size	938	504	427

Source: Detroit Area Household Financial Services study.
Note: Standard errors are in parentheses. "Savers" are individuals who contributed at least once to their savings in the twelve months prior to the survey.

Income plays a significant role in both the regularity of savings and in the amount contributed to savings. Respondents who contributed to savings had a higher mean and median income than respondents who did not contribute. More than three-quarters of respondents who saved were above the poverty line, while one-quarter remained below the poverty line. Of those who contributed to savings in the past twelve months, the average amount of savings was $2,474 and the median amount was $1,000. Savers with incomes above the poverty level contributed an average amount of $2,852 and a median amount of $1,000. For savers who were below the poverty level, the amount contributed was dramatically lower—with a mean contribution of $1,317 and a median of $300.

While the debate over national savings policy is often focused exclusively on retirement saving, households save for a variety of reasons, and many LMI households have savings needs other than retirement; for example, they may save for investment, precautionary reasons, or future consumption. Savings policy for LMI households should encompass the range of the savings needs of these households. The Detroit survey demonstrates that most LMI households were saving for precautionary reasons. About 78 percent saved to feel financially secure, 70 percent saved for emergency and medical expenses, and 51 percent saved for unanticipated job loss. Nearly three-quarters of respondents also saved for consumption in the near future—in order to make purchases that year or the next. This included special events (53 percent), house or home improvements (49 percent), or furniture and household appliance (33 percent). Still, a sizable portion of respondents also saved for investment purposes. About 40 percent were saving to invest in education or training, while roughly 16 percent were saving to invest in business. Nearly half were saving for retirement.

Saving is challenging for low- and moderate-income households, many of which face income volatility, start from a low base of asset-holding, shoulder high debt service burdens, and have ongoing informal financial obligations, such as the 45 percent of households that saved in order to help family or friends in need. Strikingly, nearly one-quarter had lost their job in the year prior to the interview, and 46 percent had seen their income go down (or go up and down). One of the main reasons families find asset development a challenge is simply that they are poor and saving is difficult with little income. Roughly 86 percent of respondents found it hard to save because most of their money went toward basic necessities. About 27 percent of respondents found it "very difficult" to live on current household income, while 44 percent found it "somewhat difficult." Nearly two-thirds of respondents had experienced a financial hardship in the year prior to the survey, such as having utilities or phone service shut off, not having enough food, or being evicted, and about 18 percent viewed themselves as being in "deep financial trouble."

Nearly 30 percent of the sample had monthly expenses that exceeded income during most of the year. For half of these households, family and friends played a significant role in contributing to basic living expenses. If they could not rely on family or friends, 25 percent of respondents spent down assets, while 15 percent borrowed from the bank or used their credit card. While 45 percent reported that they were always able to cover their expenses out of current income, about 40 percent of households were in debt on their credit cards. The median debt burden among LMI households, excluding home and automobile, was $500, and the mean debt outstanding was more than ten times that amount. Looking forward, a significant portion of households (37 percent) anticipated a major expense over the next five to ten years for which they would be unable to save.

Poor health and major illness can also negatively affect a household's ability to save. At the time of the interview, 28 percent of respondents had a health condition that inhibited their ability to work, and in the previous year 27 percent had faced a major illness or medical expense. About 20 percent did not have insurance and therefore were likely to be extremely vulnerable to major medical expenses if an illness occurred.

ASSET-HOLDING AMONG LMI HOUSEHOLDS

Despite the difficulty of asset accumulation, many LMI households are able to build savings. About 90 percent of the LMI households accumulated physical and financial assets in both formal and informal ways; 75 percent held formal or informal financial assets. Nearly half had a savings account, 36 percent had retirement savings, and 30 percent had life insurance, while only 17 percent had money market funds, bonds, or CDs, and 15 percent saved through holding cash, jewelry, gold, appliances, or electronics. Nonfinancial assets are more valuable than financial assets for LMI households. Roughly 75 percent of respondents owned a car, and 45 percent owned a home. Owning a car and home significantly increased the median value of assets for respondents—to about $68,000—but that amount falls to $2,500 when the value of homes and automobiles is excluded.

We would predict that LMI households would need liquid assets in case of emergencies, given their relative lack of insurance or other supports. In the Detroit study, a higher proportion of households held immediately liquid assets as compared to assets with other liquidity levels. For households above the poverty line, the median amount of asset holdings was $1,000, which might be helpful in the event of an unexpected emergency. However, with a median liquid asset holding of only $400, households below the poverty line might not be able to cover a serious emergency. Even lower proportions of poor households held financial assets that were not immediately liquid and that generated higher rates of return. While the average amount of asset holdings increases from $1,636 to $4,277 when examining assets that are not immediately liquid, the proportion of those who held these assets drops from 44 to 13.7 percent.

Generalizing from the Detroit study, we could argue that national savings policy needs to be nuanced for LMI households, many of which are simply too poor to save and must rely as much as possible on friends or family and the social safety net. For many of these households, that safety net appears to be weak, and financial crises often lead to further deterioration in their lives. At the same time, for some LMI households, saving—and even asset accumulation—is possible. Rather than focusing on retirement saving, as national policy tends to do, savings policy for LMI households should focus on the wide range of their savings needs, includ-

TABLE 3.7 / Borrowing and Alternative Financial Services

	All	Banked	Unbanked
Borrowing			
Looking to borrow	61.5%	62.7%	58.6%
Actually borrow	51.0	51.0	51.5
Method considered			
Bank	27.5	33.9	11.6
Finance company	13.6	16.6	6.3
Short-term credit	47.0	44.7	52.7
Cash advance from credit card	7.9	10.1	2.3
Borrow from pension or retirement	6.9	8.4	3.1
Payday loan	4.4	4.9	3.4
Buy on layaway	25.7	27.2	21.9
Pawn anything	11.2	7.2	21.1
Refund anticipation loan	21.8	18.9	29.1
Rent-to-own	5.3	5.4	5.2
Overdraft from account	20.3	24.1	10.9
Land contract on house	1.9	2.0	1.5
Sample size	938	668	270

Source: Detroit Area Household Financial Services study.

ing the need for liquid savings for emergencies as well as the need for illiquid savings for medium- and longer-term savings goals. Also, given the breadth of saving approaches taken by LMI households, savings policy needs to develop a range of alternative savings products to meet the needs of LMI households, including direct deposit initiatives, automatic saving plans, and tax refund saving programs. These issues are taken up in more depth later in this chapter in the discussion of policy.

DEBT PATTERNS AMONG LMI HOUSEHOLDS

Although access to credit can help households smooth consumption, invest in human capital development, and build assets through homeownership and other investments, the high cost of credit presents another obstacle for low- and moderate-income households. Reduced access and increased cost of credit limit how much households can borrow and increase debt service burdens, crowding out both current consumption and savings. Dissaving through borrowing may be necessary for many LMI households, but its toll on these households needs to be better understood. The median debt outstanding (excluding home and automobile loans) among LMI households in the Detroit study was a mere $500, but the mean was more than ten times that amount.

Households in the sample used a variety of alternative financial services providers to meet their credit needs (table 3.7), based in part on whether or not

TABLE 3.8   /   Users of Other AFS Providers Who Use Payday Loans

AFS Use	Users Who Use Payday Loans	Non-Users Who Use Payday Loans
Pawnshop[a]	16%	3%
Cash advance[a]	14	4
Refund anticipation loan[a]	9	3
Rent-to-own[a]	16	4
Cash out pension[a]	12	4
Overdraft[a]	13	2

Source: Detroit Area Household Financial Services study.
[a]Means significant difference at 10 percent level after controlling for age, race, gender, and income.

they had a bank account and on their available collateral. Rather than utilizing each alternative service as a substitute, low-income borrowers used payday loans, pawnshops, refund anticipation loans, rent-to-own contracts, and other formal and informal credit services as complementary products. While payday lending services have driven growth in the AFS sector over the last fifteen years and garnered significant public attention, payday loan services are still a lending practice on the financial fringe for LMI households. As table 3.7 shows, only 4.4 percent of DAHFS respondents said they had recently sought out a payday loan. Part of the reason so few respondents approached payday lenders might have been because of the restrictive eligibility qualifications, including holding a bank account and a steady job. African Americans were much more likely to use payday lenders than whites.

An open question in the literature on alternative financial services is whether these AFS providers act as substitutes for one another and for formal-sector financial services, or whether borrowers use a range of services depending on the situation. The DAHFS suggests that the services are usually interrelated. Tables 3.8 and 3.9, for example, show that, overall, respondents who used other types of credit were also more likely to use payday loans. For instance, those using a pawnshop were much more likely to use a payday loan (16 percent versus 3 percent). Those who used a credit card for a cash advance were much more likely to use a payday loan (14 percent versus 4 percent). Households that took out a refund anticipation loan (RAL) at tax time (see Barr and Dokko 2007) were much more likely to use a payday loan (9 percent versus 3 percent), as were rent-to-own users (16 percent versus 4 percent), and those who cashed out a pension or insurance policy in the last three years (12 percent versus 4 percent). Moreover, payday usage in the AFS sector and bank overdrafts in the formal sector were often complementary: those who used an overdraft from their bank account were more than five times more likely to use a payday lender than those who had not overdrafted.

Uses of these various alternative financial services are interconnected with each other as well as with respect to payday borrowing. Table 3.10 shows a correlation matrix of alternative financial services. The highest correlation is between pawn-

TABLE 3.9 / Payday Loan Users Who Use Other AFS Providers

AFS Use	Payday Users	Non-Users
Pawnshop[a]	40%	10%
Cash advance[a]	24	7
Refund anticipation loan[a]	45	21
Rent-to-own[a]	20	5
Cash out pension[a]	19	6
Secured card[a]	37	9
Credit card late fee	43	21
Overdraft[a]	57	19

Source: Detroit Area Household Financial Services study.
[a]Means significant difference at 10 percent level after controlling for age, race, gender, and income.

shop use and payday borrowing. Payday borrowing is also correlated with using an overdraft from a bank account. Nearly every entry in the table is positive, suggesting that individuals who used one were more likely to use another. Although usage appears complementary, most of the correlations are not large, implying relatively weak direct relationships within the network of financial services.

In addition, certain credit card behaviors are related to payday borrowing. Those who had paid late fees on a credit card were more likely to have used a payday loan than those who had a credit card and had not missed payments (9.2 percent versus 3.4 percent). Nearly 8 percent of those who said they never paid off the entire balance on their credit card had looked into using a payday loan, compared with fewer than 4 percent of those who paid off their entire credit card balance each month. Payday loans were used by 12.5 percent of those who paid only the minimum amount due. In addition, the least creditworthy cardholders—those whose cards required a deposit, known as "secured" credit cards—were much more likely to use payday lending: 17.4 percent compared with 3.3 percent of the rest of credit card users. These relationships to credit suggest that payday borrowers have a history of credit problems that make it difficult for them to acquire short-term credit elsewhere. In addition, the higher rate of credit problems among payday borrowers suggests that this group exhibits riskier borrowing behavior. Riskier credit card behavior also translates into difficulty acquiring loans from mainstream providers; once denied, over 10 percent of those who were rejected by mainstream loan providers (banks, savings and loan companies, credit unions, finance and mortgage companies) sought payday loans. Although payday borrowers contributed to savings as frequently as non-borrowers, payday borrowers had lower levels of financial assets and home-ownership rates than non-payday borrowers. In short, payday borrowers tend to seek more borrowing opportunities than non-payday borrowers, exhibit riskier credit behavior, have lower asset levels, and face higher rates of rejection from mainstream lenders.

TABLE 3.10 / Correlation Matrix of Alternative Financial Service Usage

	Payday Loan	Pawnshop	Refund Anticipation Loan	Rent-to-Own	Layaway	Cash Advance on Credit Card	Overdraft	Cash Out on a Pension
Payday loan								
Pawnshop	0.200							
Refund anticipation loan	0.124	0.151						
Rent-to-own	0.136	0.171	0.187					
Layaway	0.027	0.041	0.192	0.086				
Cash advance	0.133	0.073	-0.009	-0.014	0.105			
Overdraft	0.196	0.057	0.092	0.105	0.144	0.193		
Cash out a pension	0.105	0.017	0.077	0.040	0.021	0.119	0.065	
Any AFS	0.101	0.184	0.276	0.125	0.306	0.076	0.141	0.011

Source: Detroit Area Household Financial Services study.
Notes: "Any AFS" includes pawnshops, rent-to-own stores, refund anticipation loan, money orders, and layaway.

TABLE 3.11 / Use of Recent Loan (Up to Two Responses), Conditioned on Having Most Recently Taken Out a Payday Loan

Use of Loan	Percentage
Everyday expenses (bills, food, gas, and so on)	59.5%
Gift to a relative or friend	3.2
Car or transportation	7.7
Auto repair	2.3
Vacation, entertainment, casinos, dog racing, leisure	3.2
Education, tuition	7.7
Legal expenses, tickets	3.2
Medical or dental expenses	5.9
Debt consolidation, credit card debt, bank debt	10.9
Just to have money, to have cash, "just to see if I could get it"	3.2

Source: Detroit Area Household Financial Services study.

Individuals reported that they took out payday loans to pay for necessities (table 3.11). Of those who had most recently looked into getting a payday loan, 60 percent said that they needed the money for everyday expenses such as food and gasoline or for regular bills. About 5 to 11 percent of respondents cited paying off credit card or bank debts, car expenses, education costs, and medical or dental expenses. Although this evidence is consistent with the view that payday borrowers take out loans when their income cannot meet their expenses, it is possible that their prior spending on non-necessities crowded out spending on necessities and thus led to high-cost borrowing through payday loans. Future research would need to include data on consumption patterns to better understand these borrowing decisions.

Respondents who used payday lenders often used them multiple times, including by "rolling over" existing loans into new ones. The most common number of loans or cash advances (for those with at least one) in the past year was two (31 percent), with three and four times being the next most common (19.9 percent and 14.2 percent). Our estimates regarding repeat loans are far smaller than is found in other studies. The median number of loans in our sample was three in the past year, in stark contrast to studies such as Elliehausen and Lawrence (2001, 39, table 5.11), which reports a median between five and six loans.

It is possible that our measure did not fully capture rollovers when we asked, "How many times have you taken a loan . . . ?" Separately, we asked specifically about rollovers: of those who used a payday lender, 40.2 percent paid a fee to postpone paying back the loan, but we do not know how many times; an additional 14.3 percent took a loan from one payday lender to pay back a loan from a different payday lender. Overall, the rollover experiences of the payday borrowers in the DAHFS sample suggest that the costs of repeated borrowing may be high. Nonetheless, we did not find evidence that rollovers are as extensive as reported elsewhere.

TABLE 3.12 / Total Indebtedness and Net Assets, by Banked Status

Characteristic	Banked	Unbanked
Total indebtedness		
Mean	$35,056	$8,365
	(7,407)	(1,392)
Median	10,230	0
Net assets (assets minus debts)		
Mean	103,965	25,029
	(42,278)	(4,404)
Median	38,800	1,500
Sample size	668	270

Source: Detroit Area Household Financial Services study.
Notes: Standard errors are in parentheses. "Total indebtedness" is an aggregated dollar value of all debts and liabilities. "Net assets" aggregates the value of assets and subtracts the respondent's debts and liabilities.

The most important reasons given for going to payday lenders among other credit options were the convenience and accessible hours of the payday outlet (23.6 percent), the expectation of being approved for the loan (22 percent), and the need for a small amount of money or money to pay a bill (19.2 percent).

Despite the high costs, customers choose payday lenders over other possible sources of credit in part because they have often been recently turned down by other, lower-priced alternatives and are confident that they will be approved for a payday loan. To the extent that borrowers need access to credit during emergencies, payday lenders may fill a critical need. At the same time, payday lenders charge high fees, and many borrowers find it difficult to repay payday loans when they come due. These borrowers often pay additional fees to postpone or "roll over" payments, or they borrow from one payday lender to pay back another. Payday borrowers may get into further financial difficulties.

OVERALL LEVELS OF INDEBTEDNESS AND NET WORTH

Given significant debt levels and low levels of asset-holding, not surprisingly, net worth among LMI households is relatively low. As table 3.12 shows, banked households carry significantly more debt than unbanked households. Median indebtedness is approximately $10,000 among the banked and approaches $0 for the unbanked; the means are about $35,000 and $8,000, respectively. Given their higher level of asset-holding, the banked have greater net worth (nearly $39,000) than the unbanked (only $1,500); the respective means are about $100,000 and $25,000. Net worth is strongly connected to income. The mean and median net worths of respondents are significantly higher for those above the poverty level as compared to those below. The median net worth of those whose income is above the poverty line is about $38,000, while those with incomes below the poverty line hold about $1,000.

DIRECTIONS FOR POLICY

The results of the Detroit study suggest that LMI households would benefit from a range of financial services products to meet their needs to receive their income, pay bills, and save their hard-earned funds. The private sector should begin with an initiative to provide straightforward and affordable bank accounts. Such accounts would be federally insured and carry straightforward, up-front fees. Rather than promoting traditional checking accounts, which often are high-cost and high-risk for these households, the initiative would encourage debit card–based bank accounts with no check-writing, no overdraft, and no hidden or back-end fees. These accounts would not require a minimum balance or account opening balance, and given the no-overdraft restriction, they would not require complicated reviews to open. The accounts should be made available to those who have had difficulty managing a checking account in the past, given that these accounts would not permit check-writing. Funds could be accessed at ATMs and at the point-of-sale. Over time, the accounts could increase in functionality. The accounts could provide for bill payment, an automatic savings plan, and reasonable consumer credit options to compete with the AFS sector. For example, banks could offer a six-month, self-amortizing consumer loan up to $500 with direct debit from the account; such a loan would be relatively low-risk and paid automatically, could be offered without the need for labor-intensive interaction with the customer, and could be offered at reasonable interest rates. The credit option could also include a savings component, in which monthly payments would include the borrower's contribution to a savings account (see Bair 2005; Barr 2004, 2007).

The primary goal of public policy changes to strengthen the financial security of LMI families should be to facilitate the provision of safe and affordable bank accounts that meet the transactional, savings, and short-term credit needs of these households. Given the relatively low profit margins available to the financial sector for offering such accounts, public policy needs to provide incentives to the financial sector to provide them and should also be focused on making it easier for LMI households to get access to them. In the remainder of this section, I offer three examples of policies that would promote these twin goals.

A New Tax Credit for Safe and Affordable Accounts for Working Americans

To overcome the financial services mismatch, Congress should enact a tax credit for financial institutions to offer safe and affordable bank accounts to LMI households (see Barr 2004, 2007). The tax credit would be pay-for-performance, with financial institutions able to claim tax credits for a fixed amount per account opened by a low- to moderate-income household. The tax credit program would be administered by the Financial Management Service, which would track bank performance, in cooperation with the IRS, which would administer the reduction in the bank's quarterly withholding tax to adjust for the credits earned. The initiative could be coupled with outreach to employers to encourage direct deposit and automatic savings plans.

A New Opt-Out, Direct Deposit Tax Refund Account

Congress should enact a new "tax refund account" plan to encourage savings and expanded access to banking services, while reducing reliance on costly refund loans (see Barr 2007). Under the plan, unbanked low-income individuals who file their tax returns would have their tax refunds directly deposited into a new account. Banks agreeing to offer safe and affordable bank accounts would register with the IRS to offer the accounts, and a fiscal agent for the IRS would draw from a roster of banks offering these services in the taxpayer's geographic area in assigning the new accounts. On receiving the account number from its fiscal agent, the IRS would directly deposit the Earned Income Tax Credit (EITC) and other tax refunds into that account.

Taxpayers could choose to opt out of the system if they did not want to deposit their refund directly, but the expectation is that the accounts would be widely accepted since they would significantly reduce the costs of receiving one's tax refund. Once the tax refund account is set up through the IRS mechanism at tax time, households would receive their refund in the account weeks earlier than if they had to wait for a paper check. Moreover, once it is established, the account could continue to be used long past tax time. Households could also use the account just like any other bank account—to receive their income, to save, to pay bills, and the like. By using an opt-out strategy and reaching households at tax time, this approach could dramatically, efficiently, and quickly reach millions of LMI households and bring them into the banking system.

State Strategies to Move Families into the Financial Mainstream

States can adopt access to financial services as a core element of welfare-to-work strategies. For example, states now use card-based products for many state benefits, but there are several problems with many of these accounts: they do not permit direct deposit of other sources of income; they are pooled accounts not owned by the customer; and they cannot be used for other purposes or retained when benefits end. In addition, the household does not develop any transactional or credit history and cannot use the card as a means of taking care of daily financial needs. Instead of using these pooled accounts, states should increasingly use individually owned, safe, and affordable bank accounts to receive direct deposit of TANF (Temporary Assistance for Needy Families) and related state benefit payments as an essential component of their electronic benefit transfer (EBT) programs. In addition, many states are considering linked deposit programs, using their fiscal relationships and leverage with banks, to encourage more responsible banking products. Lastly, states employ millions of LMI households that would benefit if they were automatically signed up for bank accounts with direct deposit and automatic savings programs.

CONCLUSION

High-cost financial services, barriers to saving, lack of insurance, and credit constraints may contribute to poverty and other socioeconomic problems. Low-income individuals often lack access to the financial services they need from banks and thrifts and turn to alternative financial services providers such as check-cashers, payday lenders, and money transmitters. Many low-income households live paycheck to paycheck and are vulnerable to emergencies that might endanger their financial stability. Often lacking access to insurance, reasonably priced credit, or regular savings plans, low-income households suffering emergencies suffer worse outcomes. Moreover, the lack of longer-term savings options tailored to low-income households may undermine their ability to invest in human capital or build assets over time. More generally, heavy reliance on alternative financial services reduces the value of take-home pay as well as government assistance programs, such as the Earned Income Tax Credit.

With the right mix of policies, the financial services system could better meet the needs of low- and moderate-income households. In particular, Congress should enact a new tax credit to financial institutions for offering safe and affordable bank accounts. Congress should also develop a new initiative under which the IRS would directly deposit the tax refunds of unbanked households into low-cost bank accounts offered by insured depositories. Furthermore, the states should deploy electronic benefit transfer strategies that move low-income households into the banking system. Implementation of these strategies should lead to households being able to utilize a range of financial services that will lower their costs, enable them to manage their finances better, and increase their ability to save.

This chapter is based on joint work with Jane K. Dokko and Benjamin Keys. Any errors are the author's alone. Data are from Michael S. Barr, principal investigator in the 2006 Detroit Area Household Financial Services (DAHFS) study conducted by the Survey Research Center of the University of Michigan. The DAHFS was supported by the Ford Foundation, the MacArthur Foundation, the Annie E. Casey Foundation, the Fannie Mae Foundation, the Mott Foundation, the Community Foundation of Southeast Michigan, the National Poverty Center, CLOSUP, the provost and vice president for research of the University of Michigan, and the Law School of the University of Michigan. The views presented here are those of the author and not of the supporting organizations.

NOTE

1. Household income largely mirrors tractwide medians, but the data reported here are not restricted with respect to the income of households in LMI tracts.

REFERENCES

Aizcorbe, Ana M., Arthur B. Kennickell, and Kevin B. Moore. 2003. "Recent Changes in U.S. Family Finances: Evidence from the 1998 and 2001 Survey of Consumer Finances." *Federal Reserve Bulletin* 89(January): 1–32.

Bair, Sheila. 2005. *Low-Cost Payday Loans: Opportunities and Obstacles.* Report by the Isenberg School of Management, University of Massachusetts at Amherst, to the Annie E. Casey Foundation. Baltimore, Md.: Annie E. Casey Foundation.

Barr, Michael S. 2004. "Banking the Poor." *Yale Journal on Regulation* 21(1): 121–237.

———. 2007. "An Inclusive, Progressive National Savings and Financial Services Policy." *Harvard Law and Policy Review* 1(1): 161–84.

Barr, Michael S., Ed Bacheldor, and Jane K. Dokko. 2007. "Consumer Choice in Payment Cards." Working paper. Ann Arbor: University of Michigan.

Barr, Michael S., and Jane K. Dokko. 2007. "Paying to Save." University of Michigan Public Law Working paper 100, University of Michigan Law and Economics, Olin Working paper 07-22. Ann Arbor: University of Michigan. Available at http://ssrn.com/abstract=997866.

Bucks, Brian K., Arthur B. Kennickell, and Kevin B. Moore. 2006. "Recent Changes in U.S. Family Finances: Evidence from the 2001 and 2004 Survey of Consumer Finances." *Federal Reserve Bulletin* 92(February): A1–38.

Caskey, John. 1994. *Fringe Banking: Check-Cashing Outlets, Pawnshops, and the Poor.* New York: Russell Sage Foundation.

Dunham, Constance R. 2001. "The Role of Banks and Nonbanks in Serving Low- and Moderate-Income Communities." In *Changing Financial Markets and Community Development: A Federal Reserve System Research Conference,* edited by Jackson L. Blanton, Sherrie L. Rhine, and Alicia Williams. Richmond, Va.: Federal Reserve Bank of Richmond.

Dunham, Constance R., Fritz J. Scheuren, and Douglas J. Willson. 1998. "Methodological Issues in Surveying the Nonbanked Population in Urban Areas." In *Proceedings of the American Statistical Association, Survey Research Methods Section:* 611–16.

Elliehausen, Gregory A., and Edward C. Lawrence. 2001. "Payday Advance Credit in America: An Analysis of Customer Demand." Monograph no. 35, McDonough School of Business. Washington, D.C.: Georgetown University.

Green, Paul E. and V. Srinivasan. 1978. "Conjoint Analysis in Consumer Research: Issues and Outlook." *Journal of Consumer Research* 5(2): 103–23.

Luce, R. Duncan, and John W. Tukey. 1964. "Simultaneous Conjoint Measurement: A New Type of Fundamental Measurement." *Journal of Mathematical Psychology* 1(1): 1–27.

Seidman, Ellen, Moez Hababou, and Jennifer Kramer. 2005. "A Financial Services Survey of Low- and Moderate-Income Households." Center for Financial Services Innovation. Chicago, Il. Available at: www.cfsinnovation.com (accessed January 28, 2009).

U.S. Department of Health and Human Services. 2004. "The 2004 HHS Poverty Guidelines: One Version of the (U.S.) Federal Poverty Measure." Available at: http://aspe.hhs.gov/poverty/04poverty.shtml (last revised January 23, 2006; accessed January 28, 2009).

Chapter 4

Banking Low-Income Populations: Perspectives from South Africa

Daryl Collins and Jonathan Morduch

When Muhammad Yunus was starting Grameen Bank in Bangladesh in the late 1970s, Mary Houghton and Ron Grzywinski, founders of Shorebank, the leading community development bank in the United States, made repeated trips to Bangladesh to assist the novice banker and his funders. The international exchange went two ways. In the mid-1980s, Muhammad Yunus met Bill and Hillary Clinton in Washington, and Yunus inspired the Clintons to help launch a replication of the Grameen Bank in Arkansas (Taub 2004; Yunus 1999). Since then, exchanges have proliferated as the Grameen model has been replicated elsewhere in the United States, including Project Enterprise in New York City and Count-Me-In, a nationwide replication (Jurik 2005). The fundamental argument—that low-income households can be reliable bank customers and that access to finance can be a catalyst to help reduce poverty—has taken wider hold.

This chapter provides evidence on the soundness of this argument by providing a better understanding of the financial lives of poor households: their constraints, objectives, and aspirations. We draw on a study of "Financial Diaries" that details the financial lives of poor households in three low-income communities in South Africa.[1] The study includes households in low-income urban township and rural areas, drawing a sample from the (relatively) wealthiest households in the areas to the poorest.[2] We argue that poor households have surprisingly active financial lives and use a variety of tools to manage their money. These tools are often informal, devised between families and neighbors, but hold potential keys to innovation in the formal banking sector.

For the most part, conversations about poverty and finance in the United States and conversations in developing countries run along different lines. The asset-building framework—focusing on helping households build long-term assets to support investments in businesses, housing, and education—has been particularly influential in the United States. Policy initiatives like individual development accounts (IDAs, a subsidized long-term saving mechanism for low-income households) and children's savings accounts have captured the imaginations of policymakers and activists, in part because they promise to reorient social welfare systems to foster greater autonomy for recipients (Sherraden 1991, this volume).

The push to build long-term assets, however, has not been a top focus in poorer countries. Instead, policymakers in low-income countries focus on more immediate and instrumental concerns, especially on raising incomes through business loans (so-called micro-credit) and, to an increasing extent, expanding access to general-purpose savings accounts and insurance.

Microfinance advocates argue that reliable financial access can have strong positive social and economic impacts even when households, in the end, build few lasting assets.[3] A second push away from the asset-building framework comes from a strong emphasis on commercially viable interventions. Rather than finding ways to redirect systems of public grants and subsidies (as with IDAs in the United States), policymakers in low-income countries have, of necessity, focused on delivering affordable, basic retail financial services to poor households—and doing so with limited subsidies.

Our research on global microfinance leads us to argue that a strong focus on expanding reliable access to banks, credit unions, and other basic finance providers makes strategic sense in the United States as well. In principle, the vision entered legislation as the Community Reinvestment Act (CRA) of 1977 (Barr 2005), but while the CRA has spurred an expansion of banking in poor communities, there is still far to go. A recent study of bank branches in New York City, for example, finds that neighborhoods where half of households have incomes above $60,000 have one bank branch for every 2,165 people and that neighborhoods with a median income under $19,000 have just one bank for every 14,153 people (Office of Anthony Weiner 2007). Where banks are absent, residents turn to friends and relatives or the pawnshops, payday lenders, and check-cashers that serve as "fringe" banks (Caskey 1996), often with high costs. Deploying subsidies for long-term asset-building can complement expanding access to reliable banks but will not substitute for such access. Even where bank or credit union branches are located nearby, and despite the fact that a customer stands to save as much as $40,000 over time by replacing high-cost check-cashing services with a checking account, many individuals still find that the high-cost services deliver features missing elsewhere (Fellowes and Mabanta 2008).

If there is growing international convergence around the need for a wider distribution of banks, the priorities in providing services remain ambiguous. Muhammad Yunus's stress on the importance of loans for productive purposes (to seed and expand small businesses) has proved popular with a wide audience from both the left and right. It strikes particular chords with people worried that entrepreneurship and self-reliance are values missing in traditional government transfer programs.

We argue that business investment is important but only one of the needs for finance in low-income communities, and it is not particularly helpful for employed people who work for others. In the United States, many would-be small-scale entrepreneurs are hobbled by regulation and a lack of management and marketing skills, in addition to a lack of capital (Schreiner and Morduch 2002). Even without those limits, the need for credit extends beyond business needs. U.S. households that use pawnshops, for example, spend the funds to buy groceries, travel to work, pay utility bills, and keep up on rent payments (Fernandez 2007). The evidence presented in this chapter shows that the pattern is also broadly true in South Africa. The poor households we have studied face substantial ups and downs of income, both month to month and week to week, and cash flow management is a priority. Not surprisingly, a growing consumer finance industry is aggressively filling the voids left by banks (Porteous and Hazelhurst 2004).

We argue that household financial needs begin with the need for basic, reliable ways to manage cash flows and short-term expenses. When households lack ways to do that easily, they are often forced in emergencies to rely on the mercy of predatory lenders or the kindness of friends and relatives with little of their own to spare. Both paths can be expensive in their own ways, and when neither path is sufficient, we too often see emergencies triggering downward spirals toward destitution. In less extreme cases, we see ongoing instability that hinders future-looking investment. Facilitating basic cash flow management is thus an often-neglected foundation for other initiatives. With that in place, the next steps will necessitate going beyond Yunus's focus on "micro-enterprise" loans—a process that has already started at the Grameen Bank itself and that holds lessons for U.S. finance as well.

SOUTH AFRICA AND THE UNITED STATES

The United States is, of course, a much wealthier country than South Africa, with a gross national product (GNP) per capita of $28,000, nearly three times that of South Africa. Still, the wide income disparities in both countries mean that households in the lowest income ranges in the United States have income and asset levels similar to those covered in the South African Financial Diaries. On average, the Financial Diaries households have an annual income of $12,400, measured on a purchasing power parity (PPP) basis.[4] The 2004 Survey of Consumer Finances (SCF) reports that the mean income for U.S. households below the twentieth percentile was $10,800.[5] While there are certainly differences—politically, historically, and culturally—households in the United States and South Africa have similarly low incomes, juxtaposed against a sophisticated financial system that does not adequately cater to their needs.

In both South Africa and the United States, lack of access to banks has emerged as a major policy issue. Roughly 15.3 million South African adults—half of the adult population—are "unbanked," that is, they lack a bank account in a regulated financial institution (Finscope 2006). In the United States, 2004 SCF estimates place 8.7 percent of families in the same category (Bucks, Kennickell, and Moore 2006), though there is wide regional variation (Caskey, Duran, and Solo 2006).[6]

Important differences, however, limit direct comparisons. Most central is South Africa's legacy of apartheid and the ethnic divides that remain. Another is economic: in South Africa the labor market is loose—official unemployment rates run about 30 percent, though the figure probably undercounts informal employment. In the Financial Diaries sample, even when we account for informal jobs, only

42 percent of the adult population earns an income from regular, steady employment. In the South African context, having a regular job is a strong marker of success: you generally earn much more than others and have access to a wider variety of financial services. In contrast, the U.S. labor market is much tighter: as we write this in January 2008, the official unemployment rate was reported at 4.9 percent.[7] But unlike in South Africa, having a job in the United States is not as strong a marker of success—it can still be difficult to make ends meet with a regular job—and it is not uncommon for low-income households to struggle to manage money and save for the future even with two earners. We thus do not seek direct parallels between South Africa and the United States. Instead, we focus on insights about the importance of access to money management tools, structured ways to accumulate, and flexible devices for addressing emergencies. These fundamental ideas bear on ways to improve financial access in the United States. They have emerged in our research across a variety of financial landscapes and, for the most part, transcend race, location, ethnicity, and class.

Our starting point is understanding the financial arrangements in which households are already engaged. The financial lives of the poor are complex. Household membership and sharing arrangements are fluid and often ambiguous, incomes come from a variety of sources and livelihoods, and cash flows are often small and irregular. Michael Barr (this volume) points out that the financial practices of the low-income households in Detroit are not fixed, and we show similar evidence from South Africa. Households combine formal and informal services and move in and out of using them as needed. This chapter describes how these factors play out with regard to credit and saving and ultimately with regard to income, assets, and poverty.

THREE OBSERVATIONS

The first and most important finding in our research is that the households we studied are active financial managers. It would be easy to assume that individuals who live in low-income households have little in the way of financial lives, given their income levels. But that logic gets it backward. It is because incomes are so low that households devote considerable energy to strategizing around their financial lives. As described here, households juggle "portfolios" of financial relationships; some are with formal banks and other financial institutions, and others are with friends and family. The formal financial mechanisms do not tend to easily displace the informal. Even the wealthiest households in the sample, which were using an extensive portfolio of bank accounts, formal loans, retirement annuities, and insurance, still tended to interact with the informal financial sector, primarily in savings clubs and burial societies. These respondents suggested to us that they continued to use informal mechanisms not only out of a desire to maintain social solidarity, but also because these mechanisms suited their needs in a way that formal instruments did not. All mechanisms, taken together, are needed to provide the kind of reliability, flexibility, and discipline that households demand. Households seek flexible ways to address unexpected events, on the one hand, and structured devices that impose discipline in order to save, on the other. This finding on the centrality of basic money management tools also emerges in closely related studies in two very different contexts: Bangladesh and India.[8]

Second, the households we studied often saved diligently, though not always in banks. They needed no particular incentives to save, but they did need appropriate mechanisms. These were safe and convenient, and they often built in commitment devices. Informal "savings clubs" organized among neighbors, for example, help households discipline themselves to accumulate in small amounts over time. Strikingly, we find that many households accumulate largely through informal devices even when they have access to reliable savings accounts in banks. One of the problems with these devices is that they are set up for accumulating short-term savings, leaving households to accumulate higher-value assets (like a house) incrementally or to augment savings with funds from other sources during an emergency. The evidence here suggests that there is a demand by low-income households in poor countries for structured, long-term savings devices (of which the IDA is an example). Public subsidy, however, need not be a part of the equation.

Third, with respect to policy in both developed and developing countries, consumer finance often carries negative associations—in the United States through association with "predatory lenders" and mountains of credit card debt, and in poorer countries through tales of exploitative moneylenders. In contrast, credit for productive purposes, most importantly micro-loans to support micro-enterprises, has been widely embraced by policymakers. But as noted earlier, when we look more closely, the households we studied in fact strongly preferred consumer finance over loans for micro-enterprise. Even loans that are nominally made to support small businesses are often diverted to other purposes—and often with good reason. In South Africa, low-income households often use loans to cope with health shocks, pay school fees, put food on the table, or participate in communal and religious activities. The choices made by these households suggest that the need is for access to credit that can be used for flexible purposes. In this way, the international conversation on microfinance has been too limited—as has been, we believe, the U.S. conversation on microfinance.[9] A beginning step is to reimagine "consumer finance" in a more constructive light—while not dismissing the serious and ongoing concerns with overindebtedness and predatory lending.

These three observations characterize important elements of the financial lives of the low-income households we came to know in South Africa. They are not much different, in fact, from important elements of the financial lives of richer South Africans, nor from the financial lives of typical Americans. These observations mesh with what we are learning about how "fringe" banks are used in the United States, as well as with lessons from the emerging literature in behavioral economics (see, for example, Mullainathan and Shafir, this volume). The implications align with movements away from a strict focus on asset-building toward improvements in access to basic banking services and the spread of simple tools like debit cards, ATMs, structured ways to save, and, especially abroad, mobile phone banking (on a range of such mechanisms, see Tufano and Schneider, this volume).

THE FINANCIAL DIARIES DATA

Valuing the assets of poor households in poor countries is more difficult than doing so in wealthier countries, where prices, ownership, and asset qualities are more easily established. Large household surveys have been collected, but precision is variable. The Financial Diaries begin with a complementary approach; the aim is to collect rich data on a very small set of households such that the richness of the analysis compensates for the relative smallness of the sample (Collins 2005).

The Financial Diaries studies continuously track a small number of households across an extended time period. The word "diaries" is something of a misnomer—respondent households do not actually keep a diary themselves. They are interviewed by field researchers every other week for one year. These field researchers ask respondents detailed questions about their financial flows during the prior two weeks: Did they take a loan? Did they deposit money into an account? Did they take goods on credit? The first Financial Diaries study took place in Bangladesh in 1999, led by Stuart Rutherford. Households were interviewed across two research sites—one in the slums of Dhaka and the other in a rural village. The next study, led by Orlanda Ruthven in India, took the lessons learned from Bangladesh and applied a more rigorous framework, particularly in the area of livelihoods. Both studies used small samples of 42 and 48 households, respectively, and used qualitative data collection methods.

The South African Financial Diaries, designed by Daryl Collins, built on both studies, tracking daily cash flows across 152 households from November 2003 to December 2004.[10] The households were drawn from three different areas: Langa, an urban township; Lugangeni, a rural village; and Diepsloot, a suburban township. This chapter uses the South African data, with supplementary information from the Indian and Bangladesh diaries.

Several key innovations were brought into the South African Financial Diaries. Data collection was aided by a specially built relational database that allowed for a substantial improvement in data quality. First, questionnaires were generated for each household, based on data from the previous interview. This meant a higher precision of recall, even for small financial transactions. Second, field workers calculated an on-the-spot reconciliation of household cash flow statements and thus could easily target cash flows that households might have forgotten or had avoided discussing. As shown in figure 4.1, measurement errors, even after three or four visits, are initially large, but after six interviews (about three months) the margin of error across the sample falls to an average of 6 percent of sources of funds. This method allowed us to track, with high precision, a set of more than two hundred income, expenditure, and financial transaction daily time series for each household.[11] Note that most of the errors at the start of the study were negative, meaning that the uses of funds (expenditures and financial outflows) were higher than the sources (income and financial inflows). This came largely from an initial underreporting of income from irregular and informal sources and from financial inflows. These are both particularly difficult data to collect from households in any context.

FIGURE 4.1 / Financial Diaries' Margin of Error

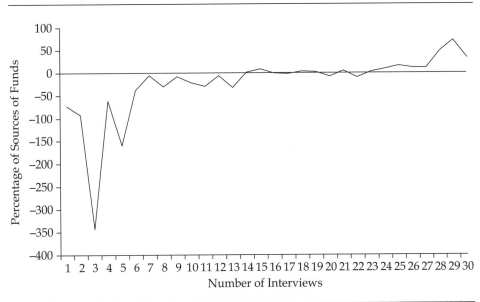

Number of Interviews

Source: Financial Diaries Database 2004, authors' calculations.
Note: After about six interviews, the margin of error of data collection decreases to an average of 6 percent.

The diaries allowed us to do more, however, than increase data quality. The structure also gave us the opportunity to spend part of the interview time in open-ended conversations with households, which elicited rich qualitative data. We were able to follow households' financial dilemmas, opportunities, and strategies as they played out from week to week. In this way, the diaries revealed a diversity of activities that usually remain hidden in onetime cross-sections or even in annual longitudinal studies.

As with all longitudinal survey research, the survey method, based on fortnightly visits, could induce changes in behavior among the respondents over the study year. The research team saw little that explicitly appeared to be such behavioral change, but we acknowledge the possibility as a trade-off entailed in gathering detailed data.[12]

PORTFOLIOS OF THE POOR

With reliable data in hand, we calculate the value of the net worth of Financial Diaries households. "Net worth" is defined as the sum of physical assets (such as livestock, land, housing material, and furniture) and financial assets (such as balances in bank accounts and savings clubs plus informal loans or credit given),

TABLE 4.1   /   Median Financial Assets Versus Annual Cash Flows, South Africa
                (U.S. Dollars, Converted at PPP Rates)

	Year-End Financial Assets	Annual Flows
Rural	$526	$8,247
Urban	$1,895	$14,987

Source: Financial Diaries Database 2004, authors' calculations.

less liabilities (balances on loans or credit outstanding). The median net worth value for the South African Financial Diaries sample was $3,401 (converted at market exchange rates). Adjusting for purchasing power parity, this number rises to $8,187 for South Africa. The South African Financial Diaries sample thus compares roughly to households below the twentieth percentile in the United States, whose median net worth is reported by the 2004 Survey of Consumer Finances to be $7,500.

An interesting picture presents itself when we look at both the stock of financial assets and the value of the financial flows. Table 4.1 shows the median value of financial assets versus the median value of flows through financial instruments over the year for both rural and urban areas of the Financial Diaries sample. From the numbers just cited and the figures in table 4.1, one might assume that the households are not financially active, but looking at cash flows reveals a different story. The table shows that the households "push" and "pull" significant amounts of money through financial instruments over the course of a month (depositing, withdrawing, borrowing, and repaying) more than might be expected from the relatively low value of their financial assets.

Table 4.1 shows that households may not hold large values of financial assets but do have higher turnover in financial instruments than might be expected. (Table 4.2 demonstrates this even more starkly with data from a single household.) The turnover is largely driven by the need to match small and often irregular income inflows to household consumption needs. The financial lives of the poor and low-income households that we have studied thus largely revolve around managing cash flows within the year. Neither financial assets nor net worth by themselves give a full or accurate picture of the financial lives of those in our sample.

Basic money management is achieved by patching together diverse financial strategies. In South Africa, households use an average of seventeen different financial instruments over the year in their ongoing financial portfolios.[13] These include, for example, loans from neighbors and relatives, membership in burial societies, savings accounts in banks, and consumer finance loans. Note that, even though South Africa has a sophisticated and substantial banking system, most of the financial instruments are informal ones. Low-income households are managing their money, but in ways that are not always visible through official banking statistics. Instead, the most important "portfolios" are composed of personal relationships that can be called on to help manage income flows, to match them to the timing of expenditures, and, as best possible, to accumulate for future needs.

TABLE 4.2 / Sylvia's Financial Net Worth at the Start and End of the Research Year
(U.S. Dollars, at Market Rate)

	Starting Amount	Ending Amount	Share of End Portfolio Balances[a]	Turnover[b]	Share of Turnover
Assets					
Formal					
Bank account	$1,373	$2,086	62%	$10,353	54%
Savings plan	153	369	11	182	1
Funeral plan	—	—		68	<1
Informal					
Saved at home	84	483	15	4,875	25
Savings clubs	0	246	7	1,206	6
Using a money guard	0	153	5	153	1
Burial society	—	—		68	<1
Interest-bearing loans	0	0	0	2,404	13
Total	1,611	3,338	100	19,314	100
Liabilities					
Formal					
Credit cards	214	0		248	99
Informal					
Shop credit	0	0		1	1
Total	214	0		249	100
Financial net worth	1,397	3,338			
Total turnover				19,564	

Source: Financial Diaries Database 2004, authors' calculations.
[a]End-year value of assets or liabilities divided by the total.
[b]Inflows into instruments plus outflows out of them.

Consider Sylvia, a very disciplined thirty-nine-year-old woman living in a shack
in Diepsloot, South Africa, outside of Johannesburg.[14] She earns about $370 per
month as a house cleaner for two separate clients. Her income puts her at about the
average for her community, and she uses a similar number of financial instruments, but she is a particularly active and effective money manager. Every month
she has her employers pay her into two different bank accounts. One she uses for
all her expenses, and the other she tries not to touch. Keeping two different bank
accounts is more expensive in terms of bank fees, but the practice has given her a
mechanism with which to save half her salary every month—a mechanism in keeping with the notion of "mental accounts" prominent in behavioral economics (see,
for example, Thaler 1990).

Sylvia also contributes to a formal savings plan, which will come due when her daughter is sixteen and needing money for university. By requiring deposits at regular intervals, this device builds commitment, another feature that has become central to the behavioral economics literature (Thaler 1990). Sylvia tries to keep aside money in the house, but this is a mechanism that requires an extremely disciplined budget. She concentrates on paying off her two credit cards that she used the past Christmas. Other important savings mechanisms include five different informal savings clubs organized by neighbors, a financial device common in South Africa and across the developing world (Rutherford 2000). As table 4.2 demonstrates, Sylvia manages a portfolio of financial activities, borrowing and saving with a diversity of financial instruments. The result has paid off: she more than doubled her financial net worth over the research year.

BUILDING SAVINGS AND ASSETS

Having low incomes does not mean that poor households do not have aspirations. The South African Financial Diaries households have financial goals similar to ones that we see in better-off households, particularly with regard to acquiring a home and paying for important events like weddings, funerals, and holiday celebrations (a finding seen in many countries with regard to spending by the very poor; see Banerjee and Duflo 2007). We saw that a substantial proportion of monthly income can be diverted in an effort to attain these goals. In an average month, 26 percent of monthly income goes into savings instruments, primarily bank accounts and informal savings clubs. Because incomes are small (an average of $1,040 per month, converted at PPP rates), savings represent a relatively small absolute amount of $270 per month. More important, these small amounts are usually not given an opportunity to accumulate for more than one year before they are diverted to short-term needs or unexpected events. One implication has been raised before: viewing changes in year-end balances only may greatly underrepresent the need for and use of savings vehicles.

A second implication is that, although households are able to set aside proportionately large amounts of money every month, they are not as able to accumulate for the long term. We found that savings tend to be short-term in nature and that poor households are left without a pool of accessible savings. Thus, when unexpected events do hit, as we show later in this chapter, households augment savings with funds from a variety of sources—borrowing (often under less than ideal terms), selling assets, and looking for help from friends and family. None of these solutions is cost-free. Borrowing is expensive; South African households borrow at informal rates of 30 percent per month. Selling assets in emergencies can hamper income generation and financial protection later on. And help from family and friends is not always forthcoming without conditions attached. Likewise, when an unexpected opportunity arises, such as the chance to start a business, there is rarely a pool of savings to draw upon to take advantage of it. Finding

TABLE 4.3 / Mimimi's Typical Monthly Budget (U.S. Dollars, at Market Rate)

Source of funds	$509
Business profits	324
Regular wages	185
Uses of funds	$486
Cell phone	6
Cigarettes	3
Electricity	16
Food	49
Send money to Eastern Cape	31
Transport to shopping	1
Transport to work	13
Savings clubs	367
Net savings in bank	$23

Source: Financial Diaries Database 2004, authors' calculations.

ways to convert short-term accumulations into a pool of accessible savings is thus a continuing concern.

We saw in the previous section that Sylvia saves successfully by contributing to a formal savings plan in anticipation of her daughter's university expenses. There is an important commonality and difference with the individual development account approach in the United States (Sherraden 1991, this volume). Sylvia seeks a device that allows her to save in ways that make sense to her, with discipline and a clear set of goals. IDAs share that possibility. The devices used by Sylvia, however, are unsubsidized. Of course, she would probably be happy with a subsidy, but it is not a necessary component of her interest in saving nor of her ability to save in quantity. One implication is that there are contexts in which it makes sense to separate the roles of the subsidy and product design in considering alternatives to (or innovations in) devices like IDAs.

In other cases, discipline and incentives to save are instilled through informal devices. A third point is that most households use a combination of financial instruments, both formal and informal, to attain their financial goals. Jonas and Mimimi are an excellent example of a household that is successful in using all the financial devices available to them, both formal and informal, to generate substantial savings. They are a married couple who run a shebeen (township bar) in Langa, a township of Cape Town. As table 4.3 shows, they have an impressive capacity to save money. Mimimi usually earns profits from the shebeen business of about $324 per month, while Jonas works as a gardener and is paid $185 per month. Their combined income makes them slightly better off than their neighbors, but income from the shebeen business can be unpredictable. Mimimi typically manages to send home about $31 per month for either building their home in the Eastern Cape or supporting their children living there. She then manages to stretch about $88 for their living expenses every month. A typical monthly budget is detailed in table 4.3.

The share of income that Jonas and Mimimi are able to save is unusual in this sample, but their strategies are not. Their most important savings devices are two informal savings clubs. Savings clubs are commonly found all over the world (for many examples, see Rutherford 2000). In South Africa, they tend to come in two forms: rotating clubs (rotating savings and credit associations, or ROSCAs) and accumulating clubs (accumulating savings and credit associations, or ASCAs) (see Armendáriz and Morduch 2005, ch. 3; Rutherford 2000). In a rotating club, each member contributes a set amount of money each period, and one person walks away with the entire sum of the contributions, the "pot." The next month another person will get the pot, and so on, until everyone has had a turn. The money is always taken by someone so that it does not need to be kept anywhere, nor is interest earned. In an accumulating club, members contribute a set amount each period, and the money accumulates for the duration of the club, usually a year or six months. In this case, the money may be deposited in the bank in a club account and earn a small amount of interest, or it may be kept at a member's house.

Jonas and Mimimi belong to one of each type of club, and between these two savings clubs they save about $367 per month. A total of $3,065 was paid out from one of the savings club during 2004, and they used all of it to build the house in the Eastern Cape. The other savings club paid out $725 in December 2004. From this payout, they spent the majority on a Christmas feast and Christmas presents when they went to the Eastern Cape for the holidays, and then they left behind about $260 to buy doors for the house and cement for the floors.

At the end of the year, this young couple had built up in a bank account about $4,000 in savings between the two savings clubs and the saving they retained from Jonas's salary. Of this savings, 12 percent was spent on Christmas, 6 percent was retained in the bank, and 82 percent was used to build the Eastern Cape house.

The reliance of this couple on local savings clubs is striking, since they also have a savings account in a bank. One may wonder why savings clubs have been a larger generator of savings for them than the bank, particularly given the risks associated with the transfer of cash at meetings or in storing money in a member's home. Unlike the bank account, however, the savings clubs offer social pressure to make steady deposits, and they provide structure for steady accumulation. In Jonas and Mimimi's case, these savings were invested immediately in the house they were building in a rural area, although we use the word "investment" with caution. For households in the United States and other countries, investment in a home is clearly seen as building a long-term asset, but in rural South Africa such an investment is seen differently. Homes in rural South Africa are not sold, nor can they be mortgaged to borrow money. They are important to people working in urban areas because they represent a tie back to their village. As Mimimi said, "You need a home in your village so they can bury you from that home."

As noted, Jonas and Mimimi's experience with savings clubs is not unusual among low-income South African households. Two-thirds of the sample used at least one savings club during the study year. Savings clubs are a huge part of savings growth, but by their very structure, most of these savings are set up to be short-term, with payouts saved and used within a year. On average, over the course of 10 months, savings cycles in savings clubs last only 6.6 months before the money is used for the purpose for which it has been saved.

Incremental Asset-Building over Time

Because savings get diverted to other uses along the way, most large purchases are built up incrementally. A key example of this is a home. Many other households in South Africa, India, and Bangladesh would save to build a house in ways similar to how Jonas and Mimimi went about it, using a similar proportion of their savings, but the typical pattern in the United States is quite different. Raising lump sums is one way to get cash together to acquire housing, but housing is also improved or obtained incrementally. Nearly half of South African Financial Diaries homeowners say that they acquire their homes by buying the housing supplies bit by bit over time. Other means of acquisition might be saving a lump sum—that is, saving up through a savings club, as Jonas and Mimimi did—or getting a payout from a pension scheme. Households also use retail credit from stores, usually a local supply store. Rarely do households acquire their home through an informal loan from a moneylender or family member. Some have access to a formal loan from a bank, and about one-quarter, mostly in the rural areas, inherit their homes.

The South African Financial Diaries data allow us to estimate how much households tend to put aside from their monthly cash flow for housing improvement and acquisition. Often these amounts quickly add up to a new room or a wall around the property. Many homeowners in different areas and income levels had been building up their homes by bits and pieces throughout the year. At least half the Financial Diaries households made some sort of expenditure on housing improvement or acquisition during the study year. The amount spent, if prorated on a monthly basis, is between 4 and 6 percent of monthly income. This spending is not just undertaken by the wealthier households in the sample. Although the relatively poor are less likely to spend on their homes, half of the poorest households still manage to find enough funds for home improvement.

Mary Tomlinson (1999) adds evidence to this picture. She interviewed focus groups of 150 beneficiaries of the South African government housing subsidy. Contrary to conventional wisdom, the number of people who told her they did not want a mortgage loan outnumbered those who did by three to one. Respondents were concerned about a number of issues involved in having a mortgage: the high interest charges, the control that the bank would have over their lives, and fears of repossession. These concerns did not indicate any lack of intention to improve their homes, but only a desire to be in charge of their finances and not take on more than they could handle. Like the Financial Diaries households, the respondents in Tomlinson's study preferred to buy the material they needed when they could afford to do so, incrementally.

As noted, this mode differs from homeownership strategies in low-income communities in the United States. Building a home, a common course in South Africa, is different from buying one. The South African example serves as a reminder of the possibilities for simple home improvement loans as a complement to mortgages.

COPING WITH EMERGENCIES

Perhaps because low-income households face so many risks—health, accidents, theft—they cannot afford to insure against each of these risks individually. The rise of HIV/AIDS-related deaths in South Africa has made funerals an increasingly common event in the lives of low-income households. Over the study year, 81 percent of the Financial Diaries households contributed to a funeral at least one time. These funerals are expensive, usually costing up to seven months of income. Such costs cannot be met out of cash flow; if they are to be met at all, a financial instrument, or a combination of financial instruments, must be brought into play. In response to this situation, South African households invest in specialist instruments that we refer to generally as "funeral insurance." No less than 79 percent of the South African Financial Diaries sample had at least one funeral insurance scheme of some kind in place during the research year, and most had more than one. Many households are multiply covered, using more than one kind of plan or having more than one account in any one type of plan. Out of an overall portfolio of eight to twelve financial instruments, households usually have at least two types of funeral insurance. Funeral coverage makes up at least 10 percent of the instruments that compose the household portfolio, with households spending, on average, 3 percent of gross monthly income on all of their funeral coverage instruments.

Yet these funeral plans are only one source of the funds brought together to pay for a funeral. In considering insurance products, it is not necessary for a product to cover the entire cost of an event in order to alleviate the burden of an emergency. The funeral insurance devices we see provide partial coverage only, but add importantly to the financial mix. An example of the expenses and funding sources demonstrates how much funerals cost and how households pay for them. Thembi is one of the urban respondents, a fifty-year-old woman who lived with her forty-seven-year-old brother. The major source of income for the household during the study year was the disability grant of $114 per month that each received, plus Thembi's part-time job.[15] Thembi belongs to a burial society and a savings club, but she hadn't managed to accumulate much savings. She struggled with depression and a host of other chronic ailments, such as high blood pressure, and often spent money on medication. When Thembi's brother died, reportedly of tuberculosis, in June 2004, she was left scrambling for funds to pay for his funeral.

A set of consolidated accounts for the funeral is shown in table 4.4. Of the sources of funds, only 11 percent came from Thembi's burial society. The majority of the costs (54 percent) were paid for through relatives' contributions. Thembi was able to scrape together a bit more by borrowing, both with interest and without, and by using money remaining from her own grant and that of her brother, which she

TABLE 4.4 / Sources and Uses of Funds for Thembi's Brother's Funeral
(U.S. Dollars, at Market Rates)

Sources of Funds	Amount	Uses of Funds	Amount
Cash contribution from relatives	$538	Undertaker	$538
In-kind contribution from relatives	225	Tent	91
Burial insurance payout	154	Pots	35
Borrowed from aunt's burial society (no interest)	154	Food	750
Borrowed from cousin's savings club (30 percent per month)	92		
Borrowed from cousin (no interest)	108		
Leftover money from grant	92		
Leftover money from brother's grant	50		
Total	$1,413		$1,414

Source: Financial Diaries Database 2004, authors' calculations.

found among his things. She managed to pay for the funeral but was left with a significant debt that she struggled to repay for the remainder of the year.[16]

As these examples show, low-income households have aspirations and the budgeting ability to start realizing them. Because the instruments tend to be focused on
funding short-term expenditures, however, there is very little savings left unallo-
cated toward a specific expenditure or for the much longer term, such as retirement.
We found that only about 15 percent of adult singles and 18 percent of married couples in the Financial Diaries sample are forecast to have greater than five years of
retirement support. Most of those are able to secure their future with retirement
annuities and provident funds put in place by their employer. The others depend
heavily on the old-age grant provided by the state, worth about $114 per month at
the time of the study. This is not much, particularly considering that several other
household members may also depend on it.

The bottom line is that households have needs to save for the short, medium,
and long terms. Although having a house is important, other needs, like life-cycle
events, are also central to household members' aspirations about how they want
to live their lives. Commitment devices are effective, but by their very nature
they are also constraining and leave households vulnerable to unexpected events.
Households have many different goals to give their attention to and are well aware
that as a result it may take more time to acquire assets over the long term.

CONSUMER AND BUSINESS FINANCE

Microfinance for micro-enterprise has been trumpeted as a solution to poverty
worldwide. Muhammad Yunus has spoken passionately about creating "poverty
museums" one day after microfinance has helped to wipe out global poverty. The

FIGURE 4.2 / Number and Average Monthly Profit of Small Businesses
(U.S. Dollars, at Market Rates)

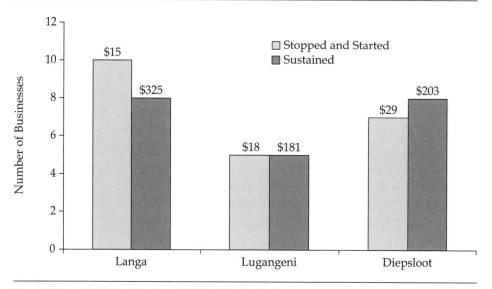

Source: Financial Diaries Database 2004, authors' calculations.

words fire the imagination, but many of the small businesses we encountered over the study year were not sustained.[17] Many were started and stopped within the study year. Figure 4.2 divides the small businesses that were in process at the start of the survey year and those that were started during the survey year into two categories: those that were sustained during the entire year and those that were started during the year but then stopped. In total, we observed forty-six businesses over the course of the year. For businesses to be considered sustained, they must either have been running when we first met respondents or started and in business until the end of the study.[18] In most of the three areas of the study, just as many small businesses—or more—were started and stopped as were sustained. As the average monthly profits above the bars in figure 4.2 suggest, profitability was closely linked to sustainability. We found that many households would start a small business, mostly selling small things from home to try to find a way to generate extra income, but without a clear plan or any sense of whether the business would work.

The greatest need was for flexible working capital rather than capital finance for fixed costs. Part of this need was to fund the "debtor's book," a crucial link to sustaining small businesses. One key feature of entrepreneurial success entails managing the credit given to customers. Figure 4.3 shows that over half the small businesses in the sample gave credit. However, only about 10 percent in all areas felt compelled to charge interest. Of those that did, many simply rounded up the cost of the product rather than charging an interest rate, as can be seen in the following case study.

FIGURE 4.3 / Giving Credit and Charging Interest

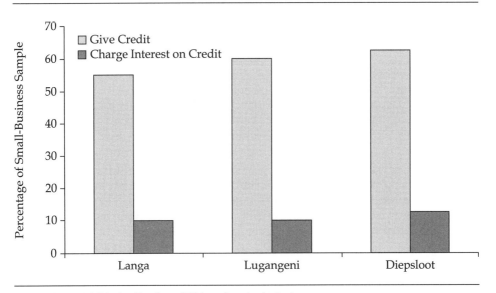

Source: Financial Diaries Database 2004, authors' calculations.

We see these points play out in the case of two beer sellers. We met Jonas and Mimimi at the start of this chapter. As mentioned, Mimimi runs a shebeen—a township bar. From her business, she usually has profits of about $370, more than her husband earns in his full-time job. One reason for Mimimi's success is her credit policy. She gets the bulk of her customers on Friday night, Saturday, and Sunday. Her credit rules are very clear: she only gives credit on Sundays, and you must pay by Friday or you don't get served that weekend. Also, she charges interest: instead of costing 70¢ cash, a beer costs 77¢ on credit. This policy differs significantly from that of Busi, who makes and sells traditional beer several shacks away from Mimimi. Like Mimimi, she tries to keep track of the credit in a book, but unlike Mimimi, Busi does not enforce a credit rule. At one point in the study, we counted sixteen people who owed Busi money. She does not charge any extra from those who take on credit. As a result, she barely earns enough to justify her efforts. Not everyone is a natural entrepreneur.

Even for those households with ongoing businesses, when we asked how they would use a capital loan, most said that they would use additional funds for their personal needs rather than to expand their business. This indicates a growing need for consumer finance, exactly what many policymakers in both South Africa and the United States fear. A key argument in debates on overindebtedness centers on whether debt is used for "productive" debt, like business loans and mortgage debt, or "consumption" debt, such as installment credit for buying consumer items like TVs and clothes. However, when looking into the lives of Financial Diaries households, we found that this distinction is often difficult to make. Installment credit is often used to buy school uniforms, which are necessary for children to attend school. Similarly, a savings club loan may be taken to pay for a funeral. Or credit at the local store may be taken to buy food. This reality does not mesh easily with the distinction between productive and consumption debt. If lacking a school uniform would prevent children from attending school, then it is difficult not to see this debt as productive—though sending a child to school does not generate a short-term cash flow to service the loan. The key issue for success in repaying loans is having a sufficiently steady cash flow to service debt, whatever its purpose.

For one household, access to credit is crucial. Mapeyi is a seventy-two-year-old woman living in a house in the established part of an urban area with her three grandchildren. All four members of this household are supported by Mapeyi's monthly old-age grant, worth about $114 at the time of the study. We witnessed Mapeyi's struggle to contribute to the funeral of her daughter-in-law, which happened in June 2004. She took $40 from her grant and received $155 from her daughter, who borrowed at work. Mapeyi also borrowed $155 from the local grocery shop, from which she used to take groceries on credit every month. When she borrowed the $155, however, she stopped taking credit because she wanted to pay back the loan first. She did not pay any interest for either the loan or the credit. She took the loan in June and managed to pay back the loan from her grant by October.

The shop owner reports that she rarely gives credit to anyone without a salary, but Mapeyi is a special case because she has been in the neighborhood so long and the shop owner knows that she will pay. The shop owner does, however, restrict the credit given to Mapeyi every month to $30 because she worries that Mapeyi cannot pay more than that. As figure 4.4 shows, Mapeyi tends to manage her credit fairly tightly, paying back 10 to 20 percent of her income to the shop. During the four months she was paying back the loan, she used 30 to 60 percent of her income to pay the loan and severely restricted her household expenditures.

Several observations come out of this case. First, we see that even households that manage money carefully can be thrown into high levels of debt when a sudden emergency arises. As mentioned earlier, having to pay for a funeral was something we observed frequently during the Financial Diaries study, and Mapeyi's situation was not an unusual one. However, we also saw that Mapeyi's financial discipline paid off after the funeral—she was able to move herself out of this debt situation fairly quickly, within four months. Second, we saw that informal finance can be crucial to poor households. Mapeyi was able to secure a loan from the first place she asked, but had she not succeeded, what were her options? One possibility is that she might have had to borrow from the local moneylender at interest of 30 percent per month. But Mapeyi's relationship and good credit standing with the grocery shop owner, along with her own self-discipline, allowed her to pay for the funeral without putting herself in a debt trap. We rarely saw other households in the Financial Diaries study, however, being able to borrow such a large sum of money, both hassle- and interest-free. Usually households needed to draw on a larger number of loan sources, paid substantially more in interest, and were under far more pressure from lenders to repay quickly. Finally, we underscore that access to reasonably priced credit for people like Mapeyi can be critical. Her use of it,

FIGURE 4.4 / Mapayi's Debt Payments as a Percentage of Her Income

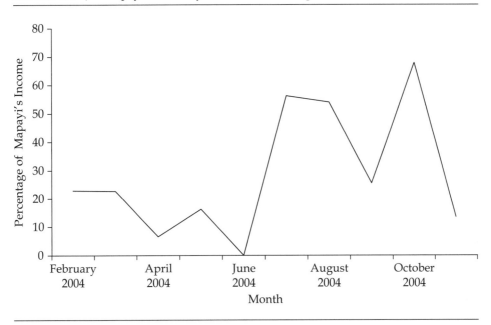

Source: Financial Diaries Database 2004, authors' calculations.

however, had nothing to do with the business-focused claims typically invoked to justify expanding credit access to low-income communities.[19]

CONCLUSIONS

The Financial Diaries study uncovered no households that live "hand to mouth" despite their low incomes. Even households that live "from payday to payday," like the households in Michael Barr's analysis of low-income communities in Detroit (this volume), still use informal financial devices like storing money at home for short term financial needs and borrowing and lending with friends and neighbors to bridge cash flow to address the mismatched timing of income and expenditures. Because of their financial circumstances, they need to manage money much more actively than we might expect. They make frequent transactions through a variety of financial instruments in order to save money, insure against adverse events, and manage cash flow constraints.

Often, low-income households must turn to informal markets and institutions, which are seldom as reliable as formal institutions. Consider the case of one respondent who supported her family of five by cooking and selling sheep intestines on the street. Often she would find that after a day of sparse sales or a day when she sold on credit, she did not have enough cash to buy the ingredients for the next day's business. To better manage her cash flow needs, she joined a savings club (a ROSCA) with four other street sellers. Each contributed $8 every day, making a total pot of $40. Club members took turns getting the pot each of the five working days of the week. It was a clever solution to a binding financial constraint. However, not everyone contributed on time, and the club soon fell apart. We found many businesses in this situation, forced to rely on an assemblage of imperfect financial instruments.

The introduction and take-up of new formal instruments that can help households manage cash flow, insure against adverse events, and save would yield obvious gains. But we also saw that it would not necessarily lead households to abandon their informal instruments. As we noted earlier, even when households become wealthier and are exposed to more formal instruments, they do not entirely drop their informal instruments. This continued adherence to informal instruments is not so much a matter of price as a matter of convenience—households, having found an instrument that suits some needs, are loathe to abandon it entirely. The convenience of informal instruments, for example, often trumps formal instruments.

However, even though the introduction of new formal instruments into the household portfolio does not cause a complete abandonment of informal mechanisms, it does change the portfolio balance—in a direction that we suspect is less risky and has more diversity. First, informal mechanisms can be risky. They can fall apart, as the example of the sheep intestine seller shows, or they can fail entirely. Sylvia, who wanted to send her daughter to college, saved a tremendous amount in a savings club, but the club suffered a robbery at payout time and half their savings were lost. Second, with respect to savings, the very element that makes informal savings clubs work—their time-bound, inflexible nature—is also their downfall in contributing to a well-diversified portfolio. Moreover, savings clubs are useful for savings in the medium term (less than a year), but they are not helpful for short-term cash management, and they do not allow households to save for the longer term or for open-ended purposes. This leaves a large hole in the savings portfolios of the poor. Lastly, formal financial instruments can often be better value in terms of cost and reward, including the interest costs on short-term loans and the fees for other instruments, such as insurance. An analysis of formal burial insurance against informal burial insurance in the South African Financial Diaries data set shows that formal insurance pays out at least as much as informal insurance, with some plans showing far better value (Collins and Leibbrandt 2007).

The results of the studies in South Africa provide general insights into the financial management practices of low-income households. Most policy debates center on the "big-ticket items" such as financing a home or obtaining a capital loan for a business, but this focus misses most of the action. Households have a variety of different needs and aspirations, not just for housing or businesses. They cope with adverse events, manage everyday cash flow, save for weddings, and borrow for funerals. The important innovations need to do more than get incentives right and encourage discipline. They also should focus on developing truly reliable and flexible financial instruments for a wide variety of purposes. The first aim should be to help low-income households simply manage their money dependably. The next steps are to provide better ways for households to cope with unexpected risk and seize opportunities, whether those financial transactions take the form of supporting a migrating family member, paying for a doctor's visit, or taking advantage of a chance to start a business.

NOTES

1. The work described here is part of a collaborative project on collecting and analyzing "Financial Diaries" that also took place in Bangladesh and India. See Ruthven (2002) and Rutherford (2002) for more details and findings from the Indian and Bangladesh Financial Diaries studies. Collins and her colleagues (2009) synthesize lessons from the three Financial Diaries studies. We are grateful for the collaboration of Stuart Rutherford, Orlanda Ruthven, and David Hulme, and we have drawn substantially on their insights and ways of framing evidence, though the views here are ours. We know of no similar research program with regard to financial conditions in the United States, but we find common themes in the ethnographic work of Sudhir Venkatesh (2006), for example, and in the analysis of fringe banks by John Caskey (1996).

2. To select the sample, we first chose two urban townships and one rural village with very low monthly income figures from national surveys. We then randomly chose five neighborhoods in each township or village. Within those neighborhoods, we took advantage of the reality that in poor communities people know their neighbors well, so we were able to use "wealth ranking" to determine our selection of households. Wealth ranking is a technique that relies on comparing key informants' estimates of the relative wealth of their neighbors to compile a ranked list of households from the most to the least wealthy. We then randomly selected equal numbers of households from the most wealthy, the middle-income, and the poorest in those wealth rankings. This provided us with a good selection of all three levels of incomes within each neighborhood.

3. Beatriz Armendáriz and Jonathan Morduch (2005, ch. 8) survey evidence from impact evaluations of microfinance.

4. Numbers that are compared directly with U.S. numbers are converted from South African rand to U.S. dollars at the purchasing power parity rate of 2.7. All others are converted at the market exchange rate, which at the time of the study was R6.5/US$1.

5. All U.S. data quoted in this chapter are from the SCF of 2004, the same year the South African Financial Diaries study was conducted.

6. Note that this estimate is for all households. In the lowest quintile, the estimated unbanked population is about 25 percent.

7. As this book goes to print, it has been reported that the unemployment rate in the United States rose sharply to 7.2 percent in December 2008, its highest level since 1993. Nonetheless, even these historically high levels of unemployment are far lower than those in South Africa. Moreover, even though in the United States the unemployment rate is much higher in low-income communities than in the general population, the broader point about the relative tightness and looseness of the labor markets remains.

8. Our debt to Stuart Rutherford on this score will be apparent to those familiar with his writings.

9. Caskey (1996) is an important exception.

10. For more details on the data set, including survey instruments, see www.financial diaries.com and Collins (2005). One of the key advances made in the South African Financial Diaries and its use of a specially conceived and built relational database is its ability to give the researcher on-the-spot indicators while still in the field. Our key indicator for data collection assessment is the margin of error. This measures all the sources of cash flowing into the house (not only income but also withdrawals from bank accounts, getting paid back from friends, savings club payouts) as well as uses of income (not only expenditures but also making deposits into the bank account or "house account," paying premiums, giving a loan), less cash on hand. Ideally, this measure, from interview to interview, should be 0, or at least a small number. Each week, when we do our assessment of each data set, we pinpoint those households with large margins of error to determine whether there is a data capture error or whether the household is simply holding something back. Errors such as the former are corrected during a site trip each month. Errors such as the latter are noted and filed. Although the data collection is not perfect in these households, we focus on "knowing what we don't know" and return repeatedly to the "problem" households to get better information.

11. Income and financial flows are collected on an individual basis, and expenditure and physical assets are collected on a household basis. Because each household has different numbers of income sources and financial instruments, there is a wide variance in the number of time series collected per household. A household with two adults and two children and an average number of financial instruments would have about two hundred time-series observations of cash flow data.

12. During the survey year, we wondered how much households changed their financial behavior as a result of being constantly asked about their money. In our year-end interview, we probed this issue by directly asking respondents whether being involved in the Financial Diaries had changed their behavior or not. Many said that it had indeed, and that being involved in the project had made them think more carefully about their financial decisions. A few respondents said that involvement in the project had had no effect on their financial management at all. However, without a controlled experiment that would allow us to measure the size of this effect, we cannot comment on whether our persistent questioning caused households to manage their money more, or less, conservatively.

13. In Bangladesh, Rutherford found that households used, on average, ten different financial instruments. Even with a large number of microfinance institutions in Bangladesh, the most frequently used financial instruments were informal.

14. The names of all respondents cited in this chapter have been changed to protect their identities.

15. For a description of the South African transfer system and its benefits for low-income families, see Case and Deaton (1998).

16. This case study is used in Collins et al. (2009).

17. This observation is also reflected in a broader survey conducted by the Graduate School of Business of the University of Cape Town and reported in Acs et al. (2005). For a view from Indonesia, see Johnston and Morduch (2008).

18. Three businesses were started within two months of the end of the study year and so are not included in figure 4.2.

19. This case study is used in Collins (2008).

REFERENCES

Acs, Zoltan J., Pia Arenius, Michael Hay, and Maria Minniti. 2005. "Global Entrepreneurship Monitor 2004." Unpublished paper, Babson College and London Business School.

Armendáriz, Beatriz, and Jonathan Morduch. 2005. *The Economics of Microfinance.* Cambridge, Mass.: MIT Press.

Banerjee, Abhijit, and Esther Duflo. 2007. "The Economic Lives of the Poor." *Journal of Economic Perspectives* 21(1): 141–67.

Barr, Michael S. 2005. "Credit Where It Counts: The Community Reinvestment Act and Its Critics." *New York University Law Review* 80(2): 513–652.

Bucks, Brian K., Arthur B. Kennickell and Kevin B. Moore. 2006. "Recent Changes in U.S. Family Finances: Evidence from the 2001 and 2004 Survey of Consumer Finances." *Federal Reserve Bulletin* 92(February): A1–38.

Case, Anne, and Angus Deaton. 1998. "Large Cash Transfers to the Elderly in South Africa." *Economic Journal* 108(450): 1330–61.

Caskey, John. 1996. *Fringe Banking: Check-Cashing Outlets, Pawnshops, and the Poor.* New York: Russell Sage Foundation.

Caskey, John, Clemente Ruiz Duran, and Tova Maria Solo. 2006. "The Urban Unbanked in Mexico and the United States." Policy research working paper 3835. Washington, D.C.: World Bank.

Collins, Daryl. 2005. "Financial Instruments of the Poor: Initial Findings from the South African Financial Diaries Study." *Development Southern Africa* 22(5): 717–28.

———. 2008. "Debt and Household Finance: Evidence from the Financial Diaries." *Development Southern Africa* 25(4): 469–79.

Collins, Daryl, and Murray Leibbrandt. 2007. "The Financial Impact of HIV/AIDS on Poor Households in South Africa." *AIDS* 21(supp. 7): S75–81.

Collins, Daryl, Jonathan Morduch, Stuart Rutherford, and Orlanda Ruthven. 2009. *Portfolios of the Poor: How the World's Poor Live on $2 a Day.* Princeton, N.J.: Princeton University Press.

Fellowes, Matt, and Mia Mabanta. 2008. "Banking on Wealth: America's New Retail Banking Infrastructure and Its Wealth-Building Potential." Washington, D.C.: Brookings Institution.

Fernandez, Manny. 2007. "Cash to Get By Is Still Pawnshop's Stock in Trade." *New York Times,* September 14.

Financial Diaries Database. 2004. Distributed by the University of Cape Town, South Africa. Available at: http://www.datafirst.uct.ac.za/data_fdiaries.html#database (accessed January 2007).

Finscope. 2006. *Finscope 2006 Findings Brochure.* Johannesburg: Finmark Trust. Available at: http://www.finscope.co.za/southafrica.html (accessed January 2007).

Johnston, Don, and Jonathan Morduch. 2008. "The Unbanked: Evidence from Indonesia." Working paper. New York: New York University, Wagner School of Public Service, Financial Access Initiative.

Jurik, Nancy C. 2005. *Bootstrap Dreams: U.S. Microenterprise Development in an Era of Welfare Reform.* Ithaca, N.Y.: Cornell University Press.

Office of U.S. Representative Anthony D. Weiner. 2007. "Many More Banks in New York City (but Only for Some)." Washington: U.S. House of Representatives (September 9).

Porteous, David, and Ethel Hazelhurst. 2004. *Banking on Change: Democratizing Finance in South Africa, 1994–2004 and Beyond.* Cape Town: Double Storey.

Rutherford, Stuart. 2000. *The Poor and Their Money.* Delhi: Oxford University Press.

———. 2002. "Money Talks: Conversations with Poor Households in Bangladesh About Managing Money." Working paper 45. Manchester, U.K.: University of Manchester, Institute for Development Policy and Management, Finance and Development Research Program.

Ruthven, Orlanda. 2002. "Money Mosaics: Financial Choice and Strategy in a West Delhi Squatter Settlement." *Journal of International Development* 14(2): 249–71.

Schreiner, Mark, and Jonathan Morduch. 2002. "Replicating Microfinance in the United States: Opportunities and Challenges." In *Replicating Microfinance in the United States,* edited by Jim Carr and Zhong Yi Tong. Baltimore, Md.: Woodrow Wilson Center/ Johns Hopkins University Press.

Sherraden, Michael. 1991. *Assets and the Poor: A New American Welfare Policy.* Armonk, N.Y.: M. E. Sharpe.

Taub, Richard. 2004. *Doing Development in Arkansas: Using Credit to Create Opportunity for Entrepreneurs Outside the Mainstream.* Fayetteville: University of Arkansas Press.

Thaler, Richard H. 1990. "Anomalies: Saving, Fungibility, and Mental Accounts." *Journal of Economic Perspectives* 4(1): 193–205.

Tomlinson, Mary R. 1999. "From Rejection to Resignation: Beneficiaries' Views on the South African Government's New Housing Subsidy System." *Urban Studies* 36(8): 1349–59.

Venkatesh, Sudhir. 2006. *Off the Books: The Underground Economy of the Urban Poor.* Cambridge, Mass.: Harvard University Press.

Yunus, Muhammad. 1999. *Banker to the Poor: Microlending and the Battle Against World Poverty.* New York: PublicAffairs.

Chapter 5

Savings Policy and Decisionmaking in Low-Income Households

Sendhil Mullainathan and Eldar Shafir

Theories about poverty, held both by social scientists and by regular folks, typically fall into one of two camps: those who regard the behaviors of the economically disadvantaged as calculated adaptations to prevailing circumstances, and those who view these behaviors as emanating from a unique "culture of poverty" that is rife with deviant values. The first view presumes that people are highly rational, hold coherent, well-informed, and justified beliefs, and pursue their goals effectively, with little systematic error and no need for help. The second view attributes to the poor a variety of psychological and attitudinal shortcomings, presumed to be endemic, that render the views of the poor misguided and ill informed, their behaviors impulsive and lacking, and their choices fallible, and that leave them in need of paternalistic guidance.

Both camps are likely to capture some important elements some of the time. There are, no doubt, important circumstances in which people—the poor included—are methodical and calculating, and other circumstances in which they are fallible or misguided. But both camps fail to explain important phenomena. We propose an alternative perspective, one largely informed by recent behavioral research. According to this perspective, the behavioral patterns of the poor may be neither perfectly calculating nor especially deviant. Rather, the poor may exhibit fundamental attitudes and natural proclivities, including weaknesses and biases, that are similar to those of people from other walks of life. One important difference, however, is that in poverty the margins for error are narrow, so that behaviors shared by all often manifest themselves in the poor in more pronounced ways and can lead to worse outcomes (see Bertrand, Mullainathan, and Shafir 2004, 2006).

Whereas the "rational" view assumes that the poor are doing as well as they can and ought to be left to their own devices, the "culture of poverty" perspective is motivated by the impulse to change how the poor function. In contrast, the central gist of the "behavioral" perspective is that much of the time the poor are not functioning optimally, nor are they any more in need of behavioral change than everyone else. Instead, it is the interaction of fundamental behavioral proclivities with the context in which they function that produces the particularly destructive circumstances in which the poor often find themselves. According to this behavioral view, people who live in poverty are susceptible to many of the same impulses and idiosyncrasies as those who live in comfort, but whereas people who are better off function in the midst of a system—composed of consultants, reminders, cooperative employers, "no-fee" options, incentive awards, and automatic deposit—that is increasingly designed to facilitate their decisions and improve their outcomes, people who are less well off typically find themselves without easy recourse to such "aids" and often are confronted by obstacles—institutional, social, and psychological—that render their economic choices all the more overwhelming and their economic conduct all the more fallible.

In what follows, we explore some insights provided by a behaviorally more realistic analysis of the economic conditions of the poor. Our perspective draws on empirical research on judgment and decisionmaking and is supplemented by lessons from social and cognitive psychology. We first review the psychological insights and then consider their implications for a variety of financial products and services that feature prominently in the financial context of the American poor. Of course, insights generated by experimental research and empirical observation need to be carefully tested and evaluated before they can be relied on to shape policy. Even when an intervention succeeds in shaping some intended outcomes, there is always the possibility that other, unforeseen patterns will emerge. Bearing that in mind, we propose some guidelines for thinking about the future design and regulation of financial services.

THE BEHAVIORAL PERSPECTIVE

The Importance of Context

Human behavior proves to be heavily context-dependent, that is, a function of both the person and the situation. One of the major lessons of modern psychological research is that situation exerts impressive power; we have a persistent tendency to underestimate that power relative to the presumed influence of personality traits. Various studies have documented the stunning capacity of situational factors to influence behaviors that are typically seen as reflective of deep personal dispositions. In his now-classic obedience studies, for example, Stanley Milgram (1974) showed how decidedly mild situational pressures sufficed to generate persistent willingness on the part of regular people to administer what they believed to be grave levels of electric shock to innocent subjects. Along similar lines, John Darley and Daniel Batson (1973) recruited seminary students to deliver a practice sermon on the parable of the Good Samaritan. While half the seminarians were told that they were ahead of schedule, others were led to believe that they were running late. On their way to give the talk, all participants passed an ostensibly injured man slumped in a doorway, coughing and groaning. Whereas the majority of those with time to spare stopped to help, a mere 10 percent of those who were running late stopped; the remaining 90 percent stepped over the victim and rushed along. In contrast with these participants' ethical training and biblical scholarship, the contextual nuance of a minor time constraint proved decisive in the decision to stop and help a suffering man.

The Role of Construal

A simple but fundamental tension between classical economic analyses and modern psychological research is captured by the role of "construal." Agents in classical economic analyses are presumed to choose between options in the world, objectively represented. People do not respond directly, however, to objective circumstances; rather, stimuli are mentally construed, interpreted, understood (or misunderstood), and then acted upon. Behavior is directed not toward actual states of the world but toward our mental representation of those states; moreover, mental representations do not bear a one-to-one relationship to the thing they represent, nor do they necessarily constitute faithful renditions of actual circumstances. As a result, many well-intentioned interventions can fail because of the way in which they are construed by the targeted group—for example, "as an insulting and stigmatizing exercise in co-option and paternalism" (Ross and Nisbett 1991) or as an indication of what the desired or expected behavior might be, or of what it might be worth. Thus, people who are rewarded for a behavior they find interesting and enjoyable can come to attribute their interest in the behavior to the reward and consequently to view the behavior as less attractive (Lepper, Greene, and Nisbett 1973). In one classic study, for example, children who were offered a "good player award" to play with magic markers, which they had previously done with great relish in the absence of extrinsic rewards, subsequently showed little interest in the markers when these were introduced as an unawarded classroom activity—in contrast with children who had not received an award and showed no decrease in interest.

Mental Accounting and Finances

One domain that is of great relevance to our present topic and where construal can prove of great consequence is that of mental accounting. Mental accounting research documents the variety of ways in which the assumption of the fungibility of money fails, leading people to view cash, credit, and debit differently depending on the "mental account" in which the money is perceived to be. People's representation of money systematically departs from what is commonly assumed in economics. According to the fungibility assumption, which plays a central role in theories of consumption and savings, "money has no labels"; all components of a person's wealth can be collapsed into a single sum. Contrary to this assumption, people appear to compartmentalize wealth and spending into distinct budget categories, such as savings, rent, and entertainment, and into separate mental accounts, such as current income, assets, and future income (Thaler 1985, 1992). These mental accounting schemes lead to differential marginal propensities to consume (MPC) from one's current income (where MPC is high), current assets (where MPC is intermediate), and future income (where MPC is low). Consumption functions thus end up being overly dependent on current income, and people find themselves willing to save and borrow (at a higher interest rate) at the same time (Ausubel 1991).

A variety of other experimental findings are relevant to a better understanding of financial behaviors, but a full summary of those findings is beyond the purview of the present brief exposition. To list just a few, people are loss-averse—the loss of utility associated with giving up a good is greater than the utility associated with obtaining it (Tversky and Kahneman 1991)—and loss aversion yields "endowment effects," wherein the mere possession of a good can lead to higher valuation of it than if it were not in one's possession (Kahneman, Knetsch, and Thaler 1990). This, in turn, leads to a general reluctance to depart from the status quo, because the disadvantages of departing from it tend to loom larger than the advantages of the alternatives (Knetsch 1989; Samuelson and Zeckhauser 1988). People often also fail to ignore sunk costs (Arkes and Blumer 1985), fail appropriately to consider opportunity costs (Camerer et al. 1997), and show money illusion, wherein the nominal worth of money interferes with a representation of its real worth (Shafir, Diamond, and Tversky 1997). Furthermore, people often prove weak at predicting their future tastes or at learning from past experience (Kahneman 1994), and their intertemporal choices exhibit poor planning (Buehler, Griffin, and Ross 1994) and high discount rates for future as opposed to present outcomes, yielding dynamically inconsistent preferences (Loewenstein and Prelec 1992; Loewenstein and Thaler 1989).

An understanding of such proclivities may be further harnessed to help make sense of behaviors that might otherwise appear perplexing, and this understanding may also help produce more desirable behaviors and outcomes. For example, numerous studies of middle-class savings show that, as a consequence of faulty planning and procrastination, saving works best as a default. Thus, participation in 401(k) plans is significantly higher when employers offer automatic enrollment (Madrian and Shea 2001), and because participants tend to retain the default contribution rates, savings can be increased as a result of agreeing to increased default deductions from future raises (Benartzi and Thaler 2004). As we discuss later, the poor tend to have little recourse to just this kind of default savings and saving programs, but the general notion that context can be designed so as to ameliorate outcomes is a central and important one.

Channel Factors

As it turns out, the pressures exerted by apparently trivial situational factors can create restraining forces that are hard to overcome, or they can promote inducing forces that can be harnessed to great effect. What is particularly impressive is the fluidity with which construal occurs and the sweeping picture it imposes.

Alongside the remarkably powerful impact of context is a profound underappreciation of the effects of construal. When interpreting others' behavior, we tend to exhibit the "fundamental attribution error": we overweight the influence of internal, personal attributes and underappreciate the influence of external, situational forces. As explained by Lee Ross and Richard Nisbett (1991), where standard intuition would hold that the primary cause of a problem, or the particular weakness of a group of individuals, is human frailty, the social psychologist would often look to situational barriers and to ways to overcome them.

The behavioral perspective, with its emphasis on context and construal, suggests that in opposition to major interventions that prove ineffectual, seemingly minor situational changes can have a large impact. Kurt Lewin, in the middle of the last century, coined the term "channel factors." Certain behaviors, Lewin (1952) suggested, can be facilitated by the opening up of a channel (such as an a priori commitment or a small, even if reluctant, first step), whereas other behaviors can be blocked by the closing of a channel (such as the inability to communicate easily or the failure to formulate a simple plan). A well-known example of a channel factor was documented by Howard Leventhal, Robert Singer, and Susan Jones (1965), whose subjects received persuasive communications about the risks of tetanus and the value of inoculation and were told where they could go for a tetanus shot. Follow-up surveys showed that the communication was effective in changing beliefs and attitudes. Nonetheless, only 3 percent actually took the step of getting themselves inoculated, compared with 28 percent of those who received the same communication but were then also given a map of the campus with the infirmary circled and urged to decide on a particular time and route to get there. Related findings have been reported in studies of the utilization of public health services: a variety of attitudinal and individual differences rarely predict who will show up at a clinic, whereas the mere distance of individuals from a clinic proves to be a strong predictor (Van Dort and Moos 1976.) Consistent with this interpretation, Derek Koehler and Connie Poon (2006) argue that people's predictions of their future behavior overweigh the strength of their current intentions relative to situational or contextual factors. As it turns out, seemingly inconsequential contextual features can have a profound influence on the likelihood that intentions will be translated into action. (It is worth noting the complicating implications of these and related findings for standard assumptions of revealed preference: Did the students in the study conducted by Leventhal and his colleagues "want" to get the inoculation? And which observed preference is the "right" one—the 3 percent observed in the control condition or the 30 percent observed when handed a map?)

Individual psyches can be understood as "tension systems" (Lewin 1951), composed of coexisting proclivities and impulses, in which incentives, if they run against substantial opposing forces, will have little influence, whereas other interventions, when the system is finely balanced, can have a profound impact. In other words, big interventions can sometimes have negligible effects, whereas apparently small manipulations can make a big difference.

The basic insights outlined here have important corollaries for our present concerns. For one, they suggest that the same tendencies and weaknesses express themselves differentially in diverse circumstances. For example, the tendency to avoid action and resort to the status quo leads to inferior outcomes when context is structured so that the most beneficial outcomes require action, and this tendency leads to more desirable outcomes whenever the default is set naturally to produce them. Similarly, the same tendencies and weaknesses have different repercussions in different circumstances. A person who is well off but fails to formulate a farsighted plan may have a more modest though still comfortable nest egg upon retirement, whereas a poor person who exhibits similar failures may end up with too little cash to pay a phone bill, accrue large fines for reconnection, become increasingly unable to pay bills, and descend further into poverty.

In this chapter, we examine the specific implications of the behavioral perspective for the financial lives of the poor at three different levels. At the individual level, how does this perspective affect their choices about savings and borrowing? At the institutional level, what does this perspective say about how financial services ought to be designed? And at the regulatory level, what are the implications of this perspective for how financial services ought to be regulated?

Individual psychology is relevant at each of these levels. It directly affects the choices and actions that compound to generate a pattern of saving and borrowing. It affects how individuals respond to various features of a financial product, from its pricing to the transaction costs in acquiring it to its intertemporal consequences. It also gives us a different perspective on the channels by which financial services can affect behavior. All of these insights generate implications for design. Finally, since individual psychology generates deviations from the traditional economic model, it also provides different rationales and guidance for regulation, and not always in the direction of traditional consumer protection. Interestingly, by helping to elucidate specific psychological mechanisms, individual psychology undercuts some of the previous motivations for consumer protection.

INSTITUTIONAL FINANCIAL ACCESS FOR THE POOR

The Role of Financial Access

Financial services may provide an important pathway out of poverty. Such services facilitate savings to mitigate against shocks and promote asset development, and they facilitate borrowing to purchase durables or help weather tough times. In short, financial services allow individuals to smooth consumption and invest (for more on the financial instruments used by low-income Americans, see Barr 2004, this volume). Improvement of financial services, then, provides two key advantages. First, for individuals who already have access to these services, improvement would lower the costs they pay. For example, improved financial services may enable them to use a credit card rather than the more expensive payday lender. Second, individuals who have not had access to financial services would get the direct benefits of access, such as the ability to borrow to smooth shocks (such as health shocks).

Some Features of Financial Access

Our perspective highlights the importance of contextual nuance and consequently the emergence of circumstances in which benefits and costs emanate from the interaction between behavioral tendencies and contextual structure. We briefly consider some simple contextual features that are pertinent to financial access.

INSTITUTIONS SHAPE DEFAULTS   It is well established that defaults can have a profound influence on the outcomes of individual choices. Data available on decisions ranging from retirement savings and portfolio choices to the decision to be a willing organ donor illustrate the substantial increase in market share of default options (Johnson and Goldstein 2003; Johnson et al. 1993). This is likely to prove of great importance for the design of financial services, which often shape default financial behaviors.

Consider, for example, two individuals with no access to credit cards: one has her paycheck directly deposited into a savings account, and the other does not. Whereas cash is not readily available to the first person, who needs to take active steps to withdraw it, cash is immediately available to the second, who must take active measures to save it. The greater tendency to spend cash in the wallet compared to funds deposited in the bank (Thaler 1999) suggests that the first, banked person will spend less on impulse and save more easily than the person who is unbanked. Holding risk- and savings-related propensities constant, the first person is likely to end up a more active and efficient saver than the second.

INSTITUTIONS SHAPE BEHAVIOR   Many low-income families are in fact savers, whether or not they resort to banks (Berry 2004). Without the help of a financial institution, however, their savings are at greater risk (from theft, impulse spending, access by household members), will grow more slowly, and may not be readily available to support access to reasonably priced credit in times of need. Institutions provide safety and control. In this sense, institutional context may be even more critical for the poor than for the comfortable. In circumstances of dearth, temptation, distraction, and difficult management and control, those savers who are unbanked are likely to find it all the more difficult to succeed on the path to long-term prosperity.

In fact, a recent survey conducted by the American Payroll Association (2002) shows that "American employees are gaining confidence in direct deposit as a reliable method of payment that gives them greater control over their finances, and that employers are recognizing direct deposit as a low-cost employee benefit that can also save payroll processing time and money." The employers of the poor, in contrast, often neither require nor propose electronic salary payments. Instead, they prefer not to offer direct deposit to hourly or non-exempt employees, temporary or seasonal employees, part-timers, union employees, and employees in remote locations—categories which often correlate with being low-paid. The most frequently stated reasons for not offering direct deposit to these employees include lack of processing time to meet standard industry ("Automatic Clearing House") requirements, high turnover, and union contract restrictions. All these factors create a clearly missed opportunity to offer favorable defaults to needy individuals whose de facto default procedure for pocketing the money they have earned is to take a check, often after hours, to a place, often inconvenient, where it can be cashed for a hefty fee.

INSTITUTIONS PROVIDE IMPLICIT PLANNING As it turns out, a variety of institutions provide implicit planning, often in ways that address potential behavioral weaknesses. Credit card companies send customers timely reminders of due payments, and clients can elect to have their utility bills automatically charged, allowing them to avoid late fees if occasionally they do not get around to paying in time. By contrast, the low-income buyer who has no credit card, no automatic billing, and no Web-based reminders risks missed payments, (high) late fees, disconnected utilities (accompanied by high reconnection charges), and so on.

Interestingly, context can also be detrimental by providing debt too easily. Temporal discounting in general and present bias in particular can be exploited to make cash more attractive in the present than the future costs appear menacing. Whenever this happens, the increased availability of debt could especially lower the well-being of the poor, since overspending by the poor may entail subsequent cutbacks in far more essential consumption than overspending by the rich.

One fundamental lesson of such a behavioral analysis is a new appreciation for the impact and responsibilities of financial institutions. These should not simply be viewed from a financial cost-saving point of view but instead should be understood to affect the lives of people by easing their planning, facilitating their desired actions, and enabling their resistance to temptation. Such effects, furthermore, may have substantially different implications for those who are wealthier, who get professional help, and who, at the same time, can afford to err or be tempted than they do for the poor, who resort to fewer professionals and may pay dearly even for infrequent temptations or minor mistakes.

These considerations form part of a more general view of why financial institutions can be so important in the lives of the poor. Access to financial institutions allows people to improve their planning by keeping money out of temptation's way. In some cases (such as direct deposit and automatic deductions), one may not even notice the moment the money "arrived" in the savings account or was invested in the long term. The recourse to financial institutions provides the opportunity to make infrequent, carefully considered financial accounting decisions that can prove resistant to intuitive error or to momentary mental accounting impulses. In this sense, improving financial institutions can have a disproportionate impact on the lives of the poor. Moving from a payday lender and check-casher to a bank with direct deposit and payroll deduction can have benefits that far exceed the transactional costs saved (for further discussion and more examples of savings instruments aligned with behavioral principles, see Tufano and Schneider, this volume).

SOME NON-INSTITUTIONAL ASPECTS OF THE FINANCIAL LIVES OF THE POOR

Aided by these insights, we aim to further understand the interactions of the poor with specific financial institutions. To begin, we discuss three stylized facts about the financial lives of the poor that are non-institutional but that we think are especially important to the behavioral perspective. These stylized facts are not necessarily psychological. (Two of them have very straightforward economic interpretations.) Rather, they are facts that may render the impact of the relevant psychology particularly interesting and consequential.

Lack of Financial Slack

Though it is hard to define precisely in an economic model, the notion of "economic slack" is central to the lives of the poor. We define slack as the ease with which one can cut back consumption to satisfy an unexpected need. Under this definition, the poor appear to have less economic slack than the rich. Whereas a rich person can often cut back on (by their own admission) more frivolous spending, a poor person faced with a financially demanding situation is forced to cut back on essential expenses. There are two ways to understand this mechanism. The first, more traditional vehicle is via diminishing returns: if a rich person and a poor person face equivalent shocks and cut back on consumption by the same amount, the rich person will be cutting back on lower marginal utility consumption. The second, more psychological vehicle concerns temptations: if the incidence of temptation spending is increasing in income, the rich will be cutting back on precisely those goods that are less valuable from the point of view of past or future selves.

This analysis abstracts from the role of savings. We could argue that the poor, exactly because they face a more volatile environment, would put aside enough buffer-stock savings to handle that excess volatility. This in turn would mean that the same size shock is less likely to result in a poor person running out of savings. While plausible, we ignore this factor in the following conceptualization because a large amount of data show that poorer families tend to have negligible liquid savings. The lack of buffer-stock savings is, we feel, one of the more interesting puzzles to understand in the financial lives of the poor; we return to this issue briefly later in the chapter.

A lack of financial slack is particularly consequential when we consider the type of expenditures the poor might be forced to cut back on. One common finding in the literature is that late payments, some resulting in phone and gas disconnections (and ensuing costly reconnections), are frequent in the lives of the poor. Kathryn Edin and Laura Lein (1997) estimate that 5 percent of annual income is spent on the costs of reconnection. Many financial services impose fees for late payments. This ranges from the expected (on credit card bills) to the unexpected (the penalty for a late payment imposed by rent-to-own stores of repossessing the item, thereby forcing a loss of all previously made payments). Landlords can impose late fees, and all sorts of bills, from utility to medical bills, usually have steep fees for late payments. The key observation about fees is that they are usually disproportionate. For example, a 5 percent late fee for a monthly bill is effectively a 100 percent APR on a loan. In other words, if the poor cut back by skipping a bill payment, they are effectively borrowing at very high rates.

High-interest borrowing, however, may be the *least* costly consequence of late payments. In fact, what makes the lack of financial slack particularly onerous are the indirect but linked consequences. Consider a household that has had its phone disconnected. The members of this household now face several difficult consequences. First, they need to make a large lump-sum payment to get the phone reconnected. Acquiring this large lump sum poses extra difficulties to an already stretched budget. Second, and more importantly, the lack of a phone could have other consequences for their lives. For example, if they happen to be unemployed (not unlikely for a household that was unable to pay its phone bills), they are now far less effective job-searchers. Even if they are employed, the employer may not be able to reach the home in case shifts change and they are needed at work, making them a less valuable employee. In other words, one action—paying the phone bill late—can have dynamic consequences, amplifying the initial cost and further depressing income. Low-income households struggling with the chronic lack of slack that comes with being low-income are thus always at risk of becoming ever more destitute.

There are profound consequences to being on the edge of further destitution. The first is that any failures to plan well can have quite severe consequences. A rich person who fails to plan, or who plans poorly, may simply cut back on frivolous expenditures. A poorer individual may face a domino effect of consequences that can amplify an otherwise small misplanning step. The lack of slack makes the poor walk a planning tightrope: they must in effect be super-planners, in less conducive and less helpful surroundings, lest they slip deeper into poverty.

A second consequence is empirically easier to identify. The individual who is facing the prospect of having his phone shut off, paying a hefty late fee to have it turned on again, and dealing with the assorted difficulties that arise from a lack of phone service may well be willing to borrow at high rates to keep this sequence of events from happening—or to get the phone reconnected if it has already happened. In fact, not only are low-income individuals sometimes willing to borrow at very high rates, it may be rational for them to do so. The desire to borrow at high rates is interesting: it can easily be confused with myopia, but in some contexts it can constitute a perfectly rational, even if undesirable, response to financial difficulty. This is also relevant to payday loans, an issue we return to later in the chapter.

Small to Big Transformations

One of the fundamental services that financial institutions provide is to allow for the gradual transformation of small amounts of cash, which are easier to come by, into larger lump sums, which can be hard to attain. As Stuart Rutherford (1999) explains, individuals often need to transform small cash amounts into "usably large" amounts. Such transformation is particularly needed by the poor because of the nature of their cash inflows and needs. The urban poor typically deal with cash inflows in relatively small amounts, receiving weekly or biweekly paychecks. Net of the "necessary" rent, utility, and other bills, they are typically left with only small amounts of cash on hand. Many of the durables they may wish to purchase—washing machines, cars, televisions—require more than what they have left at any point in time. Consequently, the poor need to transform small amounts into usably large sums.

According to traditional economic theory, such transformation is straightforward: individuals simply save the cash they come by until they have accumulated enough. Alternatively, if credit is available, individuals borrow against future income streams to finance the transformation. Whether debt or savings are used depends on the flow value of the durable to be purchased, relative to the interest rate on debt. Of course, because the poor often do not have access to credit, they would need to save their way up.

The psychology of planning and self-control suggests that such savings may be more difficult than traditional theory is prone to assume. An individual saving to buy a durable over a long period of time would have large amounts of cash continuously accessible. And accessible cash can be extremely tempting and thus easy to spend on things that are mostly valued at the moment of spending. As such, temporal inconsistency and self-control problems make savings a weak vehicle on which to rely for small-to-big cash transformations. These factors turn savings accounts into highly leaky budgets.

Many institutions that are popular among the poor and that may otherwise look like less than perfectly rational solutions can be understood as alternative methods for making small-to-big transformation more feasible in a world of imperfect planning and limited control. First, consider the purchase of lottery tickets, which, as many have noted, the poor are especially likely to engage in (Blalock, Just, and Simon 2007; Kearny 2005). What is particularly interesting is the type of lottery ticket the poor typically buy—tickets with maximum payoffs of $200 to $500. If the poor are "buying dreams" through lottery tickets, these are quite modest dreams. Such small maximum payoffs are more consistent with lottery tickets as a vehicle for small-to-big conversion. An individual who struggles to save up to buy a $400 item, for example, would find it easy to buy a lottery ticket periodically. The recurring ticket costs are the "deposits," which eventually lead to a win and the ability to buy the expensive item with the winnings. Notice the dominance of this method of "saving" over the typical savings account. There is no money accumulating and providing recurring temptation to dip into it to satisfy one's own needs or those of family and friends. The individual loses his outlay until he (effectively) wins the desired item, the lottery ticket essentially serving as a commitment device, albeit an expensive one.

Notice that this explanation is very similar to a self-control explanation for the prevalence of ROSCAs in developing countries (Basu 2008). In a typical ROSCA, each participant contributes a fixed amount each week or month, with one participant taking the entire pot. The winner is determined by lottery or by bidding, with each participant eligible to win once throughout the ROSCA. This is much like a lottery ticket except that one is guaranteed to win once in a given number of times. Both these institutions reinforce the view that a bigger lump of money is worth more to the poor than many small amounts.

Perhaps most telling is the prevalence of layaway plans. In a typical layaway program, an individual picks a particular durable he would like—for example, a washing machine. He then opens a layaway account, to which he deposits money on a payment schedule that depends on the particular store. Once the client has accumulated enough, he is given the durable. This is quite similar to the SEED commitment savings product offered to clients of a Philippine bank (Ashraf, Karlan, and Yin 2006). Some stores offer a price lock-in feature so that prospective buyers are guaranteed the initial posted price, but many others do not. Individuals who do not save enough to buy the item often forfeit their cash. It appears that the primary benefit of the layaway account is its illiquidity.

The popularity of layaways emphasizes the difficulty that simple myopia models face in explaining the behavior of the poor. In resorting to such arrangements, the poor are showing remarkable farsightedness. They are opting to save, without interest, in order to purchase a durable good, which they do not even get to enjoy as they save up to buy it. As with other examples in this section, there is apparently a willingness among the poor to pay large costs to transform small amounts of cash into larger sums.

Of course, the need to make such transformations is not unique to the poor. And surely some of the phenomena we discuss here may also appear among the middle class. We conjecture, however, that in the United States they are much more common among the poor. With access to a variety of institutions intended to facilitate such transformations—from store credit for durable purchases to automatic savings deductions—the well-off are less likely to resort to more exotic, and costly, institutions.

No Buffer-Stock Savings Despite High Volatility

One of the fundamental observations of behavioral research is the exceedingly "local" nature of everyday decisions. More global perspectives and considerations about the long term are often discounted in favor of issues salient at the moment. Thus, even when long-term decisions are made, they tend to be influenced by minor contextual nuances at the moment of decision that often have little relevance for the long run. Furthermore, long-term forecasts and predictions often fail to take into account the relevance and impact of foreseeable future developments. Along with mental accounting, this tendency typically yields consumption patterns that are overly dependent on current income.

The narrow focusing that emerges has clear implications for planning. Great energy can be spent on decisions of the moment—where to go for dinner or what brand to buy—with relatively little attention allocated to arguably more important decisions that are less immediate, such as how to invest one's retirement savings, or whether to save at all. And the failure to plan can be exacerbated when circumstances are highly uncertain and the future less clear, as is often the case in the lives of the poor. With this month's rent proving of great concern, saving for the children's education or for retirement is naturally left until some better point in the future that may arrive. The tendency to leave financial planning for a more appropriate moment is particularly common among low-income individuals, whose finances afford little slack with which to do much planning. An outcome of this highly volatile struggle with the moment is a lack of buffer-stock savings even, or especially, among these people who, in some ways, need it most.

FROM A BEHAVIORAL PERSPECTIVE

The Unbanked

A little over 10 percent of American households are unbanked and have to rely on alternative financial institutions, such as check-cashers, to cash or process their checks (see also Scholz and Sheshadri, this volume). These alternative financial institutions usually charge high fees, and the households that use them typically have no recourse to formal borrowing instruments. Instead, they may resort to high-interest loans, borrow from friends and relatives to make ends meet or to cover emergency spending, or, in the worst case, simply live without access to credit even during tough times.

This pricey nonparticipation in banking could be the result of a rational choice based on cost-benefit analysis. If households have little to save, then the benefits of being banked may simply be outweighed by the financial costs of maintaining an account, such as the minimum balance fees required by most banks. Alternatively, the decision to remain unbanked could be due to sheer hassle; for example, since few banks have branches in disadvantaged neighborhoods, too much travel time may be involved in using a bank account. Low participation rates may also reflect various cultural factors. Some have attributed to the poor a persistent culture of distrust of financial institutions, or they argue that the poor have not internalized a culture of savings and simply prefer living one day at a time, doing little planning for the future. What is common to these arguments is a tendency to explain a "big" problem (millions of unbanked households) through appeal to "big" factors, such as the dearth of attractive banking options or a deep mistrust combined with a culture of living from day to day.

In contrast, a behavioral perspective suggests that even in the context of big problems, small factors may sometimes play a decisive role. From a normative perspective, defaults are seen as largely irrelevant and easily alterable, but it turns out that, descriptively speaking, the status quo, bolstered by loss aversion, indecision, procrastination, or even a simple lack of attention, has a force of its own (Samuelson and Zeckhauser 1988). Thus, the mere perception that banks are mostly intended for people of greater wealth may reinforce the impression that banking is not meant for, and ought not appeal to, those of lesser means. Indeed, decisions that involve being subjected to scrutiny, interviews, requests, and applications are all likely to have a nontrivial affective component. And those who are most vulnerable are likely to feel the weight of such sentiments even more than the rest. As a number of ethnographic studies suggest (DeParle 2004; LeBlanc 2004), the poor often are painfully aware of society's norms and of their own inability to abide by them. A single mother who, without access to child care, needs to present herself at a bank in the company of her small children may be aware of the fact that, ideally, children are not brought into a bank. Along with a severely limited understanding of financial instruments, a poor client may feel reluctance, even shame, and a general sense that she can never be a valued bank customer.

Of course, that perception may not be terribly distant from the truth. There is, after all, a built-in asymmetry in banks' incentives between credit and savings for the poor and the rich. Regarding poorer clients, banks have a greater incentive to promote debt (which can be lucrative, delayed, and compounded) rather than savings (which are bound to remain modest), as opposed to the treatment of the wealthy, whose debt is likely to be repaid with little penalty and whose savings promise to be large and valuable.

In fact, when it comes to bank accounts, the default option is often different for the poor than it is for those who are better off. Consider, for example, the simple option of direct deposit. As mentioned earlier, the employers of the poor often do not make electronic salary payments, giving their employees one less important reason to pursue the default option of maintaining a checking account. Given the well-established power of default options, even among the comfortable, it seems safe to assume that such defaults would have at least as substantial an impact on the poor, whose options are inherently inferior and who may be less informed about available alternatives.

From a public-sector perspective, the government could play an important role by further encouraging the automatic transfer of tax (including the Earned Income Tax Credit) refunds to bank accounts. This would also provide a way to facilitate the opening of bank accounts. Some evidence from the First Account program in Chicago provides cautious optimism on this front. For many years, the Center for Economic Progress has been providing free tax preparation services for those eligible for EITC refund. Over the last couple of years, the center has been trying to combine this tax preparation service with the First Account program. Specifically, the center has been singling out individuals who are eligible for a refund but lack a bank account. These individuals are informed that they could get their refund much sooner if they were to open a bank account to which their refund would be directly deposited. Data obtained from the bank handling the First Account program suggest that those individuals who opened an account in this "quick refund carrot" context were not less likely to still be using their account compared with those individuals (more positively self-selected) who opened an account following a financial education workshop (further, related findings are reported later in the chapter).

In light of this discussion, it is clear that a behavioral view would predict positive effects on saving from the opening of bank accounts. Such accounts should generate a "good" savings default to replace the "bad" money-on-hand situation. In addition, the transfer of cash from, say, checking to savings could trigger a propensity to save more. In fact, bank accounts could be designed specifically to conform to people's mental accounting schemes (Thaler 1999). People might choose to label one account their housing account, another their education account, and yet another their car account. The labeling of accounts, while nonsensical from the perspective of standard fungibility assumptions, could provide a salient reminder and help with the allocation of specific funds. Such labeling is reminiscent of other, already existing schemes such as education funds, Christmas clubs, and even layaways, and indirect evidence suggests that it may have real consequences. For example, increased child allowance payments in Sweden were found to have disproportionate effects on how the recipients spent on children (discussed in Thaler 1990).

It is fair to note at this juncture that, despite preliminary empirical support, these proposals would need to be tentatively implemented and seriously evaluated before their full consequences could be fully understood. Behavioral outcomes, after all, tend to be multifaceted and complex. Thus, for example, although the appropriate default arrangements may indeed increase savings, it is possible that people with newly automated savings might only come to feel more empowered to take on greater debts, presumably to be covered by the new savings. The dynamic and malleable nature of behavior often necessitates a pilot testing and evaluation prior to full implementation before the construal and ultimate impact of new instruments can be fully understood.

To summarize thus far, being unbanked typically means that whatever little cash is available is readily available. The storage mechanisms that the poor have access to are highly fungible. Keeping money in cash rather than in the bank increases the ability and temptation to spend immediately, making it difficult to achieve any asset accumulation. Furthermore, even among the non-poor, small amounts, as compared to large amounts, are more likely to be spent than saved, and since the poor typically deal with small amounts, savings is thereby further discouraged. In contrast with classical analyses, which impute substantial planning and control, numerous studies of middle-class savings suggest that saving works best as a default (Benartzi and Thaler 2004; Madrian and Shea 2001). Thus, 401(k)s seem to be effective because the cash is automatically deposited into savings. Yet the poor typically have little recourse to "good" savings defaults. And with good defaults less available to those without bank accounts, the poor have to revert to alternative and typically expensive commitment schemes to try to save toward big purchases. We can view participation in programs such as rent-to-own or layaway schemes as such alternative commitment devices, and some have argued that the purchase of actuarially unattractive lottery tickets may serve as a saving mechanism because they occasionally leave purchasers in possession of larger amounts than they would be able to save otherwise.

Payday Loans

Payday loans are a commonly used financial vehicle among lower- and middle-income households (for an analysis, see Skiba and Tobacman 2007; Stegman 2007). The typical payday loan involves receiving an advance on one's paycheck for a week or two, but this advance comes at a steep price, an effective interest rate that can be more than 7,000 percent APR. Such loans are highly contentious from a policy point of view and are often implicitly used to point out the myopia of the poor. We make two basic observations about this widespread institution.

First, as noted earlier, the highly credit-constrained sometimes find themselves at the edge of poverty. In these circumstances, there may be no myopia in taking out a payday loan. Instead, the local cost-benefit calculus, however painful, may be sound. Lack of cash at crucial times can result in disastrous and mounting consequences—such as having one's telephone service cut off. In these circumstances, even (especially!) the farsighted would take out a loan at high interest rates. The "error" happened earlier, through a sequence of actions that left the individual without a buffer stock to deal with shocks. In this view, therefore, there will be circumstances in which the question is not why the poor take out payday loans but why they find themselves in situations where they need them.

This perspective poses an interesting challenge to policymakers, who should want borrowers to have access to loans *at the time of borrowing*. Suppose payday loans are taken by people in severe need, and that the need they face is real, and that failure to meet it will have even more severe consequences. Put in this light, payday loans may be a lesser evil compared with policies that use interest-rate caps (or other vehicles) to drive out payday lenders, which could make the poor *worse off*.[1] Interestingly, unless interest-rate caps are accompanied by policies that solve the fundamental lack of a buffer stock among the poor, such principled arguments against payday loans are, once again, predicated, even if only implicitly, on the expectation that the poor ought to act more "rationally," and they could render the poor only more vulnerable to the various shocks they face. Note that a counter to this argument would be that perhaps the unavailability of payday loans would somehow make those who resort to them into better planners. While this is a priori possible, it seems unlikely, and it should certainly at least not be straightforwardly assumed. If, despite facing huge consequences, individuals still fail to plan, why would the addition of yet another cost have the desired effect?

To further understand the relative lack of reluctance to resort to such loans, we should ask: in what sense are payday loans so very costly? What we refer to here is not the question of whether such fees reflect marginal costs or monopoly profits. Instead, we are asking: what is the psychologically accurate way to view such costs? Do they really reflect an individual making a net present value calculation at such high (more than 7,000 percent APR) rates? Or is the behaviorally most compelling perspective one that suggests more bearable debts? As much research on mental accounting and related behavioral proclivities has shown, magnitudes are often evaluated in a narrow context. People may be willing to travel thirty minutes to save $10 on a $30 purchase, but not to save $20 on a $500 purchase. Just as we should not impute a low value of time (less than $20 per hour) from the first behavior or a high value of time (more than $40 per hour) from the second, we should not necessarily impute discount rates to the intertemporal trade-offs implicit in specific payday loans.

Consider someone who is thinking about paying $20 to get a one-week advance on his $200 paycheck. Such a transaction could be psychologically coded in nominal levels: $20 for a one-week, highly beneficial advance. Viewed in these terms, it may not seem like such a bad transaction. (After all, when the wealthy individual pays $2 to withdraw $100 from an ATM machine out of town, she is really stating a willingness to pay $2, not a general proneness to pay 2 percent to withdraw her own cash.) Of course, when put into annual rates, this payday loan implies an APR of over 14,000 percent! The disjunction between the absolute amount and its APR is the result of compounding. But, of course, the individual is not actually making this decision over a year: he typically makes this decision a few times a year, and each for a short period, so the actual compounding is more of a technical than an experienced cost. In short, while the pricing of payday loans may raise economic as well as ethical questions about competition (supply-side issues), psychology can shed light on why individuals would be willing to pay such high rates, without necessarily suggesting immense if not stunning discount rates. Especially for short-horizon loans, computed APRs may not appropriately capture how individuals naturally frame the intertemporal trade-off.

Check-Cashing

Like many other services provided to the poor, check-cashing is a costly option that provides a service the well-to-do get for less. In a survey of households living in low- and moderate-income census tracts in Chicago, Los Angeles, and Washington, D.C., Christopher Berry (2004) found that people often have a fairly accurate understanding of the relative costs of products provided by banks and check-cashers. Nonetheless, for many individuals who would be unable to adhere to banks' minimum requirements, costly check-cashing arrangements may prove to be the lower-cost option.

The willingness to engage in costly arrangements may be further facilitated by some of the behavioral proclivities reviewed here. Loss aversion is likely to increase the attractiveness even of fairly costly ways to delay or altogether avoid permanent losses. And the high costs of financial services may be aggregated with the perceived gains to which they would contribute in the short run, thus leading to an accounting that at least locally may prove more attractive.

While alternatives to costly check-cashing often exist, they may be less familiar, less common, and less readily available, especially to low-income individuals. A behavioral analysis suggests that it is not that the mere existence of good alternatives makes the greatest difference, but that, in addition, what is often required is the design of effective channels, perhaps combined with directed marketing. For example, in a recent intervention intended to increase elderly

Americans' enrollment in Medicare Part D prescription drug coverage, Jeffrey Kling and his colleagues (2008) documented significantly higher enrollment rates, with an average of at least $230 savings, among participants who were mailed personalized information regarding their current plan and costs, as compared to a control group who were provided with information regarding the official website where comparable information could be obtained.

For another illustration, credit unions and check-cashers in New York have pioneered the use of the point-of-banking machine to facilitate deposits for credit union members at check-cashing stores, providing immediate liquidity of funds and greater convenience for consumers (Stuhldreher and Tescher 2005). Although such arrangements can prove highly beneficial, other partnerships between banks and nonbanks to facilitate payday loans have at times had negative consequences for consumers. Taking the implications of behavioral research seriously, regulators need to focus on promoting partnerships between banks and nonbanks that provide a more responsive and beneficial range of services to unbanked and underbanked consumers.

AN ILLUSTRATION OF A CHANNEL FACTOR

In the attempt to increase take-up of bank accounts among the poor, the behavioral discussion suggests that more attention should be devoted to making the task of "meeting with the bank" an easier and more appealing one and, if possible, perhaps one that does not feel like a "decision" at all. This suggests a variety of small, low-cost interventions that could have first-order effects on the take-up of bank accounts among the poor.

An illustration of the potential impact of small channel factors comes from a brief study of the First Account program implemented by the Center for Economic Progress in the Chicago area. As described earlier, the goal of this program was to entice an unbanked, lower-income population that was mostly dependent on check-cashers to open low-fee accounts at a local bank. To evaluate this program, we first conducted, in collaboration with Marianne Bertrand, a phone survey of a random sample of individuals who had participated in the financial education workshops organized by the Center for Economic Progress. In the workshops, participants took part in a lecture and discussion covering the mechanics of opening a bank account, basic banking products, personal budgeting, and goal-setting. They were also introduced to the First Account program and told that, if interested, they could obtain a referral letter to take to the bank to start the process of opening a First Account. In the survey, we hoped to glean a better understanding of why some participants decided to open First Accounts and others did not.

A promising illustration of small channel factors emerged from our analysis. First, while roughly 50 percent of respondents reported having opened a First Account following the workshop, close to 90 percent reported *thinking* they would do so. We asked those who had planned to open an account but had not done so why they had not. Among those who responded, a large fraction reported some form of time mismanagement as the main cause (missing the deadline, too busy to complete the take-up process, and so on). Taken at face value, these responses suggest that take-up could have been higher had small hurdles to take-up been removed.

More direct evidence came from comparing take-up and usage of the First Accounts across two types of workshops. As mentioned, in the standard workshop participants interested in opening an account received a referral letter they could take to the bank to complete the take-up process. In an experimental subset of workshops, we gave participants interested in opening an account the opportunity to complete most of the paperwork at the workshop location with an available bank representative before heading to the bank to complete the process. From an economic perspective, the mere presence of a bank representative should have little effect on take-up, as it does not alter the cost-benefit analysis at the core of the First Account decision. From a behavioral perspective, however, this small change in implementation could have a large effect on take-up, as it would increase participants' perceived dedication to the program and reduces the likelihood that they would be derailed by procrastination or forget the initial intention.

In fact, we found a large positive effect on take-up associated with the presence of a bank representative on site. Of course, a higher take-up may not have the intended effects if people who open an account end up not using it (or rapidly closing it). As it turns out, we found that having the bank representative at the workshop was associated with a higher likelihood of having an account open at the time of the survey. In addition, a bank representative on site was positively correlated with usage of the complementary services offered by the bank, such as electronic fund transfer, direct deposits, and ATM cards. Contrary to the notion that the unbanked are plagued by "cultural norms" or a general distrust of banks, those who attended a workshop with a bank representative on site were more likely to open an account and to use it.

BEHAVIORALLY INFORMED REGULATION

The behavioral perspective has regulatory consequences, which must be handled with care for three reasons. First, the psychology underlying specific phenomena can be more involved than lay intuition allows. For example, suppose payday loans are in fact the result of individuals "overborrowing." If excess expenditures—spending "too much" on discretionary items (by the person's own admission)—occur throughout the week, then the payday loan is merely a symptom, not the source of the problem. In such circumstances, regulation of payday loans, if it has no impact on excess expenditures early in the week, could make the problem worse. When payday loans are used to deal with rent or phone bills, regulating them may generate problems of late fees or eviction.

Second, as we argue at greater length elsewhere (Barr, Mullainathan, and Shafir 2008a, 2008b), this thinking needs to be embedded in the logic of markets, through a framework that takes into account firm incentives and responses to behaviorally motivated regulation. Outcomes are an equilibrium interaction between individuals' psychology and firms' responses to that psychology. Such interactions may or may not produce outcomes that are socially optimal, and they may even produce real harms. Depending on the bias and the context, the biases of individuals can either help or hurt the firms with which they interact. Hence, the interests of firms and of publicly minded regulators are sometimes aligned and other times are not. Consider, for example, a consumer who does not understand the profound effects of the compounding of interest and is thus led both to undersave and to overborrow. In one context—savings—investment firms have an incentive to correct the bias, since they can generate fees from the investment. In another context—borrowing—lenders have an incentive to exaggerate that bias, since they can generate revenues from the loan (we abstract here from fee structures and collection costs). A notable example of such positive interactions is the finding that firms are happy to help boost participation in 401(k) retirement plans. The Truth in Lending Act (TILA) of 1968, in contrast, attempts to force disclosure of hidden and complicated prices of credit in contexts where lenders have strong incentives to avoid such thorough disclosure.

Finally, regulation must recognize that firms "move last": they can respond to regulation by subtly altering the context (see Barr, Mullainathan, and Shafir 2008a, 2008b). For example, consider the power of defaults. In one context—401(k) choices—the setting of defaults appears to have large effects, compounded by the compliance of firms, if not their active participation. In other contexts—for example, car rentals—firms have greatly facilitated getting rid of mandated "defaults," to the point where placing one's initials in specially provided boxes on the form indicates the waiver of "defaults" and could be argued to have become the new default. This reinforces an earlier observation: When firms have incentives to take advantage of or even exacerbate a bias, they will explore ways to circumvent regulations intended to avoid the problem. And regulators, of course, do not have sole access to behavioral insight. In fact, the firm, often in a position to deal directly with customers and operating after regulations have been set, is well situated to circumvent regulatory intent.

CONCLUDING COMMENTS ON THE DESIGN AND REGULATION OF FINANCIAL SERVICES

Assuming a context where no further redistribution is about to take place, our perspective suggests some potential alterations to the way financial institutions for the poor are designed. These institutions could include for-profit banks attempting to gain footholds in a lucrative market, nonprofits providing financial and other services, and government service providers. We think several principles are relevant to the design of financial access. What is particularly important about these principles is that they often stand in contrast to classical economic assumptions, and to common intuition.

One such principle, underappreciated by program designers, is that information provided does not necessarily constitute knowledge attained. Individuals often do not fully process data put before them. Either they do not attend to it or they do not fully understand it. This, combined with the curse of knowledge—the tendency of those who know something to overestimate the probability that others know it— can result in underinvestment in outreach programs that serve to educate individuals about financial services and costs.

Another principle concerns the relevance of people's construal processes. As discussed at the outset, individuals' internal representations of stimuli are, by necessity, interpretations of the "objective" reality. As a consequence, how information is framed systematically alters how it is construed. In an earlier paper (Bertrand, Mullainathan, and Shafir 2006), we focused on the role that marketing plays in the construal of contexts in which decisionmakers find themselves. On the one hand, marketing has been used profusely and effectively by for-profit firms and contributed, at least on occasion, to making the lives of the poor even poorer. Aggressive marketing campaigns have targeted the poor on products ranging from fast food, cigarettes, and alcohol to predatory mortgages, high-interest credit cards, payday loans, rent-to-own plans, and various other fringe-banking schemes (see, for example, Caskey 1996; Mendel 2005). On the other hand, significantly less has been done by marketing firms to promote more positive options aggressively, such as healthful diets, various not-for-profit services, union banks, prime-rate lenders, and so on.

Existence need not imply availability. Whereas most programs focus on the options that are available, a large behavioral literature emphasizes the importance of channel factors and small costs. Specifically, take-up of a program can be importantly influenced by the perceived nature of these small costs. Thus, an otherwise beneficial program with small "channel blockages" may de facto be a program that is not "available." Related to this principle is another touched on earlier: the existence of more options may not entail their availability. As options proliferate in what becomes a difficult choice, people may avail themselves of those options less rather than more.

This, in fact, is an area where recent trends have moved in a direction opposite to that suggested by behavioral analyses. In contrast with the economic truism that having more options is always good, behavioral research suggests that a greater number of alternatives can increase decisional conflict and overload decisionmakers, leading to deferral, procrastination, or inferior choices (see, for example, Bertrand, Mullainathan, and Shafir 2006; Kling et al. 2008 for further discussion). Consider, for example, the case of shopping for mortgages discussed earlier. To the extent that decisions are multi-attribute and complex and need to be simplified, the required monthly payment is probably the best attribute to rely on, since the affordability of payments is a good way to assess risk of foreclosure. If a client has to pick a simplifying heuristic in a sea of complicated alternatives, this would be it. Of course, apart from the ability to pay on a month-by-month basis, monthly payment conveys little information about the price of the loan. Consequently, shopping based on monthly payment might have worked adequately when home loans (say, thirty-year, fully amortizing) were roughly comparable products. But as the number and type of loans available quickly increases, sellers of loans can take advantage of this simplifying heuristic to extract substantially larger profits from borrowers (Willis 2006).

Related to the notion of channel factors is another important issue, that of the distinction between intention and action. In particular, problems of self-control, poor planning, forgetfulness, distraction, and habit can often intercede to produce observable actions that do not match underlying intentions. This tension may help produce a variety of "counterintuitive" venues intended to help people commit to their "better" intentions, such as a demand for financial services that provide illiquidity as a form of "commitment device." As in other contexts, such questionable venues, with their mixed benefits, are more likely to arise in the context of poverty, where superior institutional arrangements are often less immediately available. In addition, interventions that focus heavily on altering intentions, such as financial planning or education, may prove unsuccessful whenever context leads to actions that are in tension with these newly formed, even if genuine, intentions. Context-sensitive behavior, in other words, may run counter to people's true intentions. As a result, revealed preference fails.

A fundamental implication emanates from the present perspective that has direct consequences for issues of regulation and design: whereas the classical perspective assumes that people are rational and doing as well as should be expected, the "culture of poverty" perspective is motivated by the perception that people need to be changed. The central gist of the behavioral perspective is that the poor are neither irrational nor in need of change (not any more, that is, than the rest of humanity). Instead, it is the context in which people function—ranging from financial institutions, benefits programs, and the design of default structures to the availability of child care and transportation and the complexity of application forms—that merits careful attention and constructive work. Such a perspective is likely both to enrich and to complicate our views of the role of institutions and of regulation. As long as these are founded on a better understanding of decision-makers and generate novel policies intended to help them, it clearly seems worth trying.

We thank Michael Barr, Rebecca Blank, Christopher Carroll, and two anonymous reviewers for helpful comments. We thank the Russell Sage Foundation, the William and Flora Hewlett Foundation, and people at Ideas42 for financial, technical, and research support.

NOTE

1. Of course, if one believes that payday lenders are local monopolists, interest-rate caps could have other positive benefits. We are focusing here on the reduction in payday lending that would accompany caps in a competitive situation.

REFERENCES

American Payroll Association. 2002. "Survey Results: American Payroll Association 2003 Direct Deposit Survey." Available at: http://legacy.americanpayroll.org/pdfs/paycard/DDsurv_results0212.pdf (accessed January 28, 2009).

Arkes, Hal R., and Catherine Blumer. 1985. "The Psychology of Sunk Cost." *Organizational Behavior and Human Performance* 35(1): 129–40.

Ashraf, Nava, Dean Karlan, and Wesley Yin. 2006. "Tying Odysseus to the Mast: Evidence from a Commitment Savings Product in the Philippines." *Quarterly Journal of Economics* 121(2): 635–72.

Ausubel, Laurence M. 1991. "The Failure of Competition in the Credit Card Market." *American Economic Review* 81(1): 50–81.

Barr, Michael S. 2004. "Banking the Poor." *Yale Journal of Regulation* 21(1): 121–237.

Barr, Michael S., Sendhil Mullainathan, and Eldar Shafir. 2008a. "Behaviorally Informed Financial Services Regulation." White paper. Washington, D.C.: New America Foundation.

———. 2008b. "An Opt-Out Home Mortgage System." Hamilton Project discussion paper 2008-14. Washington, D.C.: Brookings Institution.

Basu, Karna. 2008. "Hyperbolic Discounting and the Sustainability of Rotational Savings Arrangements." Unpublished paper, University of Chicago (May 12). Available at: http://home.uchicago.edu/karna/karnabasu-rosca-may12.pdf (accessed January 28, 2009).

Benartzi, Shlomo, and Richard H. Thaler. 2004. "Save More Tomorrow: Using Behavioral Economics to Increase Employee Saving." *Journal of Political Economy* 112(1): 164–87.

Berry, Christopher. 2004. "To Bank or Not to Bank? A Survey of Low-Income Households." Working Paper Series. Cambridge, Mass.: Joint Center for Housing Studies.

Bertrand, Marianne, Sendhil Mullainathan, and Eldar Shafir. 2004. "A Behavioral Economics View of Poverty." *American Economic Review* 94(2): 419–23.

———. 2006. "Behavioral Economics and Marketing in Aid of Decisionmaking Among the Poor." *Journal of Public Policy and Marketing* 25(1): 8–23.

Blalock, Garrick, David R. Just, and Daniel H. Simon. 2007. "Hitting the Jackpot or Hitting the Skids: Entertainment, Poverty, and the Demand for State Lotteries." *American Journal of Economics and Sociology* 66(3): 545–70.

Buehler, Roger, Dale Griffin, and Michael Ross. 1994. "Exploring the 'Planning Fallacy': Why People Underestimate Their Task Completion Times." *Journal of Personality and Social Psychology* 67(September): 366–81.

Camerer, Colin, Linda Babcock, George Loewenstein, and Richard H. Thaler. 1997. "A Target Income Theory of Labor Supply: Evidence from Cab Drivers." *Quarterly Journal of Economics* 112(2): 407–441.

Caskey, John P. 1996. *Fringe Banking: Check-Cashing Outlets, Pawnshops, and the Poor.* New York: Russell Sage Foundation.

Darley, John M., and C. Daniel Batson. 1973. "From Jerusalem to Jericho: A Study of Situational and Dispositional Variables in Helping Behavior." *Journal of Personality and Social Psychology* 27(1): 100–108.

DeParle, Jason. 2004. *American Dream: Three Women, Ten Kids, and a Nation's Drive to End Welfare.* New York: Viking.

Edin, Kathryn, and Laura Lein. 1997. *Making Ends Meet: How Single Mothers Survive Welfare and Low-Wage Work.* New York: Russell Sage Foundation.

Johnson, Eric J., and Daniel Goldstein. 2003. "Do Defaults Save Lives?" *Science* (November 21): 1338–39.

Johnson, Eric J., John Hershey, Jacqueline Meszaros, and Howard Kunreuther. 1993. "Framing, Probability Distortions, and Insurance Decisions." *Journal of Risk and Uncertainty* 7(1): 35–51.

Kahneman, Daniel. 1994. "New Challenges to the Rationality Assumption." *Journal of Institutional and Theoretical Economics* 150(1): 18–36.

Kahneman, Daniel, Jack L. Knetsch, and Richard H. Thaler. 1990. "Experimental Tests of the Endowment Effect and the Coase Theorem." *Journal of Political Economy* 98(6): 1325–48.

Kearny, Melissa Schettini. 2005. "State Lotteries and Consumer Behavior." *Journal of Public Economics* 89(11–12): 2269–99.

Kling, Jeffrey R., Sendhil Mullainathan, Eldar Shafir, Lee Vermeulen, and Marian V. Wrobel. 2008. "Confusion in Choosing Medicare Drug Plans." Working paper. Cambridge, Mass.: Harvard University.

Knetsch, Jack L. 1989. "The Endowment Effect and Evidence of Nonreversible Indifference Curves." *American Economic Review* 79(5): 1277–84.

Koehler, Derek J., and Connie S. K. Poon. 2006. "Self-Predictions Overweight Strength of Current Intentions." *Journal of Experimental Social Psychology* 42(4): 517–24.

LeBlanc, Adrian N. 2004. *Random Family: Love, Drugs, Trouble, and Coming of Age in the Bronx.* New York: Scribner.

Lepper, Mark R., David Greene, and Richard E. Nisbett. 1973. "Undermining Children's Intrinsic Interest with Extrinsic Reward: A Test of the 'Overjustification' Hypothesis." *Journal of Personality and Social Psychology* 28(1): 129–37.

Leventhal, Howard, Robert Singer, and Susan Jones. 1965. "Effects of Fear and Specificity of Recommendation upon Attitudes and Behavior." *Journal of Personality and Social Psychology* 2(2): 20–29.

Lewin, Kurt. 1951. *Field Theory in Social Science.* New York: Harper & Row.

———. 1952. *Field Theory in Social Science: Selected Theoretical Papers.* London: Tavistock Publications.

Loewenstein, George, and Drazen Prelec. 1992. "Anomalies in Intertemporal Choice: Evidence and an Interpretation." *Quarterly Journal of Economics* 107(2): 573–97.

Loewenstein, George, and Richard H. Thaler. 1989. "Intertemporal Choice." *Journal of Economic Perspectives* 3(4): 181–93.

Madrian, Brigitte C., and Dennis F. Shea. 2001. "The Power of Suggestion: Inertia in 401(k) Participation and Savings Behavior." *Quarterly Journal of Economics* 116(4): 1149–87.

Mendel, Dick. 2005. *Double Jeopardy: Why the Poor Pay More.* Baltimore, Md.: Annie E. Casey Foundation.

Milgram, Stanley. 1974. *Obedience to Authority.* New York: Harper & Row.

Ross, Lee, and Richard E. Nisbett. 1991. *The Person and the Situation: Perspectives of Social Psychology.* New York: McGraw-Hill.

Rutherford, Stuart. 2001. *The Poor and Their Money.* New Delhi: Oxford University Press.

Samuelson, William, and Richard J. Zeckhauser. 1988. "Status Quo Bias in Decisionmaking." *Journal of Risk and Uncertainty* 1(1): 7–59.

Shafir, Eldar, Peter Diamond, and Amos Tversky. 1997. "Money Illusion." *Quarterly Journal of Economics* 112(2): 341–74.

Skiba, Paige M., and Jeremy Tobacman. 2007. "Measuring the Individual-Level Effects of Access to Credit: Evidence from Payday Loans." *Federal Reserve Bank of Chicago Proceedings* (May 2007): 280–301.

Stegman, Michael A. 2007. "Payday Lending." *Journal of Economic Perspectives* 21(1): 169–90.

Stuhldreher, Anne, and Jennifer Tescher. 2005. "Breaking the Savings Barrier: How the Federal Government Can Build an Inclusive Financial System." Washington, D.C.: New America Foundation and Center for Financial Services Innovation (February).

Thaler, Richard H. 1985. "Mental Accounting and Consumer Choice." *Marketing Science* 4(3): 199–214.

———. 1990. "Savings, Fungibility, and Mental Accounts." *Journal of Economic Perspectives* 4(1): 193–205.

———. 1992. *The Winner's Curse: Paradoxes and Anomalies of Economic Life.* New York: Free Press.

———. 1999. "Mental Accounting Matters." *Journal of Behavioral Decision Making* 12(3): 183–206.

Tversky, Amos, and Daniel Kahneman. 1991. "Loss Aversion in Riskless Choice: A Reference Dependent Model." *Quarterly Journal of Economics* 106(4): 1039–61.

Van Dort, Bernice E., and Rudolph H. Moos. 1976. "Distance and the Utilization of a Student Health Center." *Journal of American College Health Association* 24(3): 159–62.

Willis, Lauren E. 2006. "Decisionmaking and the Limits of Disclosure: The Problem of Predatory Lending: Price." Loyola Law School Los Angeles Legal Studies Paper 2006-27. Los Angeles: Loyola Law School.

Part II

Exploring Patterns of Use
and Policies by Type of Asset

Chapter 6

Using Financial Innovation to Support Savers: From Coercion to Excitement

Peter Tufano and Daniel Schneider

In certain stylized economic models, household savings emerge mechanically and effortlessly as informed rational agents maximize lifetime consumption in light of their likely income streams, their needs, and the hazards they might encounter. In other models, households are massively confused about intertemporal trade-offs. They employ a set of time-inconsistent discount rates to evaluate options that vary greatly from period to period, and their resultant decisions may be time-inconsistent (Mullainathan and Shafir, this volume). Although these are both useful observations about household decisionmaking, they abstract away from the messiness of saving (Collins and Murdoch, this volume). Families—and of particular interest to us here, low-income families—save for a wide variety of reasons, including identifiable reasons such as education and retirement and others that they cannot even articulate (like "rainy days" or "mad money"). Definitions of what constitutes "enough"—enough material possessions, enough services, enough savings—vary widely from person to person.

In this messy world, where companies never exhort us to "spend less," savings is hard work, and it is no surprise that household savings is low. In 2007 the U.S. personal savings rate dipped to 0 percent—a fifty-year low (U.S. Bureau of Economic Analysis 2007). Although there is some debate over the proper measurement of the saving rate (Guidolin and La Jeunesse 2007), there is little dispute that large shares of Americans have very little saved. In 2004, 10 percent of households had less than $100 in financial assets (authors' calculations from the 2004 Survey of Consumer Finances [SCF]). Even larger shares of the population are "asset-poor" or lack sufficient financial assets to survive at the poverty line for three months (Oliver and Shapiro 1990). Over the last ten years, the asset poverty rate has generally been well in excess of 25 percent for the population as a whole, and it has been approximately 60 percent for blacks and for households headed by someone without a high school diploma (Caner and Wolff 2002, 2004; Haveman and Wolff 2001). Lacking savings may make it more difficult for families to respond to emergencies, to invest in education and business opportunities, and to retire comfortably.

Some analysts are pessimistic about the potential to address this problem. It may seem as though providing sufficient financial incentives to encourage low- and moderate-income families to save is too expensive and politically unlikely. Similarly, it can be difficult to imagine that the private sector will jump on board because there is not enough money to make it worth their while.

While these concerns are real, we believe that they do not close the book on savings policy. Given that pressures to consume are not likely to abate, what realistically can stakeholders—governments, nonprofits, social institutions, and financial institutions—do to help families save? Given the diversity among people, it is unlikely that there is a single solution to the savings problem. Rather, we lay out a range of solutions in this chapter, illustrating this conceptual framework with concrete real-world examples of programs and products—many of which have great promise in supporting household savings. The continuum ranges from solutions that force families to save (coercion) to others that seek to work consumers into a frenzy about savings (excitement.) These varied solutions emphasize different elements of human behavior or impediments to savings. Some require massive government intervention, some require small changes in existing regulations, and still others are completely market-oriented. Some require large subsidies, while others might be profitable on their own. We discuss each program from the perspective of would-be savers as well as from that of other key stakeholders.

Our notion of savings in this piece is explicitly broad: savings is the deferral of consumption today to enable the use of funds later. That later period may be decades away, as in retirement. Or, in low-income communities, the deferral may be only a matter of weeks or months until a water heater breaks. We make no value judgments that only "long-term" savings can be helpful to families. To the contrary, short-term savings can be critical. An emergency fund that allows a family to quickly repair a car needed to get to work can be essential. Also, while most of the concepts we discuss could apply to people of all income levels, our emphasis is on savings structures that would be relevant to low- to moderate-income households rather than high-net-worth households. For example, we discuss "excitement" as a means to foster savings but emphasize lottery-like structures rather than the rush of a "ten-bagger" hedge fund investment (that is, an investment that quickly increases in value by a factor of ten) whose risk characteristics and economic structure render it unavailable to low-income families.

THE RANGE OF SAVINGS INNOVATIONS:
FROM COERCION TO EXCITEMENT

Beyond merely listing a number of savings programs, our work attempts to organize them along a variety of dimensions to emphasize their common features. Figure 6.1 provides a quick summary of the various dimensions. The first dimension is the mechanism by which the innovation changes the ability or motivation of the saver. At one extreme are "process" innovations that *take the savings decision away from the family,* through either outright transfers or government-mandated

FIGURE 6.1 / Savings Program Alternatives

	Force to Save	Make It Hard Not to Save	Make It Easier to Save	Bribe to Save	Provide Social Support for Saving	Make It Fun or Exciting Savings
Current Barrier	All (ability and will)	Institutional impediments, inertia		Savings not "worth it"; would rather consume		
Saver's Role	No choice	Must refuse to save	Given more convenience, but must decide	Given different savings opportunities, but must decide		
Intervention	Change the savings decisionmaking process		Change the time and place for savings	Change the cost-benefit of savings itself		
Likely Partner	Government	Workplace, government, vendors of products and services	Retail sector, workplace, tax sites, schools	Government, foundations	Communities and social networks	Financial service firms, possibly government
Cost or Profit Potential	High-cost (grants), medium-cost (mandate)	Generally low-cost	Medium-cost (new channels), low-cost (tax channel)	High dollar cost (matches, bonuses)	Low dollar cost, high effort by community	Potential for profits in long run
Example	Mandate (Social Security), grant (Child Trust)	Opt-ins, bundling, commitment products	New distribution channels, SMarT, buying savings	401(k), IDAs, Saver's Credit	ROSCAs and gifting savings	Prize-linked saving, collectible savings

Source: Authors' compilation.

savings. Other process innovations do not coerce savings but rather make it *easier to save* or *harder not to save*. These interventions leave the decision to save in the consumers' hands but change the process with respect to the time and place of savings. Finally, "product" innovations reengineer the cost-benefit calculation of savings by adding *financial, social, or psychological incentives.* This set of six types of saving innovations represents the primary dimension along which we compare the interventions and provides the organizing structure of the chapter.

Lurking behind these innovations are varied notions about the fundamental barriers that inhibit saving. Innovations that take away the need to decide at all, by either giving or mandating savings, are blunt instruments that address all possible impediments. Other process innovations, which tend to take an institutional view of impediments, hold that the time, place, or manner in which the savings offer is made is suboptimal. These innovations seek to increase savings by making it "easier," either by using an alternative way to frame the decision (for example, setting up saving as a default) or by making the offer at a better time and place (for instance, when people have money and are thinking about their family finances). Product innovations, which all try to make the savings "deal" more attractive, vary in the dimensions along which the savings transaction is defined. If individuals are rational economic actors who prefer more to less, financial incentives may induce savings. (Even here, however, the logic is not clear-cut, since income and substitution effects may come into conflict.) If we conceive of individuals embedded in a social context, the deal can be enhanced by giving people a return in the form of stronger ties to a group. If we think of individuals as responding to psychological incentives, then product innovations can leverage behavioral quirks, such as individuals' tendencies to misestimate low-probability events, be overly optimistic about their own abilities, or draw mental fences around otherwise comparable activities.

Another dimension by which programs differ is in the stakeholders involved. By "stakeholder" we mean a party, apart from the saver herself, who must act to implement the innovation. Some programs involve governmental entities—for example, programs that deliver financial incentives through the tax system or change eligibility for government benefits. Other programs involve financial institutions, such as those that bundle savings with other financial products. Still others involve nonprofits or social networks that leverage relationships to spur on savings.

These stakeholders almost always need to bear costs to support family savings. Some solutions require substantial financial resources (for example, programs that grant savings or provide financial incentives) and may cost not only dollars but political capital as well. Other programs may require that social groups draw upon their social capital. Still others may require investments by financial services in systems and marketing, and some may be costly in the form of potential formal and informal liabilities borne by stakeholders attempting to support family savings.

Any categorization exercise is prone to imprecision. In practice, many savings interventions incorporate both product and process innovations. Some product innovations simultaneously change the economic, social, and psychological features of the product bundle. In illustrating our categories by discussing specific products, we may emphasize a predominant element of the product while recognizing other features as well.

This chapter is about innovations, but we use the word broadly and charitably. In financial services, there is rarely anything that is truly new. Rather, seemingly new ideas are sometimes updated versions of old programs (such as the prize-linked savings concept, which goes back to 1694), or they build upon other innovations. The economist Robert C. Merton (1992) speaks of an innovation spiral: the existence of one financial innovation permits another. The innovation of debit cards ultimately made possible bundled products like the Bank of America Keep the Change program, which combines this payment system device with a savings component.

In each of the following sections, we briefly describe the class of savings innovation, provide a few examples, and give a sense of the success of the program, from both the point of view of generating savings and the point of view of the stakeholder with an eye toward program costs and returns. For government-organized programs, these costs might be the governmental outlays required; for the private sector, they are the costs and profitability of each product or program. Unfortunately, many of these data are somewhat sketchy, as formal evaluations have not been done for most of these programs and firms are reluctant to release product line profitability data. Nevertheless, our intent is to provide a tour of the options that we hope will leave the reader with optimism that while increasing savings may be hard work for all concerned, it is not an impossible task. And in some cases it may actually be fun.

COERCING SAVING

The first class of innovations does not require the individual to make a decision to save. These interventions literally compel individual savings, under the assumption that without paternalistic government mandate, individuals would fail to accumulate adequate savings. Often, these programs offer universal participation to redistribute individual savings so as to lessen inequality and build a political base of support (for a more general discussion of universalism and social welfare policy, see Korpi and Palme 1998). Involuntary programs, overseen and funded by the government, tend to fall into two categories: those that force families to spend less to save, and those that give families additional funds but only in the form of savings. These general characteristics are summarized in the first column of figure 6.1. These two process innovations are exemplified by two innovations—one relatively old, one quite new.

Taxing to Force Savings: Social Security

While not savings in the traditional sense, Social Security provides the functional equivalent of savings. Workers in the United States are legally required to make regular contributions to Social Security of 6.2 percent of the first $102,000 of income (in

2008), with the income ceiling increasing automatically each year. This mandatory contribution is matched by employers (or doubled in the case of the self-employed), who also generally deduct and withhold the employee portion. These funds are savings in the sense that current consumption is deferred with the goal of ensuring future consumption. The actual dollars are not saved but are rather used to support a pay-as-you-go system of retirement insurance. Savings is coerced in that the only way not to participate is not to work or to break the law.

There is a substantial literature about Social Security and the economics of this particular system, and a review of that literature is beyond the scope of this chapter. Furthermore, there have been extended debates about modifying the Social Security system to create a more standard "savings" program—for example, the debate over private accounts. Even so, it is important to note a few things about this means of saving. First, as a universal program that literally forces people to save, it requires government action. Second, with this as with nearly all of the other innovations, it is difficult to determine the incremental savings generated, since it is hard to observe hypothetical savings in its absence. Third, Social Security is largely a retirement-focused program, unlike some of the other programs that focus on less-distant savings goals.

Giving to Force Savings: The Child Trust Fund

The United Kingdom's Child Trust Fund (CTF) is an involuntary program as well, but in giving rather than mandating savings, it takes a different approach. The CTF was designed to ensure that all British children will have savings upon reaching their eighteenth birthday and to facilitate the development of good savings habits (HM Treasury 2003). It meets these goals through a policy of "progressive universalism": it is broadly inclusive with benefits apportioned according to need (Barr and Sherraden 2005).

Beginning in April 2005, every British child born after September 1, 2002, receives a grant of at least £250 at birth and will receive subsequent grants of similar value at age seven. Children born into households with annual incomes of less than £14,000 receive awards twice as large (Sodha 2006). A voucher for these initial funds (of either £250 or £500) is provided to parents after the birth of a child. Voucher in hand, parents can choose from three different types of accounts: an interest-bearing savings account, a shares account (invested in equities), or a "stakeholder" account (conservatively invested equities). Vendors are approved by the government, but accounts are offered privately by banks, building societies, or brokerages (Mensah, Schneider, and Aboulfadi 2004). As of 2006, 119 providers offered some type of account (HM Treasury 2006).

If parents fail to select an account within one year of receiving the voucher, a stakeholder account is automatically opened for the child by the government (with the provider chosen on a rotating basis). Once a CTF account is established, relatives, the children themselves, or others can deposit up to £1,200 (in after-tax pounds) each year, with interest and gains accruing tax-free. Deposits cannot be withdrawn until the child reaches the age of eighteen, at which point he or she may withdraw the funds without limitation (Mensah, Schneider, and Aboulfadi; 2004).

The costs of the CTF can be viewed from the perspective of account holders or the government. Stakeholder account owners pay a 1.5 percent management fee per annum on the account. Annual fees are also assessed on share accounts, but these fees are not capped by the government (U.K. Parliament 2007). Savings accounts do not carry explicit annual fees, but the interest rate paid builds in a spread for the vendor. These expenses are revenue sources for financial service vendors.

From the perspective of a taxpayer, the costs of the CTF are considerable. The Department of Inland Revenue reported that the initial administration costs would be £114 million for the period 2004 through 2007, tapering off to £15 million per year through 2010. Much larger costs arise from government contributions to CTF accounts, estimated at £240 million per year through the first several years of the program and then roughly doubling to £480 million once the first cohort of enrollees begins to qualify for the age seven top-up contributions (HM Treasury 2006).

As of June 2007, approximately 2.85 million CTF accounts had been opened, including 2.2 million accounts opened within one year of the receipt of voucher by parents; the rest were opened by the Treasury upon the expiration of unredeemed vouchers (HM Treasury 2007). A substantial share of families (35 percent) received the bonus funds due to lower-income households (HM Treasury 2006). Although many parents successfully opened a CTF account, preliminary analysis indicates that they were uneasy about choosing an account, with half of all parents feeling that they did not know enough to choose one of the three products (Kempson, Atkinson, and Collard 2006). Nevertheless, most chose some kind of account. By 2006, 74 percent of the 1.7 million accounts then open were stakeholder accounts, 22 percent were savings accounts, and 4 percent were of other design (including share accounts) (HM Treasury 2006). Approximately one-quarter of the accounts were receiving regular monthly voluntary contributions, with higher-income families more likely to contribute than lower-income families (Sodha 2006; Tax Incentivized Savings Association 2007).

The early data are in some ways encouraging. Advocates make the case that 75 percent of parents choosing an account (rather than triggering the automatic enrollment) speaks to high levels of parental support. One account provider has gone so far as to claim that "there is absolutely no doubt that child trust fund is transforming the nation's saving habits and fundamentally changing the way parents think about saving for their children" (White 2006).

However, the CTF raises a number of issues. First, deposits may simply reflect a reshuffling of assets in family financial portfolios. Second, though designed to be equity-enhancing, the CTF may in fact raise a number of equity issues. In the short run, the CTF may cause some intercohort inequality by awarding funds to prospective cohorts but not existing cohorts. In the longer run, although the CTF may increase the absolute level of asset ownership among low-income children, it may spur greater contributions among more well-off families than among poorer, increasing differences between these groups. Finally, some commentators have expressed concerns about "stake-blowing"—the possibility that upon turning eighteen CTF holders will gain access to their funds and promptly squander them, possibly as a side effect of the funds being granted rather than consciously accumulated (White 2004).

Though the United States does not have a program analogous to the CTF, advocates have pressed for Congress to pass the ASPIRE (America Saving for Personal Investment Retirement and Education) Act, which would create a similar system of national accounts for children. Accounts would be established for all children at birth and endowed with a $500 initial deposit, with more for children in low-income families. These funds could be augmented over the child's life by up to $1,000 a year with matching funds available to encourage saving by low-income parents. Funds could only be used for asset development purposes, such as purchasing a home, paying for education, or saving further for retirement (Cramer 2006). Although the bill has been stalled legislatively, private-sector efforts to establish children's savings accounts have moved forward. Established in 2003, the Saving for Education, Entrepreneurship, and Downpayment (SEED) program is a partnership between academia, national policy organizations, local not-for-profit groups, financial institutions, and foundations. These groups offer a mix of savings accounts, 529 accounts, and investment accounts to participating children in twelve states and territories. The accounts are endowed with an initial deposit of between $500 and $1,000, with further deposits by participants and their relations matched by the program (CFED 2007). It is no coincidence that these account terms and the product structure are quite similar to those proposed in the ASPIRE Act: SEED is designed to provide preliminary evidence on the efficacy of such a policy.

The CTF and the various American proposals along the same lines compel savings but do so in a way that is not likely to inspire much complaint—they simply give savings away. Nonetheless, these policies are coercive in that individuals end up with savings without having taken affirmative steps to build assets and are unable to opt out of that asset creation. Granted, these innovations differ from a program like Social Security in that they incorporate design elements, like automatic enrollment, that are derived from other theories of saving. We take up one of these approaches in the following section.

MAKING IT HARD NOT TO SAVE

With Social Security or the U.K. CTF, it is nearly impossible not to save except by not working or not being born. Closely related would be the concept of making it difficult for people *not* to save, that is, making not saving an affirmative decision. In this section and the following one, we present a set of innovations that are slightly less coercive than either granting savings or forcing people to save. First, we discuss those that make it hard not to save through the use of defaults and bundling, and then we turn to those that make it easy to save (or harder to dissave) by offering commitment savings products and lowering the impediments to savings. These programs tend to change the manner in which the savings decision is made.

Innovations of this sort proceed from a slightly different set of behavioral assumptions than coercive savings innovations. People are subject to certain behavioral biases, such as a susceptibility to procrastination, problems of self-control, orientation toward the status quo, and other tendencies that have a powerful effect on human behavior (see Mullainathan and Shafir, this volume). This behavioral logic is summarized in the first row of column 2 in figure 6.1, which also details the other key programmatic aspects of innovations of this sort. If behavioral flaws predominate, then the concept of libertarian paternalism developed by the economist Richard Thaler and the legal scholar Cass Sunstein (2003; Sunstein and Thaler 2003; Thaler and Sunstein 2003) sketches out a philosophical basis for exploiting these flaws. Arguing that humans are generally "irrational" decisionmakers, Thaler and Sunstein (2003) assert that intervention by third parties in decisionmaking is difficult to avoid and that, when designed carefully, policy can thus guide choices in a way that is beneficial (and therefore paternalistic) yet still leaves room for individual choice (and therefore is libertarian). We see this embodied in 401(k) defaults and opt-outs.

Defaults and Opt-Ins/Opt-Outs

Inertia makes us "go with the flow," continuing on the same course or avoiding decisions, especially when faced with complex or unpleasant choices. In savings processes where the inertial or default behavior is "savings," saving increases. This idea is popular in retirement savings, although the setting of defaults has a long heritage, embodied in the old adage of "paying yourself first." An increasing number of U.S. companies are changing their 401(k) enrollment policies from ones that require employees to "opt in" to plan participation to new ones that automatically enroll employees upon hire and require them to choose affirmatively not to participate, or to "opt out," if they would like to avoid enrollment.

Companies' interest in opt-out plans is partly driven by a desire to help their employees save for retirement. But other considerations also enter into the calculus. In particular, employers may face significant costs if their retirement programs are not in compliance with government nondiscrimination rules. Firms must increase participation among lower-paid employees to avoid limiting retirement benefits for executives (Madrian and Shea 2001).

However, broadening plan participation may create new administration costs. Automatic enrollment may increase employee participation, but because default contribution rates are generally quite low, it may also create a large number of new small-balance accounts whose cost to serve on a per dollar basis will be high (Anderson et al. 2003).

A number of studies have assessed the effect of automatic enrollment plans, generally with an eye toward participation rates, contribution rates, and asset allocations (Choi et al. 2006; Madrian and Shea 2001; Vanguard Center for Retirement Research 2001). These evaluators conclude that automatic enrollment dramatically increases participation, raising initial enrollment rates significantly above both initial and subsequent rates for standard opt-in plans. For example, the economists James Choi, David Laibson, Brigitte Madrian, and Andrew Metrick (2004) find that plan enrollment rates rose to 90 percent at three companies that adopted automatic enrollment plans, versus previous rates of 20 to 40 percent at six months' tenure or 60 percent at thirty-six months' tenure.

Automatic enrollment leverages inertia to increase participation rates dramatically. However, defaults also exert a powerful effect on contribution rates and investment allocations. Large shares of employees enrolling in plans under automatic enrollment tend to stay at the default contribution rate (Choi, Laibson, and Madrian 2004). For example, Choi, Laibson, Madrian, and Metrick (2004) find that a large plurality of employees at one company hired under automatic enrollment maintained the default rate—in this case shifting the modal rate from 6 percent before automatic enrollment to the new default rate of either 2 or 3 percent after automatic enrollment. The literature finds that most employees also stick with the initial investment choices (Beshears et al. 2007). Newer concepts build in automatic adjustments in contributions and some automatic rebalancing, which can also be accommodated through life-cycle investing products.

Nationally, retirement account ownership is highly correlated with household income. In 2004 only 10 percent of households in the lowest income quintile and 30 percent in the second quintile had retirement accounts, compared with between 70 and 90 percent of households in the top two quintiles (Bucks, Kennickell, and Moore 2006). Nevertheless, the 401(k) defaults literature does present some interesting findings with regard to low-income families. Automatic enrollment seems to equalize participation across income and racial groups, raising participation rates for lower-paid and African American and Latino employees far more than for their higher-paid and white colleagues (Madrian and Shea 2001). Lower-income participants were also more likely to maintain default contribution rates than other employees. In sum, automatic enrollment has ambiguous effects on aggregate account balances: they are driven up by increased enrollment, but driven down by low contribution rate defaults. However, defaults increase balances for those who would otherwise not participate (Choi, Laibson, Madrian, and Metrick 2004).

There has been little research that examines defaults in the context of overall household saving, which is a general challenge that can be leveled against many savings programs. However, evidence that participation in company stock plans is unaffected by opt-outs suggests that automatic enrollment probably does not simply reshuffle workplace saving (Madrian and Shea 2001).

The concept of defaults can be used far beyond retirement saving. Businesses have long used the concept of defaults to affect consumer behavior, for example, by capitalizing on inertia to keep us with the same phone service, cable television provider, or magazine subscriptions. If defaults can be used to increase consumption, their use to increase savings seems quite natural. But there are a number of high-level questions surrounding defaults. First, how does one ensure that the defaults are in the best interests of consumers? In particular, how does a default strategy work for very heterogeneous consumers who might need different defaults? Second, what is the liability of the program designer if the participant complains ex post? While new regulations begin to address this question, it remains a broader concern than the immediate change in pension reform.

One proposal for a more widespread adoption of the concept of defaults and opt-outs is the automatic IRA (individual retirement account). This concept (Iwry and John 2007), which is embodied in various legislative proposals, would compel employers to facilitate the opening of IRAs for workers who do not have retirement plans. These workers would be automatically enrolled in the program, though they could voluntarily opt out. As compensation, employers would receive certain tax credits. The proposal, aimed at addressing retirement savings for the 75 million Americans working at jobs that do not offer employer-sponsored retirement plans, would leverage the existing infrastructure of direct deposits and IRA vendors.

Bundling

A second strategy makes it difficult to avoid saving by bundling saving with a product or service that consumers would typically otherwise purchase when they shop, use a credit or debit card, or borrow. This type of product innovation is embodied simply in amortizing mortgages. A person who wants to buy a house can get a loan whereby, over time, she essentially "pays herself," or saves by investing in the equity in her home, as she pays off the loan. Each month, the mortgage bill not only covers interest, tax, and insurance escrows but is also effectively a "savings bill" that cannot be ignored (Campbell and Henretta 1980; Chen and Jensen 1985; Moore et al. 2001; Parcel 1982).

Similarly, certain loyalty programs bundle spending and savings. In the past, some grocery stores rewarded shoppers for their purchases with "S&H Green Stamps," which could be used to make future purchases. By shopping, the store patron could support future consumption, just as if saving. Credit card and airline loyalty programs that offer cash rewards are modern innovations on this type of saving.

The basic logic of bundling is to leverage demand for highly desirable activities to spur less enjoyable savings. Given natural complementarities, many bundled savings products are offered by financial service firms, although loyalty programs are more widely offered. When these schemes work, individuals get a product and a bonus of savings, and firms differentiate their offerings and generate profits and perhaps customer loyalty. Bundling has elements of both process and product innovation. As process innovations, they combine decisionmaking about savings with decisions about other products. Framed as product innovations, these products change the costs and benefits of the extended product bundle.

BUNDLING: KEEP THE CHANGE AND UPROMISE   In October 2005, Bank of America introduced the Keep the Change program. Designed to enhance debit card usage while spurring savings, the program allows enrollees to authorize the bank to automatically round up the value of every debit card purchase to the nearest dollar and transfer the difference from their checking accounts to traditional savings accounts. Under the terms of the program, Bank of America matches these transfers at 100 percent for the first three months of enrollment and at 5 percent thereafter, up to an annual maximum of $250 (Enrich 2005). In spirit, the program is a successor to both home mortgage structures and loyalty programs. Like a home mortgage, the customer is essentially paying herself. Yet, like a loyalty structure, savings is proportional to customer activity.

Modern versions of S&H Green Stamps are common. Some allow consumers to "save" for consumption of a single type of item (like additional airline travel), while others offer less constrained savings. For example, some reward programs pay back cash, use the rewards to buy savings bonds, or invest the arrangement in long-term savings accounts. An example of the last type of scheme is Upromise. Launched in 2001, Upromise enables users to save for college by earning rebates of up to 10 percent on consumer purchases from local and national partners, including AT&T, McDonald's, ExxonMobil, and General Motors. Participants sign up through Upromise; the company collects the rebates and invests the funds in a 529 college savings account (Bulkeley 2001; Kim 2006). The firm also offers a loyalty credit card in conjunction with CitiBank, with rewards deposited into a 529 plan.

Products of this kind have had some success. Bank of America attributes 1.8 million new savings accounts to the Keep the Change program (Mierzwa 2007), and as of April 2007, its 4.3 million program participants had saved $400 million collectively, or about $93 on average—a steady rise from average savings of $30 in April 2006 and $67 in October 2006 (Davis 2006; McGeer 2007; Tescher 2006). Part of this uplift probably comes from the general increase in the use of debit cards over time, as well as from the initial appeal of matching. It is too early to measure the long-run impact on total savings, but we suspect that the program may be attractive as a commercial proposition.

Enrollment in Upromise has grown rapidly since its inception, reportedly by as much as 50 percent per year to 8 million in mid-2007 (Chaker 2004; Upromise 2007). While Keep the Change is credited for being relatively easy to join, critics point out that Upromise has a more involved enrollment process: customers must register their credit cards and preexisting company-specific loyalty cards with Upromise (Davis 2001). Further, given current reward rates and annual caps on rebates, savings accumulation for any family may be modest (Wyatt 2001).

There are no direct costs for customers of either program. Nevertheless, both programs offer their parent corporations several revenue streams. Upromise receives a portion of the member rebate, per enrollment fees from some partners, and the float on consumer rebate funds that are not yet invested in 529 accounts (Sahlman 2003). As an indication of its profitability, Upromise was acquired by Sallie Mae in 2006 for $308 million (Sallie Mae 2006, F-33).

The Keep the Change program also appears to have fairly attractive economics. Bank reports indicate that the program is a valuable customer acquisition tool, having brought in 1.8 million new savings accounts and 1.3 million new checking accounts over nineteen months of program operation (Mierzwa 2007). The program has the potential to increase debit card use, can reduce the bank costs associated with processing paper checks, and generates incremental interchange revenues from each debit card transaction (*ATM and Debit News* 2006; Lubasi 2005). Although the deposits generated by Keep the Change pale relative to Bank of America's total assets of $1.46 trillion, the funds currently earn an interest rate of just 0.20 percent in the bank's regular savings account, permitting the bank to profit from the net interest margin (Bauerlein 2007; Bank of America 2007; Freeman 2005).

Keep the Change and Upromise are fascinating examples of bundled savings programs, but they raise some concerns. As a psychological matter, they may further confuse consumers. In our own recent market research, we found general confusion among low-income consumers between saving in the form of putting money away and saving in the form of paying less for goods (see Maynard and Zinsmeyer 2007). Consumer advocates fear that these programs may encourage people to spend more, to ignore the need to accumulate more substantial savings, or to further conflate savings and spending (Enrich 2005; Singletary 2001, 2005).

BUNDLING: THE SALARY ADVANCE LOAN The North Carolina State Employees Credit Union (NCSECU) offers an innovation that bundles savings and credit. NCESCU entered the $40 billion to $50 billion payday lending market in 2001 with the Salary Advance Loan (SALO). The credit union offers the SALO at a 12 percent annual percentage rate (APR), far less than the 400 to 1,000 percent APRs standard in the industry (Stegman 2007). Loans of $500 or less are available with a maximum term of one month and with fees capped at $5 per loan. The program is available to members with direct payroll deposit. Repayments are due at the time of the next payroll payment.

There has been significant demand for these loans, with nearly $400 million loaned out since the program's inception in 2001. Each month, approximately $12 million to $13 million is loaned to individuals in the pool of 53,000 SALO-registered members (out of a total of 1.25 million members). The bundled saving element was added in 2003, with all SALO borrowers required to deposit 5 percent of each loan into a share account. The bundled cash account makes SALO borrowers save, with the goal of helping them to accumulate sufficient savings "to break the payday loan cycle" (NCSECU 2006). The share account also secures the payroll loan. Although the account is interest-bearing, withdrawals must be approved by a lending official. Under the terms of the contract, withdrawals can trigger suspension of borrowing privileges on the Salary Advance Loan. Observers report that in practice withdrawals lead to ineligibility for SALOs for six months (Fellowes and Brooks 2007).

In terms of its economics, the credit union has earned $2.5 million in interest income on loans of $400 million, with charge-offs of just 0.27 percent combined with overhead and funding costs of 2.00 percent and 2.75 percent, respectively (Stegman 2007).

In terms of its scale, both the payday loan balances and the savings in the SALO program have grown. The 53,000 enrolled members grew their savings deposits from $5.5 million in June 2004 to approximately $9.7 million in June 2006 (NCSECU 2004, 2005, 2006). These savers (and borrowers) are predominantly low-income and low-asset, with annual earnings usually below $25,000 and savings of about \$130 on average (Stegman 2007). About 75 percent of SALO users said that the funds that have accumulated in their SALO accounts make this the "first time in their lives that they have had any significant savings" (Fellowes and Brooks 2007).

Like an amortizing mortgage, the SALO encourages borrowers to pay themselves, in the form of the bundled share account. Like the home in a mortgage, the share account provides the bank with some security. The withdrawal restriction presumably prevents careless dissaving (discussed more in the following section), but the denial of loans to savers who make withdrawals may raise interesting issues. In particular, it is important to see whether participants tap other credit sources to maintain their access to SALO rather than draw down their savings; if so, it is important to assess the total impact on the entire family balance sheet. If the program, like other secured credit programs, encourages consumers to borrow high and lend low, its overall impact might be unclear.

Making It Hard to Dissave: Withdrawal Commitments

While the spirit of this section is about innovations that make it hard not to save through defaults and bundling, there is a complementary set of products that make it hard to dissave through withdrawal commitments. These commitments take many forms, such as the requirement for bank officer sign-off for saving withdrawals in the SALO; term deposits in banks with early withdrawal penalties; tax-advantaged programs, like individual retirement accounts (IRAs), that have withdrawal penalties; or private equity investments with limited opportunities for exit by limited partners. If the key behavioral problem causing a lack of savings is self-control, then bonding in the form of commitment savings products can provide a solution. The lack of self-control can come from the saver, or it can arise from the demands placed upon the saver by his or her social network of family and friends. The economists Nava Ashraf, Nathalie Gons, Dean Karlan, and Wesley Yin (2003) reviewed the evidence on commitment savings products (including both withdrawal commitments and savings commitments, which we discuss elsewhere in this section). Ashraf, Karlan, and Yin (2007) then conducted a randomized study of a withdrawal commitment project in the Philippines. About 28 percent of those offered the restricted withdrawal product took it up and after a year had saved 81 percent more than the control group.

From the perspective of financial service firms, withdrawal commitment products may be attractive in a variety of ways. In particular, the need to respond to redemptions forces banks to hold liquid assets and plan for the uncertainty of asset runoff. Commitment savings products offer a form of core deposits that many banks find attractive, both to model and to hold.

At the same time that withdrawal commitment savings programs are seen as a way to discourage dissaving, there may be seemingly contradictory evidence that easy access to funds can, under some circumstances, increase savings. Some have argued that the increases in holdings of money market funds are partly attributable to making the funds easier to liquidate, in the form of adding features like check-writing to the product. Similarly, there is some evidence that 401(k) programs that allow loans are more attractive to potential savers. Specifically, being able to take a loan against 401(k) deposits seems to increase contributions, with estimates ranging from a less than one-percentage-point increase to a ten-point increase (Holden and VanDerhei 2001; Mitchell, Utkus, and Yang 2005; Munnell, Sundén, and Taylor 2001–2002). By giving would-be savers the assurance that they can gain access to their funds if they need them, these innovations might increase the demand for certain savings products.

These two observations need not be contradictory. Different people may have varying preferences for commitment versus liquidity. Furthermore, the increased saving may come from the relative attractiveness of the baseline product. Some products are framed as having substantial withdrawal restrictions, while others are framed as being nearly as liquid as cash. The "optimal" product may be somewhere in between these extremes, offering some liquidity and some element of commitment. Either adding an element of commitment to an otherwise liquid product or adding some liquidity to an otherwise illiquid product could enhance saving by moving closer to the preferred product.

Taken together, defaults, bundling saving with other products, and commitment savings products seek to make not-saving more difficult.

MAKING IT EASY FOR PEOPLE TO SAVE

Innovations that make it easy for people to save may lower the impediments to savings, but they still require individuals to make a conscious, unbundled savings decision. Making saving easy involves making savings products available when and where people can save, that is, where they have "free" money. These attributes are described succinctly in column 3 of figure 6.1. In this section, we discuss three strategies and associated savings innovations for "going where the free money is": the workplace, tax preparation sites, and retail point-of-sale (POS). These innovations typically open up new convenient distribution channels and make savings less of a hassle. In the extreme, consider how quickly one can walk into a retailer and spend $2,000. The spirit of these innovations is to make it just as simple to save that money.

The Workplace As a Distribution Channel

For most Americans, the primary source of savable funds comes from their employment income. Workplace saving options, whether in the form of retirement plans, tax-deferred annuities, on-site banks and credit unions, or employer-based savings bond distribution, all attempt to divert funds at this source. Groups such as the Employee Benefit Research Institute (EBRI) and the Center for Business and Poverty at the University of Wisconsin, as well as firms such as pension administrators, occupational credit unions, and start-ups like EDuction (Tufano and Schneider 2005a), focus on the potential of the workplace as a channel for providing financial services. The Auto IRA discussed previously is a proposal aimed at expanding the use of the workplace as a distribution channel for savings products.

One clever innovation that marries product and process innovations in the workplace is the Save More Tomorrow (SMarT) plan proposed by the economists Richard Thaler and Shlomo Benartzi (2004), which allows people to save easily with "free" money, that is, their future raises. Behavioral research has illuminated two key insights relevant to encouraging savings. First, though individuals may want to save, many also have difficulty exercising the self-control necessary to forgo consumption (Thaler and Shefrin 1981). Mechanisms that allow people to precommit to savings may help to circumvent this lack of self-control. Second, funds are not in fact fungible, and certain sources of money may be mentally classified differently than others (Thaler 1999). For instance, people may act differently with "house money," such as unanticipated winnings, than with regular income flows. First implemented in 1998, SMarT leverages these behaviors by allowing workers to precommit to saving a portion of *future* salary raises. The program designers argue that because enrollment occurs well before the salary increase takes place, and because employees often discount future funds quite heavily, the dollars committed to savings feel less "real" than present dollars. Furthermore, employees who think of the raises as windfalls might spend them differently than current income. Once enrolled in the program, employees may opt out, but given inertia, such decisions are uncommon (Thaler and Benartzi 2004). In essence, the program is designed to mitigate or capitalize on well-known behavioral phenomena in order to increase savings.

Assessing three implementations of SMarT, Thaler and Benartzi (2004) find that take-up was strong and that participants' savings increased dramatically relative to pre-take-up levels and relative to other employees. Take-up varied with the level of marketing and the enrollment process. At one firm where employees met one on one with a financial adviser, take-up rates were as high as 80 percent. However, at a second firm where marketing was limited, take-up was lower, at about 18 percent of 401(k) participants and 10 percent of nonparticipants. At a third company, take-up rates were about 25 percent but varied considerably by employee characteristics. Lower-income workers had higher take-up rates, at 36 percent, than more highly paid employees (20 to 29 percent). These findings may be explained by the hypothesized tendency of less financially skilled workers to interpret changes to company savings plans as advice (Madrian and Shea 2001).

SMarT participants saved more in their 401(k) accounts. In the first administration of the program, participants had a pre-enrollment savings rate of 3.5 percent, lower than the rate for those workers who did not participate at all and for those who attended an initial meeting but declined to participate. But participants increased their saving more than any other group—up to 13.6 percent after four pay raises. Thaler and Benartzi (2004) found similar, though not as dramatic, results at two other research sites. Although these savings rates are a dramatic increase over prior levels, the research on SMarT to date lacks a baseline survey of household assets and savings, and so it is difficult to determine if these deposits into 401(k)s represent new household savings dollars.

Although intriguing on its own, an automatic enrollment feature could be added to SMarT to streamline the savings process completely—what some have called the autopilot 401(k) (Utkus and Young 2004), whereby enrollment and increased contributions are determined in advance.

Tax Preparation Sites As a Distribution Channel

The Internal Revenue Service (IRS) distributed over $230 billion in tax refunds in 2005, with $110 billion going to families with adjusted gross incomes (AGIs) of less than $40,000 (IRS 2005a), largely through the Earned Income Tax Credit (EITC) and the Additional Child Tax Credit (ACTC). Large in total, these refunds are also financially meaningful at the family level. In 2005 over 20 million low- to moderate-income families claimed and qualified for the EITC, receiving an average EITC refund of nearly $1,900 (IRS 2005b). Compared to the savings figures per participant attainable in other programs, such as Keep the Change and Upromise, these numbers suggest the potential to generate meaningful savings through refunds.

Refund dollars may be particularly "savable." Scholars have hypothesized that lump-sum distributions may be easier to save because individuals mentally account for these funds differently from regular income flows, seeing them as surplus or bonus funds—money that can be saved if processes are in place to facilitate such investment (Shefrin and Thaler 1988; Thaler 1994). Refund recipients do some of this saving without any intervention. Research on the uses of the EITC has found that many recipients either save a portion of their refund or use refund dollars to purchase relatively expensive durable goods such as appliances or autos (Barr and Dokko 2006; Barrow and McGranahan 2000; Robles 2005; Romich and Weisner 2000; Schneider and Tufano 2006; Smeeding, Ross-Phillips, and O'Conner 2000).

However, because the large majority of refund recipients file for refunds through intermediaries such as commercial or volunteer income tax assistance programs, this saving could be made even easier (Kneebone 2007). Specifically, these professionals could both provide filers with access to savings products and allow filers to precommit to savings months or weeks before refund receipt. By agreeing to save well before having dollars in hand, filers may be more likely to save if they evaluate their choices using extremely high mental discount rates. In this sense, refund precommitment programs tap into the same behavioral logic that drives the SMarT plan.

Scholars and practitioners as well as businesses have made several efforts to facilitate this type of tax-time saving through process innovations. One set of efforts has focused on using the tax preparation process and the eventual receipt of a refund to motivate unbanked filers to open savings accounts. A series of pilot tests at volunteer income tax assistance (VITA) sites around the country have demonstrated that many low-income tax filers have a demand for savings accounts and are interested in opening accounts during the tax preparation process. For instance, 15 percent of unbanked filers who were offered a savings account in New York took up the offer (Rhine et al. 2005), as did 20 percent of low-income filers offered an account in Chicago (Beverly, Tescher, and Romich 2004). Although most account holders in the Chicago pilot quickly drew down their account balances, a small percentage began to accumulate balances. We note, however, that declining balances may not indicate failure but rather saving for short-term goals. There is a larger movement at VITA sites toward combining tax refunds and savings (for a partial listing of such programs, see Beverly, Schneider, and Tufano 2006). Additionally, some private firms, most notably H&R Block, offer savings programs at tax time. Block's 15.5 million retail clients can open IRAs, and in 2007 the company reported that it had opened 120,000 of its new Easy IRA and Easy Savings accounts since May 2006, and a total of 600,000 such accounts between 2001 and 2005 (H&R Block 2006, 2007a, 2007b).

However, the mechanics of the tax-filing process have limited the efficacy of these efforts. Until recently, the IRS required that all refund dollars be sent to a single destination. Filers could elect to receive their entire refund in the form of a check, or they could have it all deposited to a checking or savings account. But filers were not able to earmark a portion of their refund for spending (in, say, a checking account) and another portion for saving (in a savings account). Although this might seem like a minor issue, decisionmaking biases could make it a significant hurdle to saving. An analogous problem might be if employers gave employees their entire paycheck and then left it up to them to contribute to their 401(k) program after receiving their pay, rather than offering automatic deduction of contributions.

In the not-for-profit sector, the Doorways to Dreams (D2D) Fund and the Community Action Project of Tulsa County (CAPTC) piloted a split-refund option in 2004. This small test found relatively high take-up rates, on the order of 20 percent, and participants made initial savings allocations worth 47 percent of refund dollars on average. However, while these participants proved to be more effective savers than members of comparison groups who had no access to the splitting service, account balances still diminished significantly over time (Beverly, Schneider, and Tufano 2006). In the private sector, H&R Block has also created a way for its clients to split their refunds; its clients generally divide their funds between a savings product, such as an IRA or a savings account, and deposits to a checking account or a paper check (Tufano and Schneider 2004).

While these not-for-profit and private-sector initiatives have found a way to split refunds for some tax filers, the process is generally cumbersome and costly. However, these efforts have sparked policy advocacy, and in turn, starting in January 2007, the IRS began facilitating multiple destinations for refunds with its introduction of Form 8888. This policy change substantially lowered the administrative and technical costs that not-for-profit and business groups previously faced in trying to facilitate split refunds to spur savings (Barr 2007). There are some indications that filers will be interested in using this new split-refund capability. Nearly two-thirds of low- and moderate-income filers surveyed in Detroit expressed interest in using the split-refund option (Barr and Dokko 2006).

To realize the potential for refund-splitting to spur savings, additional steps are necessary. First, financial institutions need to do a better job of tapping the potential of using split refunds to fund current-year IRA accounts by incorporating the receipt of tax refunds from Form 8888 into their processes. Second, to fully exploit the potential of split refunds, the government must clarify the legal obligations faced by banks and other financial institutions under customer identification requirements, making it clear when tax preparers must satisfy the requirements of FINRA (Financial Industry Regulatory Authority, formerly the National Association of Securities Dealers, or NASD) as well as know your customer (KYC) requirements.

Finally, low-income refund recipients who lack existing accounts need a simple universal savings option that has a very low minimum initial deposit requirement and does not impose a debit record check (Schneider and Tufano 2007). Savings bonds would fit the bill and, in fact, were easily available to all at tax time as recently as the 1960s, when tax filers could buy savings bonds right off of the tax form (Tufano and Schneider 2005b). The bonds have no fees, are low-risk, earn competitive, inflation-indexed rates, have no credit or debit check requirement, and can be purchased for as little as $25.

A series of pilot tests conducted in partnership between H&R Block, VITA sites, and D2D Fund has begun to address the operational issues of offering U.S. savings bonds at tax time and to gauge consumer interest in savings bond purchase. A 2007 experiment at H&R Block sites found a savings bond take-up rate of 7.05 percent of eligible clients offered the product, significantly above the 0.74 percent take-up rate for other H&R Block savings products such as Easy IRA. Bond buyers saved on behalf of other people, such as children or grandchildren, in about two-thirds of all cases (Tufano 2008a). Bond buyers were also more likely to receive the EITC than nonpurchasers and more likely to have had a savings account in the past, but not currently—raising the possibility that these clients had been barred by Chex Systems (Maynard 2007). A contemporaneous test at five VITA sites found a 6.0 to 9.6 percent take-up rate. These bond purchasers invested an average of $185, mostly on behalf of children or grandchildren. These deposits, though fairly small, were significant savings for many participants. Thirty-five percent of purchasers lacked savings accounts, and 55 percent reported having no savings or investments. Interestingly, when the bond offer was subsidized so that it appeared that the bonds were offered at "20 percent off," take-up rose significantly, to 15 percent of eligible filers (Zinsmeyer and Flacke 2007).

Retail Point-of-Sale Savings

Think of how many steps you need to go through to buy almost anything except for a house or a car. You give the merchant your money (or a credit card), and you either walk out with the product or arrange for its delivery. In contrast, to save, you typically have to show various documents, fill out a number of forms, and go through some other time-consuming steps. Would it be possible to create point-of-sale savings where a consumer could "buy" savings in the same way that he buys a cup of coffee, a pack of cigarettes, or a lottery ticket? This concept is being brought to life in prepaid cards and mobile banking products. More generally, can we make it as easy to "buy" savings as to buy anything else? If so, can we make the economics of POS savings attractive to low-income savers? This would expand the point-of-sale savings "outlets" from depository institutions to a much wider range of possible places, such as supermarkets, convenience stores, Wal-Marts, and other retail locations. Furthermore, once a consumer "bought" the savings, it would be possible to give the savings as a gift, in the way that you give prepaid spending cards (like iTunes or mall cards).

Technologically, payment cards can now accommodate some rudimentary savings in the form of non-interest-paying prepaid cards. For example, Green Dot offers a line of prepaid cards that are sold through neighborhood retailers such as Walgreens, CVS, and RiteAid or through the Internet. MasterCard- or VISA-branded Green Dot cards are available and usable at millions of locations. Fees include a onetime activation fee of $9.95, retail reload fees of $4.95, a monthly maintenance fee of $4.95, and ATM cash withdrawal fees of $2.40.[1] The structure and economics of this product emphasize its use as a means of effecting payments. NetSpend and Financial Service Centers of America (FISCA) already offer a prepaid debit card with an associated savings component, marrying payments and savings features. However, an alternative card could be constructed that emphasizes savings; this alternative card could be branded differently, pay interest, and restrict withdrawals, earning most of its economics from net interest margin. The appeal, if such a card could be constructed, would be the ability to "buy savings."

BRIBING PEOPLE TO SAVE

Financial economists seem especially fond of monetary incentives (bribery) to change behavior. The private sector is generally less enamored with bribery, but uses it in the form of promotions and discounting. For example, banks sometimes offer attractive bonuses in the form of teaser rates on CDs and other products. Incentives of this type proceed from a set of behavioral assumptions embodied in the notion of homo economicus, the rational economic actor underlying much of neoclassical economics. While recognizing complex utility functions, this perspective judges that most outcomes can somehow be denominated in money.

Savings product innovations based on financial incentives are fairly well studied in economics. We discuss them briefly, not because they are unimportant, but because they have received considerably more attention than other innovations and because they tend to require large outlays. In the extreme form, compelling saving through outright grants would be the ultimate bribe. Here we discuss less extreme bribery in the form of individual development accounts (IDAs) and the Saver's Credit. We conclude by discussing a set of very different innovations—anti-bribes that discourage saving among low-income families. These interventions, and the underlying behavior assumptions, are listed in column 4 of Figure 6.1.

Financial Incentives for Low-Income Asset-Building: Individual Development Accounts

In matching the savings deposits of low-income participants, IDAs are an explicit application of financial incentives to encourage poorer households in the United States to save. However, IDAs are more than simply matched savings accounts for low-income people; they also include financial education, high-touch case management, and restrictions on the use of accumulated funds. These other features address other institutional impediments to saving, as discussed by the economist Mark Schreiner and the social welfare scholar Michael Sherraden (2007). A fuller discussion of IDAs can be found in Sherraden's chapter in this volume. Here we give a general accounting of the policy in order to situate it within our framework of savings innovation.

The IDA field first received governmental funding in 1996, and since then it has grown to encompass between 500 and 1,000 IDA programs serving 15,000 active participants in 2005 (Grinstein-Weiss and Irish 2007). IDAs have been found to have mixed success, with most participants accumulating fairly modest savings, but some evidence suggests that IDAs may help to close the black-white homeownership gap (Mills et al. 2008; Schreiner, Clancy, and Sherraden 2002). IDA programs have also remained quite small, leading to high per account costs for the financial institutions that administer the accounts. These expenses, ranging from $64 to $45 per participant per month, are alone between two and three times greater than the average monthly net deposits of $19 reported for the American Dream Demonstration (ADD) project (Boshara 2005; Grinstein-Weiss and Irish 2007).

There are more efficient ways to administer IDA accounts, such as using technology (as in the Online IDA program developed by D2D Fund in conjunction with Sungard). Furthermore, there are more streamlined ways to conduct financial education and to support savers. Innovations to date have been constrained by limited governmental IDA funding. We suspect that were large-scale funding available, many of these more efficient models could emerge.

IDAs are one of a small number of financial incentives targeted to low-income consumers. Much of the federal budget for asset-building goes to the wealthiest Americans; in fact, CFED calculates that less than 1 percent of the $335 billion spent by government on incentivizing asset-building goes to households in the bottom two income quintiles (Woo, Schweke, and Buchholz 2004). However, there are a few other asset-building programs for less-well-off Americans using financial incentives. For example, the U.S. Department of Housing and Urban Development's (HUD) Family Self-Sufficiency (FSS) program is designed to help residents of public housing increase their savings by abating rent increases to residents' savings accounts (Cramer and Lubell 2005). But perhaps the largest program is the Saver's Credit, which we turn to next.

Financial Incentives for Retirement Saving

When asked to list their most important savings purposes, over one-third of households list retirement—more than any other choice (Bucks, Kennickell, and Moore 2006). The federal government and private business have put a number of savings incentives in place to try to support this goal. Reviews of the literature on the effectiveness of these innovations by the economists Douglas Bernheim (2002), Glenn Hubbard and Jonathan Skinner (1996), and Eric Engen, William Gale, and John Karl Scholz (1996) generally conclude that IRAs and 401(k)s may have had effects on saving, but for all of the incentives offered, these effects are probably small. The majority of the tax benefits offered by these savings policies are also targeted to higher-income savers. In an effort to provide lower-income savers with incentives to build retirement assets, Congress in 2001 passed the Retirement Savings Contribution Credit (the Saver's Credit), a progressively structured tax benefit that awards the largest credits to the lowest-income taxpayers (Gale, Iwry, and Orszag 2004).

However, the ability of the credit to serve low-income savers is constrained in part by its nonrefundability. Approximately 5 million filers claimed the Saver's Credit in each of its first two years (2002 and 2003), and about one-quarter of these claimants had incomes of less than $10,000. However, these low-income claimants received very little benefit, in large part because they lacked a tax burden for the credit to offset (Gale, Iwry, and Orszag 2005). The credit is also hampered by its apparent complexity. Nearly 60 million taxpayers were eligible for the credit in 2002, about twelve times the number who actually claimed the credit, and 2.7 million filers could have claimed the credit given their actual retirement saving but failed to do so (Koenig and Harvey 2005).

A recent pilot experiment attempted to resolve some of these issues through testing the design of a substantially simplified retirement savings credit for low-income households. In 2005, H&R Block partnered with a team of academic researchers to test the effect of offering tax clients a match (of 20 percent or 50 percent) on their contributions to IRAs. The presence of a match raised average contributions among participants, but there was no substantial difference in contribution level between those who were matched at 20 percent and those matched at 50 percent. However, even though a large number of participants seemed to "leave money on the table," declining very high match rates, participation was still markedly higher than for the Saver's Credit, which also offers high match rates to some filers (Duflo et al. 2006).

The Universal 401(k) proposal builds on these insights. It seeks to establish a simple program that matches contributions to retirement savings accounts. One version of the Universal 401(k) would provide a match to retirement savings in the form of a fully refundable tax credit that would be directly deposited into the tax filer's 401(k), IRA, or new government-sponsored account (Calabrese 2007).

The Elimination of "Anti-Bribes"

Financial disincentives to save may also influence low- and moderate-income families. Public assistance programs regulate the amount of assets that recipients may hold in an effort to ensure that only the neediest families receive aid. However, asset-building advocates argue that even families receiving public assistance are well served to have emergency savings and that the ownership of certain assets, such as a car, can be crucial for finding work and achieving self-sufficiency (Chen and Lerman 2005; McDonald, Orszag, and Russell 2005).

Since 1996, states have had the ability to set their own asset tests for Temporary Assistance for Needy Families (TANF), food stamps, and Medicaid, covering areas such as liquid assets, IDA ownership, and car and home ownership. These thresholds have come to vary considerably, but in general the trend has been toward exempting illiquid assets. For instance, in 2003, twenty-six states exempted IDAs, thirty exempted homes or businesses, and twenty-nine exempted vehicles from welfare program limits (McKernan and Margrabe 2007). Over the same period, however, the real value of limits on liquid assets has fallen from an average maximum of $2,779 for TANF in 1998 to $2,592 in 2003 (McKernan and Margrabe 2007).

These limits might be irrelevant if few low-income families could save. A number of studies have found evidence, however, that asset tests of this type do discourage saving among low-income families. An effect of asset tests on liquid savings is evident in the case of supplemental security income (SSI) (Neumark and Powers 1998), public health insurance (Gruber and Yelowitz 1999), and public assistance (Powers 1998; Ziliak 2003; but see Hurst and Ziliak 2006). Additionally, there is some evidence that asset limits affect vehicle ownership (Sullivan 2006; Hurst and Ziliak 2006). Asset tests may also be confusing to welfare recipients and may create a desire to try to conceal assets from public authorities, leading to a resistance to using formal financial institutions for saving and exacerbating the problem of the unbanked (O'Brien 2006). Further, these tests are both costly to administer and often inequitable: because they ignore household debt and net worth, families with some assets but significant debt are penalized (Chen and Lerman 2005).

It seems counterproductive to both encourage and discourage saving through financial incentives. This problem is germane for recipients of public assistance, but it is also more widely relevant. Federal financial aid for college tuition is determined by a complex formula that takes into account both household income and assets, effectively imposing a "tax" on wealth. A number of papers have uncovered some evidence that this tax has an effect on saving (Dick, Edlin, and Emch 2003; Feldstein 1995; Long 2003; Monks 2004; Reyes 2007). These effects are most relevant for higher-income households, however, since few families earning less than $25,000 a year face an asset penalty in financial aid calculations (Reyes 2008). Similarly, eligibility for certain Medicare benefits for senior citizens includes asset tests, forcing seniors either to spend down or to create elaborate structures to qualify for benefits. Although it may be appropriate to provide benefits only to certain people, we must be mindful of their impact on incentives to save.

MAKING SAVINGS A GROUP ACTIVITY

Whereas economists tend to see money as a universal motivator, psychologists and sociologists see other quantities as the building blocks of motivation. Whereas behavioral economics tends to view these other factors as leading to various decisionmaking "biases," other disciplinary perspectives see fear, greed, guilt, excitement, and belonging as the determinants of behavior. These other lenses provide inspiration for a variety of savings programs, including those that leverage groups' approval and norms.

Leveraging the power of groups, rotating savings and credit associations (ROSCAs) are found in communities around the world. A number of people come together for regular ROSCA meetings. At each meeting, each member of the group contributes funds that are aggregated and presented to one member of the group. These meetings continue until each member has been awarded the pooled sums. For instance, a ten-member group may meet weekly. At each meeting, every member contributes $25. In the first week, these funds are awarded to member A; in the second week, everyone again contributes $25 (including A) and the "pot" is awarded to B. This process continues until all ten members have received the pot. In this way, members who received the pot early on become debtors to those members who have not (who are essentially creditors). This basic structure has been modified extensively. The order of receipt can be set by seniority, lottery, or bidding. The amount of the pot can be fixed over time or adjusted to compensate members who receive it later in the process. The group's savings can be regularly distributed or saved up to serve as capital for loans (Bouman 1995).

ROSCAs are widespread—they are found in South America, Asia, and Africa particularly (Biggart 2001)—and membership in many countries is high. The microfinance scholar Fritz Bouman (1995) reports that upward of 50 percent of the adult population in Congo and as much as 95 percent of the population in many rural African areas belong to a ROSCA. These groups also have a substantial economic impact and are essential sources of funds for households to purchase durable goods, invest in business, pay school fees, and meet other asset development goals (Bouman 1995). These features of ROSCAs are summarized in column 5 of figure 6.1.

Some explain ROSCA participation in terms of individual maximizing behavior, particularly in the absence of formal financial institutions. This research posits that a rotating structure increases the welfare of all group members except the last one, helping them to get the desired good more quickly than if they were saving alone (Besley, Coate, and Loury 1993). But this formulation breaks down when we consider ROSCAs in which the order of award is fixed (Anderson and Baland 2002). It seems that far more than this neoclassical economic approach, behavioral economics and economic sociology matter—with financial transactions embedded in a web of social relations.

From a sociological perspective, ROSCAs may help people manage intrafamily relations. ROSCA members take their free cash out of the home and invest it in a form that is fairly illiquid—at least until they receive the pot. This structure may help members avoid the financial demands of family members without explicitly denying their requests, a form of withdrawal commitment (for evidence of the impact of intrafamily demands on saving in the United States, see Chiteji and Hamilton 2005). For instance, the economists Siwan Anderson and Jean-Marie Baland (2002) find that Kenyan wives protect their income from their husbands by joining ROSCAs. More broadly, the sociologist Viviana Zelizer (2005) suggests that money is often used to define intimate ties. For instance, intrafamily transfers may be used to affirm family relationships (as when, say, a son enacts his fidelity to his parents by giving them money). ROSCAs may then be useful because they allow members to keep their money without inflicting overt damage on these relationships.

ROSCAs have a readily apparent financial goal, but they may also have an equally important social purpose (Ardner 1995). In his seminal overview of ROSCAs, the anthropologist Clifford Geertz (1962) argues that group savings structures allow participants to perform traditional norms about reciprocity and group help—what he calls "rotating communalism." Perhaps more clearly, ROSCAs are often tied to social occasions. The recipient of the pot is frequently required to host the group at her home and provide food and drink (Biggart 2001). The law scholar Sandra Burman and her coauthor Nozipho Lembete (1995, 34) note that in their study of South African ROSCAs, "meetings were considerable occasions, with impressive party fare and photographs of the six recipients dressed in their most elegant clothes." A similar story emerges about ROSCA members in Kenya, where establishing a ROSCA was a means by which to "develop unity among members" and not solely a means of building savings (Gugerty 2003, 10). Americans see saving as almost exclusively a way of earning money. But elsewhere social rewards and group feeling (not just peer approval) may be a powerful motivator of savings as well.

Finally, upholding one's duties as a member of the ROSCA may help participants to situate themselves relative to other group members. ROSCAs may help a member show responsibility (by contributing regularly), generosity (by joining a ROSCA organized by someone in need), or competence (by setting up a successful group) (Ardner 1964). In all cases, saving is not just an end unto itself, but also a means by which individuals establish social standing and define their relationships with others.

Lessons from behavioral economics are also useful in understanding the potential of ROSCAs. Behavioralists identify a lack of saving with self-control problems, and scholars have proposed that ROSCAs function as commitment savings devices that lock members into a fixed savings schedule (Ambec and Treich 2007; Gugerty 2003; Mullainathan, forthcoming). People would keep these commitments for a variety of reasons. ROSCAs are deeply embedded in community and friendship networks, so groups can screen potential members to determine whether they are responsible and creditworthy (Biggart 2001; Chiteji 2002). This social embeddedness allows members to impose social sanctions on deadbeats (Anderson, Baland, and Moene 2003; Ardner 1964; Besley, Coate, and Loury 1993; Karlan 2007). But members can also exploit their social ties to differentiate between defaults due to genuine hardship and those due to fraud (Gugerty 2003).

The social nature of ROSCAs also provides a measure of peer support, not just peer censure (Battaglini, Benabou, and Tirole 2005). Savings is a "not" activity, that is, not consuming. Other "not" activities are supported by social support. Consider Weight Watchers, Alcoholics Anonymous (AA), and various other cessation programs. For people who have trouble saving, ROSCAs can be more than a commitment device: they can also provide social rewards for successful asset accumulation (Biggart 2001). That said, ROSCAs are not without flaw. Daryl Collins and Jonathan Morduch (this volume) describe the disintegration of a ROSCA over late payment, and Erik Bahre (2007) documents similar disagreements and conflict in his ethnographic account of informal savings groups in South Africa.

Most of the literature on ROSCAs focuses on developing countries, where formal finance is often lacking. ROSCAs also exist in the United States, however, especially in immigrant communities (Bonnett 1981; Light, Kwuon, and Zhong 1990). This savings innovation could also be successfully implemented in non-immigrant low-income communities in the United States. The sociologist Nicole Woolsey Biggart (2001) identifies five factors that should be in place for ROSCAs to function effectively: (1) the social structure is communally based; (2) obligations are collective; (3) community members are stable economically and socially; (4) the community is socially and geographic isolated; and (5) members have equal social status. These conditions are likely to be met where there are dense kin networks, relative isolation from formal financial institutions, and an economically homogenous population.

In the United States, there are groups that use peer groups to encourage saving and try to create social rewards and support for savings. One well-known example of this is the America Saves! campaign. Begun in 2001, the program encourages people to save by setting up citywide savings campaigns centered on providing education and encouragement (Fox, Bartholomae, and Lee 2005). Approximately sixty-seven thousand people have enrolled in the program in the United States, made a savings plan, and pledged to meet their savings goals (Consumer Federation of America 2007). These savers are supported by one thousand organizations in fifty areas around the country (Consumer Federation of America 2007) that provide print media, one-on-one meetings, and, interestingly, savers clubs (Consumer Federation of America 2003). The specific content of the program varies across sites, but the individual initiatives are similar in their focus on creating a movement around savings; they emphasize that individuals are joining a "network of individuals who are interested in building wealth and reducing debt" and becoming "part of a growing community . . . realizing their dreams."[2] Although the social bonds forged by saving this way are less obvious than in ROSCAs, this innovation tries to frame savings in the form of membership in a larger community.

In Cleveland, the first city to sign on to America Saves!, about one-third of families made less than $30,000 per year (36 percent), and more than half were nonwhite. Notably, participants in savings clubs were far more likely to report making progress on their savings goals (Cude and Cai 2006).

Peer-supported savings has also shown favorable results in the IDA context. Attending meetings with peers increased the savings of IDA participants by more than any other institutional or personal factor (Grinstein-Weiss, Wagner, and Ssewamala 2006). Though the effect may be due in large part to self-selection, the finding is promising.

For low-income families, savings circles may perform many functions: support, education, fewer demands on the family saver, peer pressure, and social reward. In addition, pooling resources might give low-income savers access to financial choices that are otherwise unavailable. Furthermore, pooling monies may enable low-income families to bargain with—or be more attractive to—more financial institutions. Existing social groups, such as tight-knit faith-based organizations, might be useful settings for these efforts (Fondation, Tufano, and Walker 1999).

Finally, social bonds can be leveraged to encourage savings in the form of gifts. Savings is almost always conceived as an activity done by a person for herself or on her immediate family's behalf. Yet, in many cultures, extended social groups periodically "save" on behalf of newly married couples at weddings, parents at the time of the birth of their children, and children on the occasion of their birthdays and secular or religious transitions (such as graduation, communion, or bar or bat mitzvah). Recent market research on low- and moderate-income adults, especially women, suggests that these savings-gifting motives are very strong (Maynard and Zinsmeyer 2007). We see them manifested in the savings bond research cited earlier, in which many of the deposits into this commitment savings vehicle were made in the name of children.

MAKING SAVINGS EXCITING OR FUN

The savings innovations in the preceding sections take various approaches to trying to help people save. But whether they coerce savings, make it difficult to avoid or easy to engage in, or make sure it is financially lucrative, most of these innovations (perhaps with the exception of group saving) still require that people believe that savings will help them. This is not necessarily an unfair requirement. Americans do seem to want to save: most can rattle off a list of saving goals, and many own some kind of savings product (Bucks, Kennickell, and Moore 2006). But a bigger challenge is to find savings products that do not require that people particularly want to save. ROSCAs may appeal to nonsavers who want social approval. More boldly, can savings products be created that induce people to save simply because they enjoy it? Is it possible to make savings exciting? Even addictive? Are we willing to experiment with concepts of marketing (including some faddish or gimmicky concepts)?

In this final section, we discuss two product innovations that seek to create fun saving products. One is more than three hundred years old. The other is described for the first time ever (as far as we know) in this chapter. Both have the potential to be "disruptive innovations," as defined by the business strategist Clayton Christensen (1997). Disruptive innovations are "second best" innovations that have enough features to be attractive to new or existing customers but seem inferior relative to the leading products in a market. Ultimately, they prevail over seemingly superior products. For instance, finance theorists might consider lottery-linked savings or even saving bonds far inferior to the panoply of advanced products in the market. By virtue of their simplicity, however, they appeal to nonsavers.

Lottery-Linked Savings

In 1694 the British government offered investors the chance to join a "Million Adventure." One million pounds was raised in the United Kingdom, with investors receiving a 10 percent return and a chance at winning a large raffle prize (Allen and Gale 1994). That experiment has since spurred more than three hundred years of product offerings. The form of the product has settled on a fairly simple construction: investors purchase a savings product with no risk of principal loss and either forfeit or accept reduced interest payments in exchange for the chance to win one or several large prizes allocated randomly.

The "Million Adventure" was followed by prize-bond offerings in France and England during the eighteenth century. These offerings were popular, encouraging new investors to purchase bonds, but they were relatively costly compared with nonprize government debt and were primarily geared toward fairly well-off individuals (Cohen 1953). Prize-bonds were next offered in 1864 by the Russian government. These bonds were offered at a relatively low purchase price, and bondholders were eligible for biannual prize drawings. The prizes varied in value and volume from a single 200,000-ruble prize (roughly 100 times a middle-class household's income) to approximately 250 prizes worth 500 rubles. The bonds sparked significant public interest at the time, and a recent study has documented investors' willingness to pay significantly for the risky bonds—as much as eight times the expected value (Ukhov 2002). By the late nineteenth century, this structure was used throughout continental Europe (Levy-Ullmann 1896). The twentieth century saw governments reintroduce prize-bonds across Europe—in Sweden in 1918 (Chacko et al. 2004), in Denmark in 1948 (Florentsen and Rydqvist 2002), and in 1956 in the United Kingdom, where they are still offered (Tufano 2008b). Britain's "Premium Bond" is available in denominations of £1, with a minimum purchase of £100. Each bond represents a chance to win a prize, with drawings held monthly and roughly 1.2 million prizes distributed at each drawing. The prizes range in value from two £1 million prizes to more than a million £50 prizes. Ownership of the bonds is widespread, with £31.1 billion outstanding held by one-quarter of British households. Peter Tufano (2008b) analyzes the determinants of Premium Bond sales in an effort to distill both what drives investments and how consumers view the product. He finds that sales are driven both by factors that correlate with a savings perspective, such as the aggregate interest rate (or prize rate), and by factors that are more gambling-oriented, such as the amount of the largest prize.

In addition to bonds retailed by governments, private financial institutions also market prize-linked savings products. Such products are sold with great success internationally, including in Kenya, Mexico, Venezuela, Colombia, and Japan.

Focusing on Central and South America, the sociologist Mauro Guillen and the business economist Adrian Tschoegl (2002) describe the prize-linked deposit products of two banks. Both products offered daily prizes (of a car and $22,000, respectively) and larger monthly prizes (of $220,000 and $250,000, respectively). The odds of winning were quite low for both, around .000032 percent. Each also paid reduced interest on the account, between one-half and two-thirds of the standard rate. In general, it appears that the prize-linked accounts were particularly appealing to low-income individuals and served to attract the unbanked as well as to take customers from other banks. Data presented for one of the banks show fairly rapid deposit growth. A Mexican bank reported 485,000 accounts and deposits of $178 million over two years; similar amounts were reported in Colombia over one year, and even larger amounts in Venezuela (697,000 accounts and $646 million on deposit) over one year (Guillen and Tschoegl 2002).

A more recent iteration of the prize savings concept in South Africa also shows evidence of strong demand and illustrates the importance of marketing in making this kind of product offering successful. First National Bank (FNB), one of the four largest retail banks in the South African market, introduced its Million-a-Month-Account (MaMA) in 2005. The MaMA account is a no-fee savings account that pays a nominal interest rate, 0.25 percent, and rewards savers with one prize entry for every 100 rand invested. Prize drawings are held monthly, and at each drawing 114 prizes are awarded, ranging in value from 1 million rand to 1,000 rand. Since the product's debut, FNB has opened 750,000 accounts and collected 1.2 billion rand of deposits (Mabuza 2007). The economics of the program can apparently be attractive, once at scale, especially if the campaign to sell product has ancillary marketing or selling benefits (for additional details on this program, see Cole et al. 2008).

There is extensive evidence that low-income families in the United States play lotteries, and recent survey evidence suggests that these families believe that they are more likely to become affluent from playing lotteries than by saving. In 2003 alone, U.S. residents spent nearly $80 billion on legalized forms of gambling (Kearney 2005). Though large shares of the U.S. population engage in some form of gambling annually, evidence suggests that low-income Americans are likely to spend a larger percentage of their income on gambling activities such as state jackpots.

This lottery-playing may actually substitute for savings for many families. Research conducted in 1999 suggests that low-income individuals may see gambling and saving as closely related. Some low-income respondents thought it was fruitless to save and so concluded that their best chance of accumulating wealth lay in winning jackpots or bets (Holton 2000). More recent surveys confirm this perception. Asked if they would be more likely to accumulate $500,000 by saving or by playing the lottery, 38 percent of low-income adults felt that they stood a better chance of reaching that savings level by playing the lottery, compared with just 30 percent who picked savings (Consumer Federation of America 2006). In some sense these data speak to the difficulty that low-income families may face in trying to motivate themselves to save—putting away $10 or $20 a month may just not feel like it will ever amount to enough to bother. Lotteries, on the other hand, hold out the promise, however remote, of accumulating truly life-changing sums of money.

Lottery-linked programs permit an interesting blend of classical economic and behavioral elements. As emergency savings vehicles, these structures can offer no principal loss and liquidity. Leveraging the concept of loss aversion, they offer a highly asymmetric payout: heads—you win; and tails—you don't lose. While they do not offer the familiar and powerful concept of compound interest, this trade-off may be appropriate for savers who would (a) otherwise earn very low nominal returns—owing to the size of the account and their demands for liquidity—and thus have to wait years for material accumulation through interest-on-interest, and (b) have relatively short and uncertain holding periods, thus leaving little time for the monies to compound.

A number of current research projects, including those we are engaged in, are studying lottery-linked products in the United Kingdom and South Africa. Currently, exact structures of the type used in these countries would probably be deemed in the United States to be in violation of most state laws that prohibit private lotteries. Research experiments in the United States using similar structures need to test whether low- and moderate-income Americans respond to these incentives like savers elsewhere in the world. If so, changes in state and federal law could permit, rather than prohibit, these potentially interesting structures. However, they raise interesting issues. For example, this product might be appropriate for certain savers but less appropriate for others—say, people with a thirty-year horizon who are saving for retirement.

Wilder Concepts

People react to sight, smell, taste, and touch—yet while life is tangible, much of our thinking about savings is ethereal. Perhaps there is a way to make saving more concrete. Taking this concept literally, the cement maker CEMEX designed Patrimonio Hoy, a savings program for poor families (see Segel, Chu, and Herrero 2006). The program has many of the elements discussed elsewhere in this chapter: it leverages a ROSCA-like structure, combines savings with credit, and offers new saver-friendly distribution channels. At the heart of the program is the requirement that families band together to save to purchase construction materials to expand their small homes. After making some progress toward saving (but before paying for all the materials), savings materialize in the form of building materials on-site. The program appears to be quite successful, by many metrics. Although CEMEX advances credit, default rates are reported to be extremely low, with only 0.4 percent of sales written off in 2003 (Segel, Chu, and Herrero 2006). The quality of housing has improved, and the efficiency of building has increased. Although it is difficult to attribute the program's success to any one element, it seems plausible that making savings tangible played a role. Savers could see and touch the product of their saving.

American savers might not be motivated by deliveries of cement blocks, but we can imagine other tangible manifestations of savings that might work. For example, some people are very motivated by the concept of collectibles, whether they be stamps, plates, Beanie Babies, or beer labels. Could a collectible savings program be created, whereby each increment of savings is marked by a physical object and the goal is to "collect them all"? Before rejecting this concept, consider the satisfaction (now largely gone) of getting enough entries on a passbook savings account that you moved to the next page, or flipping through a stamped passport to be reminded of your international travels. By setting concrete, incremental, and achievable goals, we might set up families for success rather than the failure of always falling short of large lifetime aspirations. With a physical marker, it might be possible for savers to keep track of their progress easily. With an attractive physical collectible, the item itself might keep savers motivated. Although faddish, newer concepts like this (which are summarized in column 6 of figure 6.1) might be useful in supporting savings. Furthermore, while the economics of the program would need to be addressed, the private sector might be able to bring its formidable marketing skills to bear.

FROM IDEAS TO ACTION

Our goal in writing this chapter was to acknowledge the wide range of solutions to the problem of low family savings. All too often, we focus on one type of savings (such as retirement or education) or one type of program (such as a tax credit or a default scheme) without acknowledging the breadth of families' savings goals or the range of available savings mechanisms. Some solutions are best suited to government action (savings bonds at tax time), others to the private sector (collectibles or point-of-sale), and some to social groups or nongovernmental organizations (NGOs) (social network savings). Some solutions might appeal to lower-income families, and others to more moderate-income families. Some might appeal to "analytic types" (for example, inflation-indexed savings bonds), while others might appeal to savers with other preferences (collectible savings or prize-linked savings).

If there is such a wide range of good ideas, then why do we not see more of them? In part we do: virtually all of the examples cited here are taken from practice, albeit not always scaled up. Expanding some of these policies in place does not seem particularly far-fetched. The private sector can offer lottery savings, distribute savings products at tax time, offer point-of-sale savings, and provide bundled savings vehicles like the SALO and Keep the Change. The private sector can design effective marketing strategies around the psychological factors that are emerging as salient to savings, and it can also support, but not deliver, social savings schemes—for example, by facilitating the paperwork done by savings groups in communities.

Firms will be motivated because they believe that these products can deliver profits. Our observations, based on working with financial service firms for savings products for low- to moderate-income savers over the past decade, suggest that the barriers to adoption are real but surmountable. In part, many private organizations lack basic information about low- to moderate-income families simply because they have not previously served them. In part, many financial service firms are more set up for delivery than innovation. Both of these barriers can be addressed through partnerships with other organizations. As examples, the non-profits Center for Financial Services Innovation (a unit of ShoreBank Corporation in Chicago) and D2D (founded by one of the authors) create organizations that produce new market insights, support new product development, and link untra-ditional partners in support of new product innovation. Beyond this, we have witnessed firsthand how these process and product innovations may require rel-atively minor changes to existing regulations and laws. Splitting refunds to mul-tiple destinations or permitting savings bond sales off of the 1040 form are not revolutionary changes. We have spoken to many financial institutions interested in lottery savings programs, but existing laws make offering these products prob-lematic. Finally, even small innovations that simplify the process of point-of-sale or tax-time savings (and thereby make the cost of customer acquisition and account opening lower) can be thwarted by the unintentional consequences of KYC. Even clarifying the liability around defaults, as has recently been done in pension reform legislation, can have a positive impact on employers' willingness to support savings.

As optimists, we are hopeful that effective bipartisan alliances can increase sav-ings for low-income families—but as realists, we can observe that this alliance may hold only so long as the innovation requires minimal governmental involvement and investment. For instance, recent regulatory changes facilitated automatic enrollment in IRAs and simplified the refund-splitting process. On the right, mak-ing these small changes may be seen as a way forward on President George Bush's "ownership society" agenda. By increasing private savings with little governmen-tal outlay, these fixes can be seen as a way to reduce reliance on social insurance in favor of private insurance (Hacker 2002, 2006). On the left, these small changes may be seen as all that can be practically done to help the poor in an otherwise unsympathetic political environment. These small-scale policies can be conceptu-alized as patches to the welfare state.

There is a more complicated political economy around the "big-money" gov-ernmental interventions discussed in this chapter. Child savings accounts and nationwide IDA programs have not succeeded in Congress, perhaps in part because these policies have both support and opposition on both the left and the right. By increasing individual and family savings, these programs may advance the right's "ownership society" agenda—reducing social insurance in favor of pri-vate insurance (often in the form of private savings)(Hacker 2002, 2006). However, they do so not through small regulatory changes but through multibillion-dollar governmental expenditure—hardly small social welfare state policies. At the same time, by transferring funds to the poor, these programs also advance the tra-ditionally left goal of assisting the poor and maintaining the role of government in providing social insurance. However, there appears to be suspicion that adopting asset-based social welfare policy means reducing traditional income supports. We are writing well before the elections of November 2008, and so it is impossible to gauge how the election results might change this political dynamic. It is probably safe, however, to bet that small "technical" changes in regulations are always more likely than large expensive programs, which require broader constituencies and can be undone by national and international crises.

In the recent past, proponents of these interventions and other large-scale asset policies have surveyed the political landscape and adopted two strategies. The first is to appeal to "progressive universalism." The logic here is that even though social programs that provide their benefits to all citizens achieve less targeting of the poor, they may still distribute more to the poor in the end because the political support for such programs extends more broadly. Essentially, though the share of social spending directed to the poor may be smaller, it is a share of a bigger pie (Korpi and Palme 1998). The "progressive" aspect of the Child Trust Fund and the proposed ASPIRE accounts simply accentuates this. The second strategy is to frame these policies in such a way as to neutralize the typical American objection to social welfare spending—that it goes to an undeserving poor (Gilens 1999). The ASPIRE act does this by distributing funds to children, a more sympathetic population than poor adults. IDAs restrict the use of funds to specific "worthy" purposes, such as education, home purchase, or small business development. These remain promising strategies for achieving more far-reaching asset-building policy.

Government policies are likely to be key for some of these innovations, but we cannot wait for government action alone. We need to compare innovations from the perspectives of those involved: would-be savers, for-profit businesses, and NGOs. The cost-benefit equation for these partners must be clear, considering direct and indirect costs (including opportunity costs) as well as benefits, which might be revenues or customer retention (for private-sector firms), progress toward mission objectives (for NGOs), or impact on national savings or public assistance programs (for governments).

Whichever innovation is considered, it is important to research its impact on total *saving.* Just because a product is adopted does not mean that it is increasing saving—it could be cannibalizing savings from elsewhere. While measuring savings levels may be the primary goal, it is important to adopt a broad perspective when measuring "impact." If seen as a long-run investing vehicle, then measuring wealth impact may be appropriate. If seen as a short-run emergency buffer, then the measurement of success may be very different. Furthermore, it is critical to consider saving in the context of other financial decisions, especially credit management. Were we to induce families to take out debt at high rates to save at low rates, we might be working against their best interests. Research should also focus on how new savings initiatives affect family well-being more generally. New savings at the expense of reduced consumption of nondiscretionary items (like health care) can reduce family welfare. Where the money for savings comes from remains an important concern.

Additionally, though this chapter looks at savings broadly, we did not fully consider the interplay between other government programs and savings. We should. From a purely economic perspective, a dollar in potential government benefits may offset the need for a dollar in savings. From a psychological or sociological perspective, however, these may not be the same at all. We suspect that while a dollar of TANF grants might offset a dollar of drawn-down savings, on an emotional level, they might be experienced quite differently.

Finally, researchers need to focus their work on providing guidance about how much savings, and what type, is optimal for families. There is some research on this topic for long-horizon retirement savings, but we need to focus the same level of attention and rigor on the full range of saving. In doing so, we must be sensitive to the needs of low- and moderate-income families, whose concerns about short-term emergencies are just as legitimate as their need to plan for a retirement that may be decades away.

This chapter was prepared for the National Poverty Center Conference "Access, Assets, and Poverty," and it has benefited from comments from the conference organizers (Rebecca Blank and Michael Barr), the discussant Jeff Kling, conference attendees, and two anonymous reviewers. We have also benefited from discussions and comments over the past years with many groups, including students, faculty, and alumni at Harvard Business School, our colleagues at Doorways to Dreams Fund, and conference attendees at the Consumer Federation of America's Financial Services Conference, the Boston Economic Club, the University of Wisconsin Institute for Research on Poverty, the Harvard Joint Center on Housing Studies Consumer Credit Symposium, the National Conference of State Legislatures, the meeting of the FDIC Advisory Committee on Financial Inclusion, and the 2008 annual meeting of the American Sociological Association. Peter Tufano is grateful for the ongoing support of the Harvard Business School Division of Research; Daniel Schneider thanks Princeton University, the National Institute of Child Health and Development (NICHD), and the National Science Foundation (NSF) Graduate Research Fellowship Program for support; and the National Poverty Center Conference is grateful for funding by the Assistant Secretary for Planning and Evaluation (ASPE) and the Ford Foundation.

NOTES

1. Details are available at Green Dot Online: http://www.greendotonline.com/Contents/Products.aspx#Fees_English.
2. Details are available at DC Saves: http://www.dcsaves.org/default.asp.

REFERENCES

Allen, Franklin, and Douglas Gale. 1994. *Financial Innovation and Risk Sharing*. Cambridge, Mass.: MIT Press.

Ambec, Stefan, and Nicolas Treich. 2007. "ROSCAs as Financial Agreements to Cope with Self-Control Problems." *Journal of Development Economics* 82(1): 120–37.

Anderson, Siwan, and Jean-Marie Baland. 2002. "The Economics of ROSCAS and Intrahousehold Resource Allocation." *Quarterly Journal of Economics* 117(3): 963–95.

Anderson, Siwan, Jean-Marie Baland, and Karl Ove Moene. 2003. "Enforcement in Informal Savings Groups." Working paper 2007/11. Vancouver, Canada: The University of British Columbia.

Ardner, Shirley. 1964. "The Comparative Study of Rotating Credit Associations." *Journal of the Royal Anthropological Institute of Great Britain and Ireland* 94(2): 201–29.

———. 1995. "Women Making Money Go Round: ROSCAs Revisited." In *Money-Go-Rounds: The Importance of Rotating Savings and Credit Associations for Women,* edited by Shirley Ardner and Sandra Burman. Oxford: Berg Publishers.

Ashraf, Nava, Nathalie Gons, Dean S. Karlan, and Wesley Yin. 2003. "A Review of Commitment Savings Products in Developing Countries." *Asian Development Bank Economics and Research* working paper 45. Manila, The Philippines: Asian Development Bank.

Ashraf, Nava, Dean S. Karlan, and Wesley Yin. 2007. "Tying Odysseus to the Mast: Evidence from a Commitment Savings Product in the Philippines." *Quarterly Journal of Economics* 121(2): 673–97.

ATM and Debit News. 2006. "BofA Earnings Flat, Debit Up." January 26.

Bahre, Erik. 2007. *Money and Violence: Financial Self-Help Groups in a South African Township.* Leiden, Holland: Brill.

Bank of America. 2007. "Regular Savings Rates and Fees." Available at: http://www.bankof america.com.

Barr, Michael S. 2007. "An Inclusive, Progressive National Savings and Financial Services Policy." *Harvard Law and Policy Review* 1: 161–84.

Barr, Michael S., and Jane K. Dokko. 2006. "Tax Filing Experiences and Withholding Preferences of Low- and Moderate-Income Households: Preliminary Evidence from a New Survey." Paper presented to the 2006 IRS research conference. Washington, D.C.: Georgetown University Law School (June 14–15, 2006).

Barr, Michael S., and Michael Sherraden. 2005. "Building Assets, Building Credit: Creating Wealth in Low-Income Communities." In *Building Assets, Building Credit: Creating Wealth in Low-Income Communities,* edited by Nicolas P. Restinas and Eric S. Belsky. Washington, D.C.: Brookings Institution Press.

Barrow, Lisa, and Leslie M. McGranahan. 2000. "The Effects of the Earned Income Credit on the Seasonality of Household Expenditures." *National Tax Journal* 53(4): 1211–43.

Battaglini, Marco, Roland Benabou, and Jean Tirole. 2005. "Self-Control in Peer Groups." *Journal of Economic Theory* 123(2): 105–34.

Bauerlein, Valerie. 2007. "Vault to the Top: Bank of America CEO in Spotlight After Deal." *The Wall Street Journal* A1(27 August).

Bernheim, Douglas B. 2002. "Taxation and Saving." *Handbook of Public Economics* 3: 1174–1249.

Beshears, John, James J. Choi, David Laibson, and Brigitte C. Madrian. 2007. "The Impact of Employer Matching on Savings Plan Participation Under Automatic Enrollment." Working paper. Cambridge, Mass.: Harvard University.

Besley, Timothy, Stephen Coate, and Glenn Loury. 1993. "The Economics of Rotating Savings and Credit Associations." *American Economic Review* 83(4): 792–810.

Beverly, Sondra, Daniel Schneider, and Peter Tufano. 2006. "Splitting Tax Refunds and Building Savings: An Empirical Test." *Tax Policy and the Economy* 20: 111–62.

Beverly, Sondra, Jennifer Tescher, and Jennifer Romich. 2004. "Linking Tax Refunds and Low-Cost Bank Accounts: Early Lessons for Program Design and Evaluation." *Journal of Consumer Affairs* 38(2): 332–41.

Biggart, Nicole Woolsey. 2001. "Banking on Each Other: The Situational Logic of Rotating Savings and Credit Associations." *Advances in Qualitative Organization Research* 3: 129–53.

Bonnett, Aubrey. 1981. *Institutional Adaptation of West Indian Immigrants to America: An Analysis of Rotating Credit Associations.* Washington, D.C.: University Press of America.

Boshara, Ray. 2005. "Individual Development Accounts: Policies to Build Savings and Assets for the Poor." Washington, D.C.: Brookings Institution.

Bouman, Fritz J. A. 1995. "Rotating and Accumulating Savings and Credit Associations: A Development Perspective." *World Development* 23(3): 371–84.

Bucks, Brian K., Arthur B. Kennickell, and Kevin B. Moore. 2006. "Recent Changes in U.S. Family Finances: Evidence from the 2001 and 2004 Survey of Consumer Finances." *Federal Reserve Bulletin* 92(March 22): A1–38.

Bulkeley, William M. 2001. "Large Companies Join Rebate Plan for College Savings." *Wall Street Journal,* April 21.

Burman, Sandra, and Nozipho Lembete. 1995. "Building New Realities: African Women and ROSCAs in Urban South Africa." In *Money-Go-Rounds: The Importance of Rotating Savings and Credit Associations for Women,* edited by Shirley Ardner and Sandra Burman. Oxford: Berg Publishers.

Calabrese, Michael. 2007. "A Universal 401(k) Plan." In *Ten Big Ideas for a New America.* Washington, D.C.: New America Foundation.

Campbell, Richard T., and John C. Henretta. 1980. "Status Claims and Status Attainment: The Determinants of Financial Well-Being." *American Journal of Sociology* 86(3): 618–29.

Caner, Asena, and Edward Wolff. 2002. "Asset Poverty in the United States, 1984–1999: Evidence from the Panel Study of Income Dynamics." Working paper 356. Annandale-on-Hudson, N.Y.: Bard College, Jerome Levy Economics Institute.

———. 2004. "Asset Poverty in the United States: Its Persistence in an Expansionary Economy." Policy brief 76. Annandale-on-Hudson, N.Y.: Bard College, Jerome Levy Economics Institute.

CFED, Corporation for Enterprise Development. 2007a. "Individual Development Accounts: Providing Opportunities to Build Assets." Washington: CFED.

———. 2007b. "The Seed Policy and Practice Initiative." Available at: http://www.cfed.org (accessed January 21, 2009).

Chacko, George, Peter Hecht, Vincent Dessain, and Andres Sjoman. 2004. "Swedish Lottery Bonds." Case 204-048. Boston: Harvard Business School Press.

Chaker, Anne Marie. 2004. "How Shopping Can Pay for College." *Wall Street Journal,* September 23.

Chen, Alexander, and Helen H. Jensen. 1985. "Home Equity Use and the Life Cycle Hypothesis." *Journal of Consumer Affairs* 19(1): 37–56.

Chen, Henry, and Robert I. Lerman. 2005. "Do Asset Limits in Social Programs Affect the Accumulation of Wealth?" Washington, D.C.: Urban Institute.

Chiteji, Ngina. 2002. "Promises Kept: Enforcement and the Role of Rotating Savings and Credit Associations in an Economy." *Journal of International Development* 14(4): 393–411.

Chiteji, Ngina, and Darrick Hamilton. 2005. "Family Matters: Kin Networks and Asset Accumulation." In *Inclusion in the American Dream: Assets, Poverty, and Public Policy,* edited by Michael Sherraden. Oxford: Oxford University Press.

Choi, James J., David Laibson, and Brigitte C. Madrian. 2004. "Plan Design and 401(k) Savings Outcomes." *National Tax Journal* 52(2): 275–98.

Choi, James J., David Laibson, Brigitte C. Madrian, and Andrew Metrick. 2004. "For Better or for Worse: Default Effects and 401(k) Savings Behavior." In *Perspectives in the Economics of Aging,* edited by David Wise. Chicago: University of Chicago Press.

———. 2006. "Saving for Retirement on the Path of Least Resistance." In *Behavioral Public Finance: Toward a New Agenda,* edited by Edward McCaffrey and Joel Slemrod. New York: Russell Sage Foundation.

Christensen, Clayton M. 1997. *The Innovator's Dilemma.* Boston: Harvard Business School Press.

Cohen, Jacob. 1953. "The Element of Lottery in British Government Bonds, 1694–1919." *Economica* 20(79): 237–46.

Cole, Shawn, Daryl Collins, Daniel Schneider, and Peter Tufano. 2008. "First National Bank's Golden Opportunity." Case study 208-072. Boston: Harvard Business School.

Consumer Federation of America. 2003. "New Analysis Reveals Wealth Gap Between Hispanic and Other Americans." Washington, D.C.: Consumer Federation of America.

———. 2006. "How Americans View Personal Wealth Versus How Financial Planners View This Wealth." Washington, D.C.: Consumer Federation of America.

———. 2007. "National Survey Reveals Emergency Savings Needs and Effective Saver Strategies." Washington, D.C.: Consumer Federation of America.

Cramer, Reid. 2006. "Net Worth at Birth: Creating a National System for Savings and Asset Building with Children's Savings Accounts." Washington, D.C.: New America Foundation.

Cramer, Reid, and Jeffrey Lubell. 2005. "Shoring Up HUD's Family Self-Sufficiency Program." Washington, D.C.: New America Foundation.

Cude, Brenda J., and Yi Cai. 2006. "Assessing the Outcomes of a Social Marketing Program: Lessons Learned from Cleveland Saves." Paper presented to the meeting of the Eastern Family Economics and Resource Management Association (February 23–25).

Davis, Kristin. 2001. "A Not-So-Easy College Freebie." *Kiplinger's Personal Finance,* November 1.

Davis, Paul. 2006. "In Brief: 2 Million Sign-Ups for B of A Program." *American Banker,* April 6.

Dick, Andrew W., Aaron S. Edlin, and Eric R. Emch. 2003. "The Savings Impact of College Financial Aid." *Contributions to Economic Analysis and Policy* 2(1): 1–29.

Duflo, Esther, William G. Gale, Jeffery Liebman, Peter Orszag, and Emmanuel Saez. 2006. "Saving Incentives for Low- and Middle-Income Families: Evidence from a Field Experiment with H&R Block." *Quarterly Journal of Economics* 121(4): 1311–46.

Engen, Eric M., William G. Gale, and John Karl Scholz. 1996. "The Illusory Effects of Saving Incentives on Saving." *Journal of Economic Perspectives* 10(4): 113–38.

Enrich, David. 2005. "Credit-Card Savings Accounts Reward Spending." *Wall Street Journal,* October 11.

Feldstein, Martin. 1995. "College Scholarship Rules and Private Saving." *American Economic Review* 85(3): 552–66.

Fellowes, Matt, and Terry I. Brooks. 2007. "The High Price of Being Poor in Kentucky." Washington, D.C.: Brookings Institution, Metropolitan Policy Program (July).

Florentsen, Bjarne, and Kristian Rydqvist. 2002. "Ex-Day Behavior When Investors and Professional Traders Assume Reverse Roles: The Case of Danish Lottery Bonds." *Journal of Financial Intermediation* 11(2): 152–75.

Fondation, Larry, Peter Tufano, and Patricia Walker. 1999. "Collaborating with Congregations: Opportunities for Financial Services in Inner Cities." *Harvard Business Review* 77(4): 57–68.

Fox, Jonathan, Suzanne Bartholomae, and Jinkook Lee. 2005. "Building the Case for Financial Education." *Journal of Consumer Affairs* 39(1): 195–214.

Freeman, Lisa. 2005. "CUs Slow to Match Rival Cards' Savings Feature." *Credit Union Journal,* November 26.

Gale, William G., Mark Iwry, and Peter Orszag. 2004. "The Saver's Credit: Issues and Options." *Tax Notes* 103(5): 597–612.

———. 2005. "The Saver's Credit: Expanding Retirement Savings for Middle- and Lower-Income Americans." Washington, D.C.: Retirement Security Project.

Geertz, Clifford. 1962. "The Rotating Credit Association: A 'Middle Rung' in Development." *Economic Development and Cultural Change* 10(3): 241–63.

Gilens, Marty. 1999. *Why Americans Hate Welfare: Race, Media, and the Politics of Anti-Poverty Policy.* Chicago: University of Chicago Press.

Grinstein-Weiss, Michal, and Katie Irish. 2007. "Individual Development Accounts: Frequently Asked Questions." St. Louis: Washington University, George Warren Brown School of Social Work, Center for Social Development.

Grinstein-Weiss, Michal, Kristen Wagner, and Fred M. Ssewamala. 2006. "Saving and Asset Accumulation Among Low-Income Families with Children in IDAs." *Children and Youth Services Review* 28(2): 193–211.

Gruber, Jonathan, and Aaron Yelowitz. 1999. "Public Health Insurance and Private Savings." *Journal of Political Economy* 107(6): 1249–74.

Gugerty, Mary Kay. 2003. "You Can't Save Alone: Testing Theories of Rotating Savings and Credit Associations in Kenya." Working paper. Seattle: University of Washington.

Guidolin, Massimo, and Elizabeth La Jeunesse. 2007. "The Decline in the U.S. Personal Saving Rate: Is It Real and Is It a Puzzle?" *Federal Reserve Bank of St. Louis Review* 89(6): 491–514.

Guillen, Mauro, and Adrian Tschoegl. 2002. "Banking on Gambling: Bank and Lottery-Linked Deposit Accounts." *Journal of Financial Services Research* 21(3): 219–31.

Hacker, Jacob. 2002. *The Divided Welfare State: The Battle over Public and Private Social Benefits in the United States.* Cambridge: Cambridge University Press.

———. 2006. *The Great Risk Shift: The Assault on American Jobs, Families, Health Care, and Retirement.* Oxford: Oxford University Press.

H&R Block. 2006. "H&R Block Defends Its Express IRA Product and Delivers Strong Rebuttal to New York AG's Attack." St. Louis: H&R Block Media Relations.

———. 2007a. "H&R Block Annual Report." St. Louis: H&R Block.

———. 2007b. "H&R Block Serves Record Total U.S. Clients in 2007 Tax Season." St. Louis: H&R Block Media Relations.

Haveman, Robert, and Edward Wolff. 2001. "Who Are the Asset Poor? Levels, Trends, and Composition, 1983–1998." Discussion paper 1227-01. Madison: University of Wisconsin, Institute for Research on Poverty.

HM Treasury. 2003. "Detailed Proposals for the Child Trust Fund." London: HM Treasury and Inland Revenue.

———. 2006. "Child Trust Fund Statistical Report." London: HM Revenue and Customs.

————. 2007. "The Child Trust Fund: Total Number of Vouchers Issued and Accounts Opened by Parents." London: HM Treasury (June).

Holden, Sarah, and Jack VanDerhei. 2001. "Contribution Behavior of 401(k) Plan Participants." *ICI Perspective* 7(4): 1–19.

Holton, Lisa. 2000. "Redefining the Rainy Day." *American Demographics* 22: 6.

Hubbard, Glenn R., and Jonathan Skinner. 1996. "Assessing the Effectiveness of Saving Incentives." *Journal of Economic Perspectives* 10(4): 73–90.

Hurst, Eric, and James P. Ziliak. 2006. "Do Welfare Asset Limits Affect Household Saving? Evidence from Welfare Reform." *Journal of Human Resources* 41(1): 46–71.

Internal Revenue Service (IRS). 2005a. "All Returns: Tax Liability, Tax Credits, and Tax Payments, Statistics of Income, Table 3.3." Washington: IRS.

————. 2005b. "Individual Income Tax Returns with Earned Income Credit, Statistics of Income, Table 2.5." Washington: IRS.

Iwry, J. Mark, and David C. John. 2007. "Pursuing Universal Retirement Security Through Automatic IRAs." Washington, D.C.: Retirement Security Project.

Karlan, Dean S. 2007. "Social Connections and Group Banking." *Economic Journal* 117(517): F52–84.

Kearney, Melissa S. 2005. "The Economic Winners and Losers of Legalized Gambling." *National Tax Journal* 58: 281–302.

Kempson, Elaine, Adele Atkinson, and Sharon Collard. 2006. "Saving for Children: A Baseline Survey at the Inception of the Child Trust Fund." Bristol, U.K.: University of Bristol, Personal Finance Research Centre.

Kim, Jane J. 2006. " 'Loyalty' and College Savings—Buying at Some Retailers Helps a 529 Plan, but It Takes Work." *Wall Street Journal,* February 11.

Kneebone, Elizabeth. 2007. "A Local Ladder for Low-Income Workers: Recent Trends in the Earned Income Tax Credit." Washington, D.C.: Brookings Institution, Metropolitan Policy Program.

Koenig, Gary, and Robert Harvey. 2005. "Utilization of the Saver's Credit: An Analysis of the First Year." *National Tax Journal* 53: 787–806.

Korpi, Walter, and Joakim Palme. 1998. "The Paradox of Redistribution and Strategies of Equality: Welfare State Institutions, Inequality, and Poverty in the Western Countries." *American Sociological Review* 63(5): 661–87.

Levy-Ullmann, Henri. 1896. "Lottery Bonds in France and in the Principal Countries of Europe." *Harvard Law Review* 9(6): 386–405.

Light, Ivan, Im Jung Kwuon, and Deng Zhong. 1990. "Korean Rotating Credit Associations in Los Angeles." *Amerasia* 16(2): 34–54.

Long, Mark. 2003. "The Impact of Asset-Tested College Financial Aid on Household Saving." *Journal of Public Economics* 88(1–2): 63–88.

Lubasi, Victor. 2005. "Debit Card Competition: Signature versus PIN." *Chicago Fed Letter* 221.

Mabuza, Ernest. 2007. "FNB 'Lottery' Still on Pending New Appeal." *Business Day* (Johannesburg), April 18.

Madrian, Brigitte C., and Dennis F. Shea. 2001. "The Power of Suggestion: Inertia in 401(k) Participation and Savings Behavior." *Quarterly Journal of Economics* 116(4): 1149–87.

Maynard, Nick. 2007. "Tax Time Savings: Testing U.S. Savings Bonds at H&R Block Tax Sites." Boston: D2D Fund.

Maynard, Nick, and Jeff Zinsmeyer. 2007. "The Mind of Low- and Moderate-Income Savers." Madison, Wisc.: Filene Research Institute.

McDonald, Gordon, Peter Orszag, and Gina Russell. 2005. "The Effect of Asset Tests on Saving." Washington, D.C.: Retirement Security Project.

McGeer, Bonnie. 2007. "Bankers Hope a Dollar Saved Is a Customer Earned." *American Banker,* May 31.

McKernan, Signe-Mary, and William Margrabe. 2007. "How Have Asset Policies for Cash Welfare and Food Stamps Changed Since the 1990s?" Washington, D.C.: Urban Institute.

Mensah, Lisa, Rachel Schneider, and Magda Aboulfadi. 2004. "The Child Trust Fund: A Universal Long-Term Saving Policy." New York: Aspen Institute, Initiative on Financial Security.

Merton, Robert C. 1992. "Financial Innovation and Economic Performance." *Journal of Applied Corporate Finance* 4(4): 12–22.

Mierzwa, Erin. 2007. "Bank of America Wants Customers to Keep Their Change." *Cascade* 64: 8.

Mills, Gregory, William G. Gale, Rhiannon Patterson, Michael D. Erikson, and Emil Apostolov. 2008. "Effects of Individual Development Accounts on Asset Purchases and Saving Behavior: Evidence from a Controlled Experiment." *Journal of Political Economy* 92(5–6): 1509–30.

Mitchell, Olivia S., Stephen P. Utkus, and Tongxuan Yang. 2005. "Turning Workers into Savers? Incentives, Liquidity, and Choice in 401(k) Plan Design." Philadelphia: Pension Research Council.

Monks, James. 2004. "An Empirical Examination of the Impact of College Financial Aid on Family Savings." *National Tax Journal* 57: 189–207.

Moore, Amanda, Sondra Beverly, Mark Schreiner, Michael Sherraden, Esther Y. N. Cho, Lissa Johnson, and Rebecca Vonderlack. 2001. "Saving, IDA Programs, and Effects of IDAs: A Survey of Participants." St. Louis: Washington University, George Warren Brown School of Social Work, Center for Social Development.

Mullainathan, Sendhil. Forthcoming. "Psychology and Development Economics." In *Yrjo Jahnsson Foundation 50th Anniversary Conference on Economic Institutions and Behavioral Economics,* edited by Peter Diamond and Hannu Vartianinen. Princeton, N.J.: Princeton University Press.

Munnell, Alicia H., Annika E. Sundén, and Catherine Taylor. 2001–2002. "What Determines 401(k) Participation and Contributions?" *Social Security Bulletin* 64(3): 64–75.

Neumark, David, and Elizabeth Powers. 1998. "The Effect of Means-Tested Income Support for the Elderly on Pre-Retirement Saving: Evidence from the SSI Program in the U.S." *Journal of Public Economics* 68(2): 181–206.

North Carolina State Employees Credit Union (NCSECU). 2004. "Annual Report." Raleigh, N.C.: NCSECU.

———. 2005. "Annual Report." Raleigh, N.C.: NCSECU.

———. 2006. "Annual Report." Raleigh, N.C.: NCSECU.

O'Brien, Rourke. 2006. "Ineligible to Save? Asset Limits and the Savings Behavior of Welfare Recipients." Washington, D.C.: New America Foundation.

Oliver, Melvin L., and Thomas M. Shapiro. 1990. "Wealth of A Nation: A Reassessment of Asset Inequality in America Shows at Least One-Third of Households Are Asset-Poor." *American Journal of Economics and Sociology* 49(2): 129–51.

Parcel, Toby L. 1982. "Wealth Accumulation of Black and White Men: The Case of Housing Equity." *Social Problems* 30(2): 199–211.

Powers, Elizabeth. 1998. "Does Means-Testing Welfare Discourage Saving? Evidence from a Change in AFDC Policy in the United States." *Journal of Public Economics* 68(1): 5–21.

Reyes, Jessica Wolpaw. 2008. "College Financial Aid Rules and the Allocation of Savings." *Education Economics* 16(2): 167–89.

Rhine, Sherrie, Sabrina Su, Yazmin Osaki, and Steven Lee. 2005. "Householder Response to the Earned Income Tax Credit: Path of Sustenance or Road to Asset Building?" New York: Federal Reserve Bank.

Robles, Barbara. 2005. "Latino Family and Community Wealth Building: Linking the Earned Income Tax Credit to Asset Building." Paper presented to the fall research conference of the Association for Public Policy Analysis and Management. Washington, D.C. (November 3–5, 2005).

Romich, Jennifer, and Thomas Weisner. 2000. "How Families View and Use the EITC: Advance Payment Versus Lump Sum Delivery." *National Tax Journal* 53: 1245–66.

Sahlman, William A. 2003. "Upromise 2002." Boston: Harvard Business School Press.

Sallie Mae. 2006. "Sallie Mae 10-K." Available at: http://www.salliemae.com/about/investors.

Schneider, Daniel, and Peter Tufano. 2006. "The San Francisco Working Families Credit: Analysis of Program Applicants." Report to SFWorks and the City of San Francisco.

———. 2007. "New Savings from Old Innovations: Asset Building for the Less Affluent." In *Financing Low-Income Communities,* edited by Julia S. Rubin. New York: Russell Sage Foundation.

Schreiner, Mark, Margaret Clancy, and Michael Sherraden. 2002. "Final Report: Saving Performance in the American Dream Demonstration." St. Louis: Washington University, George Warren Brown School of Social Work, Center for Social Development.

Schreiner, Mark, and Michael Sherraden. 2007. *Can the Poor Save? Saving and Asset Building in Individual Development Accounts.* New Brunswick, N.J.: Transaction Publishers.

Segel, Arthur I., Michael Chu, and Gustavo Herrero. 2006. "Patrimonio Hoy." Case study 207-059. Boston: Harvard Business School.

Shefrin, Hersh M., and Richard H. Thaler. 1988. "The Behavioral Life-Cycle Hypothesis." *Economic Inquiry* 26(4): 609–43.

Singletary, Michelle. 2001. "Spend to Save? Why Not Just Save?" *Washington Post,* April 15.

———. 2005. "Spend and Save Don't Go Together." *Washington Post,* October 30.

Smeeding, Timothy, Katherine Ross-Phillips, and Michael O'Conner. 2000. "The EITC: Expectation, Knowledge, Use, and Economic and Social Mobility." *National Tax Journal* 53: 1187–1209.

Sodha, Sonia. 2006. "Lessons from Across the Atlantic: Asset-Building in the U.K." Paper presented to the 2006 Assets Learning Conference, "A Lifetime of Assets: Building Families, Communities, and Economies." Phoenix (September 19–21).

Stegman, Michael A. 2007. "Payday Lending." *Journal of Economic Perspectives* 21(1): 169–90.

Sullivan, James X. 2006. "Welfare Reform, Saving, and Vehicle Ownership." *The Journal of Human Resources* 41(1): 72–105.

Sunstein, Cass R., and Richard H. Thaler. 2003. "Libertarian Paternalism Is Not an Oxymoron." *University of Chicago Law Review* 70(4): 1159–1202.

Tax Incentivized Savings Association (TISA). 2007. "TISA CTF Statistics Project: Subscription Profiles." Available at: http://www.tisa.uk.com/statistics.html?stat_type=clf (accessed January 21, 2009).

Tescher, Jennifer. 2006. "Viewpoint: Behavioral Studies: Raising the Savings Rate." *American Banker,* December 1.

Thaler, Richard H. 1994. "Psychology and Savings Policies." *American Economic Review* 84(2): 186–92.

———. 1999. "Mental Accounting Matters." *Journal of Behavioral Decision Making* 12(3): 183–206.

Thaler, Richard H., and Shlomo Benartzi. 2004. "Save More Tomorrow (TM): Using Behavioral Economics to Increase Employee Saving." *Journal of Political Economy* 112(1): 164–87.

Thaler, Richard H., and Hersh M. Shefrin. 1981. "An Economic Theory of Self-Control." *Journal of Political Economy* 89(2): 392–406.

Thaler, Richard H., and Cass R. Sunstein. 2003. "Libertarian Paternalism." *American Economic Review* 93(2): 175–79.

Tufano, Peter. 2008a. "Just Keep My Money! Supporting Tax-Time Savings with U.S. Savings Bonds." Working paper 09-059. Boston: Harvard Business School.

———. 2008b. "Saving Whilst Gambling: An Empirical Analysis of U.K. Premium Bonds." *American Economic Review* 98(2): 321–26.

Tufano, Peter, and Daniel Schneider. 2004. "H&R Block and Everyday Financial Services." Case study 9-205-013. Boston: Harvard Business School.

———. 2005a. "EDuction." Case study 206-006. Boston: Harvard Business School.

———. 2005b. "Reinventing Savings Bonds." *Tax Notes,* October 31.

U.K. Parliament. 2007. "Hansard Written Answers, Child Trust Funds." *British House of Commons,* January 16.

Ukhov, Andrey. 2002. "Time-Varying Risk Aversion: Evidence from Russian Lottery Bonds." Working paper. New Haven, Conn.: Yale School of Management.

Upromise. 2007. "Upromise Reaches Record 8 Million Members." *Upromise,* July 18.

U.S. Bureau of Economic Analysis. 2007. "Personal Income and Its Disposition, Table 2.1." Available at: http://www.bea.gov/national (accessed January 21, 2009).

Utkus, Stephen P., and Jean A. Young. 2004. "Lessons from Behavioral Finance and the Autopilot 401(k) Plan." Valley Forge, Pa.: Vanguard Center for Retirement Research.

Vanguard Center for Retirement Research. 2001. "Automatic Enrollment: Benefits and Costs of Adoption." Valley Forge, Pa.: The Vanguard Group for Retirement Research.

White, David. 2006. "Missing Out on Child's Play." *Financial Times.*

White, Stuart. 2004. "The Citizen's Stake and Paternalism." *Politics and Society* 32: 61–78.

Woo, Lillian F., William Schweke, and David E. Buchholz. 2004. "Hidden in Plain Sight: A Look at the $335 Billion Federal Asset-Building Budget." Washington, D.C.: Corporation for Enterprise Development.

Wyatt, Edward. 2001. "Buy Stuff, Pay for College." *New York Times,* November 11.

Zelizer, Viviana A. 2005. *The Purchase of Intimacy.* Princeton, N.J.: Princeton University Press.

Ziliak, James P. 2003. "Income Transfers and Assets of the Poor." *Review of Economics and Statistics* 85(1): 63–76.

Zinsmeyer, Jeffrey, and Tim Flacke. 2007. "A Gateway to Longer-Term Savings: Testing U.S. Savings Bonds to Help Low-Income Tax Filers Start Saving." Boston: D2D Fund.

Chapter 7

Individual Development Accounts and Asset-Building Policy: Lessons and Directions

Michael Sherraden

This chapter addresses individual development accounts (IDAs), which feature matched savings for the poor as a strategy for building assets. A large, multi-method, and continuing research project known as the American Dream Demonstration (ADD) provides the empirical foundation for the discussion. Several research methods and key results from ADD and other studies are summarized and discussed. Evidence is considered in light of current and potential policy, and future research directions are suggested.

ASSET-BUILDING AS A POLICY STRATEGY: CONTEXT AND MOTIVATION

It is a commonplace that asset accumulation and investment pave the way to household development. With few exceptions, families must save and invest in education, skills, experience, a house, land, an enterprise, financial securities, or other assets to improve their capabilities, earnings, and life circumstances over time and across generations. Not focusing on assets may do a disservice to understanding poverty and household development, perhaps particularly by race (Conley 1999; Lui et al. 2006; Nembhard and Chiteji 2006; Oliver and Shapiro 2006; Shapiro 2004). Moreover, there is evidence that asset inequality in itself may have negative consequences for well-being. For example, Juan Rafael Morillas (2007) finds that asset-holding is associated with earnings mobility and that racial inequality in asset-holding is further associated with earnings mobility.[1]

Approximately 20 percent of Americans have zero or negative net worth, with much higher percentages among people of color. Moreover, asset inequality is much greater than income inequality. For example, looking at inequality by race, at the median whites have average income roughly 50 percent greater than African

Americans and Latinos, which is a large inequality. But whites have median net worth in the range of 1,000 percent (ten times) greater than African Americans and Latinos (Caner and Wolff 2004; Kochhar 2004; Mishel, Bernstein, and Allegretto 2007; Oliver and Shapiro 2006; Scholz and Seshadri, this volume; Shapiro 2004; Wolff 2004).

Income, as a proxy for consumption, has been the standard definition of poverty in social policy. Income support is essential to provide basic necessities. But today there is increasing questioning of income as the sole definition of poverty and well-being. Amartya Sen (1993, 1999) and others are also looking toward capabilities. Asset-based policy—one measure of long-term capabilities—can be seen as part of this larger discussion. As public policy, asset-building may be understood as a form of "social investment" (Midgley 1999; Sherraden 1991). From this perspective, asset-based policy is a complement to income-based policy, each serving different purposes: income may support consumption, or "getting by," while assets may promote development, or "getting ahead."

Asset-based policy is not new. Current examples of U.S. asset-based policy include homeownership tax benefits, investment tax benefits, and defined-contribution retirement accounts with tax benefits—at the workplace in 401(k)s and 403(b)s, and away from the workplace in individual retirement accounts (IRAs), Roth IRAs, state college savings plans, and medical savings accounts. These defined-contribution policies have all appeared since 1970 and are growing rapidly. Unfortunately, the poor receive almost none of the benefits. Public subsidies operate through tax deferments and exemptions and are tied to income in a regressive way. The United States spends well over $300 billion annually in tax expenditures for asset-building in homes, investments, and retirement accounts, and over 90 percent of this expenditure goes to households in the top half of the income distribution (Corporation for Enterprise Development 2004; Howard 1997; Seidman 2001; Sherraden 1991).

THE PROPOSAL FOR INDIVIDUAL DEVELOPMENT ACCOUNTS

Insight for the proposal for IDAs came during discussions with "welfare mothers" during the 1980s. These women said that a major part of their challenge was that they could not "get anywhere" because they could not accumulate resources for long-term goals, such as finding better housing, getting more education, starting a small business, or moving to a better neighborhood. These discussions led to a proposal for individual development accounts, or IDAs. IDAs are matched savings for low-income individuals.

In response to the rapidly growing and regressive asset-based policies mentioned earlier, IDAs were proposed as a universal and progressive asset-building policy that would bring the poor into asset-building policies. As originally proposed, IDAs would include everyone, provide greater support for the poor, begin as early as birth, and be used for key development and social protection goals across the life span, such as education, homeownership, business capitalization, and retirement security in later life (Sherraden 1988, 1991). IDAs have instead been implemented in the form of short-term "demonstration" programs targeted toward the poor and as yet are far from becoming a comprehensive asset-based policy.

Typically, a community organization works with a financial institution in providing IDAs. Early funding of IDAs was from philanthropic foundations, but today IDA funding comes mostly from government, both federal and state, with significant resources coming from the United Way and other nonprofit organizations.

Features of IDAs vary depending on the funder. Matching rates are typically one-to-one, two-to-one, or three-to-one. (For example, the federal Assets for Independence Act of 1998 provides a match of three-to-one.) Allowed uses for IDA savings are typically homeownership, education, and small business capitalization, but sometimes cars or computers are allowed uses. The amount of savings that can be matched (the "match cap") is set on a monthly or annual basis (analogous to a certain level of annual IRA savings receiving a tax benefit); typical annual match caps range from $300 to $600. Sometimes IDA programs offer automatic deposit from earnings. Financial education, both "general" and "asset-specific," is required of all IDA participants. For example, an IDA participant saving for a home purchase would take classes on general financial matters (such as budgeting, credit, and investment options) as well as classes focused on homeownership (such as mortgages, maintenance, and insurance).

There is a great deal of enthusiasm among IDA program directors, and there are many positive stories about participants. Results of IDA programs to date appear to be promising in terms of saving and asset-building, but as so often occurs, program-level enthusiasm sometimes runs ahead of systematic research results.

THE AMERICAN DREAM DEMONSTRATION

A large study of IDAs known as the American Dream Demonstration (ADD) was introduced in the United States in 1997.[2] ADD involved thirteen organizations around the country selected through a competitive process to design, implement, and administer IDA initiatives in their local communities. ADD is the first large-scale test of IDAs. ADD IDA programs together established over 2,300 IDAs in low-income communities across the country, with each site starting 50 to 150 accounts and one site expanding to over 500 accounts. The demonstration saving period was from September 1997 through December 2001, with use of savings through June 2002, post-program research through 2005, and additional research currently underway.

ADD provides the most thorough research to date on an asset-building program. An intensive, multi-method research agenda has accompanied the demonstration. The purpose of ADD has been to find out whether IDAs are successful, in what ways, and for whom. Because IDAs are new and there is much to learn, research is central to the purpose of ADD. The ADD research design is multifaceted, designed by the Center for Social Development (CSD) at Washington University in St. Louis, with the advice of an expert Evaluation Advisory Committee.[3] ADD research has sought answers to the following questions: What are good design features for an IDA program? What are the barriers and facilitators in starting and operating a successful IDA program? What is the pattern of saving and asset accumulation in IDAs? What affects savings behavior (how do people save) in an IDA program? What are IDA savings used for? What are the impacts of IDAs on asset accumulation and the use of assets to meet life goals (education, homeownership, starting a business, and so on)? What are the possible additional effects (social, psychological, and economic) of asset-holding for IDA participants and their families? What are the possible community-level effects of an IDA program? What is the cost and financial return of an IDA program?

The overall ADD study has employed multiple research methods, each with a different purpose: an assessment of IDA program implementation, a cross-sectional survey of participants for self-report on their experience and effects, program and participant monitoring, an experiment with random assignment to participant and control groups to assess impacts (at one site), in-depth interviews (at the experimental site), cost analysis and plans for cost-benefit analysis (at an experimental site), and a study of possible community-level effects. Several key methods in ADD research are still in progress. This chapter covers key findings to date, current developments, and future plans in four areas of ADD research: account monitoring, in-depth interviews, cost assessment, and experimental impacts. The chapter also looks ahead to directions for this body of research.

ACCOUNT MONITORING: SAVING IN IDAS AND THE FACTORS ASSOCIATED WITH OUTCOMES

Realizing that we should track all IDA savings transactions, CSD created software known as MIS IDA that would manage IDA programs, with more than thirty management reports, account statements to participants, reports to funders, and so on, and at the same time would keep a database of all IDA account transactions (Johnson, Hinterlong, and Sherraden 2001). Our thinking was that, if the software was an effective management tool, then IDA programs would use it and collect the monitoring data (some might call this administrative data) that the researchers could then use. This has worked out. MIS IDA was used to manage all ADD programs, and as a result, account monitoring in ADD produced an exceptionally comprehensive database of all account transactions by all ADD participants for their entire time in the demonstration. To our knowledge, this is the most detailed data set available on low-income savers, with highly accurate data on all IDA savings transactions for all participants coming from records of financial institutions.

What are the IDA savings patterns and outcomes? To provide an overall picture, the average ADD participant deposits $16.60 net per month. About half of ADD participants (48 percent) are not "savers" (defined as at least $100 in net IDA savings). The savers have average monthly net deposits of $32.44. Match rates vary, with two-to-one being most typical. Homeownership or home repair has been the most popular use of IDA savings in ADD.[4]

Sometimes very simple data, rightly or wrongly, can make a difference. The simple descriptive data indicating that low-income people can save in IDAs has had a pronounced influence on the policy discussion. When IDAs and asset-building by the poor were first proposed, it was common to hear that the poor cannot save and perhaps even should not save, but as the ADD data on average monthly saving were reported, these responses have become less common.

Regarding the account monitoring results, the reader should keep in mind that all IDA participants in ADD are self-selected and program-selected. All IDA savings reported are IDA savings alone and do not speak to potential shifting of assets. (These issues are better addressed in the experiment that is also part of ADD.) The data and analyses reported here enable us to ask a different but no less important question: what individual and program features are associated with IDA savings? This question is critical for the design of public policy as well as of savings services and products that aim to include low-income households.

Many individual and program features are included in the analyses. A two-step regression first estimates the model to sort out the savers from the "low savers"— those who have less than $100 net IDA savings (most of whom are close to zero) and who can be considered not very successful. The analysis then estimates the model for savers—those who have more than $100 net IDA savings (most having well above that figure) and who can be considered successful. This strategy is an oversimplification, but it allows us first to ask what is associated with IDA success and then to ask, among those who are successful, what is associated with savings outcomes.

Observed individual variables as a whole are surprisingly weak predictors. For example, education, employment, and welfare receipt have modest or no statistical ties to savings outcomes. Also, one of the most important findings in ADD is that income (both recurrent and intermittent) is at best weakly associated with savings outcomes. The poorest participants, controlling for other variables, did not have savings outcomes statistically different from those who were not as poor, and the poorest saved a higher proportion of their income. In theoretical terms, this finding suggests that something other than the observed individual characteristics may be leading to savings outcomes.

In contrast to individual variables, program variables are often statistically related to savings outcomes in ADD, and effect sizes are sometimes surprisingly large. Here we review only a few of the most important. The matching rate is positively associated with being a saver (one-to-one versus greater than two-to-one, $p < .05$), but among savers it is negatively associated with average monthly net deposits (AMND) (one-to-one versus two-to-one, $p < .01$). This suggests that the match rate may attract and keep people saving in the IDA program; once in the program, however, participants may find that higher matches substitute for their own effort in reaching asset accumulation goals, and therefore they may not save more in response to higher matches. In other words, the matching of savings may create complex influences on savings by IDA participants. These results are similar to savings patterns in 401(k) plans, where increases in matching rate also tend not to increase savings amounts.

The match cap (the amount of saving that can be matched each month) is not associated with being a saver, but among savers it is highly and strongly associated with AMND. This is among the most striking findings in the study. Increasing the match cap by $1.00 results in an additional $0.57 in AMND (p < .01), a very large effect.

The use of automatic deposits is positively associated with being a saver (p < .01), but among savers it is unrelated to AMND. The automatic feature, once in place, tends to keep people saving, but this "autopilot" feature does not promote higher savings amounts among the savers. Perhaps the explanation of both results is that participants are on autopilot and not cognitively engaged with the saving process.

Turning to general financial education (required of all IDA participants in ADD), one to ten hours is positively associated with AMND (p <.01), with no significant relationship after ten hours. Among savers, each hour of the first ten hours is associated with an increase of $1.16 in AMND. This is a very meaningful effect. Ten hours of financial education would generate $11.60 in additional savings per month, or $139 per year. If matched at two-to-one (typical in ADD), increased asset accumulation would be $418 per year, and over a period of four years, $1,670. For a low-income IDA participant who is saving for a home, this amount of money, combined with other IDA savings and homeownership assistance programs, can make a meaningful difference. (Indeed, we find that homeownership is the most common use of IDAs.) Above ten hours of financial education, however, we find no significant relationship with AMND. This suggests that the payoff in financial education may be in the first ten hours, which is very good to know for policy purposes because financial education is costly to deliver.[5]

In practical terms, these findings suggest that saving by the very poor should not be dismissed in public policy (Schreiner and Sherraden 2007). As we discuss later in the chapter, the findings on the relationships between IDA program characteristics and IDA savings outcomes are in many ways consistent with a growing body of evidence in behavioral economics. Before exploring these connections, let us turn to another quite productive research method in ADD, the in-depth interviews.

IN-DEPTH INTERVIEWS: WHAT IDA PARTICIPANTS SAY IS HAPPENING

Another key research method in ADD has been in-depth interviews with fifty-nine IDA participants and twenty-five controls drawn from the experiment. Although the subject matter for the in-depth interviews has covered a wide range of topics, one of the most fruitful areas to date has been close examination of how participants think about IDA accounts and saving in IDAs. In this section, we point to only a couple of noteworthy findings (for a thorough report on the in-depth interviews in ADD, see Sherraden, McBride, and Beverly, forthcoming).

First, a note on participants' conceptualization of short-term and long-term savings. Although mainstream economics assumes that savings and assets are fungible, it is clear that IDA participants have "mental accounts" with savings and that IDAs are often considered long-term, that is, not available for current consumption (Sherraden, McBride, Hanson, et al. 2005). While this may be true for some, it is also the case that many IDA participants made "unapproved withdrawals," presumably for short-term purposes, thus giving up the savings match at least until they returned the money to their IDA (Schreiner and Sherraden 2007). The financial pressure of living close to the margin makes it difficult for the poor to save, and IDA balances often have to be spent. This raises a key question: what types of saving product features would make it more likely for the poor to deposit, retain, and increase "long-term" savings if they had this category as a mental account? Would it be helpful (or harmful) if IDAs were to be in some way less accessible?

The second noteworthy finding has to do with participant responses to the IDA match cap. We know from in-depth interviews with IDA participants in ADD that in the minds of many participants the match cap is transformed into a target or goal that they are striving for (Sherraden, McBride, Johnson, et al. 2005). Given the statistical relationship of match caps and savings outcomes, this psychological phenomenon may have important implications for the design of savings products and services. For example, it raises the interesting possibility that a savings target with no match might in itself have a pronounced effect on savings. In another study, we are considering studying savings targets alone, without a match, to see whether there is a positive effect.

Third, turning to potential effects of the IDA, another key area of inquiry is future orientation. If there are "asset effects," it seems likely that they operate in part through envisioning a different future (Sherraden 1991). ADD respondents say that the IDA "creates goals and purpose." Participants can "see more clearly" and "visualize a future." The IDA, because it is for a particular purpose, also provides a "road map" and a "way to reach goals." With these changes in outlook, IDA participants say they are "more able to save," "look forward to saving," and "plan to save in the future" (Sherraden, McBride, Johnson, et al. 2005). These findings may support a cognitive approach to understanding asset effects; that is, it appears that asset-holding may change the way people think, which in turn may lead to still more asset-holding. Although we know little about these dynamics, they may be giving us an empirical glimpse of a "virtuous cycle" of asset-building and household development that operates in part through positive cognition about the future.

FROM PROGRAM FEATURES TO INSTITUTIONAL CONSTRUCTS

These findings can help to inform policy design. However, the program variables discussed here are particular to IDAs. In the larger picture, it would be inefficient to build a body of knowledge about saving based on program characteristics. Instead, the challenge is to seek constructs that are more general and more useful for knowledge-building *across a range of saving policies and financial products and services.* In this regard, we have sought to identify institutional constructs that may be related to savings outcomes. The term "institutional" as used here has a specific meaning: it refers to structures and conditions that can be purposefully designed and put in place, as in a savings plan policy or private-sector financial services.

At this stage, we offer eight constructs that we believe are important aspects of institutions designed to promote saving and asset accumulation: access, information, incentives, facilitation, expectations, restrictions, security, and simplicity. These eight constructs have emerged from research on IDAs and other savings programs (Beverly and Sherraden 1999; Clancy, Cramer, and Parrish 2005; Rutherford 2000; Schreiner and Morduch 2003; Schreiner and Sherraden 2007; Sherraden and Barr 2005; Sherraden, McBride, and Beverly, forthcoming; Sherraden, McBride, Hanson, et al. 2005; Sherraden, Schreiner, and Beverly 2003). For example, we understand match rate as an *incentive* (a financial inducement), match cap as an *expectation* (an identified target), automatic deposit as *facilitation* (being helped), and financial education as *information* (learning more about it).

This may not be exactly the right list of constructs, but this list may be a step in the direction of building a practical institutional theory of saving and evidence that can guide policy. To illustrate briefly from the IDA research results reported earlier, if the goal is increased saving by participants, we have considerable reason to believe that *expectations* (in the form of a match cap) provide greater policy leverage than *incentives* (in the form of a match rate). We have reason to believe that *information* (in the form of financial education) may plateau in its effects on savings outcomes. We have reason to believe that *facilitation* (in the form of direct deposit) keeps people saving, but not increasing their savings amount. These findings have direct implications for policy design.

A key point in this discussion is that *more than incentives are involved.*[6] Indeed, incentives in an economic sense may not be the most important factor in increasing saving. Expectations and information may matter more. In any saving policy or program, individuals are interacting with a complex pattern of institutional constructs that could be affecting outcomes. To take another example, *access* to a saving opportunity can be fundamental. If a 401(k) or similar retirement plan is not offered in the workplace, the odds of retirement saving are greatly reduced. For productive work in this area, knowledge should be built for multiple and sometimes interacting constructs that may be associated with savings outcomes.

Another way to think about this is that economics, in both neoclassical and behavioral versions, addresses individuals (or other units) and how individuals make choices. These choices are made in the context of "constraints," though constraints are seldom specified; there has been little knowledge development in economics about the nature of constraints. One way of understanding the institutional context of saving is as a *specification and testing of constraints* related to saving, for the purpose of building systematic knowledge that can inform policy design (Sherraden and Barr 2005).

LINKING WITH BEHAVIORAL ECONOMICS: GETTING THE INSTITUTIONS RIGHT

Traditional theories of saving have a mixed record in explaining saving behavior, especially among the poor.[7] Promising recent developments in behavioral economics suggest that people may not have perfect knowledge and are not always rational (see, for example, Choi et al. 2001, 2004; Madrian and Shea 2000; Maital and Maital 1994; Mullainathan and Shafir, this volume; Shefrin and Thaler 1988; Thaler 2000). Aiming for a theoretical approach that would be somewhat closer to the data on how people think and behave and would serve as a guide for public policy, the perspective in this study is institutional—that saving and asset accumulation may occur in large part because of explicit access, rules, information, assistance, restrictions, and subsidies—for example, as in a 401(k) plan. It seems likely to us that the poor are not very different from the nonpoor in this regard (see also the chapters by Scholz and Seshadri and by Mullainathan and Shafir, this volume). If people are not able to save, what they may lack is not only individual capacities and virtues but also institutional structures and conditions.

Several applied scholars in the United States have made important contributions to our understanding of the marketing, uptake, and use of savings and other financial services by the poor.[8] However, product and service innovations, no matter how well designed, are probably not sufficient. If saving and asset-building are to be inclusive, the overarching policy should have characteristics of a *savings plan,* such as a 401(k) or 403(b) plan, the Federal Thrift Savings Plan, or a college savings (529) plan. Such plans are in fact the way most Americans save for the long term. Savings plans (contractual savings) have important features that lend themselves to reaching a large portion of the population. These features may include centralized and efficient accounting, outreach and education, simple and low-cost investment options, low initial and ongoing deposit requirements, automatic deposits, and opportunities to establish "defaults" and other practices that increase participation and saving performance. These desirable practices may include automatic enrollment, a savings match, a match cap (the amount of savings that can be matched, which becomes a target), a default low-cost fund, and automatic increases in savings deposits with pay raises. Such plan features are practical expressions of institutional constructs for saving, as discussed earlier.

For instance, with the "auto 401(k)" (which is about *access*), there are large increases in participation when such plans go from an opt-in to an opt-out format. ("Opt-out" means that everyone is automatically put into the plan, but individuals can choose to get out.) For females, participation rose from 35 to 86 percent; for Hispanics, from 19 to 75 percent; and for those earning under $20,000 annually, from 13 to 80 percent (Beshears et al. 2006). Similarly, precommitment to saving more later (*restriction* of future choices) in the Save More Tomorrow (SMarT) program has led to substantial increases in contribution rates over time (Thaler and Benartzi 2004). Overall, 401(k) plan features can have large influences on savings outcomes.[9]

There may be potential in using college savings (529) plans as a platform for inclusion in asset-building, especially for children's savings accounts. To be sure, some state 529 plans have high fees and high investment costs, and such high-cost plans are undesirable. But some state 529 plans keep costs low, have very low deposit requirements, provide outreach to state residents, and match savings for the poorest savers. These state plans, or something like them, have the potential to be a platform for an inclusive child development account (Clancy, Cramer, and

Parrish 2005; Clancy, Orszag, and Sherraden 2004; Clancy and Sherraden 2003). It is encouraging that the overall trend in 529 plans, as they mature, appears to be toward offering simple choices with lower annual fees.

Ultimately, savings outcomes result from the interaction of individual and institutional characteristics. But the policy effort should lean toward creation of effective institutions for saving and, to a somewhat lesser extent, toward improving individuals so that they save more effectively. To take an example of highly institutional saving, most everyone on university faculties saves regularly and successfully in a TIAA-CREF retirement plan, and this has very little to do with individual behavior. Once we have signed up, it happens regularly and automatically month after month and year after year, regardless of what information we may know or how rationally or prudently we may think and behave. Those of us who enjoy these paternalistic and subsidized benefits, and who may even feel accomplished in our saving, should ask in our research programs whether the poor might also be able to save successfully under such conditions.

THE COST OF IDAS IN ADD: EXPENSIVE IN THE FORM DEMONSTRATED?

ADD has featured one of the most thorough cost assessments of a social demonstration. All identifiable costs, including the volunteer time of board members, are included (Schreiner 2002, 2006; Schreiner, Ng, and Sherraden 2006). The key finding is that IDA programs as implemented in the demonstration form of ADD are costly to operate. A thorough assessment of program costs (not counting matching funds) is $64 per participant per month. Arguably, this figure is distorted by the cost of demonstration research, the inefficiencies of starting something new, requirements for communication and policy involvement in a national demonstration, and other special circumstances (Sherraden 2000). Perhaps over time and with efficiencies of scale, the monthly cost of IDAs would decrease. Some IDA programs are reporting costs much less than this figure, though the research might not be as thorough.

How does the cost of IDAs compare to other similar programs? The cost is high compared to 401(k)s and similar financial plan products, which are under $10 per month. The cost is low compared to many intensive family service programs, which can reach $400 per month (Ng 2001). As another useful comparison, the administrative cost of the food stamps program, which operates "at scale" and with no financial education, has been assessed at $34 per household per month (Abt Associates 2002). Ultimately, whether the cost of IDAs is high or low depends on documented impacts of participation compared to costs. If the asset effects, both economic and social, turn out to be substantial, it could be that even $64 per month is a good public investment. We do not yet know.

It is useful to bear in mind that IDAs as proposed and demonstrated are more than matched savings and include a high level of staff involvement, especially in financial education. We have seen evidence that about ten hours of financial education is associated with positive saving performance in IDAs, but we do not know yet if this positive result is worth the policy investment. We also know that much of the high cost of IDAs lies in the fact that community agencies serve as de facto financial service providers by running MIS IDA and calculating the match, sending out statements, and so on. This is a dysfunctional aspect of the IDA demonstration format and should be avoided in an IDA policy at scale. We do not yet know if a more streamlined IDA format would have the same outcomes and impacts as the IDA format demonstrated in ADD.

The next phase of ADD research will include a cost-benefit analysis. Looking ahead, it seems unlikely that survey research could document benefits that could be monetized (and therefore included in the cost-benefit analysis) and would exceed the measured $64 per month. Perhaps asset effects do not even exist; if they do exist, the measurement challenges are great. Moreover, even if an IDA program at $64 per month were determined to be cost-beneficial, allocating public resources in these sums to tens of millions of people in an inclusive IDA policy might be politically unlikely.

CSD has published these IDA cost figures without hesitation, often to the consternation of our policy colleagues who work on Capitol Hill and in the states. So far, the cost figures do not seem to have impeded resource flows to IDAs. Apparently there is enough positive information and sentiment in favor of using public and private resources to create a "social market" that supports IDAs at current levels. But the resources supporting IDAs are not very great—in total not more than $2 billion per year from all sources—and a major increase is not on the immediate horizon.

In short, IDAs are probably too costly to be scalable in the form demonstrated, and CSD has been making this point for some time. The initial proposal for IDAs was for a large-scale, efficient public policy, not for the small, intensive, community-based applications in ADD and elsewhere. Especially, it is inefficient (and unwise) to have community-based organizations undertaking financial service functions; they are not trained for it, and the costs and risks are too great. The ideal direction is to create an overarching saving plan structure with centralized accounting, simple investment options, and low fees. Then community organizations can interact with this structure when interests and resources permit, but the core policy itself should not depend on community providers (Sherraden 2000).

IDA EXPERIMENT: IMPACTS ON HOMEOWNERSHIP, ASSETS, AND NET WORTH

For some policy scholars, only experimental impacts matter. Although we need not learn from experiments alone, we can all agree that a clear claim of impacts can only be made when there is a proper counterfactual. In this regard, ADD has featured an experiment at one program site in Tulsa, Oklahoma. ADD experimental data were collected using a longitudinal design where 1,103 participants were randomly assigned to a treatment or control group after they completed a baseline interview (wave 1). The treatment group participated in the IDA program, while the control group participants did not.[10] The experiment ran for four years (1998 to 2002), with the first follow-up interviews conducted at eighteen months (wave 2) and the second follow-up interview (wave 3) at the end of the program. Abt Associates was responsible for collecting data and reporting impacts for the first three waves of ADD. Here we discuss three key areas of experimental impacts: homeownership, assets and liabilities, and net worth (for further details, see Mills et al. 2004).

Regarding homeownership, to date experimental results from ADD indicate that, compared to a randomly assigned control group, IDA participants have increased their rate of homeownership from six to eleven percentage points, which would be a large impact in the context of national policy. The positive impact on homeownership appears to be stronger for African Americans, depending on how analyses are conducted (Mills et al. 2004, 2006, 2008). While encouraging, this may or may not turn out to be a positive result. If IDA participants in ADD keep their homes over time, this would be positive. But it is possible that the IDA merely rushed a few extra people into homeownership who would have purchased a house eventually even without the IDA (Mills et al. 2006). It is also possible that the subprime mortgage lending market that existed during the first waves of ADD enticed IDA participants into homeownership with undesirable mortgage loans; consequently, their homeownership might be at risk. Especially during this subprime period and its aftermath, it will be interesting to know whether the increased homeownership of the IDA group in ADD is sustained at a rate higher than that of controls. Regarding homeownership over time, wave 4 of ADD will contribute one more piece of useful information to this larger picture.

Increased asset holdings may lead to positive effects—economic, psychological, and social. This is the underlying rationale of IDAs and inclusive asset-building policy (Sherraden 1991). One way to think about this is that increased asset-holding represents a higher level of economic functioning and possibly a better quality of life. For example, an individual might own a home and have little net equity, yet she might enjoy the quality of the home and her residential stability. In terms of human capital, the experience of owning is probably a valuable learning experience, and in terms of psychological and social impacts, homeowning may be positive— certainly many people believe it to be so, including ADD participants. In this regard, one of the important results of ADD to date is its impacts on assets and liabilities. Gregory Mills and his colleagues (2004) find positive impacts on real assets overall (+$6,310, p < .10) and on real assets and total assets for blacks and those over age thirty-six, but also positive impacts on liabilities for these groups. (For IDA balances that are not yet matched—that is, that are still in the IDA account—matching funds are not included in these impact calculations.) Mills and his colleagues (2006) report a positive impact on home equity for black renters (+$4,073, p < .05), but also a negative impact on financial assets for this group (−$1,348, p < .10). Mills and his colleagues (2008) report a negative impact on financial assets for the IDA group (−$1,925, p < .05). These findings taken together are consistent with a view that IDA participants have shifted some of their financial assets into real assets in the form of homeownership. Although homeownership has been the traditional pathway to the American dream, whether this turns out to be so for IDA participants in ADD over the long run remains to be seen.[11]

Economists appropriately want to know whether a saving policy has an impact not just on saving but on net worth—although impact on net worth is not tested in most saving initiatives and policies. Prior to enactment, impact on net worth was not systematically assessed for 401(k)s and other asset-building policies that serve primarily the nonpoor. Existing experiments on saving (most of which are not in the United States but in developing countries) fail to test impact on net worth even in the short term, much less over a period of years. ADD provides one of the few experimental tests of the impact of a saving strategy on net worth over time.

What are the results? Mills and his colleagues (2004, 2006, 2008) find nonsignificant impacts (ranging from +$29 to +$1,339). One possible interpretation of this finding is that investment of IDA assets in a home, for example, might require the use of a participant's ADD savings to pay closing and moving costs, and over a short time horizon these costs might not be recovered by increased equity in the home. This might be even more the case with educational use of IDAs—money saved and then spent on education would have no short-term positive effect on net worth and indeed might reduce it (Mills et al. 2004, 2006). In the case of both homeownership and education, we might expect that net worth would be positively affected over time, though this remains to be seen. It is possible that a home purchase in a declining neighborhood or education from a marginal school leads to depleted rather than increased assets. Along these lines, a key question in ADD is whether IDAs might in fact push participants to make unwise asset purchases. We do not yet see evidence of this, but it could be happening and if so should become apparent at wave 4.

We should also consider whether out-of-range and extreme values in the ADD experimental data create large standard errors that make statistical relationships hard to find. For a large number of ADD respondents (all of whom are in low-income households), the measured value of a particular asset, and hence of net worth, implausibly changes by $100,000 or more over a relatively short period of time. Under these circumstances, one analysis strategy is to adjust or remove out-of-range or extreme data values. The Abt team did this in a "sensitivity analysis," but did not publish the results. In one of the Abt sensitivity analyses in which 3 percent of the most extreme net worth values were deleted (the top 1.5 percent and the bottom 1.5 percent) and out-of-range independent variable values were imputed to the mean, a positive impact on net worth (+$5,390, p < .01) was found. Thus, when out-of-range and extreme values are removed or imputed to the mean as described, a meaningful positive impact on net worth appears to emerge. Bill Gale at the Brookings Institution has undertaken numerous alternative regression specifications on these data (Mills et al., 2008) and does not find a pattern that would suggest an impact on net worth. In light of all this, the latest version of impact analyses concludes that the data do not permit a clear assessment of the impact on net worth in ADD at this time. Fortunately, wave 4 of ADD may help to sort out this important question going forward.

THE INFLUENCE OF IDAS AND THE ADD DEMONSTRATION

Since asset-building and IDAs were first proposed, there has been modest policy progress in the United States. Perhaps most noteworthy, nearly all states, influenced in part by the changed discussion of assets and public policy, have increased welfare asset limits. Regarding direct public resource allocation, IDAs were included as a state option in the 1996 Personal Responsibility and Work Opportunity Reconciliation Act (PRWORA). The Assets for Independence Act, the first public IDA demonstration, became law in 1998. Other bills to extend IDAs are regularly before the U.S. Congress (Boshara 2003; Cramer, Parrish, and Boshara 2005), and more than forty U.S. states have adopted some type of IDA policy (Edwards and Mason 2003). All of this signals a change in thinking, though not yet a major change in policy. Most IDA programs in the United States are in a demonstration mode and very small.

Perhaps the most important change to date is that saving and asset accumulation by the poor, which was seldom discussed fifteen years ago, is today almost a mainstream idea in the United States, and political support is bipartisan. Both Republicans and Democrats use the language of "asset-building," "asset-based policy," "stakeholding," and "the ownership society." The policy environment is buzzing with variations on this theme, and the contribution of IDAs is the idea that the poor should be included.

Research in ADD has been important for policy development in IDAs and similar matched saving policy on both the state and federal level in the United States (Sherraden 2001). IDA research results from CSD contributed to President Bill Clinton's 1999 proposal for universal savings accounts and his 2000 proposal for retirement savings accounts (Clinton 1999, 2000).[12] Beyond the United States, research on IDAs has considerably influenced asset-based policy developments, including the Saving Gateway and the Child Trust Fund in the United Kingdom (HM Treasury 2001, 2003; Kelly and Lissauer 2000; Kempson, McKay, and Collard 2003, 2005; Paxton 2003; Sherraden 2002),[13] family development accounts in Taipei (Cheng 2003), IDAs and the Learn$ave demonstration in Canada (Kingwell et al. 2004; Leckie, Dowie, and Gyorfi-Dyke 2008), and asset-building programs for the poor in Australia, Uganda, Peru, China, Korea, Hungary, and elsewhere.[14]

IDA and other matched savings policies, services, and products continue to develop in the United States. Examples are very common and part of a widespread discussion. To take some recent examples, Federal Deposit Insurance Corporation (FDIC) chairman Sheila C. Bair suggests that "IDAs are a relatively low-risk way for banks to introduce underbanked individuals to the financial mainstream. IDAs can help people of modest means build assets and can help banks tap into new markets" (Federal Deposit Insurance Corporation 2007). In the 2008 presidential campaigns, Hillary Clinton and John Edwards proposed matching savings in 401(k) plans of middle- and low-income workers. In addition, the United Way of America has announced a $1.5 billion initiative on family financial stability that includes IDAs and savings.

THE NEXT STEP: WAVE 4 OF THE ADD EXPERIMENT

Wave 4 of ADD is an assessment of the long-term impact of participation in an IDA program for low-income individuals.[15] The investigation is conducting follow-up interviews with both the experimental and control groups who participated in ADD between 1998 and 2002. Wave 4 of ADD is guided by four research questions: What effects do IDAs have on long-term asset-building and net worth? What percentage of IDA graduates who used their savings to invest in an asset have been able to maintain and sustain that asset? What factors are associated with the ability of these low-income households to maintain their assets? And what are the long-term social, psychological, economic, and health effects of IDAs and asset-holding for low-income families? Wave 4 is particularly important because, at the time of the wave 3 interviews, many ADD participants either had not yet invested their IDA savings in a home, education, or business or had only recently done so.

Wave 4 is being conducted approximately eighty-four months after initial enrollment in the IDA program. For treatment group participants, wave 4 interviews take place at least three years after graduating from the program and purchasing assets. Collecting these additional data enables us to test crucial questions about the long-term effects of IDAs and asset accumulation for low-income households by building on the advantage of the original randomized experimental design. Dependent variables include measures of asset ownership, such as homeownership or home improvement, business ownership, education advancement, retirement savings, and net worth. Additional measures related to housing include housing tenure, stress related to housing payments, trends of deferred maintenance, home equity and its uses, and incidence of mortgage default.

To date, research on IDAs has focused on the more immediate performance and outcomes for IDA participants during the program. As a result, we know very little about long-term effects of IDAs. Following IDA graduates beyond program graduation will inform not only the research knowledge base but also the broader field of asset-building and social policy. There is a need for long-term studies that use experimental designs (Scanlon and Page-Adams 2001). In addition, since asset-building is a relatively new field, few studies include measures to test asset effects. Will Paxton (2003) offers a persuasive argument that, because of the possible temporal nature of asset effects, a longitudinal approach should be used to study their influence.

ANOTHER NEXT STEP: TESTING
CHILD DEVELOPMENT ACCOUNTS

Asset-building policy makes the most sense across a lifetime, beginning with children.[16] In this regard, the visionary and bipartisan ASPIRE (America Saving for Personal Investment Retirement and Education) Act, which would create a savings account for every newborn in the United States, has been introduced in Congress since 2004.[17]

As previously mentioned, a serious discussion of asset-based policy began in the United Kingdom in 2000 (Blunkett 2000; Kelly and Lissauer 2000; Nissan and LeGrand 2000). In a major policy development in April 2001, Prime Minister Tony Blair proposed the Child Trust Fund for all children in the United Kingdom, with progressive funding, and two years later, in April 2003, Blair announced that he would go forward with the Child Trust Fund. Beginning in April 2005, each new-born child in the United Kingdom has been given an account, retrospective to children born since September 2002 (Blair 2001). The children receive an initial deposit of at least £250, and children in the bottom third of family income receive £500. Additional government deposits are not yet specified. In addition to the United Kingdom, other countries are expanding or adopting CDAs (Loke and Sherraden 2007). Currently, Yunju Nam of CSD is working on CDAs with the government of South Korea, where the plan is to provide coverage for the bottom half of the population by 2010 (Nam 2007; Sherraden 2006). In the United States, universal and progressive accounts for all children at birth have been proposed for some time (Boshara and Sherraden 2003; Cramer 2004; Goldberg 2005; Lindsey 1994; Sherraden 1991). Policy discussion on children's accounts is bipartisan and active (Boshara, Cramer, and Parrish 2005; Cramer, O'Brien, and Boshara 2007; New America Foundation 2006).

Children's development accounts may be a promising pathway to inclusive asset-building in the United States. The United States is one of the few economically advanced nations without a children's allowance (monthly cash payment to all families with children); the average children's allowance in western Europe is 1.8 percent of GDP. The United States is unlikely, for ideological and political reasons, to adopt a children's allowance, but a CDA is ideologically and politically much more likely. Even 0.1 percent of U.S. GDP would be enough to open an account for every newborn with $3,000 (see Curley and Sherraden 2000).

What do we know about the effects of CDAs? In-depth study of first- and second-graders in applied research in a CDA program finds that young children engage in saving behavior for the long-term goal of college education (Sherraden et al. 2007). Based on this study, there is empirical evidence that young children can articulate that the purpose of their saving is for college (Elliott and Sherraden 2007) and that this ability is associated with their aspirations and expectations (Elliott 2007).

Studies using the Panel Study of Income Dynamics (PSID) to look at the impact of wealth on child developmental outcomes find that, controlling for many other factors, parental wealth is positively associated with the cognitive development, physical health, and socioemotional behavior of children (Shanks 2007; Williams 2003). Using the PSID Child Development Supplement to look at three- to twelve-year-olds, these studies find that household wealth is associated with improved math outcomes and reduced problem behaviors. These results support the proposition that assets lead to better well-being for offspring—in this case, above and beyond economic well-being. The study finds these effects even among very income-poor families, and in fact wealth seems to be a better predictor of well-being as children grow older. A study using the National Survey of Families and Households (NSFH) finds that asset accumulation in low-income, single-parent families is associated with higher educational expectations on the part of the mother and, later, with higher educational achievement of the children (Zhan and Sherraden 2003). In this research, when assets are included in regression models, the effects of income become nonsignificant, indicating that those studies that predict the social outcomes of economic conditions but do not include assets—as is true of the vast majority of them—may be underspecified.

Amy Orr (2003), using the National Longitudinal Survey of Youth (NLSY), looks at the influence of household wealth on math achievement scores and finds significant positive results. Orr's interpretation is that wealth may influence "cultural capital" (being culturally appropriate in the Bourdieu sense), which tends to enhance academic achievement over time. She suggests that household wealth may explain a good portion of the black-white achievement gap. From a somewhat different perspective, Thomas Shapiro (2004), relying on in-depth interview research, documents that many parents use wealth, sometimes even modest amounts, to create "transformative" opportunities for their children—for example, moving to a better school district. Consistent with this, Dalton Conley (1999) uses the PSID to look at the influence of childhood household wealth on adult outcomes. He finds that parental wealth in childhood helps to predict both high school graduation and college graduation. The effects of wealth are stronger than the effects of income. In sum, wealth appears to influence both the outlook and the behaviors of parents regarding their children's education, from early education to all subsequent education.

A growing body of evidence indicates that early childhood education may be among the best investments in long-term development.[18] CDAs would not provide early childhood education but rather create assets for education, which we hypothesize would change how parents think about and engage with their children's early development. Whether these hypotheses will be supported by the evidence we cannot say at this time. If so, then early asset accumulation might take its place alongside early childhood education as a policy tool for educational development.

In applied research, the Ford Foundation and several other foundations are supporting a large demonstration of CDAs in the form of the SEED (Saving for Education, Entrepreneurship, and Downpayment) initiative. The goal of SEED is to model, test, and inform a universal and progressive CDA policy for the United States. SEED is a demonstration and research partnership of CFED,[19] CSD, the School of Social Welfare at the University of Kansas, the New America Foundation, the Research Triangle Institute, the Institute for Financial Security of the Aspen Institute, and others. The goal of SEED is to model, test, and inform a universal CDA policy for the United States.[20] SEED has several components, including SEED accounts at twelve community-based sites, tracking of savings transactions and performance, a survey of parents, a quasi-experiment, a true experiment, and in-depth interviews. In addition to research, SEED includes work in state policy, federal policy, market development, and communications.

Interest in a universal, progressive CDA has been long-standing at CSD, going back to the original proposal for IDAs. SEED for Oklahoma Kids, or SEED OK, is a large experiment to test this important idea. It may be important to emphasize three points: First, this study is about the long-term investment in and development of children; it is not about short-term amelioration of income poverty. Second, we anticipate meaningful positive outcomes within the seven-year horizon of this study in addition to longer-range outcomes beyond the seven-year period. Third, this is a true experiment in a population without any selection in the initial sample. Experiments in a population are uncommon, and this project will therefore be of considerable interest to policy scholars; furthermore, research results will directly inform the potential of a universal policy of CDAs in the United States.

By the end of seven years, we hypothesize, SEED OK savings will have positive impacts on parental attitudes and behaviors related to education, on the cognitive and educational development of children, and, within the seven-year window of the study, on children's educational achievement. There will be some key impacts to test: savings for children's education; total household savings; other household assets, liabilities, and net worth; parents' financial knowledge; children's financial knowledge; parents' aspirations for their children; children's aspirations, especially for education; children's cognitive development; children's socioemotional development; and children's preschool and early school performance.

The SEED OK experiment, in a competitive RFP (request for proposal) process, selected the state of Oklahoma as the research site because of a very good state college savings (529) plan, which is the policy vehicle for SEED OK; large subpopulations of African Americans, Hispanics, and Native Americans; and dedicated interest from the state treasurer and other Oklahoma state officials. In late 2007 and early 2008, 1,350 randomly selected SEED participants received $1,000 shortly after birth, with an additional $1,000 available in matching funds. Families are now being encouraged to make additional deposits. The same number of randomly selected controls receive no treatment but are free to enroll in the state 529 plan as they choose. At this writing, the baseline SEED OK survey data are collected. The plan is to follow the respondents for seven years, but other researchers may follow later. Ideally, researchers will resurvey this group when they are older, perhaps at age twelve, eighteen, and twenty-four. With quality data collection at wave 1, SEED OK will be set up as a long-term public good yielding useful knowledge over time. This is the beauty of a social experiment.

CONCLUSIONS

This body of work is in the early stages of development. A new policy direction—in this case, asset-building by the poor—requires many years to articulate, design, implement, study, and, as the evidence warrants, change policy in a meaningful way. Based on IDA research thus far, there is reason to believe that the poor can save if they are embedded in institutional conditions that promote saving. Incentives may not be as important as several other institutional constructs, especially access, facilitation, and expectations. In this regard, the body of IDA research findings is consistent with a number of research results from behavioral economics.

Overall, there is reason to be cautiously optimistic about long-term savings out-comes and the impacts of IDAs and similar saving strategies that include the poor. But administrative costs are high, and it will be necessary to create lower-cost versions if asset-building policy is to include tens of millions of low-income, low-asset households. A key implication is to use a centralized provider for all of the financial services, like 401(k) plans, 529 plans, or other savings plan structures, rather than community-based organizations. Community organizations can then add value through financial education and other supports where funding is available to do so.

As a policy strategy, it is challenging to suggest a new policy instrument such as IDAs. On the plus side, the IDA proposal has served the very positive purposes of defining a discussion of saving and asset-building by the poor and achieving focus and clarity in research. The resulting body of knowledge and accompanying policy discussion have put asset-building by the poor "on the table" for policy consideration. This might not have happened without IDAs.

On the minus side, defining, testing, and implementing a new policy is an uphill endeavor, especially in the American constitutional system of governance. Passing laws is very difficult, as the founding fathers intended. So IDAs have been legislated as a demonstration, and this can take on its own reality. IDAs are now understood in the public mind in their demonstration mode—as short-term savings programs targeted to the poor, operating out of community-based organizations. An entire "field" now exists to support IDAs in this mode, and it seems likely that IDAs will continue to play a meaningful role in many community-based projects. This is by and large a positive outcome, even if not the one originally intended.

In thinking about an inclusive, asset-based policy, however, a different tack will be necessary. Going forward, it may be wiser to build on a large and existing asset-based policy and extend it to the poor. For example, one approach would be to take steps toward a more inclusive 401(k) plan or a more inclusive college saving (529) plan. Regarding the latter, a universal 529 plan in the United States might one day include all newborns, like the United Kingdom's Child Trust Fund. With this potential in mind, current research being conducted by CSD and our partners in SEED builds on 529s as a promising structure for a universal CDA in the United States.

In the larger picture, it seems likely that asset-building will continue to play an expanding role in social policy in the United States and many other countries. For those concerned about the poor, it is unwise to ignore this trend. IDAs have served the purpose of articulating and providing a beginning body of evidence that the poor can be successfully included in this policy direction. Research on access to financial services and building the assets of the poor is likely to continue. This research will be all the more useful as scholars from different disciplines, with different research questions and methods, contribute evidence and understanding to inform policy development. In this regard, the authors in this volume provide the best current thinking and research.

This chapter was supported by the Ford, Charles Stewart Mott, and F. B. Heron Foundations, and indirectly by many public and private funders of IDA programs and research. The author is indebted to CFED for implementing a large IDA demonstration; to IDA program staff around the country, IDA participants, and all research respondents, especially experimental controls who have not participated in IDAs but nevertheless have helped to build knowledge; and to numerous research partners and the research team at the Center for Social Development at Washington University in St. Louis. This report has benefited from suggestions from Michael Barr and Rebecca Blank; from the contributions of participants at the preseminar and conference on "Access, Assets, and Poverty"; and from comments by Mark Schreiner, Margaret Sherraden, and two anonymous reviewers.

NOTES

1. For details on the current state of knowledge on asset-building, measurement, and outcomes, see McKernan and Sherraden (2008).
2. The ADD project was organized and implemented by CFED in Washington. The Center for Social Development (CSD) at Washington University designed the research. Abt Associates undertook data collection and reported on impacts for the experiment. ADD has been funded by twelve private foundations: Ford Foundation, Charles Stewart Mott Foundation, Joyce Foundation, Citigroup Foundation, Fannie Mae Foundation, Ewing Marion Kauffman Foundation, John D. and Catherine T. MacArthur Foundation, Levi Strauss Foundation, Rockefeller Foundation, Moriah Fund, and MetLife Foundation.
3. The members of the ADD Evaluation Advisory Committee are Margaret Clark, Claudia Coulton, Katherine Edin, John Else, Robert Friedman, Irving Garfinkel, Karen Holden, Lawrence Kotlikoff, Robert Plotnick, Salome Raheim, Marguerite Robinson, Clemente Ruiz, and Thomas Shapiro.
4. The ADD project, account monitoring data, and research results are described in considerable detail in Schreiner and Sherraden (2007).
5. This discussion of account monitoring research borrows from a more extensive presentation in Sherraden and Boshara (forthcoming), with statistical results from the analyses in Schreiner and Sherraden (2007).
6. Regarding incentives and savings pertinent to this discussion, see also Engen, Gale, and Scholz (1996) and Hubbard and Skinner (1996).
7. The traditional neoclassical models focus on preferences for consumption over time; see especially Friedman (1957) and Modigliani and Brumberg (1954). Overviews of savings theories and evidence are presented in Korczyk (1998), Beverly and Sherraden (1999), and Carney and Gale (2001).
8. See especially the contributions of John Caskey (1994, 2005), Michael Barr (2004), and several key chapters in this volume, especially the survey research by Barr,

and the marketing research of Tufano and Schneider. Saving by the poor has been studied in greater detail in developing countries; a classic example is Rutherford (2000).

9. For further discussion of the effects of 401(k)s on savings outcomes, see Joulfaian and Richardson (2001).

10. The ADD experiment, like all experiments in the field, encountered deviations from purity. Because housing programs were integrated with IDAs at CAPTC (the organizational provider), the control group did have access to homeownership counseling but was not to have access to the home buyer assistance program (though thirty participants reported that they did so anyway). Controls could participate in any other home buyer programs in Tulsa or elsewhere. Also, controls agreed not to participate in IDAs or matched savings, but four reported that they did so at locations other than CAPTC. While these deviations are not ideal, this is the reality of experiments outside the lab. Because the deviations are recorded, appropriate adjustments could be made in the analyses.

11. Another IDA experiment has taken place in Canada's Learn$ave program (see Leckie, Dowie, and Gyorfi-Dyke 2008). The major findings related to assets are increased bank savings and liquid assets. The researchers do not find evidence of shifted assets or borrowing.

12. CSD provided IDA data to the White House prior to these speeches by the president.

13. The Labor Party's Saving Gateway is based on IDAs in the United States, and ADD research informed the Offices of the Prime Minister and the Chancellor of the Exchequer on the Child Trust Fund.

14. In each of these cases, there has been reference to IDA research in the United States and advising by CSD.

15. The research partnership for wave 4 of ADD consists of the University of North Carolina, the Research Triangle Institute, the Brookings Institution, and CSD.

16. Discussions of child development accounts (CDAs) in the United States go back at least to the George H. W. Bush administration. Fred Goldberg (2005) was a proponent of CDAs in the first Bush administration, and at the request of the Bush White House, Michael Sherraden outlined a plan for a CDA with an initial deposit of $1,000 for all children in the United States.

17. An important background paper for what became the ASPIRE Act was written by Reid Cramer (2004). Ray Boshara and his team at the Asset Building Program at the New America Foundation have been very instrumental in organizing the introduction of the ASPIRE Act.

18. Steven Barnett (1995) reviews thirty-six studies of early childhood programs and finds evidence of long-term improvements in grade retention.

19. CFED is the official name of the organization formerly known as Corporation for Enterprise Development.

20. At CSD, we are especially grateful to the Ford, Charles Stewart Mott, F. B. Heron, MetLife, and Lumina Foundations for funding research on SEED, CDAs, 529s, and related topics so that we can learn as much as possible from the SEED demonstration and other research that may inform a future policy of CDAs.

REFERENCES

Abt Associates. 2002. *Food Stamp Program Costs.* Cambridge, Mass.: Abt Associates.

Barnett, Steven. 1995. "Long-Term Effects of Early Childhood Programs on Cognitive and School Outcomes." *The Future of Children* 5(3): 25–50.

Barr, Michael S. 2004. "Banking the Poor." *Yale Journal on Regulation* 21(1): 121–237.

Beshears, John, James Choi, David Laibson, and Brigitte Madrian. 2006. "The Importance of Default Options for Retirement Savings Outcomes: Evidence from the United States." Working paper 12009. Cambridge, Mass.: National Bureau of Economic Research.

Beverly, Sondra, and Michael Sherraden. 1999. "Institutional Determinants of Saving: Implications for Low-Income Households and Public Policy." *Journal of Socioeconomics* 28: 457–73.

Blair, Tony. 2001. "Savings and Assets for All" (speech). London: 10 Downing Street (April 26).

Blunkett, David. 2000. "On Your Side: The New Welfare State as an Engine of Prosperity" (speech). London: Department of Education and Employment (June 7).

Boshara, Ray. 2003. "Federal Policy and Asset Building." *Social Development Issues* 25(1–2): 130–41.

Boshara, Ray, Reid Cramer, and Leslie Parrish. 2005. *Policy Options for Achieving an Ownership Society for All Americans.* Issue brief 8. Washington, D.C.: New America Foundation.

Boshara, Ray, and Michael Sherraden. 2003. "For Every Child, a Stake in America." *New York Times,* July 23.

Caner, Asena, and Edward Wolff. 2004. "Asset Poverty in the United States: Its Persistence in an Expansionary Economy." Policy brief 76. Annandale-on-Hudson, N.Y.: Bard College, Jerome Levy Economics Institute.

Carney, Stacie, and William Gale. 2001. "Asset Accumulation Among Low-Income Households." In *Assets for the Poor: The Benefits of Spreading Asset Ownership,* edited by Thomas Shapiro and Edward Wolff. New York: Russell Sage Foundation.

Caskey, John. 1994. *Fringe Banking: Check-Cashing Outlets, Pawnshops, and the Poor.* New York: Russell Sage Foundation.

———. 2005. "Reaching Out to the Unbanked." In *Inclusion in the American Dream: Assets, Poverty, and Public Policy,* edited by Michael Sherraden. New York: Oxford University Press.

Cheng, Li-Chen. 2003. "Developing Family Development Accounts in Taipei: Policy Innovation from Income to Assets." *Social Development Issues* 25(1–2): 106–17.

Choi, James, David Laibson, Brigitte C. Madrian, and Andrew Metrick. 2001. "For Better or for Worse: Default Effects and 401(k) Savings Behavior." Working paper 8651. Cambridge, Mass.: National Bureau of Economic Research.

———. 2004. "Defined Contribution Pensions: Plan Rules, Participant Decisions, and the Path of Least Resistance." In *Tax Policy and the Economy,* edited by James M. Poterba. Cambridge, Mass.: MIT Press.

Clancy, Margaret, Reid Cramer, and Leslie Parrish. 2005. *Section 529 Savings Plans, Access to Postsecondary Education, and Universal Asset Building.* Washington, D.C.: New American Foundation.

Clancy, Margaret, Peter Orszag, and Michael Sherraden. 2004. *College Savings Plans: A Platform for Inclusive Savings Policy?* St. Louis: Washington University, Center for Social Development.

Clancy, Margaret, and Michael Sherraden. 2003. *The Potential for Inclusion in 529 Savings Plans: Report of a Survey of States.* St. Louis: Washington University, Center for Social Development.

Clinton, William Jefferson. 1999. "State of the Union Address." Washington: U.S. Executive Office of the President.

———. 2000. "State of the Union Address." Washington: U.S. Executive Office of the President.

Conley, Dalton. 1999. *Being Black, Living in the Red: Race, Wealth, and Social Policy in America.* Berkeley: University of California Press.

Corporation for Enterprise Development. 2004. *Hidden in Plain Sight: A Look at the $335 Billion Federal Asset-Building Budget.* Washington, D.C.: Corporation for Enterprise Development.

Cramer, Reid. 2004. *Accounts at Birth: Creating a National System of Savings and Asset Building with Children's Development Accounts.* Washington, D.C.: New America Foundation.

Cramer, Reid, Rourke O'Brien, and Ray Boshara. 2007. *The Assets Report 2007: A Review, Assessment, and Forecast of Federal Assets Policy.* Washington, D.C.: New America Foundation.

Cramer, Reid, Leslie Parrish, and Ray Boshara. 2005. *Federal Assets Policy Report and Outlook.* Washington, D.C.: New America Foundation.

Curley, Jami, and Michael Sherraden. 2000. "Policy Lessons from Children's Allowances for Children's Development Accounts." *Child Welfare* 79(6): 661–87.

Edwards, Karen, and Lisa Marie Mason. 2003. "State Policy Trends for Individual Development Accounts in the United States, 1993–2003." *Social Development Issues* 25(1–2): 118–29.

Elliott, William. 2007. "Examining Minority and Poor Youth's College Aspirations and Expectations: The Potential Role of College Savings." Working paper 07-07. St. Louis: Washington University, Center for Social Development.

Elliott, William, and Margaret S. Sherraden. 2007. "College Expectations Among Young Children: The Potential Role of Savings." Working paper 07-06. St. Louis: Washington University, Center for Social Development.

Engen, Eric, William Gale, and John Karl Scholz. 1996. "The Illusory Effects of Saving Incentives on Saving." *Journal of Economic Perspectives* 10(4): 113–38.

Federal Deposit Insurance Corporation (FDIC). 2007. "IDAs and Banks: A Solid Match." *FDIC Quarterly* (June).

Friedman, Milton. 1957. *A Theory of the Consumption Function.* National Bureau of Economic Research General Series 63. Princeton, N.J.: Princeton University Press.

Goldberg, Fred. 2005. "The Universal Piggy Bank: Designing and Implementing a System of Universal Accounts for Children." In *Inclusion in the American Dream: Assets, Poverty, and Public Policy,* edited by Michael Sherraden. New York: Oxford University Press.

HM Treasury. 2001. "Saving and Assets for All: The Modernization of Britain's Tax and Benefit System." No. 8. London: HM Treasury.

———. 2003. "Details of the Child Trust Fund." London: HM Treasury.

Howard, Christopher. 1997. *The Hidden Welfare State: Tax Expenditures and Social Policy in the United States.* Princeton, N.J.: Princeton University Press.

Hubbard, Robert, and Jonathan Skinner. 1996. "Assessing the Effectiveness of Saving Incentives." *Journal of Economic Perspectives* 10(4): 73–90.

Johnson, Elizabeth, James Hinterlong, and Michael Sherraden. 2001. "Strategies for Creating MIS Technology to Improve Social Work Practice and Research." *Journal of Technology for Human Services* 18(3–4): 5–22.

Joulfaian, David, and David Richardson. 2001. "Who Takes Advantage of Tax-Deferred Savings Programs? Evidence from Federal Income Tax Data." *National Tax Journal* 54(3): 669–88.

Kelly, Gavin, and Rachel Lissauer. 2000. *Ownership for All.* London: Institute for Public Policy Research.

Kempson, Elaine, Stephen McKay, and Sharon Collard. 2003. *Evaluation of the CFLI and Saving Gateway Pilot Projects.* Bristol, U.K.: University of Bristol, Personal Finance Research Centre.

———. 2005. *Incentives to Save: Encouraging Saving Among Low-Income Households.* Bristol, U.K.: University of Bristol, Personal Finance Research Centre.

Kingwell, Paul, Michael Dowie, Barbara Holler, and Liza Jimenez. 2004. *Helping People Help Themselves: An Early Look at Learn$ave.* Ottawa: Social Research and Demonstration Corporation.

Kochhar, Rakesh. 2004. *The Wealth of Hispanic Households.* Washington, D.C.: Pew Hispanic Center.

Korczyk, Sophie. 1998. *How Americans Save.* Washington, D.C.: American Association of Retired Persons (AARP).

Leckie, Norm, Michael Dowie, and Chad Gyorfi-Dyke. 2008. *Learning to Save, Saving to Learn: Early Impacts of the Learn$ave Individual Development Account Demonstration.* Ottawa: Social Research and Demonstration Corporation.

Lindsey, Duncan. 1994. *The Welfare of Children.* New York: Oxford University Press.

Loke, Vernon, and Michael Sherraden. 2007. "Building Assets from Birth: A Comparison of Policies and Proposals on Children's Development Accounts in Singapore, the United Kingdom, Canada, Korea, and the United States." Working paper 06-14. St. Louis: Washington University, Center for Social Development.

Lui, Meizhu, Barbara Robles, Betsy Leondar-Wright, Rose Brewer, and Rebecca Adamson. 2006. *The Color of Wealth: The Story Behind the U.S. Racial Wealth Divide.* New York: New Press.

Madrian, Brigitte C., and Dennis F. Shea. 2000. "The Power of Suggestion: Inertia in 401(k) Participation and Savings Behavior." Working paper 7682. Cambridge, Mass.: National Bureau of Economic Research.

Maital, Shlomo, and Sharon L. Maital. 1994. "Is the Future What It Used to Be? A Behavioral Theory of the Decline of Saving in the West." *Journal of Socio-Economics* 23(1–2): 1–32.

McKernan, Signe-Mary, and Michael Sherraden, eds. 2008. *Assets and Low-Income Families.* Washington, D.C.: Urban Institute Press.

Midgley, James. 1999. "Growth, Redistribution, and Welfare: Towards Social Investment." *Social Service Review* 77(1): 3–21.

Mills, Gregory, William G. Gale, Rhiannon Patterson, and Emil Apostolov. 2006. "What Do Individual Development Accounts Do? Evidence from a Controlled Experiment." Working paper. Washington, D.C.: Brookings Institution.

Mills, Gregory, William G. Gale, Rhiannon Patterson, Gary V. Englehardt, Michael D. Eriksen, and Emil Apostolov. 2008. "Effects of Individual Development Accounts on Asset Purchases and Saving Behavior: Evidence from a Controlled Experiment." *Journal of Public Economics* 92(5–6): 1509–1530.

Mills, Gregory, Rhiannon Patterson, Larry Orr, and Donna DeMarco. 2004. *Evaluation of the American Dream Demonstration.* Final evaluation report. Cambridge, Mass.: Abt Associates.

Mishel, Lawrence, Jared Bernstein, and Sylvia Allegretto. 2007. *The State of Working America.* Washington, D.C.: Economic Policy Institute.

Modigliani, Franco, and Richard Brumberg. 1954. "Utility Analysis and the Consumption Function: An Interpretation of Cross-Section Data." In *Post-Keynesian Economics,* edited by K. Kenneth Kurihara. New Brunswick, N.J.: Rutgers University Press.

Morillas, Juan Rafael. 2007. "Assets, Earnings Mobility, and the Black-White Gap." *Social Science Research* 36(2): 808–33.

Nam, Yunju 2007. "Child Development Accounts in Korea." Invited presentation at the conference on "Saving, Assets, and Financial Inclusion," sponsored by Citi Foundation and others. Singapore (June 27–29).

Nembhard, Jessica G., and Ngina Chiteji, eds. 2006. *Wealth Accumulation and Communities of Color in the United States: Current Issues.* Ann Arbor: University of Michigan Press.

New America Foundation. 2006. *Savings Accounts for Kids: Current Federal Proposals.* Washington, D.C.: New America Foundation.

Ng, G. Tin. 2001. "Costs of IDAs and Other Capital Development Programs." Working paper 01-08. St. Louis: Washington University, Center for Social Development.

Nissan, David, and Julian LeGrand. 2000. "A Capital Idea: Start-Up Grants for Young People." Policy report 49. London: Fabian Society.

Oliver, Melvin, and Thomas Shapiro. 2006. *Black Wealth/White Wealth.* 2d ed. New York: Routledge.

Orr, Amy. 2003. "Black-White Differences in Achievement: The Importance of Wealth." *Sociology of Education* 76(4): 281–304.

Paxton, Will, ed. 2003. *Equal Shares? Building a Progressive and Coherent Asset-Based Welfare Policy.* London: Institute for Public Policy Research.

Rutherford, Stuart. 2000. *The Poor and Their Money.* Delhi: Oxford University Press.

Scanlon, Edward, and Deborah Page-Adams. 2001. "Effects of Asset Holding on Neighborhoods, Families, and Children." In *Building Assets,* edited by Ray Boshara. Washington, D.C.: Corporation for Enterprise Development.

Schreiner, Mark. 2002. "What Do IDA Programs Cost? The First Three Years at CAPTC." Research report. St. Louis: Washington University, Center for Social Development.

———. 2006. "Program Costs for Individual Development Accounts: Final Figures from CAPTC in Tulsa." *Savings and Development* 30(3): 247–74.

Schreiner, Mark, and Jonathan Morduch, eds. 2003. *Replicating Micro Finance in the United States.* Washington, D.C.: Woodrow Wilson Center Press.

Schreiner, Mark, Guat Tin Ng, and Michael Sherraden. 2006. "Cost Effectiveness in Social Work Practice: A Framework with Application to Individual Development Accounts." *Research on Social Work Practice* 16(1): 28–37.

Schreiner, Mark, and Michael Sherraden. 2007. *Can the Poor Save? Savings and Asset Building in Individual Development Accounts.* New Brunswick, N.J.: Transaction Publishers.

Seidman, Laurence. 2001. "Assets and the Tax Code." In *Assets for the Poor: Benefits and Mechanisms of Spreading Asset Ownership,* edited by Thomas Shapiro and Edward Wolff. New York: Russell Sage Foundation.

Sen, Amartya. 1993. "Capability and Well-Being." In *The Quality of Life,* edited by Martha Nussbaum and Amartya Sen. Oxford: Clarendon Press.

———. 1999. *Development As Freedom.* New York: Knopf.

Shanks, Trina R. 2007. "The Impacts of Household Wealth on Child Development." *Journal of Poverty* 11(2): 93–116.

Shapiro, Thomas. 2004. *The Hidden Cost of Being African American: How Wealth Perpetuates Inequality.* New York: Oxford University Press.

Shefrin, Hersh M., and Richard H. Thaler. 1988. "The Behavioral Life-Cycle Hypothesis." *Economic Inquiry* 26(4): 609–43.

Sherraden, Margaret S., Elizabeth Johnson, William Elliott, Shirley Porterfield, and William Rainford. 2007. "The I Can Save Program: School-Based Children's Saving Accounts for College." *Children and Youth Services Review* 29(3): 294–312.

Sherraden, Margaret S., Amanda M. McBride, and Sondra Beverly. Forthcoming. *Striving to Save.* Ann Arbor: University of Michigan Press.

Sherraden, Margaret S., Amanda M. McBride, Stacie Hanson, and Lissa Johnson. 2005. "The Meaning of Saving in Low-Income Households." *Journal of Income Distribution* 13(3–4): 76–97.

Sherraden, Margaret S., Amanda M. McBride, Elizabeth Johnson, Stacie Hanson, Fred Ssewamala, and Trina Shanks. 2005. *Saving in Low-Income Households: Evidence from Interviews with Participants in the American Dream Demonstration.* Research report. St. Louis: Washington University, Center for Social Development.

Sherraden, Michael. 1988. "Rethinking Social Welfare: Toward Assets." *Social Policy* 18(3): 37–43.

———. 1991. *Assets and the Poor: A New American Welfare Policy.* Armonk, N.Y.: M. E. Sharpe.

———. 2000. "On Costs and the Future of Individual Development Accounts." CSD perspective. St. Louis: Washington University, Center for Social Development.

———. 2001. "From Research to Policy: Lessons from Individual Development Accounts." Colston Warne Lecture. *Journal of Consumer Affairs* 34(2): 159–81.

———. 2002. "Opportunity and Assets: The Role of the Child Trust Fund." Paper presented at a seminar organized by Prime Minister Tony Blair and dinner speech with Chancellor of the Exchequer Gordon Brown. London: 11 Downing (September 19).

———. 2006. "Asset-Based Social Policy: Potential of Child Development Accounts." Paper presented at Korean Institute of Labor and Ministry of Health and Social Welfare. Seoul (November).

Sherraden, Michael, and Michael S. Barr. 2005. "Institutions and Inclusion in Saving Policy." In *Building Assets, Building Credit: Bridges and Barriers to Financial Services in Low-Income Communities,* edited by Nicolas Retsinas and Eric Belsky. Washington, D.C.: Brookings Institution Press.

Sherraden, Michael, and Ray Boshara. Forthcoming. "Learning from Individual Development Accounts." In *Saving and Financial Education,* edited by Annamaria Lusardi. Chicago: University of Chicago Press.

Sherraden, Michael, Mark Schreiner, and Sondra Beverly. 2003. "Income, Institutions, and Saving Performance in Individual Development Accounts." *Economic Development Quarterly* 17(1): 95–112.

Thaler, H. Richard. 2000. "From Homo Economicus to Homo Sapiens." *Journal of Economic Perspective* 14(1): 133–41.

Thaler, Richard, and Shlomo Benartzi. 2004. "Save More Tomorrow: Using Behavioral Economics to Increase Employee Saving." *Journal of Political Economics* 112(1): 164–87.

Williams, R. Trina. 2003. "The Impact of Household Wealth and Poverty on Child Outcomes: Examining Asset Effects." Ph.D. diss., Washington University.

Wolff, N. Edward. 2004. "Changes in Household Wealth in the 1980s and 1990s in the United States." Working paper 407. Annandale-on-Hudson, N.Y.: Bard College, Jerome Levy Economics Institute.

Zhan, Min, and Michael Sherraden. 2003. "Assets, Expectations, and Children's Educational Achievement in Single-Parent Households." *Social Service Review* 77(2): 191–211.

Chapter 8

Homeownership: America's Dream?

Raphael W. Bostic and Kwan Ok Lee

L iving in a single-family, owner-occupied dwelling unit is central to the American conception of a secure and successful life—the quintessential "American dream." Study after study has justified the interest in homeownership among Americans by claiming that it confers benefits both to individuals and to the society as a whole. First and foremost, homeownership fosters asset-building and helps to insulate households from generally rising housing costs (Di, Yang, and Liu 2003). Homeownership is also thought to contribute to life satisfaction, psychological and physical health, positive child outcomes, and greater civic engagement (DiPasaquale and Glaeser 1999; Fannie Mae 1999; Galster 1987; Harkness and Newman 2002; Haurin, Parcel, and Haurin 2002; Kind et al. 1998; Lewis et al. 1998; Rohe and Stegman 1994a, 1994b; Rossi and Weber 1996; Saunders 1990; Tremblay, Dillman, and Van Liere 1980). On a broader scale, because homeownership limits household mobility, homeowners better maintain their properties and neighborhoods, which results in higher property values, greater neighborhood prosperity and sustainability, and reductions in crime (Boehm 1981; Galster 1983; Rohe and Stewart 1996; Rosenthal 2004). Finally, owner-occupied housing is also thought to have a beneficial effect on the local economy by increasing consumer spending, providing tax revenues and fees, and growing businesses and jobs (Collins 1998).[1]

Over the last decade, political and social efforts to promote homeownership among lower-income households have intensified, with the goal of promulgating these benefits. Questions remain, however, as to the efficacy and advisability of such efforts. For example, in spite of the potential benefits, are there risks and responsibilities associated with homeownership that lower-income families might be particularly vulnerable to and ill suited for? Mortgage payment stress and the risk of foreclosure could have significant negative impacts on lower-income homeowners and their families. Similarly, are lower-income households more likely to be subjected to geographically concentrated mortgage foreclosures, and what role does this play in the quality of the neighborhoods in which they live? More generally, what is the right framework for understanding the trade-offs between benefits and costs among different groups of low-income homeowners?

These questions and concerns have become more relevant with recent developments in mortgage markets. Delinquency and foreclosure rates have increased dramatically since 2006, with mortgage failures accelerating through 2008. As of the second quarter of 2008, a Mortgage Bankers Association (2008) survey reported delinquency and foreclosure rates never before seen in the history of the survey. These trends have been most acute among holders of adjustable-rate mortgages (ARMs), a mortgage product more commonly found among lower-income populations. In the second quarter of 2008, subprime ARMs accounted for 36 percent of foreclosure starts despite historically accounting for less than 10 percent of all mortgages outstanding (Mortgage Bankers Association 2007). As discussed later, these products differ from the standard thirty-year fixed-rate mortgage, and successfully managing the variable payment streams they feature requires considerable sophistication. The recent delinquency and foreclosure developments highlight this difficulty and point to the increasing importance of instrument risk as a serious threat to lower-income households seeking to improve their financial and personal situations through homeownership.

This chapter considers these broad questions and issues, with the goals of:

- Documenting the rapid expansion of credit in the last two decades and the rise in homeownership rates among low-income and minority households

- Summarizing trends and emerging issues in mortgage markets

- Quantifying the benefits of successful low-income homeownership and assessing the likely distribution of these benefits

- Evaluating the costs of failed low-income homeownership, including consideration of who is most likely to bear these costs

- Discussing policy options for retaining the benefits of homeownership and ameliorating the potential costs of foreclosures and their negative impacts

The main contribution of the analysis is its explicit consideration of both the benefits and costs of homeownership, particularly important in this context because low-income families are likely to be more exposed than others to the costs. The analysis details how newer tools for financing mortgages, such as the 2/28 mortgage, provide relatively limited benefits while introducing instrument risks that low-income homeowners had not previously encountered. In addition, a new, previously unused data set allows us to determine the spatial and neighborhood distribution of foreclosures. The data confirm that low-income communities have been more susceptible to negative ownership outcomes in the new mortgage-lending environment. This focus on low-income populations in the context of ownership performance is similar to research by Edwin Mills and Luan Lubuele (1994) and Harriet Newberger (2006), and our consideration of foreclosure's broader impacts is in the spirit of Dan Immergluck and Geoff Smith (2006a, 2006b). This portion of the study is similar in design to Immergluck and Smith (2005), but with more recent data and a broader geographic scope.

TABLE 8.1 / Evolution of Homeownership Rates, by Income Quintile, 1994 to 2006

	Overall	First	Second	Third	Fourth	Fifth
Year						
1994	62.4%	34.2%	50.2%	64.9%	76.8%	86.8%
2000	65.6	38.4	54.7	69.3	79.8	87.9
2006	68.8	38.0	56.7	71.9	83.9	91.1
Percentage change						
1994 to 2000	5.1	12.2	9.0	6.8	3.9	1.3
2000 to 2006	4.9	−1.1	3.7	3.8	5.1	3.6
1994 to 2006	10.3	11.1	12.9	10.8	9.2	5.0

Source: Current Population Survey 1994, 2000, and 2006 March supplements.

LOWER-INCOME HOMEOWNERSHIP: WHERE WE ARE AND HOW WE GOT THERE

According to the Current Population Survey (CPS), the homeownership rate in 2006 for households in the bottom two income quintiles stood at 38 and 57 percent, respectively (table 8.1). This reflects the culmination of a nearly fifteen-year trend of growing homeownership among poorer households. As a result, the number of low-income minority homeowners increased during this time by more than 800,000, which represents 11 percent of the net increase in all homeowners (Belsky and Duda 2002a). Indeed, low-income homeownership grew to such an extent during the last decade that it was labeled by some a "boom" (Belsky and Duda 2002a).

Table 8.1 demonstrates the extent of this boom. From 1994 to 2000, the fastest growth rates for homeownership were observed for households in the lowest income quintiles, with rates at or exceeding double the growth nationwide. This is consistent with Belsky and Duda (2002a), Retsinas and Belsky (2002), and Bostic and Surette (2001), all of whom find that homeownership among low-income and minority households has grown more rapidly since 1990 than for other groups. However, more recent trends suggest that the market has become more nuanced. Homeownership in the lowest income quintile has stabilized at around 38 percent, with no growth seen in the past six years. By contrast, homeownership has continued to become more common among households in the second income quintile, though at a slower pace than was observed in the 1990s. On balance, lower-income households have still outperformed other households in terms of homeownership attainment over the whole period, though not as dramatically as if the boom of the 1990s had continued.

When considering the growth in lower-income household homeownership, however, it is important to keep it in context. Despite this tremendous growth, homeownership among lower-income households continues to lag, and not only in terms of homeownership rates as reported in table 8.1. John Karl Scholz and Ananth Seshadri (this volume) show that housing equity accrual has also lagged for lower-income households. Their study using the Survey of Consumer Finances

(SCF) demonstrates considerable variation in the fraction of households that have positive net housing equity and indicates that the gap across income quintiles has increased over time. It is particularly noteworthy that the percentage of households that have positive net housing equity in the lowest income quintile (40 percent) has not increased at all over the last forty-two years, while the percentage of such households in other income quintiles has significantly increased by 14 to 19 percent over the same period.

The New Homeowners: A Low-Income Household Story

The growth in homeownership has meant that the benefits and challenges of owning a home have become reality for a new group of households. Data from the CPS provide information on exactly who these new lower-income households are. Within the lowest income quintiles, not surprisingly, homeowners are a relatively privileged group, and their characteristics suggest that they are more stable than the broader lower-income population. Among lower-income households, homeowners are older, more likely to be married, less likely to be headed by a single female, and less likely to have children. In addition, they tend to have higher incomes and to be better educated, though these differences are relatively small. These differences emphasize the importance of demographic, economic, and human capital considerations in determining whether one rents or owns.

Moreover, the spatial distribution of lower-income homeownership differs in significant ways. Lower-income homeowners are far more likely to live in rural areas than lower-income households overall. For example, in 1994, while 24 percent of households in the lowest income quintile lived in rural areas, 41 percent of the homeowners in this group lived in rural areas. Finally, lower-income homeowners are more concentrated in the South than the general lower-income population.

Interestingly, over time many of these differences have shrunk, such that the lower-income homeowner population and the general lower-income household population were more alike in 2006 than they were in 1994. This suggests that changes in the housing market environment allowed more lower-income households to become homeowners in more recent years. The nature of these changes is discussed later in the chapter.

Table 8.2 shows how the population of lower-income homeowners changed from 1994 to 2006. Lower-income homeownership became a more urban phenomenon, with significant increases seen in metropolitan areas, and in the central portion of cities more specifically. Consistent with the research cited earlier, minority households now make up an increasing fraction of lower-income homeowners. The Hispanic household presence grew by 40 percent in both income quintiles, while the black presence also increased by at least 20 percent. Also, the lower-income homeowner has become more likely to live in the West, which is now quite similar to the Midwest in this regard.

There has been a marked increase in the proportion of lower-income homeowners who are single and never married. This fraction increased by nearly 60 percent

Insufficient Funds

TABLE 8.2 / Homeowner Demographics for Bottom Two Income Quintiles,
1994 and 2006 CPS

	Quintile 1		Quintile 2	
	1994	2006	1994	2006
Household characteristics				
Household income (mean)	$9,539	$13,679	$23,333	$34,115
Age (mean)	48.2	48.1	45.3	45.4
Female head	18.0%	20.1%	13.1%	16.0%
With children (18 and younger)	36.8	37.1	44.2	47.8
Urban location				
Central city	16.1	20.6	17.3	19.7
Suburb	23.6	29.8	26.7	33.0
Rural	41.3	32.6	36.4	29.1
Other place	19.0	17.1	19.6	18.3
In MSA	58.7	67.4	63.6	70.9
Census region				
Northeast	14.8	14.6	18.2	15.8
Midwest	24.9	22.4	26.6	24.7
South	40.8	41.4	36.2	35.8
West	19.4	21.6	19.0	23.8
Marital status				
Married	44.1	38.7	59.6	54.7
Widowed	14.4	9.9	6.9	4.6
Divorced	23.9	25.8	18.8	21.2
Separated	5.1	6.1	3.0	2.8
Single	12.5	19.6	11.7	16.8
Education				
Less than high school	32.4	21.4	19.9	14.4
High school degree	37.4	38.3	40.9	36.2
Some college	21.0	27.2	27.4	32.0
College degree or more	9.2	13.2	11.8	17.4
Race-ethnicity				
White head	83.3	77.1	88.2	82.0
Black head	12.6	15.3	8.4	11.5
Hispanic head	11.0	15.3	10.7	14.9
Number of observations	2,990	4,420	4,421	6,778

Source: Current Population Survey 2004, 2006.

in the lowest income quintile and by more than 40 percent in the second income quintile. In addition, we observe a higher incidence of female-headed households in both quintiles and an increase in the fraction of families with children. Moreover, while income has increased by over 40 percent in both quintiles, this increase lags the nearly 65 percent increase in income found in the population at large. These trends all suggest that the new lower-income homeowners might not be as stable and secure as those of previous times and that they may be at risk of elevated exposure to delinquency, default, and foreclosure.

Causes of the Growth in Low-Income Homeownership

The differences in homeownership trends across income quintiles and time periods and the changing composition of the population of lower-income households both suggest that documenting housing market dynamics will be important for explaining lower-income homeownership and understanding the opportunities and risks faced by lower-income homeowners. For example, the divergent experiences across the two lower-income quintiles between 2000 and 2006 point to developments that advantaged one set of lower-income households, yet disadvantaged another.

In part, differences in homeownership across groups with different income levels are to be expected, since wealth and income are important factors that contribute to homeownership. There is evidence, however, suggesting that factors beyond these also are important. This section discusses the factors and forces that have shaped the evolution of homeownership for lower-income households. Aside from basic economic factors, these influences have largely involved changes to the credit markets that support the financing of home purchases and refinances.

DEMOGRAPHIC AND ECONOMIC FORCES   The growth in homeownership among lower-income households is in part a reflection of the improving fortunes of such households. For example, the CPS data indicate that among households in the lowest income quintile the share of households headed by a high school dropout fell by 22 percent and the share with some college education increased by 20 percent between 1994 and 2006. In addition, the financial capacity of lower-income households has grown. Wealth for households at the twenty-fifth percentile of the income distribution increased by 64 percent in real terms from 1989 to 2004 (Kennickell 2006). Both developments suggest that lower-income households were in a significantly better position to purchase a home at the end of the period than they were in 1990.

Despite the clear demographic improvements observed for lower-income households and for homeowners in particular, evidence suggests that a wide range of developments contributed to the growth in lower-income homeownership. As one example, while wealth has increased for lower-income households over the past fifteen years, it actually declined slightly from 2001 to 2004 (Kennickell 2006), meaning that increases in lower-income homeownership since 2000 are not due to greater financial capacity. In addition, the noted increase in the proportion of lower-income homeowning households that are headed by a single female indicates elevated exposure to trigger event risk. As discussed later, homeownership increases for this group are due in part to the evolution of the financing system that supports home-ownership. However, this new development does not come without significant potential consequences in terms of the resultant exposure to risk that these house-holds face. Given that these households already have low incomes and generally have limited savings as well, lower-income homeowners are more vulnerable to income shocks that could induce delinquency, default, and foreclosure.

MARKET INNOVATIONS   The passage of the Depository Institutions Deregulatory and Monetary Control Act of 1980 marked a turning point in the underwriting of mortgage credit (Gramlich 2007). Prior to this, lenders faced caps on the interest rates they could charge, and thus credit was rationed such that higher-risk applicants were denied. As a consequence, applicants with impaired credit or households facing income and wealth constraints—problems more frequently found among lower-income populations—were effectively shut out of the mortgage mar-ket and precluded from achieving homeownership.

Once lenders were free to charge higher interest rates commensurate with ele-vated repayment risks, however, incentives were in place for them to develop tools to quantify the risks that particular applicants posed so that they could charge them an appropriate interest rate rather than deny them. This led to renewed efforts in the area of credit scoring, which mortgage lenders rapidly adopted during the mid-1990s, such that it became the standard for mortgage underwriting by the end of the decade. The success of this technological evolution is evident in the noticeable drop in mortgage denial rates during the period (Gramlich 2007).

These developments resulted in an explosion of sorts in high-cost (high-interest-rate) lending to borrowers with lower credit quality, also known as "subprime lend-ing." In addition to the less favorable credit profiles of subprime borrowers, subprime loans typically have higher loan-to-value ratios, reflecting the greater difficulty that subprime borrowers have in making down payments and the propen-sity of these borrowers to extract equity during refinancing. These higher-risk fac-tors increase the cost of subprime loans. Evidence from surveys of mortgage lenders suggests that a weak credit history alone can add about three and a half percentage points to the loan rate.

During the 1990s, the number of subprime loans made in the United States grew by 900 percent (Hurd and Kest 2003). Moreover, subprime lending has become a much more important segment of the overall mortgage market. In 1998 subprime mortgages amounted to 2.4 percent of outstanding home mortgage loans; by the sec-ond quarter of 2006, they made up 13.4 percent (Duncan 2006). Thus, we might argue that the growth in subprime lending, by making mortgages available to groups that include many lower-income households, has enabled the expansion of lower-income homeownership and represents a natural evolution of credit markets.[2]

These developments are additionally relevant for lower-income borrowers and homeowners because subprime lending has been spatially concentrated in lower-income, and especially lower-income minority, communities. Studies of subprime lending in metropolitan areas across the United States have consistently shown the considerably greater propensity for subprime loans to be originated in lower-income and minority neighborhoods than in upper-income and predominantly white areas (Gruenstein and Herbert 2000a, 2000b; U.S. Department of Housing and Urban Development 2000a, 2000b; U.S. Department of Housing and Urban Development and U.S. Department of the Treasury 2000). For example, in 2001 over 10 percent of home purchase loans made to low-income households living in low-income neighborhoods were subprime, compared to only greater than 6 percent overall. Among refinance loans, the disparity was sharper, with subprime loans accounting for 27 percent of all loans to lower-income households living in lower-income neighborhoods and 42 percent to lower-income black households in lower-income neighborhoods (Apgar and Calder 2005). Although a geographic disparity in the prevalence of subprime lending might be reasonably expected to some degree because of systematic differences in income and credit quality across neighborhoods of different income levels, studies have shown higher propensities of lenders to originate subprime loans in minority communities even after controlling for such factors (Calem, Hershaff, and Wachter 2004).

If there are negative possibilities associated with subprime lending, then lower-income communities might face extra risks and challenges. Later in the chapter we discuss the existence of such negative potentialities, most notably but not limited to predatory lending.

GOVERNMENT POLICY   The federal government has a long record of actively promoting homeownership, particularly among lower-income households. Every president since World War II has had some type of homeownership initiative, and homeownership has been a legislative priority since the passage of the National Housing Act of 1949. In terms of key recent legislative influences, we must look to key acts that have strengthened incentives to lend to lower-income households. Research suggests that these have had been effective in increasing homeownership.

The Community Reinvestment Act (CRA) of 1977 established that federally insured depository institutions had an obligation to help meet the credit needs of the communities they were chartered to serve, including lower-income people. Many studies have shown that the incentives created by the CRA have resulted in increased access to mortgage credit for lower-income households. In perhaps the most comprehensive study of the issue of CRA impact, Robert Avery, Raphael Bostic, and Glenn Canner (2005) show that lenders have expanded mortgage credit and that this expansion has not on balance been associated with losses. Other research has corroborated the general result (Fishbein 2003; Joint Center for Housing Studies 2002; Litan et al. 2000). Similarly, Bostic and Breck Robinson (2005) show that CRA agreements, which are pledges that banking institutions make to demonstrate commitment to CRA objectives, have been associated with increases in mortgage lending activity to targeted neighborhoods, which are often lower-income and minority.

A second important piece of legislation that has influenced lending to lower-income households is the Federal Housing Enterprises Financial Safety and

Soundness Act of 1992. Also known as the GSE (government-sponsored enterprise) Affordable Goals Act, this act requires Fannie Mae and Freddie Mac (together the GSEs) to pay particular attention to those populations historically underserved by credit markets with the goal of increasing their access to such markets. Xudong An and his colleagues (2007) find that the GSEs increased their activities in response to incentives laid out by the act and that these actions produced improvements in housing market outcomes such as vacancy rates and median house values. Similarly, An and Bostic (2008) find that the GSE Affordable Goals Act has helped lower-income and minority borrowers gain access to cheaper credit, which lowers their likelihood of default and improves their ability to weather financial stresses arising from trigger events such as illness or divorce.

Other pieces of legislation have allowed the public to provide its own scrutiny of how lenders serve prospective lower-income homeowners. Revisions to the Home Mortgage Disclosure Act enacted in 1992 required lenders to disclose publicly information on all individual loan applications, including the race and income of the applicants. The public availability of this information permits community groups, advocacy organizations, and the media to conduct their own analyses of patterns and places pressure on lenders to reconsider policies that are thought to disadvantage lower-income borrowers. This facilitated the quick replication of influential reports such as the Pulitzer Prize–winning "Color of Money" series (Dedman 1988) and helped create a sophisticated advocacy community to counterbalance the interests of lenders.

Support for lower-income homeownership during the 1990s was not limited to legislative activity focused on mortgage finance. The Federal Housing Administration (FHA) is an important player for lower-income homeowners, as it guarantees mortgage loans for many borrowers who could not qualify for prime market mortgages owing to limited savings or prior credit repayment problems. During the 1990s, the FHA liberalized its rules for guaranteeing mortgages, which increased competition in the market and lowered the interest rates offered to some subprime mortgage borrowers (Gramlich 2004).

Similarly, since 1994, the Treasury Department has administered the CDFI Fund, which is designed to support the activities of community development financial institutions (CDFIs). CDFIs are private organizations with a dual mission of profitably funding projects and promoting community and economic development, and they accomplish these goals through lending, investment, service provision, and product and practice innovation. Given their mission, we might expect such support to translate into elevated lower-income homeownership. To date, however, little research has focused on this question.

A third development in the 1990s was the emergence of the individual development account (IDA) as a vehicle to promote lower-income saving and to perhaps make homeownership more accessible. The most recent comprehensive analysis of IDA programs was done by Mark Schreiner and Michael Sherraden (2007), who studied the American Dream Demonstration (ADD). These authors found that IDAs do induce lower-income households to save. However, their results indicate levels of saving that are small relative to what would be needed to purchase a home.

EMERGING ISSUES FOR
LOWER-INCOME HOMEOWNERSHIP

Because most of the evidence showing positive financial, social, and behavioral homeownership effects has been based on the experiences of middle- and high-income homeowners, it is appropriate to ask whether these benefits are generalizable to lower-income households.[3] There is evidence suggesting that they are. For example, Joseph Harkness and Sandra Newman (2002) find financial and social benefits of homeownership (less idleness and lower rates of welfare receipt and higher income) that are bigger for low-income children compared with high-income children. Similarly, a series of papers by William Rohe and Michael Stegman find positive, though limited, effects of homeownership on self-esteem and perceived control, life satisfaction, the extent of neighborhood and organizational involvement, and the intensity of organizational involvement among lower-income households (Rohe and Stegman 1994a, 1994b; Rohe and Stewart 1996).

In theory, appreciation in house values should allow lower-income households to build wealth and be insulated to some degree from rising housing values and rents. However, some studies (Belsky and Duda 2002b; Retsinas and Belsky 2002) question whether there is clear evidence that homeownership brings more economic gains to low-income households compared to renting. These authors argue that it is hard to generalize economic returns delivered from homeownership because such returns are heavily dependent on the timing and location of home purchases. Thomas Boehm and Alan Schlottmann (2004a) make a similar argument, noting that many low-income and minority homeowners return to renting. Indeed, Boehm and Schlottmann (2004a, 129) explicitly state that "homeownership may be less beneficial than it otherwise might be."

The remainder of this section examines this question in the context of recent developments in the housing and mortgage markets. Trends in both of these areas suggest that the challenges for lower-income households seeking to use homeownership as an asset- and wealth-building strategy may be increasing. We focus on the serious cost burdens to lower-income homeowners caused by an imbalance between demand and supply of affordable housing and the rapid expansion of subprime mortgage lending targeting lower-income and minority households. This latter issue has leant urgency to these concerns and also highlights how innovation in the marketplace has increased the need for consumers to be knowledgeable in order to avoid excessive exposure to risks. Overall, research in this area has shown that homeownership often involves risks and responsibilities that low-income people may be particularly ill suited for, including costly home repairs and improvements, declining house values, and being overcharged for credit or sold loans that expose them to substantial repayment risks. We conclude by highlighting the broader neighborhood-level implications of these negative impacts.

The Cost Burdens of Lower-Income Homeownership

As house prices have risen sharply in recent years, the fraction of lower-income first-time homebuyers with serious cost burdens, defined as spending more than 50 percent of household disposable income on housing, has grown to greater than 20 percent, which significantly exceeds the 12 percent rate for all households (Gramlich 2007). Edward Gramlich (2007) notes a similar imbalance among first-time homebuyers with moderate cost burdens, defined as spending 30 to 50 percent of household disposable income on housing. These figures highlight a stark reality faced by lower-income households: homeownership frequently comes with the added stress of meeting monthly payments (Doling and Stafford 1989; Hoffmann and Heistler 1988).

Financial hardships for defaulted homeowners are estimated to cost an average of $58,792 and to take eighteen months to resolve (Cutts and Green 2004). Indeed, failures in homeownership (foreclosure) can have more devastating consequences for homeowners and their families than rental eviction because foreclosure may lead homeowners not only to be evicted but also to lose their housing assets and credit (Gramlich 2007).

There is also a concern that using homeownership as a tool for revitalizing low-income areas or central cities may not be the best mechanism for low-income families to build their assets and upward social mobility. Although many low-income homebuyers buy homes in good locations for investment (Belsky and Duda 2002b), low-income housing is typically more available in neighborhoods with the least resources (Listokin and Wyly 2000; Shlay 1993). Low-income homebuyers may face greater risks in terms of costly home repairs, lower rates of appreciation, and lower-quality neighborhood amenities (Herbert and Belsky 2006). Hence, the promotion of low-income homeownership may move already at-risk households to take on even more risk under conditions of great uncertainty. As Anne Shlay (2006, 523) puts it, "It is unclear whether policy directed at helping low-income families should encourage people with the least amount of assets to take on more risk."

These high and increasing cost burdens mean that homeownership will remain unaffordable for most renters using standard underwriting and conventional mortgage products, such as the thirty-year fixed-rate mortgage. David Listokin and his colleagues (2001, 493) note that homeownership will remain elusive even using more liberal underwriting standards. "With such a trace level of assets, even a 100 per cent LTV (loan to value) mortgage will not facilitate homeownership because of the resources required to meet substantial closing costs."

An obvious reason for these high-cost burdens is a lack of adequate housing at affordable prices. In many locales, as noted by Michael Collins, David Crowe, and Michael Carliner (2002), affordable housing production has not kept pace with the loss of such units from the affordable housing stock through house value appreciation and the removal of units due to the expiration of affordable housing contracts and obligations. Noting that standard market mechanisms are failing to meet market needs, these authors further argue that "policymakers need to recognize the failure of filtering as a mechanism to expand the supply of affordable homes" (Collins, Crowe, and Carliner 2002, 198).

Instrument Risk and the Need for Increased Sophistication

The rapid evolution of the mortgage finance market through the 1990s resulted in the introduction of many new loan products. These myriad new products have variable payment patterns that differ considerably from each other and, importantly, from the payment pattern associated with the standard, fully amortizing, thirty-year, fixed-interest-rate mortgage product, which features constant payments for the entire life of the loan.

Consider, for example, the 2/28 mortgage. This mortgage has fixed mortgage payments for the first two years of the loan and then becomes an adjustable mortgage with annual interest rate resets for the remaining twenty-eight years of the loan. The interest rate for the first two years is generally significantly less than that for a thirty-year fixed-rate mortgage—this is often called the loan's "teaser rate"—and it changes during the adjustable-rate period based on prevailing mortgage rates. In environments in which interest rates are increasing, the rates during the adjustable period can be significantly higher than during the fixed-rate period, resulting in considerably higher monthly payments for borrowers. For example, initial monthly payments for a $200,000 2/28 mortgage with a teaser rate of 5.25 percent would be $1,104. If, after the two-year fixed period, prevailing interest rates were such that the adjustable mortgage interest rate was 7.25 percent, monthly payments would increase to $1,392, an increase of more than 26 percent on a monthly basis.[4]

Thus, a borrower can no longer be sure that an initial monthly payment will represent the same nominal payment over the life of a mortgage. Instead, homeowners with these newer-style mortgages must be vigilant and proactive in tracking changes in market conditions and interest rates so as to anticipate the likely changes to the mortgage payment. Those households that do this market analysis effectively will be able to determine whether troubles lie ahead and to take the necessary remedial actions to prevent or delay delinquency, default, and foreclosure. Those that do not could face significant hardships and will need to rely on serendipitous favorable market developments—otherwise known as luck—to avoid them.

The variable payment patterns associated with newer mortgage products represent a different sort of risk for borrowers that we term "instrument risk." Particularly when interest rates are rising, instrument risk can leave borrowers facing an elevated risk of default *even when their personal circumstances do not change or even sometimes when those circumstances improve.* This is quite different from other sorts of repayment risk where problems are typically triggered by some sort of event, such as divorce or job loss. Importantly, much of the discussion about the danger of subprime lending has focused on this second class of repayment risks. Instrument risk has not been elevated to the same degree as an important issue for policy to consider.

Exposure to instrument risk has increased dramatically over the past decade as the use of newer mortgage instruments has become more widespread. The use of subprime mortgages, especially 2/28s, grew considerably after 2000 (Gramlich 2007), and recent performance statistics suggest that instrument risk is real. Delinquency rates during 2007 spiked for a wide range of newer mortgage instruments, a trend due in large measure to interest rate adjustments at the expiration of the fixed-rate term that raised monthly payments sharply (Apgar and Duda 2004, 2005; Gruenstein and Herbert 2000a, 2000b; National Training and Information Center 1999). This rise in delinquency, default, and foreclosure without an associated economic shock of some sort is virtually unprecedented and accents the new terrain that mortgage borrowers find themselves having to navigate.

In this environment, there is a premium to being financially sophisticated, and unfortunately lower-income households lag in this regard. Lower-income people with a limited access to education tend to be not as adept as educated higher-income people in financial matters (Bernheim and Scholz 1992; Maki 1996). This lower degree of financial sophistication could lead lower-income borrowers to decide to buy a house without proper evaluation of their own repayment ability or to pay more than is necessary for their credit (Courchane, Surette, and Zorn 2004). The challenge is even greater in the subprime market, where borrowers, as Howard Lax and his colleagues (2004) have found, are indeed financially less sophisticated.

An added concern with the rise of the newer mortgage products and subprime lending is the increased presence of illegal, deceptive, and abusive lending practices in this market segment (Renuart 2004). These abuses, known as predatory lending, include excessive points and fees, high and extended prepayment penalties, underwriting based on asset value rather than income, loan flipping (repeated refinancing), and inflated house appraisals (Hurd and Kest 2003). Predatory lending is quite costly. Its features, coupled with the high interest rates on these loans, leave homeowners vulnerable to loss of the equity they have often spent years accruing (known as "equity stripping") (White 2004). In addition, the onerous terms often result in homeowners losing their homes through foreclosure. According to Eric Stein (2001) and Elizabeth Renuart (2004), housing equity taken by predatory lending practices is estimated to have reached $2.1 billion annually.

Predatory lending is a concern in the context of lower-income homeownership because it occurs more frequently in the subprime market segment, which is where lower-income families, as well as minorities and the elderly, more often find themselves. Borrower sophistication plays a role here as well: predatory lenders often take advantage of borrowers who lack financial sophistication (Carr and Kolluri 2001). Thus, such households are more exposed to the risks of predatory lending and the potential for significant equity loss and perhaps foreclosure.

Potential Neighborhood-Level Issues

The view that homeownership is an effective device for neighborhood stabilization and economic development has proven a powerful rationale for those who encourage homeownership in low-income and central-city neighborhoods (Rosenthal 2004). A host of public policy programs, such as the Nehemiah Program, strongly advocate homeownership as a means of revitalizing severely depressed neighborhoods. While Jean Cummings, Denise DiPasquale, and Matthew Kahn (2002) find few spillover effects on community development associated with two Nehemiah housing developments in Philadelphia, several recent studies (Ellen et al. 2003; Lee, Culhane, and Wachter 1999; Santiago, Galster, and Tatian 2001) have found positive effects of homeownership programs on surrounding communities. Ingrid Gould Ellen and her colleagues (2003) suggest that affordable homeownership programs in New York, including the Nehemiah Program, have increased property values in their immediate neighborhoods.

There are two additional neighborhood-level issues that should be discussed. First, at the household level, much research has demonstrated that homeownership reduces household mobility. Because lower-income homeowners tend to be geographically concentrated in lower-income neighborhoods, this lack of mobility can translate into their being "trapped" in communities that were once healthy but have devolved into distressed areas (Lauria 1976). Residential isolation and segregation is also an issue in these neighborhoods, and these factors can stunt homeowners' capacity to improve their neighborhood. In such cases, the decreased employment, higher incidence of families on public assistance, and higher levels of dilapidated houses associated with concentrated poverty can offset the benefits that would accrue from homeownership (Massey and Fong 1990).

At the neighborhood level, homeownership can also generate problems if large numbers of homeowners default on their mortgage loans and the properties enter foreclosure. Such a concentration of mortgage foreclosure can lead to deteriorated or vacant residential buildings in a neighborhood and so bring negative impacts on neighborhood property values (Shlay and Whitman 2004). Other researchers insist that vacant and abandoned buildings are often considered a component of the physical and social disorder in a neighborhood that leads to serious crime (Kelling and Coles 1996; Wilson and Kelling 1982). Several studies (Apgar and Duda 2004, 2005; Goldstein et al. 2005; National Association of Realtors 2004) have predicted a concentration of housing foreclosures in lower-income urban neighborhoods with particular segregation patterns. As the current subprime performance crisis is beginning to reveal elevated concentrations of foreclosed properties in several cities, this concern might be growing in significance.

BENEFITS OF SUCCESSFUL
LOW-INCOME HOMEOWNERSHIP

A motivating factor that has helped shift low-income housing policy in favor
of homeownership is an increasing interest in using homeownership as an asset-
building strategy for the poor. The key question, of course, is whether the perceived benefits of homeownership outweigh the risks and costs posed by
homeownership. This section reports on the results of an exercise in which we
explore lower-income homeownership from an asset-building perspective, with
a particular eye to the question of whether lower-income households are better
off as homeowners or renters.

The Simulation Framework

The basic approach is to simulate how the wealth of lower-income households
would evolve over time if they were homeowners as compared to renters.
Assuming that households are identical in terms of income and living expenses and
that they face the same inflationary environment, differences in wealth accumulation between homeowners and renters will derive from growth in the equity associated with ownership and differential contributions to savings. For renters, this
latter quantity is a simple function of income and living expenses. For homeowners,
however, determining savings is complicated by how the home purchase is
financed. The choice of how much to provide as a down payment and which mortgage instrument to use helps establish an interest rate and monthly payment, which
in turn determine how much money homeowners have left over to save.

Simulation implementation requires definitions of household, neighborhood,
and mortgage types. Because household expenditure patterns vary over the life
cycle and household form, we created twenty-seven prototype households defined
by the age of the primary person, the size of the household, and the relative income
of the household. We created two neighborhood types defined by relative median
income levels, since rents and house prices differ across neighborhoods of varying
affluence.[5] Finally, to evaluate the importance of mortgage instrument risk for asset-
building, we created twelve combinations of down-payment amount and type of
mortgage instrument that define mortgage payments for homeowners.[6] The specific
partitions used in defining the prototypes for the simulation exercise are summarized in the following list. The appendix to this chapter describes the details of the
simulation implementation methodology.

> Simulation Elements: Dimensional Partitions
>   Family Characteristics
>   Age of Household Head
>   Twenty-five to thirty-four
>   Thirty-five to forty-four
>   Forty-five to fifty-four

Size of Family
  One person
  Two people
  Three people (one child)
Relative Income
  High (120 percent of area median)
  Middle (median)
  Low (80 percent of area median)
Neighborhood Characteristics
  Relative Income
    Middle (median)
    Low (80 percent of area median)
Financing Characteristics
  Down Payment
    0 percent
    5 percent
    10 percent
  Mortgage Instrument
    Thirty-year fixed rate
    5/1 hybrid ARM[7]
    2/28 hybrid ARM
Housing Appreciation
  Appreciation Rate
    4.1 percent (median)
    12.3 percent (high)

To carry the simulation beyond a single year, we assume 4 percent growth in income and prices and 3 percent growth in annual rents, and we inflate income, rents and nonhousing living expenses accordingly. For mortgage payments in the out years, there are no changes required for the fixed-rate mortgage. For the adjustable-rate mortgages, we assume that the mortgages adjust when possible by the maximum amount (that is, up to the margin cap). The final piece to the simulation involves quantifying the rate of house price appreciation. Using data from the 1990 and 2000 censuses, we calculated annual house price appreciation rates for neighborhoods grouped by relative income. Surprisingly, and contrary to findings in previous studies[8] and widely held assumptions, we found little systematic variation in appreciation rates by neighborhood relative income levels (table 8.3). We therefore applied the median appreciation rate of 4.1 percent across all neighborhoods. In light of the recent house price surge, however, and recognizing the high house price volatilities observed recently in some housing markets, we also consider a higher appreciation rate of 12.3 percent. By applying these two different rates, we can observe the implications of housing price appreciation for lower-income homeowner asset-building and risk exposure.

In reviewing the simulation results, we must remain cognizant of the pros and cons of using such an approach. The obvious advantage is that a simulation allows

TABLE 8.3 / Average Annual House Price Appreciation Rates, 1990 to 2000

	Median Rate
Lower-income neighborhood	4.31%
Middle-income neighborhood	4.37
High-income neighborhood	3.46
All neighborhoods	4.10

Source: 1990 U.S. Census and 2000 U.S. Census, United States Census Bureau.
Note: Lower-income neighborhoods are those with a median household income less than 80 percent of the metropolitan statistical area (MSA) median household income, middle-income neighborhoods have median incomes between 80 and 120 percent of the MSA median income, and high-income neighborhoods are those with median incomes greater than 120 percent of the MSA median income.

us to abstract away from institutional complexity to hone in on the most relevant aspects of the problem at hand and spotlight the most important relationships. On the other hand, such abstraction means that simulation results might not reflect the experience of any single household and in this sense may project an average outcome that is not particularly meaningful. Readers should review these results with this in mind.

Simulation Results: Does Homeownership Pay for Lower-Income Households?

Given the simulation framework, we can calculate the gain to housing equity and, coupling this with the accrued savings, determine the change in housing wealth for renters and homeowners for each household prototype and compare them. Table 8.4 reports the cumulative change in wealth that would result from a two-person household purchasing a home priced at 70 percent of the median house value in a middle- or low-income neighborhood. The table presents the cumulative totals over one- and ten-year horizons, and we use the high rate of house price appreciation (12.3 percent).

The table indicates that homeownership is often but not always beneficial to lower-income households, and it identifies affordability as a key factor in determining whether homeownership offers benefits. Looking solely at the results after one year of ownership, we find that home purchases in low-income neighborhoods offer wealth benefits across all types of financing except for the zero-down-payment 2/28 product. By contrast, purchases in middle-income neighborhoods, which require larger mortgage payments because of the higher home prices, are beneficial only in cases where the homeowner provided at least a 10 percent down payment. Given the low likelihood that lower-income households will have savings sufficient to provide such a down payment, it will generally be the case that

TABLE 8.4 / Simulation Results for Cumulative Wealth Gains for a Two-Person
Household in a High-Appreciation Environment
(Using a 12.3 Percent Appreciation Rate)

	Neighborhood Income Level	
	Middle	Low
Difference after year 1		
Thirty-year, fixed-rate mortgage		
0% down	($2,317)	$132
5% down	(748)	962
10% down	820	1,747
5/1 adjustable-rate mortgage		
0% down	(1,675)	213
5% down	(139)	997
10% down	1,398	1,780
2/28 adjustable-rate mortgage		
0% down	(2,971)	(386)
5% down	(1,369)	883
10% down	232	1,714
Average	(752)	894
Difference after year 10		
Thirty-year, fixed-rate mortgage		
0% down	(6,068)	3,130
5% down	7,164	10,993
10% down	19,649	18,812
5/1 adjustable-rate mortgage		
0% down	(2,652)	3,143
5% down	9,170	10,543
10% down	20,304	17,943
2/28 adjustable-rate mortgage		
0% down	(12,252)	1,090
5% down	1,914	9,457
10% down	15,176	17,223
Average	5,823	10,259

Source: Authors' compilation.

ownership is a losing proposition in middle-income neighborhoods, especially during the early years of ownership.

The second panel in the table shows how wealth changes as the house appreci-
ates and the adjustable-rate mortgages adjust their pricing. In some cases, appreciation cures all ills. For example, after ten years of ownership in a low-income
neighborhood, appreciation has turned an initial wealth loss for the zero-down-

payment 2/28 product into a positive proposition. Even in middle-income neigh-borhoods, low-income households show wealth gains in all but three cases, with some of the gains being quite significant.

In terms of magnitudes, we find that the wealth gains associated with own-ership are significant under many financing arrangements. The average wealth gain associated with ownership in low- and middle-income neighborhoods over the ten years is $10,259 and $5,823, respectively. There is variation, how-ever, since wealth changes after ten years range from a gain of $20,304 (10 per-cent down, 5/1 hybrid mortgage, middle-income neighborhood) to a loss of $12,252 (zero-down-payment, 2/28 adjustable-rate mortgage, middle-income neighborhood). On balance, however, homeownership is a winning strategy: only seven of the eighteen financing arrangements for low- and middle-income areas yield a wealth gain of less than $5,000.

Simulation results make it clear that the extent of the wealth gain is a direct func-tion of the initial down-payment amount. For example, for a one-person house-hold, the wealth gain after five years is two to six times greater if the homeowner makes a 10 percent down payment rather than no down payment at all, depend-ing on the financing instrument (not shown). This is not surprising, since the con-tribution of homeownership to household wealth in the early years of ownership will be due to home value appreciation, given that mortgage payments contribute little to equity during this time. This dynamic is exacerbated under the more rapid price appreciation scenarios.

These results emphasize the point that homeownership is clearly more valuable as an asset-building tool if a household is able to acquire home equity early in the tenure of homeownership. The benefit of owning over renting grows increasingly larger as a greater down payment is provided up front. Unfortunately, data from many sources have made it clear that few lower-income households have the sav-ings and wealth to achieve significant accumulation and receive a maximum finan-cial benefit from owning a home. Thus, while advantageous, homeownership here seems to have less than optimal efficacy.

The simulation results also highlight the fact that innovation in the marketplace can work to the advantage of lower-income homeowners such that significant additional benefits can be realized if a household chooses the proper mortgage instrument and exercises proper financial management. Compare, for example, the relative benefits of owning in a low-income neighborhood if a 5/1 hybrid mort-gage is used rather than a thirty-year fixed-rate mortgage, holding the down-payment size constant. Consider a two-person family that puts 5 percent down. After one year, the wealth advantage to using the 5/1 is $35 ($997 versus $962; see table 8.4) and this grows to a $175 cumulative advantage by the fifth year ($5,263 versus $5,088; not shown). This advantage flips once the homeowner moves past seven years of ownership, such that by the tenth year of ownership the homeowner with a fixed-rate mortgage has a $450 wealth advantage ($10,543 ver-sus $10,993; see table 8.4). This dynamic is observed because the lower interest rate over the first five years for the 5/1 hybrid provides lower-income households with an extra income buffer and permits a slightly higher amount of savings. After five years, however, increases in the 5/1 interest rate, coupled with the more rapid equity appreciation associated with the fixed-rate mortgage, makes the fixed rate more attractive.

The simulation also shows that innovation and the introduction of new mortgage products can be potentially dangerous. While the 5/1 hybrid was shown to offer some advantages to lower-income homeowners, the 2/28 mortgage as priced during the mid-2000s is observed to pose considerable risk. Households using the zero-down-payment 2/28 mortgage generally have wealth losses, and in those cases where wealth does increase, the gains are quite small (less than $1,100; see table 8.4). Thus, households using this type of mortgage are at significant risk if a trigger event such as sickness or unemployment occurs. Consequently, we can definitively conclude that instrument risk is a legitimate concern and that consumers need to pay particular heed to the details of the mortgage contract into which they enter.

These two observations regarding innovation point to the importance of consumer sophistication for navigating today's mortgage market. The negative possibilities with the 2/28 are clear. Lower-income households must be aware of the risks with this product if they are to avoid falling into the delinquency, default, and foreclosure cycle. But there are also issues on the positive side. A sophisticated borrower might use the 5/1 hybrid for the first five years and then refinance to another product to avoid the relative loss of wealth associated with the interest rate reset. If lower-income homeowners are to maximally benefit from ownership as a wealth-building strategy, they must be cognizant of and willing to execute this type of strategy.

A second question is whether homeownership is preferred to renting for lower-income households. The data (not shown) show that homeownership is almost always preferred to renting in this scenario, independent of which financing approach is used. After one year, two-person households in low-income neighborhoods would be ahead in terms of wealth by an average of $832 if they owned a home as opposed to renting. This increases to an average advantage of about $9,403 after ten years, suggesting that homeownership is quite beneficial in terms of wealth-building on a comparative basis. Results are similar for middle-income neighborhoods, where owning is shown to be usually preferred to renting.

The importance of affordability is also reflected in the fact that owning is uniformly preferred to renting for single-person lower-income households. The simulation established a purchase price for these households of 60 percent of the area median house price, under the rationale that these households would probably purchase a house quite a bit smaller than the market median given their household size and income level. The data clearly show that ownership makes financial sense if the housing prices are low enough, which argues again for the importance of the availability of affordable units if we are to successfully promote homeownership among lower-income households. These results also suggest that savings barriers are important; without children, these households are able to consume less out of their income and save more for housing and wealth building (see appendix table 8A.1).

Conclusions relating to innovation's possibilities and risks can also be drawn in this context. For example, the zero-down-payment 2/28 mortgage is the only mortgage product in the simulation for which renting is consistently preferred to owning, even with the higher home appreciation rate of 12.3 percent. In addition, the gaps in cumulative wealth differences between owning and renting are sizable for two- and three-person households, ranging from a loss of about $1,000 in the first year (three-person) to a gain of over $7,000 after ten years (two-person). Sophistication, understanding, and awareness on the part of the consumer are of paramount importance.

THE COSTS OF FAILED LOW-INCOME HOMEOWNERSHIP: FORECLOSURE

The previous section provided information on the potential of homeownership as a wealth-building vehicle for lower-income households. The analysis showed that this potential varies significantly with neighborhood characteristics, financial capacity, and the financing instrument that is used. In particular, this strategy is most effective in lower-income neighborhoods for purchases in which equity is acquired early in the ownership tenure and in cases where features of the financing instrument can be exploited. An additional key dimension was seen to be the house value appreciation rate. We showed that high appreciation rates can swamp short-run losses in wealth over longer time horizons, even in middle-income neighborhoods.

Simulation Results: Homeownership Benefits in the Case of Low Appreciation

Along this latter dimension, we might wonder whether the same pattern of benefits is observed if appreciation rates are not so high as applied in the previous section. To examine this question, we repeated the simulation exercise using the median annual home appreciation rate of 4.1 percent that prevailed between 1990 and 2000 according to census data. The simulation results are reported in table 8.5.

The simulation results for the slower appreciation rate paint a very different picture regarding the efficacy of homeownership as a wealth-building strategy for lower-income households. As shown in the first panel, homeownership produces wealth losses or small gains for nearly all ownership scenarios in middle-income neighborhoods. More generally, homeownership in middle-income neighborhoods when appreciation rates are low is almost never a winning proposition for growing wealth. Out of the nine financing arrangements for middle-income areas, we see a wealth gain of greater than $5,000 in only one case—with a 10 percent down payment on a 5/1 adjustable-rate mortgage after ten years—and close to

TABLE 8.5 / Simulation Results for Cumulative Wealth Gains for Two-Person Household in Median-Appreciation Environment (Using a 4.1 Percent Appreciation Rate)

	Neighborhood Income Level	
	Middle	Low
Difference after year 1		
Thirty-year, fixed-rate mortgage		
0% down	($2,467)	$13
5% down	(1,542)	332
10% down	(618)	606
5/1 adjustable-rate mortgage		
0% down	(1,839)	83
5% down	(946)	356
10% down	(53)	629
2/28 adjustable-rate mortgage		
0% down	(3,107)	(495)
5% down	(2,151)	264
10% down	(1,194)	584
Average	(1,546)	264
Difference after year 10		
Thirty-year, fixed-rate mortgage		
0% down	(8,111)	1,510
5% down	(1,291)	4,288
10% down	4,781	7,022
5/1 adjustable-rate mortgage		
0% down	(4,503)	1,675
5% down	1,249	4,263
10% down	6,315	6,850
2/28 adjustable-rate mortgage		
0% down	(13,290)	267
5% down	(5,448)	3,619
10% down	(1,491)	6,372
Average	(2,090)	3,985

Source: Authors' compilation.

$5,000 in only one other case—with a 10 percent down payment on a thirty-year fixed-rate mortgage after ten years. Given the significant chance that a household will experience a loss in the early years, it is hard to make a strong case that home-ownership in middle-income neighborhoods makes sense for the average lower-income household. Indeed, simulation results (not shown) indicate that renting produces greater wealth increases than owning in all cases except when the lower-income household provides a sizable down payment.

The situation is different for homeownership in low-income neighborhoods, but only slightly so. Lower-income homeowners are not likely to lose wealth as a result of owning a home in such neighborhoods—average wealth changes are positive over every time horizon the simulation examines. However, lower-income homeowners are also not likely to gain much wealth either. Average wealth gains do not exceed $4,000 even after ten years of ownership. Importantly, unlike the case for higher-appreciation regimes, these qualitative results do not vary significantly with the choice of mortgage instrument, though the severity is considerably greater when an alternative mortgage product is used. For example, a household would gain only $267 in wealth after ten years of homeownership under the 2/28 zero-down-payment mortgage. All that noted, homeownership is found to produce greater increases in wealth than renting in nearly all cases.

Thus, in low-appreciation-rate environments, and particularly using alternative mortgage instruments, homeownership is clearly not a very effective wealth-building strategy. This means that, through their ownership tenure, lower-income homeowners do not significantly reduce their exposure to the repayment difficulties that may arise owing to trigger events like unemployment, sudden illness, or divorce. Consequently, homeownership for lower-income households in this context is coupled with an elevated risk of delinquency, default, foreclosure, and the loss of a home—the failure of homeownership.

Exposure to Foreclosure Risk

The simulation results suggest that low house value appreciation is a signal of difficulties for lower-income homeowners in terms of meeting payment obligations. In such environments, lower-income homeowners are less likely to have amassed sufficient wealth resources to be able to weather any unexpected maintenance or family-related expenses or sudden shocks to income from unemployment. Since 2006, the national housing market has slowed considerably, resulting in only slight house value appreciation in most markets and outright declines in others. If the simulation's implications in the previous section are accurate, then we should see concentrated failures of homeownership, as represented by foreclosures, among lower-income households.

To explore this further, we analyzed data on foreclosures at the zip code level for ten states that vary in their geography, size, and incidence of foreclosure.[9] The foreclosure data were obtained in two forms. First, monthly counts of new entries into the foreclosure process each month from June 2006 to May 2007 provide information on the flow of properties into foreclosure. Second, we obtained a point-in-time count of the total number of properties in foreclosure in each zip code for June 2007.[10]

The data were provided by the private vendor RealtyTrac. There have been ongoing concerns regarding the quality of the RealtyTrac data. For example, the company had a practice of counting any change in the foreclosure filing status of a property as a new foreclosure, which resulted in a significant overstatement in the number of foreclosures for some locations. Recently, however, the company

FIGURE 8.1   /   Trend in Foreclosure Rates (Entries into the Foreclosure Process),
                   June 2006 to May 2007

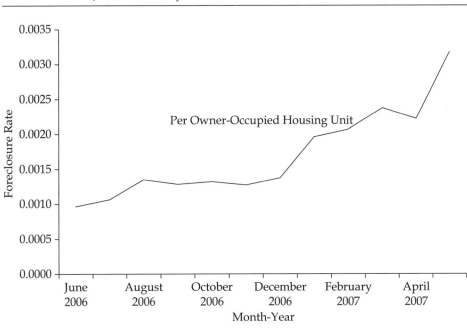

Source: Foreclosure data (2006 to 2007) by zip code from RealtyTrac. Other data from 2000 U.S.
Census, United States Census Bureau.
Note: The foreclosure rate is calculated on the number of new entries to the foreclosure process
per owner-occupied housing units.

revised this practice and now reports foreclosure data on a property basis. If a
property has multiple filing changes in a period (for example, from a notice of
default to a notice of trustee's sale to a foreclosure), it now appears as one foreclosure in the data rather than three. This approach has significantly reduced account
discrepancies between the RealtyTrac data and other information sources.[11]

Foreclosure rates are calculated as a proportion of total housing units or per
capita. All of the analyses in this section were run using both measures, and the
results are qualitatively similar. We therefore discuss only results using the
per–housing unit approach. Figure 8.1 shows the monthly progression of foreclosures into the foreclosure process and demonstrates that this period was marked
by a significant rise in foreclosure rates, whether measured on a per capita or per
housing unit basis. The annual average rate of entry into the foreclosure process
(per owner-occupied housing unit) for the ten states is 2.04 percent.

If lower-income homeowners face greater exposure to the risk of foreclosure
than other homeowners, we would expect foreclosures to be concentrated in
particular areas. Figure 8.2 reports the average foreclosure rate (1) for each state
in the sample, (2) across the MSAs in each state, and (3) across the ten zip codes

FIGURE 8.2 / Foreclosure (REO Only) Rate Medians, by State, for MSAs Within Each State and for the Ten Zip Codes in Each State with the Highest Average Rates

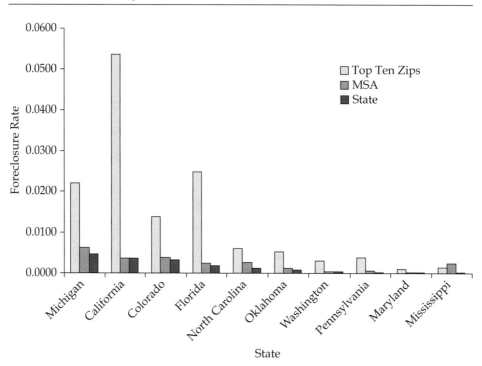

Source: Foreclosure data (2006 to 2007) by zip code from RealtyTrac. Other data from 2000 U.S. Census, United States Census Bureau.
Note: The foreclosure rate is calculated on the number of foreclosed units (REO only) per owner-occupied housing unit.

in each state with the highest foreclosure rates. The data show considerable concentrations, both across and within states. For example, while more than four out of every one hundred owner-occupied housing units had a foreclosure status in Michigan, only one of every one thousand units were in foreclosure in Mississippi. As a second example, this time demonstrating within-state concentrations, a single MSA contained nine out of the ten zip codes with the highest foreclosure rates in Colorado and Maryland.[12]

If we compare characteristics of the five states in the sample with the highest foreclosure rates and the five states with the lowest rates, we find evidence suggesting that income is an important factor (table 8.6). While the median income in the top five states is on average higher, the poverty rate is higher as well. This is consistent with the view that low-income status, as opposed to income more generally, is a key correlate with elevated foreclosure incidence. The data

TABLE 8.6 / Comparison of States in the Sample, by Magnitude of Average
Foreclosure Rate

	Five States with Highest Foreclosure Rates[a]	Five States with Lowest Foreclosure Rates
Average median household income	$42,322	$41,232
Below poverty level	12.82%	11.75%
Minority	40.49	24.26
Latino	20.91	4.31
Black	10.71	13.90
Asian	5.95	2.73
Minority fraction of owner population	30.64	17.58
Latino owner	15.06	2.56
Black owner	8.21	10.51
Asian owner	5.51	2.28
Owner within minority population	48.46	50.75
Latino population	46.12	41.71
Black population	49.09	52.95
Asian population	59.33	58.66
Annual average foreclosure rate	0.109	0.012

Source: Foreclosure data (2006 to 2007) by zip code from RealtyTrac. Other data from 2000 U.S. Census, United States Census Bureau.
Note: Sample includes foreclosure data for zip codes in ten states. The foreclosure rate is calculated on the number of REOs only per owner-occupied housing unit.
[a]Michigan, California, Colorado, Florida, and North Carolina.
[b]Oklahoma, Washington, Pennsylvania, Maryland, and Mississippi.

also show that high-foreclosure states have a greater black, Latino, and Asian presence, which suggests that minorities might similarly face elevated foreclosure exposures.

Because variables such as income and minority status are correlated, it is necessary to conduct regression analysis in order to establish the independent relationship between foreclosure rates and lower-income status. We regress the foreclosure rate at the zip code level on aggregate economic, demographic, and housing market measures characterizing the zip code. These data items were all obtained from the 2000 census. State indicator variables are also included in some specifications. For this analysis, the key indicators of interest are poverty rate and two measures of a neighborhood's income level: the median income in the zip code and whether the zip code has a relatively low median income (measured as less than 80 percent of the area median income). We consider these neighborhood variables to be reasonable proxies for lower-income homeowner exposure because of the prior analysis showing that homeownership for lower-income households makes sense less often in higher-income neighborhoods.

The results of this analysis, reported in table 8.7, show that foreclosure rates are higher in zip codes with higher poverty rates and in lower-income zip codes. Thus, if we assume that lower-income homeowners are more likely to live in such neighborhoods, the data support the view that lower-income homeowners are more vulnerable to foreclosure than other households. Surprisingly, we observe divergent relationships for blacks and Latinos. While foreclosure rates increase as a neighborhood's black presence rises, no such relationship is observed for Latino populations. Additional research might explore this relationship further.[13]

We also observe significant relationships between housing market characteristics and foreclosure rates that conform to expectations. Foreclosure rates are higher in locations with higher housing costs, and much higher in zip codes with larger fractions of homeowners facing high housing cost burdens, measured as paying more than 40 percent of their income on housing. This result again emphasizes the importance of affordability, as discussed earlier, as well as the issue of having a buffer to weather the trigger events that deplete savings and income. We also find lower foreclosure rates in zip codes with a higher median house value and in low-income zip codes with a higher appreciation rate.

CONCLUSION

Lower-income homeownership has grown dramatically over the past twenty years, allowing households that previously had been shut out of the ownership market an opportunity to enjoy its benefits, particularly in the wealth-building arena. However, our analysis has shown that these benefits are not a foregone conclusion and that considerable risks remain in some housing market environments. Indeed, the current housing environment, featuring low rates of appreciation and heavy use of alternative and subprime mortgage instruments, is one in which lower-income households can find themselves quite vulnerable to homeownership failure. Our finding that foreclosure rates are elevated in lower-income communities, holding other factors equal, supports the notion that these elevated risks have come to fruition.

Moving forward, then, it is important to take steps to shield lower-income homeowners from these potential costs. There are a number of possibilities. A vital component to any solution in this context is consumer sophistication. The current mortgage market is exceedingly complex and offers borrowers many different financing approaches. Without an independent ability to assess the benefits and risks associated with using any one of these approaches, borrowers are left to rely exclusively on the mortgage broker or loan officer in making these decisions. Because brokers and loan officers often have incentives to place borrowers in higher-cost mortgages, this reliance would seem to leave borrowers in considerable peril.

Given this, perhaps the most important initiatives will involve increasing the financial sophistication of lower-income households. These households must have a strong working knowledge of how mortgages work and be particularly well versed in the implications of using the newer alternative mortgage products. Such knowledge will help prospective borrowers make better judgments as to whether the use of a given mortgage instrument makes sense given their particular circumstances.

TABLE 8.7 / Estimated Regression Estimates for Foreclosure Rates (REO Only) per Owner-Occupied Housing Unit

Independent Variable	1	2	3	4
Poverty rate	0.019	0.015	0.015	0.012
	(4.78)**	(4.14)**	(3.67)**	(3.29)**
ln(Median household income)	0.001		0.000	
	(0.92)		(0.16)	
Income dummies	No	Yes	No	Yes
Income characteristics				
D1 (120% or more of MSA		0.000		−0.000
median household income)		(0.01)		(−0.40)
D2 (80 to 100% of MSA median		−0.000		−0.000
household income)		(−0.73)		(−0.46)
D3 (less than 80% of MSA		0.001		0.001
median household income)		(2.41)**		(2.14)**
Demographic characteristics				
Housing rate occupied	−0.000	−0.000	0.001	0.001
by blacks	(−0.16)	(−0.16)	(0.71)	(0.59)
Housing rate occupied	−0.001	−0.001	−0.003	−0.003
by Latinos	(−0.93)	(−0.88)	(−2.38)**	(−2.37)**
Vacancy rate	0.002	0.001	0.001	0.001
	(1.13)	(0.80)	(0.71)	(0.56)
Housing characteristics	0.001	0.001	0.002	0.002
Homeownership rate	(0.46)	(0.74)	(0.92)	(1.07)
Multi-family housing rate	−0.001	−0.002	−0.001	−0.001
	(−1.61)	(−1.87)*	(−0.97)	(−1.16)
Housing rate built before 1970	−0.003	−0.003	−0.002	−0.002
	(−4.60)**	(−4.82)**	(−3.27)**	(−3.48)**
ln(Median house value)	−0.004	−0.004	−0.007	−0.007
	(−4.59)**	(−4.44)**	(−7.57)**	(−7.42)**
Homeownership characteristics				
ln(Median owner cost	0.009	0.009	0.012	0.011
with mortgage)	(5.12)**	(5.75)**	(6.29)**	(6.68)**
ln(Median owner cost	−0.003	−0.003	−0.001	−0.001
without mortgage)	(−4.67)**	(−4.63)**	(−1.75)*	(−1.72)*
Ownership rate with high	0.062	0.060	0.057	0.055
cost burdens	(8.28)**	(7.98)**	(7.51)**	(7.24)**
House price appreciation rate	−0.001	−0.000	−0.000	−0.000
	(−1.52)	(−1.11)	(−0.56)	(−0.25)
Economic characteristics	−0.004	−0.004	−0.009	−0.009
Unemployment rate	(−0.74)	(−0.66)	(−1.62)	(−1.53)

(Table continues on p. 246.)

TABLE 8.7 / *Continued*

Independent Variable	1	2	3	4
Geographic characteristics				
State dummies	No	No	Yes	Yes
Interaction				
Household income*	−0.001	−0.002	−0.001	−0.001
Appreciation rate	(−2.42)**	(−3.49)**	(−2.14)**	(−2.88)**
Number of observations	3,097	3,097	3,097	3,097
R-squared	8.20%	8.47%	11.88%	12.09%

Source: Foreclosure data (2006 to 2007) by zip code from RealtyTrac. Other data from 2000 U.S. Census, United States Census Bureau.
*significant at 10 percent level; **significant at 5 percent level.

A second dimension of financial sophistication involves understanding the mortgage process, including the importance of tools such as credit scores, the roles and responsibilities of mortgage brokers, and a borrower's rights at closing. Third, we should emphasize the costs that prospective homeowners face *after* buying a home so that they can anticipate and plan for them. A fourth and more general area of focus might involve general financial literacy, to ensure that households manage their personal finances in such a way that they are well positioned to attain homeownership when they are ready to pursue it.

Development of these abilities can occur at various stages. Homeownership counseling programs could be promoted and expanded. Although such programs are mandated in some cases, a key issue is funding such services. Requiring prospective lower-income homeowners to bear such costs exclusively would be counterproductive and would actually increase the cost burden they face. Creative solutions are needed here. An alternative approach might be to introduce financial literacy as a formal part of all public school curricula. Broad introduction of such material would reduce the likelihood in the future that prospective homeowners would fall through the cracks and come to the process unprepared.

There are also measures that can ease the affordability burdens faced by many lower-income households. A clear dimension to be explored is increasing lower-income household savings rates. Higher savings would permit these households to make larger down payments, and we have shown that the risks of homeownership difficulties and foreclosure are significantly reduced if homeowners can acquire equity early in their ownership tenure. Other chapters in this volume discuss this issue in considerable depth.

Initiatives and programs to promote the production of ownership housing at prices that are affordable to lower-income households would also help reduce the number of such households that face significant housing cost burdens. Key issues accompany the question of how to produce affordable housing. Considerable evidence suggests that subsidizing new construction is an inefficient approach to housing people affordably (Olsen 2003). Thus, in most cases, if affordable homeownership subsidies are to be provided, they should not be directed toward new production. In this context, the current nonproduction housing subsidy structure must be reconsidered. Most housing subsidies emphasize rental housing over ownership product. A healthy debate as to the desirability of this pattern of subsidy would be welcome.

However, there are some areas, most typically high-cost areas on the coasts, where there is an inadequate supply of housing. In these areas, some kind of production subsidy almost certainly makes sense. Discussions here should focus on the type of housing to be produced for ownership. For example, Boehm and Schlottmann (2004b) suggest that manufactured housing would be a beneficial investment for homeowners under the right conditions. An exploration of manufactured housing or modular home options among others might lead to creative alternatives that make sense in promoting affordable homeownership.

A third area of exploration for reducing mortgage costs might be in restructuring the mortgage finance market. In particular, we might explore the possibility of allowing Fannie Mae and Freddie Mac to become more active in the subprime and alternative mortgage markets. These two secondary mortgage market players have helped standardize the prime mortgage market and reduce costs, and there is evidence suggesting that their presence in markets reduces the prevalence of more expensive mortgage products (An and Bostic 2008). Prospective lower-income homebuyers would benefit from lower costs and more standardized products if the same dynamic were to play out in the alternative and subprime mortgage markets.[14]

Finally, policymakers should consider modifying the regulatory environment to limit abuses that reduce the wealth of lower-income homeowners or leave them at risk of a loss of wealth. As one example, Bostic and his colleagues (2008) show that anti-predatory lending laws can change market behaviors in beneficial ways, but that the details of the regulatory structure matter. This suggests that carefully designed anti-predatory lending and other laws might eliminate these negative excesses without significantly reducing the beneficial aspects of homeownership. This has direct implications for both researchers and policymakers. Researchers should continue their efforts to examine prevailing regulatory incentives at the local, state, and federal levels and gain further insights into how these incentives might be altered to the benefit of lower-income homeowners. At the same time, policymakers at the state and local levels should use such knowledge to seriously assess their regulatory structures to see whether incentives are properly aligned to minimize abuses while maximizing benefits, and then make necessary changes to effect this.

Regulatory changes should also be considered for brokers, who often are the channel by which the newer mortgage products are introduced to lower-income homeowners. Currently, brokers are compensated largely independent of the outcome of the mortgage and are not penalized if a mortgage results in default and foreclosure. Policymakers should seriously review options to change this and provide an extra level of independent scrutiny regarding the prudence of some mortgage arrangements. One possibility is to require brokers to become bonded, with the bond drawn upon if a mortgage defaults and review suggests that the mortgage terms made default a distinct probability. Here brokers would have a financial incentive to limit the number of households entering into "bad" mortgages in which delinquency and default are likely. Alternatively, a reporting system could be established by which brokers would be rated according to how many of the mortgages they were associated with subsequently became delinquent and defaulted. Brokers would be required to disclose this rating to prospective homebuyers. A rating system would provide significant regulatory discipline, as poorly rated brokers would probably find it difficult to obtain customers without demonstrating some change in practices or policies.[15]

APPENDIX: THE SIMULATION METHODOLOGY

Given the population partitions by household head, household size, and income, we implemented the simulation by first estimating the annual expenditures for housing and other goods for these households. Annual income figures were obtained from 2006 data compiled by the U.S. Department of Housing and Urban Development. Average expenditures out of annual income were determined for each household type using the 2005 Consumer Expenditure Survey (CES). We partitioned the CES sample of households according to our household type categories, and then for each petition we calculated average total expenditures and total housing expenditures as fractions of total income. The estimated average expenditure and housing expense rates out of income for the various household types are reported in table 8A.1. From this, we established living expenses for households apart from housing expenses. Formally, for each sample partition, we calculated nonhousing living expenses as [(annual income) × (annual expenditures rate) × (1 − housing expenditures rate)].

Housing expenses were calculated as the prevailing fair market rent (FMR) as established by HUD for high-, middle-, and lower-income neighborhoods for renters. For homeowners, we used the monthly mortgage payment that would arise from the purchase of a median house in the relevant neighborhood given a particular mortgage and down payment combination. For the purposes of this exercise, we abstracted away from requiring private mortgage insurance. The house value was set using 2006 data as reported by Dataquick. For both rent and home purchase price, the levels were determined based on family size. For single-person households, we used the FMR for a one-bedroom unit and assumed a purchase price at 60 percent of the area median. For two-person households, the rent was set as the average of the one-bedroom and two-bedroom FMRs, and the purchase price was assumed to be 70 percent of the area median. Finally, we used the two-bedroom FMR and the purchase price of 80 percent for three-person households.

Given income, rent or mortgage payments, and nonhousing living expenses, it is straightforward to calculate the income surplus or shortfall for a household. To obtain savings, we assume a 4 percent savings rate out of this income value. We also can calculate the amount of home equity the household would have accrued given the down payment and a year's worth of mortgage payments. We can thus determine the gain to wealth associated with homeownership and renting for a single year.

TABLE 8A.1 / Estimated Total Expenditure and Housing Expenditure Rates
Using the 2005 Consumer Expenditure Survey

Type	Income Level	Family Size	Age	Average Annual Expenditure Rate	Housing Expenditure
1	High	1	25 to 34	86.12	21.64
2	High	1	35 to 44	76.47	18.91
3	High	1	45 to 54	77.21	17.79
4	Middle	1	25 to 34	94.85	24.30
5	Middle	1	35 to 44	84.22	21.23
6	Middle	1	45 to 54	85.03	19.97
7	Low	1	25 to 34	94.85	24.30
8	Low	1	35 to 44	84.22	21.23
9	Low	1	45 to 54	85.03	19.97
10	High	2	25 to 34	82.71	15.68
11	High	2	35 to 44	82.12	15.34
12	High	2	45 to 54	80.44	13.83
13	Middle	2	25 to 34	92.59	17.41
14	Middle	2	35 to 44	91.94	17.03
15	Middle	2	45 to 54	90.06	15.35
16	Low	2	25 to 34	100.46	19.50
17	Low	2	35 to 44	99.75	19.07
18	Low	2	45 to 54	97.71	17.19
19	High	3	25 to 34	97.98	17.46
20	High	3	35 to 44	82.87	14.28
21	High	3	45 to 54	76.17	12.60
22	Middle	3	25 to 34	108.47	23.25
23	Middle	3	35 to 44	91.74	16.25
24	Middle	3	45 to 54	84.32	14.34
25	Low	3	25 to 34	127.68	24.46
26	Low	3	35 to 44	107.99	20.00
27	Low	3	45 to 54	99.25	17.65

Source: Authors' compilation.
Note: High-income households have incomes greater than 120 percent of the area median, middle-income households have incomes at the median income level, and lower-income households have incomes less than 80 percent of the area median.

The authors would like to thank Michael Barr, Rebecca Blank, and participants in the University of Michigan National Poverty Center's "Access, Assets, and Poverty" conference for support, comments, and useful advice. We would also like to thank Richard Martin, John Karevoll, and Dataquick for providing data. Finally, we would like to express tremendous gratitude to the late Edward Gramlich, who provided much of the framework underlying this chapter.

NOTES

1. Although the literature often demonstrates correlations, there is a lack of consensus regarding homeownership's causal role, owing to concerns about selection bias. For more, see Dietz and Haurin (2003).
2. Evidence also suggests that to some extent the higher interest rates charged are warranted, as subprime loans have worse performance. Whereas only about 1 percent of prime mortgages are in serious delinquency, historically the rate for serious delinquency on subprime mortgages is more than 7 percent.
3. Questions are also raised out of concern that the benefits observed with homeownership are due to self-selection of households predisposed to such benefits rather than to homeownership itself (Rohe, McCarthy, and van Zandt 2001). If true, then we would need to study the selection of lower-income households into homeownership and compare this process with that for other households. This has not yet been done systematically.
4. Annual and total interest rate adjustments are typically capped as part of the mortgage contract. For example, a contract might stipulate that the interest rate cannot adjust by more than two percentage points even if prevailing rates justify a larger adjustment. For a total adjustments example, a contract might establish that the interest rate may not exceed the teaser rate plus six percentage points. Sample payments cited here were calculated using an online mortgage calculator at http://www.forsalebyownercenter.com/tools/228adjustableratemortgagecalculator.aspx.
5. Homeownership in high-income neighborhoods (those with median incomes greater than 120 percent of the area median) is generally out of reach for lower-income households. Simulation results (not shown) largely bear this out.
6. Because lower-income households have limited savings and wealth on average, we do not consider cases involving 20 percent down payments. We do note, however, that these scenarios yield the greatest benefits to homeownership.
7. Hybrid ARMs are adjustable-rate mortgages with an initial fixed-rate period, indicated in years by the first number. We assume the 5/1 ARM has a 1 percent annual rate change cap and a 6 percent lifetime interest rate change cap. We assume the 2/28 ARM has a 2 percent annual rate change cap and a 6 percent lifetime interest rate change cap. These rates mimic the prevailing loan terms in 2005.
8. For example, Karl Case (2000) reports different appreciation rates by neighborhood income level as determined for Boston, Chicago, and Los Angeles. According to his findings, high-income neighborhoods appreciate the most, low-income neighborhoods appreciate the least, and the variation between neighborhoods is significant.
9. The ten states are California, Colorado, Florida, Maryland, Michigan, Mississippi, North Carolina, Oklahoma, Pennsylvania, and Washington.
10. Although there is some variation across states, the stages of foreclosure follow this general pattern: (1) notice of default—the initial filing that starts the foreclosure process; (2) lis penden—the notification of a pending lawsuit; (3) notice of trustee's sale—the announcement of a public auction; (4) notice of foreclosure sale—the order signed by a judge allowing the property to be sold at auction; and (5) REO—officially owned by the lien-holder. For the current study, the entrance to the REO stage is

treated as a foreclosure, and all the other stages are viewed as being in the foreclosure process.
11. Issues remain regarding foreclosures in rural areas, owing to the difficulty of access-
ing these data. Fortunately, rural areas are not prevalent in our data.
12. The data show that in some zip codes the number of foreclosures recorded during the
study period exceeded the number of housing units as reported in the 2000 census.
This might be due to rapid development between 2000 and 2006, as has been the case
in parts of California.
13. Additional analysis, not shown, suggests that this is driven by variation across states.
14. The federal fiscal stimulus package enacted in February 2008 temporarily expanded
the scope of GSE activity, based on a similar rationale that the lower costs would bol-
ster housing markets.
15. Such a reporting system would be similar to the current restaurant reporting system
in Los Angeles County: restaurants receive a letter grade indicating their compliance
with public health and food preparation codes, and this grade must be posted in a
restaurant's front window, where it serves as a clear signal to consumers.

REFERENCES

An, Xudong, and Raphael W. Bostic. 2008. "GSE Activity, FHA Feedback, and Implications
for the Efficacy of the Affordable Housing Goals." *Journal of Real Estate Finance and
Economics* 36(2): 207–31.
An, Xudong, Raphael W. Bostic, Yongheng Deng, and Stuart A. Gabriel. 2007. "GSE Loan
Purchases, the FHA, and Housing Outcomes in Targeted, Low-Income Neighborhoods."
Brookings-Wharton Conference on Urban Affairs Series. Washington, D.C.: Brookings
Institution.
Apgar, William C., and Allegra Calder. 2005. "The Dual Mortgage Market: The Persistence
of Discrimination in Mortgage Lending." In *The Geography of Opportunity: Race and Housing
Choice in Metropolitan America,* edited by Xavier de Sousa Briggs. Washington, D.C.:
Brookings Institution Press.
Apgar, William C., and Mark Duda. 2004. "Mortgage Foreclosure Trends in Los Angeles:
Patterns and Policy Issues." Research prepared for Los Angeles Neighborhood Housing
Services.
———. 2005. "Collateral Damage: The Municipal Impact of Today's Mortgage Foreclosure
Boom." Washington, D.C.: Homeownership Preservation Foundation. Available at:
http://www.995hope.org/content/pdf/Apgar_Duda_Study_Short_Version.pdf.
Avery, Robert B., Raphael W. Bostic, and Glenn B. Canner. 2005. "Assessing the Necessity
and Efficiency of the Community Reinvestment Act." *Housing Policy Debate* 16(1): 143–72.
Belsky, Eric S., and Mark Duda. 2002a. "Anatomy of the Low-Income Homeownership
Boom in the 1990s." In *Low-Income Homeownership: Examining the Unexamined Goal,* edited
by Nicholas P. Retsinas and Eric S. Belsky. Washington, D.C.: Brookings Institution Press.
———. 2002b. "Asset Appreciation, Timing of Purchases and Sales, and Returns to Low-
Income Homeownership." In *Low-Income Homeownership: Examining the Unexamined Goal,*
edited by Nicholas P. Retsinas and Eric S. Belsky. Washington, D.C.: Brookings Institution
Press.

Bernheim, B. Douglas, and John Karl Scholz. 1992. "Private Saving and Public Policy." Working paper 4215. Cambridge, Mass.: National Bureau of Economic Research.

Boehm, Thomas P. 1981. "Tenure Choice and Expected Mobility—A Synthesis." *Journal of Urban Economics* 10(3): 375–89.

Boehm, Thomas P., and Alan M. Schlottmann. 2004a. "The Dynamics of Race, Income, and Homeownership." *Journal of Urban Economics* 55(1): 113–30.

———. 2004b. *Is Manufacturing Housing a Good Alternative for Low-Income Families? Evidence from the American Housing Survey.* Washington: U.S. Department of Housing and Urban Development, Office of Policy Development and Research.

Bostic, Raphael W., Kathleen C. Engel, Patricia A. McCoy, Anthony Pennington-Cross, and Susan M. Wachter. 2008. "State and Local Anti-predatory Lending Laws: The Effect of Legal Enforcement Mechanisms." *Journal of Economics and Business* 60(1–2): 47–66.

Bostic, Raphael W., and Breck Robinson. 2005. "What Makes CRA Agreements Work? A Study of Lender Responses to CRA Agreements." *Housing Policy Debate* 16(3–4): 513–45.

Bostic, Raphael W., and Brian J. Surette. 2001. "Have the Doors Opened Wider? Trends in Family Homeownership Rates by Race and Income." *Journal of Real Estate Finance and Economics* 23(November): 411–34.

Calem, Paul S., Jonathan E. Hershaff, and Susan M. Wachter. 2004. "Neighborhood Patterns of Subprime Lending: Evidence from Disparate Cities." *Housing Policy Debate* 15(3): 603–22.

Carr, James H., and Lopa Kolluri. 2001. *Predatory Lending: An Overview.* Washington: Fannie Mae Foundation.

Case, Karl E. 2000. "Real Estate and the Macroeconomy." *Brookings Papers on Economic Activity* 2000(2): 119–62.

Collins, Michael. 1998. *The Many Benefits of Homeownership.* Washington, D.C.: Neighbor-Works Publications.

Collins, Michael, David Crowe, and Michael Carliner. 2002. "Supply-Side Constraints on Low-Income Homeownership." In *Low-Income Homeownership: Examining the Unexamined Goal,* edited by Nicholas P. Retsinas and Eric S. Belsky. Washington, D.C.: Brookings Institution Press.

Cummings, Jean L., Denise DiPasquale, and Matthew E. Kahn. 2002. "Measuring the Consequences of Promoting Inner City Homeownership." *Journal of Housing Economics* 11(4): 330–59.

Courchane, Marsha J., Brian J. Surette, and Peter M. Zorn. 2004. "Subprime Borrowers: Mortgage Transitions and Outcomes." *Journal of Real Estate Finance and Economics* 29(4): 365–92.

Cutts, Amy Crews, and Richard K. Green. 2004. "Innovative Servicing Technology: Smart Enough to Keep People in Their Houses?" Working paper 04-03. Washington: Freddie Mac (July). Available at: http://www.freddiemac.com/news/pdf/fmwp_0403_servicing.pdf.

Dedman, Bill. 1988. "The Color of Money" (series). *Atlanta Journal-Constitution,* May 1–4.

Di, Zhu, Yi Yang, and Xiaodong Liu. 2003. "The Importance of Housing to the Accumulation of Household Net Wealth." Working paper W03-5. Cambridge, Mass.: Harvard University, Joint Center for Housing Studies.

Dietz, Robert D., and Donald R. Haurin. 2003. "The Social and Private Micro-Level Consequences of Homeownership." *Journal of Urban Economics* 54(3): 401–50.

DiPasquale, Denise, and Edward L. Glaeser. 1999. "Incentives and Social Capital: Are Homeowners Better Citizens?" *Journal of Urban Economics* 45(2): 354–84.

Doling, John, and Bruce Stafford. 1989. *Home Ownership: The Diversity of Experience.* Aldershot, U.K.: Gower.

Duncan, Douglas. 2006. "Fourth General Session: Economic/Housing Outlook." Slides presented to the annual convention of the Mortgage Bankers Association. Chicago (October 22–25). Available at: http://www.mortgagebankers.org/files/Conferences/2006/93rdAnnualConvention/MBA_DougDuncan4thGeneralSession_final.pdf.

Ellen, Ingrid Gould, Michael H. Schill, Amy Ellen Schwartz, and Ioan Voicu. 2003. "Housing Production Subsidies and Neighborhood Revitalization: New York City's Ten-Year Capital Plan for Housing." *Federal Reserve Board of New York Economic Policy Review* (June): 71–85.

Fannie Mae. 1999. *Fannie Mae National Housing Survey 1994.* Washington: Fannie Mae Foundation.

Fishbein, Allen J. 2003. "Filling the Half-Empty Glass: The Role of Community Advocacy in Redefining the Public Responsibilities of Government Sponsored Housing Enterprises." In *Organizing Access to Capital: Advocacy and the Democratization of Financial Institutions,* edited by Gregory D. Squires. Philadelphia: Temple University Press.

Galster, George C. 1983. "Empirical Evidence on Cross-Tenure Differences in Home Maintenance and Condition." *Land Economics* 59(1): 107–13.

———. 1987. *Homeowners and Neighborhood Reinvestment.* Durham, N.C.: Duke University Press.

Gramlich, Edward M. 2004. "Subprime Mortgage Lending: Benefits, Costs, and Challenges." Remarks delivered at the annual housing policy meeting of the Financial Services Roundtable. Chicago (May 21).

———. 2007. *Subprime Mortgages: America's Latest Boom and Bust.* Washington, D.C.: Urban Institute Press.

Goldstein, Ira, Maggie McCullough, Al Parker, and Daniel Urevick-Ackelsberg. 2005. "Mortgage Foreclosure Filings in Pennsylvania." Philadelphia: Reinvestment Fund. Available at: http://www.trfund.com/resource/downloads/policypubs/Mortgage-Forclosure-Filings.pdf

Gruenstein, Debbie, and Christopher E. Herbert. 2000a. *Analyzing Trends in Subprime Originations and Foreclosures: A Case Study of the Atlanta Metro Area.* Cambridge, Mass.: Abt Associates.

———. 2000b. *Analyzing Trends in Subprime Originations and Foreclosures: A Case Study of the Boston Metro Area.* Cambridge, Mass.: Abt Associates.

Harkness, Joseph, and Sandra J. Newman. 2002. "Homeownership for the Poor in Distressed Neighborhoods: Does This Make Sense?" *Housing Policy Debate* 13(3): 597–630.

Haurin, Donald R., Toby L. Parcel, and R. Jean Haurin. 2002. "Impact of Homeownership on Child Outcomes." In *Low-Income Homeownership: Examining the Unexamined Goal,* edited by Nicholas P. Retsinas and Eric S. Belsky. Washington, D.C.: Brookings Institution Press.

Herbert, Christopher E., and Eric S. Belsky. 2006. *The Homeownership Experience of Low-Income and Minority Families: A Review and Synthesis of the Literature.* Prepared for U.S. Department of Housing and Urban Development, Office of Policy Development and Research. Washington: HUD.

Hoffman, Lily M., and Barbara S. Heistler. 1988. "Home Finance: Buying and Keeping a House in a Changing Financial Environment." In *Handbook of Housing and the Built Environment in the United States,* edited by Elizabeth Huttman and Willem van Vleit. New York: Greenwood Press.

Hurd, Maude, and Steven Kest. 2003. "Fighting Predatory Lending from the Ground Up: An Issue of Economic Justice." In *Organizing Access to Capital: Advocacy and the Democratization of Financial Institutions,* edited by Gregory D. Squires. Philadelphia: Temple University Press.

Immergluck, Dan, and Geoff Smith. 2005. "Measuring the Effect of Subprime Lending on Neighborhood Foreclosures: Evidence from Chicago." *Urban Affairs Review* 40(3): 362–89.

———. 2006a. "The External Costs of Single-Family Mortgage Foreclosures: The Impact of Single-Family Mortgage Foreclosures on Property Values." *Housing Policy Debate* 17(1): 57–79.

———. 2006b. "The Impact of Single-Family Mortgage Foreclosures on Neighborhood Crime." *Housing Studies* 21(6): 851–66.

Joint Center for Housing Studies. 2002. *The Twenty-Fifth Anniversary of the Community Reinvestment Act: Access to Capital in an Evolving Financial Services System CRA.* Cambridge, Mass.: Harvard University.

Kelling, George L., and Catherine M. Coles. 1996. *Fixing Broken Windows: Restoring Order and Reducing Crime in Our Communities.* New York: Touchstone.

Kennickell, Arthur B. 2006. "Currents and Undercurrents: Changes in the Distribution of Wealth, 1989–2004." Working paper 2006-13. Washington: Board of Governors of the Federal Reserve System.

Kind, Paul, Paul Dolan, Claire Gudex, and Alan Williams. 1998. "Variations in Population Health Status: Results from a United Kingdom National Questionnaire Survey." *British Medical Journal* 316(7133): 736–41.

Lauria, Daniel D. 1976. "Wealth, Capital, and Power: The Social Meaning of Home Ownership." *Journal of Interdisciplinary History* 7(2): 261–82.

Lax, Howard, Michael Manti, Paul Raca, and Peter Zorn. 2004. "Subprime Lending: An Investigation of Economic Efficiency." *Housing Policy Debate* 15(3): 533–72.

Lee, Chang-Moo, Dennis P. Culhane, and Susan M. Wachter. 1999. "The Differential Impacts of Federally Assisted Housing Programs on Nearby Property Values: A Philadelphia Case Study." *Housing Policy Debate* 10(1): 75–93.

Lewis, Glyn, Paul Bebbington, Traolach Brugha, Michael Farrell, Baljit Gill, Rachel Jenkins, and Howard Meltzer. 1998. "Socioeconomic Status, Standard of Living, and Neurotic Disorder." *Lancet* 352(9128): 605–9.

Listokin, David D., and Elvin K. Wyly. 2000. "Making New Mortgage Markets: Case Studies of Institutions, Home Buyers, and Communities." *Housing Policy Debate* 11(3): 575–644.

Listokin, David D., Elvin K. Wyly, Brian Schmitt, and Ioan Voicu. 2001. "The Potential and Limitation of Mortgage Innovation in Fostering Homeownership in the United States." *Housing Policy Debate* 12(3): 465–513.

Litan, Robert E., Nicholas P. Retsinas, Eric S. Belsky, and Susan W. Haag. 2000. *The Community Reinvestment Act After Financial Modernization: A Baseline Report.* Washington: U.S. Department of the Treasury.

Maki, Dean M. 1996. "Portfolio Shuffling and Tax Reform." *National Tax Journal* 49(3): 317–29.

Massey, Douglas S., and Eric Fong. 1990. "Segregation and Neighborhood Quality." *Social Forces* 69(1): 15–32.

Mills, Edwin S., and Luan S. Lubuele. 1994. "Performance of Residential Mortgages in Low- and Moderate-Income Neighborhoods." *Journal of Real Estate Finance and Economics* 9(3): 245–60.

Mortgage Bankers Association (MBA). 2007. "Delinquencies and Foreclosures Increase in Latest MBA National Delinquency Survey." Press release (December 6). Available at: http://www.mortgagebankers.org/NewsandMedia/PressCenter/58758.htm.

———. 2008. "Delinquencies and Foreclosures Increase in Latest MBA National Delinquency Survey." Press release (September 5). Available at: http://www.mbaa.org/NewsandMedia/PressCenter/64769.htm.

National Association of Realtors. Research Division. 2004. *Rising Foreclosure Rates in Indiana: An Explanatory Analysis of Contributing Factors.* Washington, D.C.: National Association of Realtors (March). Available at:http://www.mibor.com/_pdfs/ForeclosureStudy2004.pdf.

National Training and Information Center. 1999. *Preying on Neighborhoods: Subprime Mortgages and Chicagoland Foreclosures.* Chicago: National Training and Information Center.

Newberger, Harriet. 2006. "Foreclosure Filings and Sheriff's Sales Experienced by Low-Income, First-Time Home Buyers." *Housing Policy Debate* 17(2): 341–87.

Olsen, Edgar O. 2003. "Housing Programs for Low-Income Households." In *Means-Tested Transfer Programs in the United States,* edited by Robert A. Moffitt. Chicago: University of Chicago Press.

Renuart, Elizabeth. 2004. "An Overview of the Predatory Lending Process." *Housing Policy Debate* 15(3): 467–502.

Retsinas, Nicholas P., and Eric S. Belsky. 2002. *Low-Income Homeownership: Examining the Unexamined Goal.* Washington, D.C.: Brookings Institution Press.

Rohe, William M., George W. McCarthy, and Shannon van Zandt. 2001. "The Social Benefits and Costs of Homeownership: A Critical Assessment of the Research." Low-Income Homeownership Working Paper Series 00-01. Cambridge, Mass.: Harvard University, Joint Center for Housing Studies.

Rohe, William M., and Michael A. Stegman. 1994a. "The Effects of Homeownership on the Self-Esteem, Perceived Control, and Satisfaction of Low-Income People." *Journal of the American Planning Association* 60(2): 173–84.

———. 1994b. "The Impact of Home Ownership on the Social and Political Involvement of Low-Income People." *Urban Affairs Quarterly* 30(September): 152–72.

Rohe, William M., and Leslie S. Stewart. 1996. "Home Ownership and Neighborhood Stability." *Housing Policy Debate* 7(1): 37–81.

Rosenthal, Stuart S. 2004. "Old Homes and Poor Neighborhoods: A Dynamic Model of Urban Decline and Renewal." Unpublished paper, Department of Economics, Syracuse University.

Rossi, Peter H., and Eleanor Weber. 1996. "The Social Benefits of Homeownership: Empirical Evidence from National Surveys." *Housing Policy Debate* 7(1): 1–35.

Santiago, Anna, George C. Galster, and Peter Tatian. 2001. "Assessing the Property Value Impacts of the Dispersed Housing Subsidy Program in Denver." *Journal of Policy Analysis and Management* 20(1): 65–88.

Saunders, Peter. 1990. *A Nation of Home Owners.* London: Unwin Hyman.

Schreiner, Mark, and Michael Sherraden. 2007. *Can the Poor Save? Saving and Asset Building in Individual Development Accounts.* New Brunswick, N.J.: Transaction Publishers.

Shlay, Anne B. 1993. "Family Self-Sufficiency and Housing." *Housing Policy Debate* 4(3): 457–96.

———. 2006. "Low-Income Homeownership: American Dream or Delusion?" *Urban Studies* 43(3): 511–31.

Shlay, Anne B., and Gordon Whitman. 2004. *Research for Democracy: Linking Community Organizing and Research to Leverage Blight Policy,* COMM-ORG paper series, volume 10. Madison: University of Wisconsin. Available at: http://comm-org.wisc.edu/papers2004/shlay/shlay.htm.

Stein, Eric. 2001. "Quantifying the Economic Cost of Predatory Lending." Durham, N.C.: Coalition for Responsible Lending. Available at: http://www.responsiblelending.org.

Tremblay, Kenneth R., Don A. Dillman, Kent D. Van Liere. 1980. "An Examination of the Relationship Between Housing Preferences and Community-Size Preferences." *Rural Sociology* 45(3): 509–19.

U.S. Department of Housing and Urban Development (HUD). 2000a. *Unequal Burden in Baltimore: Income and Racial Disparities in Subprime Lending.* Washington: HUD.

———. 2000b. *Unequal Burden: Income and Racial Disparities in Subprime Lending in America.* Washington: HUD.

U.S. Department of Housing and Urban Development and U.S. Department of the Treasury. 2000. "Curbing Predatory Home Mortgage Lending." Washington: U.S. Department of Housing and Urban Development and U.S. Department of the Treasury.

White, Alan M. 2004. "Risk-Based Mortgage Pricing: Present and Future Research." *Housing Policy Debate* 15(3): 503–32.

Wilson, James Q., and George L. Kelling. 1982. "Broken Windows: The Police and Neighborhood Safety." *Atlantic Monthly* (March): 29–38.

Chapter 9

Patterns of Credit Card Use Among Low- and Moderate-Income Households

Ronald J. Mann

Ensuring that the poorer segments of the population have access to financial products and services has taken on increased significance as policymakers have come to understand the broad social ramifications of inclusive financial regimes. Access not only promotes savings but also enables the poor to manage cash flows and to meet basic needs such as health care, food, and housing. In the United States, the last few decades have seen remarkable progress on that front as low- and moderate-income (LMI) households increasingly use both mainstream products like deposit accounts and "fringe" products like payday lending, check-cashing services, and pawnshops (Barr, this volume; Caskey 1996; Hogarth, Anguelov, and Lee 2004; Mann and Hawkins 2007). At the same time, because many of those products exploit cognitive and financial constraints, policymakers are now increasingly moving beyond concerns about access to emphasize the need for safety in the design and marketing of financial products (Warren 2007).

Credit cards cut across those concerns. With respect to access, the credit card is a profoundly democratizing instrument. It is only a slight exaggeration to say that any person with a Visa or MasterCard product can walk into the same stores and restaurants as the most elite trendsetters in our society and purchase the same goods and services, at the same prices. As status in a consumer society shifts to depend more heavily on consumption (rather than family wealth or occupational status), the credit card acts as a leveler of status (Cross 2000, 169–84; Frank 1999, ch. 4). The credit card also provides a remarkably flexible safety net that can be deployed in response to unexpected financial crises (Mann 2006). That protection is particularly important in the United States, where the public safety net is more porous than it is in many peer nations (Hacker 2002; Howard 2007).

At the same time, the credit card is singled out as one of the most perilous consumer financial products. The prevalence of credit card use raises concerns that consumer spending is leading to overindebtedness (Schor 1999). In previous work, I present aggregate data that suggest a significant relation between increased credit card use and consumer bankruptcy filings at a national level (Mann 2006). The flexibility that makes the credit card so useful for households faced with unexpected difficulties is central to the danger that the product can bring to those who use it in excess (Littwin 2008a; Mann 2007; Mann and Hawkins 2007). Safety concerns are particularly important in connection with financial products for the poor (McCloud 2007).

This chapter uses data from the Federal Reserve Board's Survey of Consumer Finances (SCF) for 2004 to examine the penetration of credit cards into LMI markets. The chapter has two purposes. First, I discuss the rise of the modern credit market, emphasizing the segmentation of product lines based on behavioral and financial characteristics of customer groups (for more detail, see Mann 2007). Among other things, that trend involves the use of products aimed at LMI households that differ significantly from those aimed at middle-class households.

Second, I describe the use of credit cards by LMI households: the amounts of debt they carry; the types of LMI households that carry debt; and how these households differ from higher-income households that carry debt. Despite their lower incomes, LMI households use credit cards almost as often as other households do. Indeed, measured as a share of income, the credit card balances that LMI cardholders carry are substantially higher than those of higher-income households. To refine the analysis, the chapter closes with the results of a multivariate regression analysis of the characteristics of LMI households with credit card debt. Generally, those results suggest that the demographic characteristics of LMI households that have credit card debt are different in material ways from the characteristics of those households in the overall population with credit card debt. The models I summarize here suggest that age, race, and education correlate with credit card use in the population at large. At least in these models, however, age and race become less important predictors, and education has only a marginal relation to credit card use in LMI households. In LMI households, by contrast, credit card use is most closely related to the use of other financial products: checking accounts, mortgage loans, and car loans.

THE MODERN CREDIT CARD MARKET

The rise of the credit card to dominance in American payment and lending transactions is well known. The total value of credit card transactions increased from about $800 billion in 1990 to more than $1.7 trillion in 2006. Similarly, credit card balances increased from about $450 billion in 1990 to more than $750 billion in 2006 (Nilson Report; for a more detailed discussion, see Mann 2006). As figure 9.1 illustrates, the rise in spending on cards reflects a substantial shift toward cards and away from other payment devices.

What is less widely understood is the mechanism by which this has occurred. Credit card lending is by nature risky. Unlike the home mortgage lender or the car lender, the credit card lender has no collateral to which it can look for repayment. Moreover, several factors combine to leave the credit card lender with no practical device for collecting payment. First, in most American jurisdictions,

FIGURE 9.1 / Spending on Retail Payment Systems in the United States, 1991 to 2005

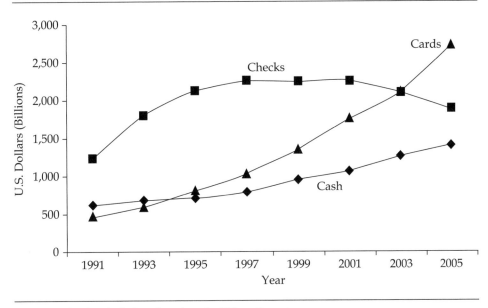

Source: Author's calculations based on the Nilson Report.

unsecured lenders have no practical remedy other than litigation, either because garnishment is illegal (the rule in some states) or because it is ineffective, especially against debtors who do not have regular incomes or bank accounts. Most jurisdictions also have schedules of exempt assets that are not subject to seizures by unsecured creditors, even when they hold unpaid judgments. Thus, exemptions in many cases cover all assets in the household. Finally, the availability of a discharge in bankruptcy means that debtors who are pushed too far normally can discharge their obligations to the credit card lender.

In practice, the most effective lever the credit card lender has is the threat of damaging the credit report of the borrower. A credit card debtor who does not pay will suffer a substantially lower credit rating. Although the lower credit card rating will have only a limited impact on the debtor's access to credit card debt, it will substantially increase the cost of subsequent borrowing. This is particularly true for mortgage lenders, which continue to use crude underwriting systems that rely directly on the credit rating system. For the sophisticated credit card lender, in contrast, the credit rating is at most one of many inputs into the underwriting process. In any event, the threat of an adverse credit report is ineffective against debtors who are in serious financial distress and whose credit rating already has been compromised because of missed payments to other creditors.

Because of the riskiness of the credit card business model, the industry, in its infancy, used a unitary business model. The product offerings of the different issuers were similar, so competition occurred mainly through marketing and customer service. Interest rates were standard and relatively high, typically in the range of 18 percent. At the same time, despite those relatively high rates, the customers to whom credit card lenders could make profitable loans were a relatively small part of the middle class. The wealthy had little interest in borrowing at 18 percent, and those who had no reliable income stream were too risky. In general, most issuers had a large group of profitable customers who borrowed and paid substantial amounts of interest, a second group of generally unprofitable customers who did not borrow but instead paid their bills each month, and a third group of highly unprofitable customers who borrowed and did not repay their debts. Profitability came from maximizing the number of customers in the first group and minimizing the number in the second and third groups.

The advent of technological underwriting tools in the 1990s changed everything. The most capable lenders developed increasingly complex statistical models that predicted more accurately the spending and repayment behavior of smaller slices of the potential cardholding population (Johnson 2005). The result has been a steady segmentation and specialization of the market. The first stage involved differential pricing, in which low-risk customers received lower interest rates (to encourage borrowing) and high-risk customers received higher interest rates (to provide a margin for delinquencies).

Differential pricing has not led to a decline in net interest margins. Although the effective annual interest rate has fallen in the last fifteen years, from about 16.4 percent in 1990 to 12.2 percent in 2006, a parallel decrease in the cost of funds means that the net interest margin has not changed substantially during that period (rising from 7.4 percent in 1990 to 7.6 percent in 2006).[1] At the same time, however, the portfolios underwritten at that margin have become considerably riskier. For example, the rate at which issuers write off unpaid balances (charge-offs) steadily increased during this period, from 3.5 percent in 1990 to about 6 percent during 2004 to 2005.[2] Essentially, improved underwriting technologies allowed the successful credit card lenders to develop reliable predictions about the repayment behavior of increasingly unreliable customers. This capability has allowed those lenders to acquire profitable portfolios filled with cardholders who would have been unacceptably risky a few decades ago.[3]

The maintenance of a relatively constant net interest margin suggests a balance of increased borrowing at lower rates by relatively creditworthy customers against new borrowing by relatively risky customers at higher rates. The ability to profit with flat interest margins despite the increase in charge-offs suggests that the card issuers have developed new revenue sources. The first is an increased reliance on fees, particularly in the subprime product lines discussed later in this chapter. Late and overlimit fees on an annual basis were only 0.7 percent of the average outstanding balances in 1990, but doubled during the 1990s to 1.4 percent or 1.5 percent of the average outstanding balances, a plateau at which they remained until they began to decline in 2005 and 2006. The second increased revenue source is fees paid by merchants that accept cards (interchange), which has risen about 70 percent faster than receivables, from 2.15 percent to 3.69 percent of average outstanding balances. In part, this reflects the ability of issuers, especially in recent years, to shift

FIGURE 9.2 / Cards Profitability Data

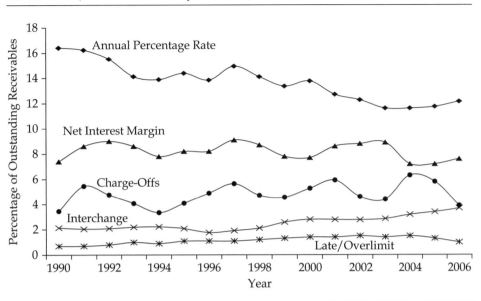

Source: Author's calculation from Cards Profitability Survey, published by *Cards and Payments*.

increasing numbers of cardholders to high-interchange premium and "platinum" products.[4]

The second stage of market segmentation involves the development of increasingly complex product attributes that tailor products to specific classes of potential cardholders.[5] Thus, different issuers are particularly expert in superprime offerings (Chase Bank and Bank of America), affinity offerings (Bank of America's MBNA division), cobranded offerings (Chase Bank), relational offerings (Wells Fargo), subprime offerings (Capitol One), and foreign offerings (CitiBank). Each issuer tailors its products carefully to make them both profitable and attractive, with a different mix of anticipated revenue streams based on the type of customer. Superprime offerings, for example, attract a portfolio of customers who spend very heavily and borrow occasionally, primarily for convenience. Issuers rely heavily on interchange and episodic interest payments, balanced against the large losses that come when a customer with a five-figure credit line becomes insolvent. Affinity products (bearing logos of universities, sports teams, or the like) are more likely to balance interchange against limited payments to sponsors, while cobranded offerings (bearing logos of airlines or leading retailers) are likely to balance annual fees and interchange against relatively high payments to sponsors. Relational offerings are part of a strategy in which a bank strives to provide many products to each customer, with a view to lowering the customer's price sensitivity on particular products.

For a study of LMI households, subprime issuers are the most interesting, because the unstable incomes and poor or spotty repayment histories of many LMI families make them likely users of those products.[6] Not surprisingly, subprime products rely heavily on interest income and fees. Indeed, a dominant share of the increase in fee revenue discussed in this chapter has come from the subprime market. In part, this reflects the reality that the stated interest rates on those products (often in the range of 18 to 24 percent per annum) are inadequate to provide a return on a portfolio with a charge-off rate in the vicinity of 15 to 20 percent. Fee revenue provides a simple way to substantially increase the effective interest rate. Take, for example, a typical subprime $500 credit card line that has been fully extended. If the cardholder incurs three late or overlimit fees per year (not an unreasonable estimate), the issuer is likely to receive approximately $100 in extra revenue.[7] Those fees add an additional 20 percent return per year on the credit line, for a total effective rate (assuming no other fees or charges) of about 35 to 40 percent.

More aggressive card issuers, targeting higher-risk customers, design products with even higher effective rates. For example, one popular subprime card has a $300 limit and a 20 percent interest rate, with $247 in up-front fees ($49 annual fee, $99 account processing fee, $89 program participation fee, and $10 monthly maintenance fee).[8] The fees are charged against the card when the cardholder receives it, leaving an available credit line of $53. If a cardholder makes a $53 purchase on the date the card arrives (thus expending the entire remaining available balance) and repays the balance in one month, the effective interest rate would be about 5,500 percent. From a marketing perspective, this card might look attractive because it offers a grace period to cardholders who pay their entire balance. Nor is this card unique. Another successful product offers a $250 limit and an interest rate of only 10 percent, with $178 in up-front fees ($29 account setup fee, $95 program fee, $48 annual fee, $6 participating fee). If that cardholder spends the entire available credit ($72) on the first day and repays the balance at the end of the first month, the effective interest rate would be about 3,000 percent. To be sure, the interest rates would fall if the cardholders took longer to repay their balances, but the large share of fees compared to the maximum amount of available credit ensures that the effective interest rate will remain substantially higher than the stated interest rate.

Collectively, these market segmentation strategies are highly effective, at least for lenders that are able to employ cutting-edge technology. Large issuers say privately that only about 25 percent of their customers are unprofitable, a substantial improvement from the early 1990s, when about half of the customers in a typical portfolio would be profitable to the issuer. One final corollary of the increasing importance of sophisticated underwriting technology is the rapid concentration of the lending market. Issuers that do not invest heavily in technology quickly fall behind, losing the ability to compete against those that do. As of 2006, the top five issuers held more than 70 percent of the outstanding credit card balances, up from only 39 percent in 1994 (Nilson Report).

The changes in the credit card market raise important questions about the role of credit cards in the finances of LMI households. It is clear, of course, that a considerable number of LMI households have held credit cards for some time. For example, the analysis by Edward Bird, Paul Hagstrom, and Robert Wild (1999) of the 1995 SCF cross-sectional study shows that 36 percent of households below the poverty line had a credit card, and about two-thirds were carrying balances. Similarly, Peter Yoo's (1997, 1998) analysis of the SCF cross-sectional studies between 1983 and 1995 shows that the share of households with credit cards and credit card debt has been increasing over time. Most importantly for present purposes, he shows that the rates of increase vary across deciles of the SCF's respondent population.

Still, relatively little is known about the extent of borrowing or the characteristics of LMI households that use credit cards. Existing research shows that credit cards play a different financial and social role in LMI households than they do in middle-class households. For example, Jeanne Hogarth and Kevin O'Donnell (1999) have studied in some detail the holdings of checking accounts among LMI households. Their work shows that a significant number (8 percent) of LMI households that do not have checking accounts nevertheless have credit cards.[9] So credit cards must present benefits that extend beyond simple retail transacting.

Angela Littwin's (2008b) research is particularly enlightening. Based on interviews with women in Boston housing projects, Littwin shows how credit cards provide a lifeline that facilitates access to or lower prices for a variety of mainstream transactions. She explains that the credit card helps LMI households remain a part of the mainstream economic community.[10] At the same time, these households have a deep-seated recognition of the risks they face if they borrow. Generally, Littwin suggests, these products would be more attractive to LMI households, and also safer for them, if they included a hard-credit line, thus precluding overlimit borrowing.

Given the rapid changes in the credit market in the last ten years, it is valuable both to update the early findings about the initial penetration of credit cards into LMI households and to analyze the available data in more detail. For example, scholars have not examined which LMI households are most likely to hold credit cards or to borrow heavily with them. The segmentation and proliferation of product models discussed earlier in this chapter suggests that the products that are attractive to LMI households function differently than the products that are attractive to the middle class. Thus, it would be useful to understand who chooses to use credit cards and how the choices that LMI households make differ from the parallel choices made by more financially secure households.

It is not easy to find data to investigate these questions with care. National aggregate data are useful to understand the conceptual relations between spending, borrowing, and financial distress but are of no use for this inquiry because they do not show how card use varies over the distribution of income (Mann 2006). I decided to look to the 2004 Survey of Consumer Finances, conducted by the National Opinion Research Center (NORC) for the Federal Reserve Board. The 2004 survey is based on a complex sample of U.S. households and includes data on income, assets, debt, and the demographic characteristics of respondents (for a general summary of the 2004 data, including the data on credit card use, see Bucks, Kennickell, and Moore 2006, table 11).[11]

There are some problems with the use of the SCF for such an inquiry. First, the SCF is not a panel survey. Rather, investigators draw a different sample of interview subjects (and train a different set of interviewers) for each edition of the survey. This limits the value of the data for analyzing trends over time—such as the changes in credit card use since 1990. Another well-known problem is the tendency of survey respondents to underreport stigmatizing behavior. Credit card borrowing, for example, is understated by about 30 percent, at least as compared to the Federal Reserve's G.19 statistics (which rely for the most part on call reports submitted by financial institutions to regulators) (Mann 2006; Zinman 2007; for details on G.19, see Furletti and Ody 2006). At first glance, the large underreporting problem seems difficult to overcome, given the likelihood that the factors that cause the underreporting will create a selection bias in the data. Jonathan Zinman's (2007) work, however, suggests that the underreporting is random with respect to other variables—so that the underreporting will affect only the weights of variables rather than the relations between them.[12] Yet another problem is the ambiguous relation between balances and borrowing on a revolving credit product like a credit card. This makes it particularly difficult for survey researchers to collect accurate information about debt: is the relevant figure the amount owed to the issuer at the time of the interview, the amount owed on the last statement, the amount that went unpaid on the last statement, the amount expected to go unpaid on the next statement, or some other figure entirely?[13] Reasonably skeptical observers will worry that use of the SCF to analyze card-related behavior is a dubious enterprise. This is particularly true for a project that focuses directly on data that are both difficult to define and collect and known to be substantially underreported. Still, the fact remains that the SCF, despite its problems, is the best available source for household-level data about national patterns of card use (Kennickell 2006a).

PATTERNS OF CREDIT CARD USE

Because the purpose of this project is to understand the pattern of credit card use among LMI households (defined as the bottom two quintiles in the income distribution), I start by dividing the SCF data set into five quintiles based on income. The two lowest quintiles (quintiles 1 and 2 in the analysis that follows) end at $18,500 and $34,000 of annual income, respectively.[14] Conversely, I use three distinct metrics to capture the penetration of credit card use in LMI households: the number of households that report a positive balance; the size of the balances reported by households that report a balance (CCBAL); and the ratio of the household's credit card balance to its income (CCSHARE) (Kennickell 2006a).

Penetration of the Market

The most basic question about credit card use by LMI households is how often they carry balances on cards, as compared to higher-income households.[15] The answer,

FIGURE 9.3   /   Households Holding Credit Card Balances

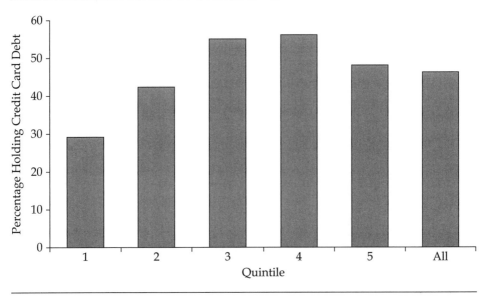

Source: Author's calculations based on Survey of Consumer Finances 2004.

in short, is that their usage patterns are surprisingly similar. The importance of income as the primary source of repayment for credit card lenders suggests that a group of households defined by low income levels should have little or no credit card debt. On the contrary, the borrowing patterns for the four lower income quintiles are surprisingly similar.

I start with the incidence of debt—the share of households reporting that they are carrying any credit card debt at all (46 percent across the entire data set). Figure 9.3 breaks down that data by quintile. Several things about this figure are interesting. First, as expected, it shows the highest rate of card balances (55 percent and 56 percent) in the second and third quintiles, long considered the principal focus of credit card lending. One notable feature of the data is the robust rate of borrowing in the two LMI quintiles. First, the 43 percent rate of borrowing by households in the moderate-income quintile is very close to the rates in the higher quintiles. This is a graphic illustration of the broadening of the traditional credit card demographic discussed earlier in this chapter. The data here display a highly similar incidence of borrowing across the interior three quintiles of the populace— with incomes ranging from $23,500 (the top of the first quintile) to $90,000 (the bottom of the fifth quintile). To be sure, the 29 percent incidence of borrowing in the first quintile is considerably lower, but even that incidence is notable given the reality that the first quintile consists of households with incomes below $23,500.

The second metric of credit card borrowing is the size of the balances carried by those households that are carrying balances.[16] This metric displays the intensity

FIGURE 9.4 / Credit Card Balances, by Income Quintile

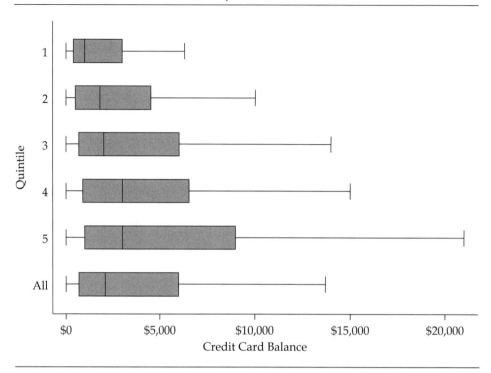

Source: Author's calculations based on Survey of Consumer Finances 2004 (excluding outliers).
Note: Endpoints of horizontal lines show minimum and maximum; box indicates twenty-fifth and seventy-fifth percentile. Vertical line within the box indicates median (fiftieth percentile).

and regularity of borrowing by the subset of respondents who report a positive balance. To set the frame of reference, the median balance for those carrying balances in the entire data set is $2,300, the 25 percent balance is $700, and the 75 percent balance is $6,300. Figure 9.4 displays a series of boxplots by quintile. These plots indicate the range of data for each quintile by vertical lines, with the boxes shading the range from the twenty-fifth to the seventy-fifty percentile and with internal vertical lines showing the median value.

Like figure 9.3, several points about the boxplots in figure 9.4 warrant emphasis. The most notable is the relative similarity of balances across the three interior quintiles. To be sure, the amounts borrowed are staggered by quintile, but the differences are relatively insignificant. Finally, the level of debt in the first quintile is surprisingly high. Press reports and industry publicity suggest that credit limits of $500 are typical for low-income households. But these data suggest that most of the lower-income (first-quintile) households that are carrying credit card balances have balances greater than $1,000. Again, combining the importance of income to credit card underwriting with the limited income of these households, it might

FIGURE 9.5 / Credit Card Balance As a Share of Income Among Those with Balances, by Income Quintiles

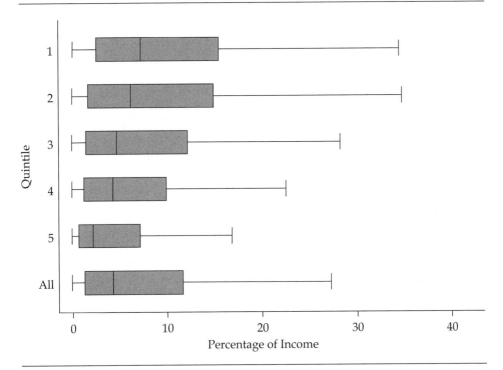

Source: Author's calculations based on Survey of Consumer Finances 2004 (excluding outliers).
Note: Endpoints of horizontal lines show minimum and maximum; box indicates twenty-fifth and seventy-fifth percentile. Vertical line within the box indicates median (fiftieth percentile).

be surprising that the median balances are so high. The most likely explanation is that, even in this quintile, most of the households carrying balances are using more than one card.

The third metric of credit card borrowing is the amount of the credit card balance as a share of income. For purposes of descriptive comparison, this metric has two advantages over the preceding metrics. First, given the role that income plays in credit card underwriting, it facilitates useful cross-quintile comparisons. To compare the extent to which customers in different quintiles are heavy borrowers, it is more useful to know what share of customers are borrowing one-tenth of their annual income than it is to know what share of customers are borrowing $5,000. Related to the first, the ratio of credit card debt to income provides a useful tool for examining overindebtedness. Thus, Bird and his coauthors (1999) use this metric to identify customers who have borrowed excessively.

The boxplots in figure 9.5 underscore this chapter's analysis. Again, the differences among the three interior quintiles are relatively slight, with typical debt loads of about one-twentieth of cardholders' annual income. Again, this suggests a relatively homogeneous willingness to take and use credit cards within these quintiles. For another, the charts show an interesting and steady decline on each of the measurement points (25 percent, median, 75 percent). Thus, using this metric, the respondents in the first quintile borrow more intensively than respondents in the higher quintiles. The median borrowing share of about one-twelfth of annual income is higher than the median for the other quintiles. Half of the respondents have debt equal to a month's income, and one-quarter of the respondents have debt equal to two months' income. Moreover, the long right tail of borrowing share in that quintile suggests that it is not uncommon for people in this group to accrue substantial debts on credit cards.

Demographic Factors

Knowing that credit cards have become a common product for LMI households tells us little about who uses them or, more importantly, whether the factors that relate to use by LMI households are the same as those that relate to use by the broader populace. For purposes of this study, I have chosen to examine four sets of demographic variables from the SCF: age, educational level, family status, and race. My goals for this analysis are modest. I do not believe, for example, that a model based on these variables can reliably predict the level of credit card use by any particular household. The models that credit card issuers use to predict card-related behavior are much more sophisticated, including dozens of variables for each potential cardholder. These variables are related not only to demographic factors like the ones included here but also, more importantly, to indicators of financial activity and creditworthiness that are not easily replicated in a survey like the SCF. To put it another way, the most important variables that issuers use to identify the persons to whom they will extend credit (and the terms on which they will extend it) are missing from this data set. The absence of these variables necessarily limits the quality of the potential models. Even more importantly, these factors cannot predict either the demand for credit cards or individual preferences and behaviors regarding borrowing and credit card use.

Nevertheless, the data can illuminate the social role of credit cards by contributing to an understanding of demographic differences between those who borrow and those who do not. I analyze those variables in two steps. First, I present data illustrating the extent to which those variables differ for those who report carrying balances on credit cards and those who do not. For comparative purposes, I also present similar data about the financial characteristics of the households: use of other financial products (checking accounts, car loans, mortgage loans), as well as employment status and stability of income. Table 9.1 presents summary descriptive statistics for each of those variables, organized by quintile. I close the chapter with a discussion of a multivariate model designed to assess the extent to which the variables explain variations in reported credit card balances when controlling for the other variables.

TABLE 9.1   /   Characteristics of Users and Non-Users of Credit Cards, by Income Quintile

	1	2	3	4	5
Age (mean years)					
With credit card balance	48	46	46	45	47
Without credit card balance	53	53	51	53	51
Education (mean years)					
With credit card balance	13	13	13	14	15
Without credit card balance	11	12	13	14	16
White					
With credit card balance	60%	66%	73%	80%	82%
Without credit card balance	60	68	76	84	90
Black					
With credit card balance	24	16	14	11	9
Without credit card balance	23	23	15	7	3
Hispanic					
With credit card balance	12	15	10	7	5
Without credit card balance	14	15	6	4	1
Married					
With credit card balance	20	40	59	80	93
Without credit card balance	23	48	55	70	90
Has children					
With credit card balance	36	40	55	57	61
Without credit card balance	30	35	36	37	50
Has checking account					
With credit card balance	85	91	96	98	99
Without credit card balance	65	80	93	98	100
Has car loan					
With credit card balance	25	36	52	63	59
Without credit card balance	8	20	33	32	34
Has mortgage loan					
With credit card balance	25	41	61	75	86
Without credit card balance	12	22	41	54	68
Employed					
With credit card balance	55	79	84	90	93
Without credit card balance	41	57	71	74	83

Source: Author's calculations based on 2004 Survey of Consumer Finances.

FIGURE 9.6 / Mean Age by Credit Card Debt Status and Income Quintile

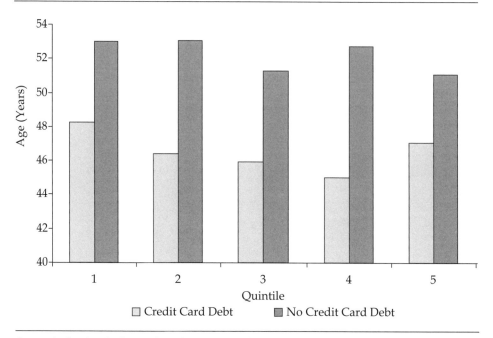

Credit Card Debt ☐   No Credit Card Debt ■

Quintile

Source: Author's calculations based on Survey of Consumer Finances 2004.

AGE   The relation between age and credit card borrowing is relatively straight-forward. On the one hand, to the extent that cardholders use credit card borrowing to smooth consumption over their life cycle, I would expect to see more borrow-ing by relatively young cardholders and less borrowing by older cardholders. Relating the consumption cycle to income levels, I would expect that young card-holders in LMI quintiles would need to borrow more frequently than young card-holders in households with more income. Similarly, cardholders in LMI households might be less likely to repay their debts and thus more likely to continue borrowing into middle and old age.

In general, the data support that understanding of the relations between age, credit card debt, and income quintile. As table 9.1 illustrates, borrowers who carry credit card balances are younger at all income levels than those who do not; the differences in each case are significant at the 0.01 percent level. Figure 9.6 illustrates the distinction graphically, showing a gap between the mean ages of those who borrow and those who do not.

EDUCATIONAL LEVEL   The relation between education and credit card borrow-ing is considerably harder to predict, primarily because it is difficult to be certain whether increased financial sophistication would lead to a greater or lower incidence of credit card debt. Similarly, it is possible that education would have a different

FIGURE 9.7 / Mean Education by Credit Card Debt Status and Income Quintile

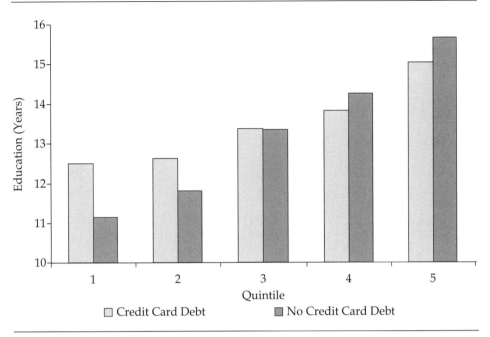

Source: Author's calculations based on Survey of Consumer Finances 2004.

relation to credit card borrowing at different levels of income. Among LMI house-holds, for example, it might be that only the relatively well educated would be in a position to obtain a credit card, while in households with higher income levels (where educational levels are likely to be higher across the board) credit cards might be readily available even to the relatively less educated.

Table 9.1 provides some support for that explanation—the mean education level of those carrying credit card balances in the LMI quintiles is higher than the educa-tion level of those who do not carry balances—but the converse is true of the highest quintile: those who carry balances tend to be less educated than those who do not. As illustrated in figure 9.7, the level of education steadily increases by quintile, but the credit card borrowers in the first two quintiles are the relatively more-educated, while borrowers are relatively less-educated in the upper quintiles.

FAMILY STATUS   The next demographic variables are family status variables—specifically whether the head of the household is married and whether there are children in the household. As with educational level, it is easy to discern conflicting possible relations. On the one hand, married families and those with children might be more stable and thus less likely to need credit card borrowing. On the other hand, the greater level of stability and higher level of consumption might make them more attractive customers. With respect to children, the data (in table 9.1 and figure 9.8)

FIGURE 9.8 / Households with Children by Credit Card Debt Status and Income Quintile

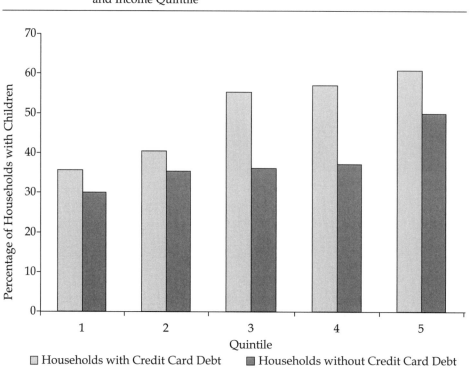

Source: Author's calculations based on Survey of Consumer Finances 2004.

suggest a relation with credit card debt; at all income levels, a greater share of households with children have credit card debt than do not. The data regarding marital status are harder to interpret. Like education, this variable seems to relate to card use differently at the LMI level than it does at higher-income levels. Thus, a lower share of LMI households in which the head is married report carrying credit card debt, while a higher share of upper-income quintiles report carrying credit card debt. Table 9.1 reports the descriptive statistics; figure 9.9 displays the data graphically.

RACE   The relation between race and credit card borrowing is most difficult to predict because of two directly conflicting intuitions. On the one hand, if markets function rationally, race would not be a useful predictor of either creditworthiness or financial behavior. On the other hand, if the effects of discrimination are present in lending or borrowing markets, or if race correlates substantially with important variables that are missing from this data set, then there might be correlations between race and credit card usage.[17] The data in table 9.1 and figure 9.10 suggest

FIGURE 9.9 / Households Headed by a Married Couple by Credit Card Debt Status and Income Quintile

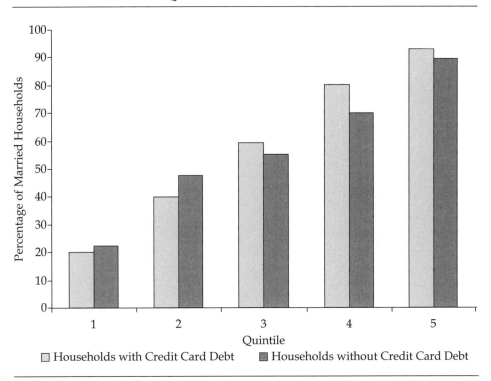

Source: Author's calculations based on Survey of Consumer Finances 2004.

that whites are less likely to borrow on credit cards than African Americans and Hispanics, especially at higher income levels. To be sure, because table 9.1 and figure 9.10 control neither for income nor education, they do not suggest any causal association between race and credit card use. They do, however, provide useful information on the demographic characteristics of those who carry balances on credit cards.

USE OF OTHER FINANCIAL PRODUCTS   As discussed earlier in the chapter, I also analyzed several variables related to the financial status of the household. Collectively, those variables should provide a valuable proxy for financial sophistication. If families are more likely to borrow on credit cards if they have previous experience with other banking products, then there should be a positive relation between having a checking account and carrying a credit card balance. As table 9.1 and figure 9.11 suggest, there is a significant correlation between credit card use and several of the variables summarized in table 9.1. The last column of figure 9.11 provides some support for that hypothesis by showing correlations between the

FIGURE 9.10 / Households Holding Credit Card Debt by Race, Ethnic Status, and Income Quintile

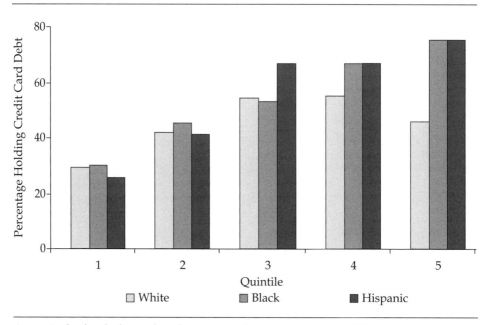

Source: Author's calculations based on Survey of Consumer Finances 2004.

most widely used of the other products, the checking account, concentrated at the lower income quintiles, apparently because almost all households in the higher income quintiles have checking accounts.

MULTIVARIATE ANALYSIS

Given the apparent variation in the relations by income quintile, multivariate analysis would be useful to refine the relations among the variables. As explained earlier, it would be surprising if the variables in the SCF data set explained most of the pattern of credit card borrowing. Credit card lenders rely on proprietary statistical models that aggregate dozens of variables from numerous sources, many of which are not in the public domain, much less in the SCF.[18] Similarly, a model that predicts consumer behavior and preferences would include many variables beyond the straightforward demographic and financial sophistication variables used here.

To examine the relation between the different groups of variables, I started with a pair of models: one for the whole data set and one limited to the two LMI quintiles, using the demographic variables (age, age-squared, education, black, Hispanic, married, and children) as the only explanatory variables. I used the existence of

FIGURE 9.11   /   Households Holding Credit Card Debt and Other Financial Products
by Income Quintile

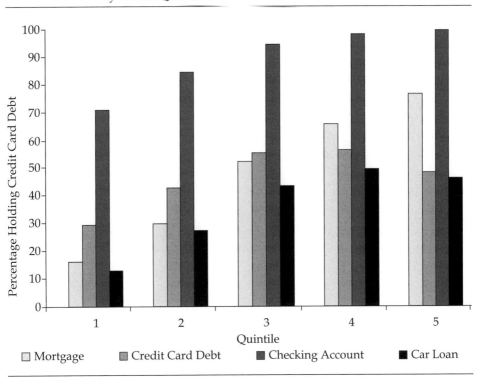

Source: Author's calculations based on Survey of Consumer Finances 2004.

any credit card balances (a binary variable) as the dependent variable and estimated logistic regression models.[19] The first two columns of table 9.2 report results from those models. I then estimated a second pair of models (columns 3 and 4 in table 9.2), which added the three financial sophistication variables (checking account, car loan, mortgage loan). I then estimated a pair of models (columns 5 and 6) that added employment and income shock. Finally, I estimated a pair of models (columns 7 and 8) to assess interactions among the variables. These models included seven additional variables in two groups: age interacted with black and with Hispanic, and education interacted with black, Hispanic, children, checking account, mortgage, and employment.[20]

Turning first to the demographic variables, the analysis suggests that the quintile-by-quintile variations discussed in the preceding section reflect statistically significant relations. For example, age has an odds ratio that is statistically significant but only slightly greater than one (in the vicinity of 1.05) in all eight models, while age-squared has a statistically significant odds ratio that is only slightly below one (in the range of 0.9995) in all of the models. This suggests a slight positive increase

TABLE 9.2 / Logistic Regression Models (Dependent Variable = 1 If Household Reports Credit Card Debt; 0 Otherwise)

	(1) All	(2) LMI	(3) All	(4) LMI	(5) All	(6) LMI	(7) All	(8) LMI
Age	1.0710***	1.0532***	1.0422***	1.0423**	1.0352**	1.0440**	1.0274*	1.0318
	(0.014)	(0.0187)	(0.0151)	(0.200)	(0.0151)	(0.0201)	(0.0157)	(0.0217)
Age-squared	0.9992***	0.9994***	0.9994***	0.9995***	0.9996***	0.9995**	0.9996**	0.9996*
	(0.00014)	(0.000184)	(0.000150)	(0.000197)	(0.000153)	(0.000200)	(0.000158)	(0.000213)
Education	1.0454***	1.1371***	0.9857	1.0789***	0.9802	1.07619***	1.2496***	1.252***
	(0.136)	(0.0238)	(0.0154)	(0.0263)	(0.0155)	(0.0265)	(0.0671)	(0.0793)
Black	1.0665	0.9629	1.3455**	1.1498	1.3645***	1.1594	0.0950***	0.1552
	(0.113)	(0.167)	(0.121)	(0.178)	(0.121)	(0.182)	(0.843)	(1.20)
Hispanic	0.9924	1.147	1.2888*	1.3641	1.2628*	1.2947	0.1030***	0.2688
	(0.133)	(0.200)	(0.140)	(0.212)	(0.140)	(0.211)	(0.816)	(1.150)
Married	0.8303**	1.0231	1.1345	1.1775	1.1520	1.1600	1.123	1.2067
	(0.0804)	(0.140)	(0.0878)	(0.151)	(0.0885)	(0.150)	(0.0893)	(0.152)
Children	1.2857***	1.1448	1.1154	1.0330	1.1088	1.0058	4.0229***	2.368
	(0.0820)	(0.156)	(0.0868)	(0.151)	(0.0868)	(0.150)	(0.452)	(0.7090)
Checking account			3.0771***	2.8548***	2.9892***	2.7566***	11.67***	4.7185**
			(0.155)	(0.181)	(0.155)	(0.181)	(0.713)	(0.780)
Car loan			2.3898***	2.4804***	2.3432***	2.3812***	2.3166***	2.402***
			(0.0830)	(0.155)	(0.0832)	(0.155)	(0.0840)	(0.155)
Mortgage			1.8460***	2.0772***	1.7828***	2.0107***	9.612***	12.513***
			(0.0863)	(0.163)	(0.0867)	(0.163)	(0.467)	(0.793)
Employed					1.4920***	1.6782**	4.5132***	6.3662**
					(0.115)	(0.166)	(0.502)	(0.742)

	(1)	(2)	(3)	(4)	(5)	(6)	(7)	(8)
Income shock					0.9440 (0.125)	0.8335 (0.166)	0.9438 (0.125)	0.8205 (0.162)
Age*Black							1.0237*** (0.00782)	1.029*** (0.010)
Age*Hispanic							1.0307** (0.0120)	1.024 (0.0169)
Educ*Black							1.1246** (0.0515)	1.0527 (0.0756)
Educ*Hispanic							1.111** (0.0485)	1.0467 (0.0704)
Educ*Kids							0.9111*** (0.0325)	0.9341 (0.0568)
Educ*Chk							0.8778** (0.0610)	0.9533 (0.0685)
Educ*Mort							0.88432*** (0.0333)	0.8635** (0.0616)
Educ*Empl							0.9235** (0.0366)	0.9033* (0.0573)
Pseudo-R-squared#	0.040	0.035	0.119	0.105	0.120	0.111	0.140	0.124
Number of observations	4,519	1,359	4,519	1,359	4,519	1,359	4,519	1,359

Source: Author's calculations based on Survey of Consumer Finances 2004.

Notes: The table reports odds ratios with standard errors in parentheses. All regressions are weighted. Similar regressions without weights (as suggested in Lindamood et al. 2007) produced generally similar results.
*significant at 10 percent; **significant at 5 percent; ***significant at 1 percent.
#pseudo-R-squared calculated based on first implicates of logit regression

in the incidence of credit card debt as households age, with a lessening of the rate of increase with advancing age. Odds ratios above one on the interactions between age and the race variables (columns 7 and 8 in table 9.2) suggest that the increasing incidence of credit card debt with age is more substantial for black and Hispanic households than it is for white households.

Similarly, at least in the LMI quintiles, education has an odds ratio that is significantly greater than one even after controlling for the financial variables; the results are more ambiguous in the models for the entire data set. This is consistent with the data presented in table 9.2, which suggests that education is positively related to credit card borrowing in lower quintiles but negatively related to it in higher quintiles. The analysis of interacted variables (columns 7 and 8 in table 9.2) suggests that the positive relation between credit card debt and education is even higher for black and Hispanic households.

Like the data in table 9.1, the data regarding the racial variables is somewhat more difficult to interpret. It is apparent, however, that after the financial variables are introduced as controls, both the black and Hispanic variables produce relatively stable odds ratios that are substantially greater than one. This suggests that blacks and Hispanics are more likely to carry credit card balances than whites with similar levels of use of other financial products. The interacted variables, however, suggest a different story. Once the interacted variables are included (columns 7 and 8 in table 9.2), black and Hispanic households (as compared to white households) have lower odds of having credit card balances (approximately 0.1). At the same time, the interacted variables suggest that the positive relations between age and education on credit card debt are substantially larger for black and Hispanic households than they are for white households.[21] This suggests that the positive relation between race and credit card debt in columns 3 through 6 is driven by the use of cards by older and more educated black and Hispanic households.

The multivariate analysis for family status is less conclusive. Married households and households with children tend to have more credit card debt than unmarried households and households without children, though the models suggest, at least after controlling for the use of financial products, that these variables are not as important as the education and race variables. The most interesting finding relates to the interaction between children and education. In the final model, the odds ratio for families with children is economically and statistically significant (4.02), but the interaction between education and that variable suggests that for more-educated families the trend toward the use of credit card debt is substantially lower than it is for less-educated families. These effects seem to be about the same for LMI quintiles and for the entire data set.

The most important finding of table 9.2 is apparent in data about the financial sophistication variables in columns 3 through 8. All three of those variables (checking account, car loan, and mortgage loan) have odds ratios that are both statistically significant and (with a single exception) much higher than the odds ratios of any of the demographic variables. This suggests, at least within this data set, that the data about the use of other financial products are much more important in predicting whether a household will report credit card balances than unrelated demographic characteristics of the household. Inclusion of the financial variables in the model also appears to alter the role of some (but not all) of the demographic variables. Thus, the odds ratios for age (and age-squared) remain relatively stable when the financial variables are added to the model. The analyses for education and race, on the other hand, change substantially with the addition of variables to control for financial sophistication. Thus, in the model for the whole data set, education has an odds ratio close to one in the model with only demographic variables, but a ratio substantially below one in columns 3 and 5 (the models that control for financial sophistication). Conversely, the odds ratios for blacks and Hispanics are substantially higher after the inclusion of financial products as controls. Interestingly, as with the interaction between education and children, the low odds ratios on the interactions between education and checking and mortgage loans (columns 7 and 8 of table 9.2) suggest that the tendency for families that use other financial products to carry credit card balances is substantially less for more-educated families than it is for less-educated families.

Columns 5 and 6 of table 9.2 reflect the addition of employment status and income shock. The income shock variable captures households in which the respondent indicated that the household's current income was at least 25 percent less than the household's normal income; the concept is that the variable might capture households for which borrowing is related to an exogenous income shock. As it turns out, the income shock variable does not appear to be economically or statistically significant in any of the models. Conversely, employment status appears to relate in a strong and positive way to carrying credit card debt; this is not surprising given the probative value that a steady job has for the lender's task of predicting the reliability of repayment. It does not appear, however, to have a substantial effect on any of the other variables, which retain odds ratios broadly similar to the odds ratios they displayed in columns 1 through 4. Like the financial variables, an interaction between education and employment status (reported in columns 7 and 8 of table 9.2) suggests that the positive relation between employment and credit card debt is less substantial for more-educated families than it is for less-educated families. The best explanation for this pattern seems to be that less-educated families with jobs are more likely to accept and use the credit cards for which their employment status qualifies them, and more-educated families are likely to refrain from using them.

CONCLUSION

This chapter provides a glimpse of the role that credit cards play in the financial lives of LMI households. Most obviously, the data show that credit cards are now a substantial factor in the economic lives of the poorest U.S. households. Indeed, at least as a share of income, the credit card debt that LMI households carry is higher than that of more affluent households. The data also illustrate the patterns by which credit card borrowing is distributed based on age, race, and other demographic factors.

The statistical analysis of the demographic characteristics of borrowers is intended to be suggestive, with a view to assessing the relation between those variables and the other types of variables in our data set. The variations in correlation and association by quintile suggest that sophisticated issuers might well wish to design and market different products to households at different income levels. The data do not, however, provide reliable information on the actual factors that credit card issuers use to underwrite their loans. Moreover, data limitations aside, the absence of panel data means that the SCF simply cannot provide the temporal evidence that might be useful for examining causal effects. Given the difficulties of using surveys to collect panel data on that question, the best source for research of that nature would probably be data from the portfolio of a major credit card issuer.

Returning to the focus on access and safety with which the chapter began, the data provide stark evidence about the high incidence and level of debt among the poorest families. Looking at the lowest quintile alone—those households with income below $23,000—31 percent of the households are carrying credit card debt. Among those that carry credit card debt, half have debt equal to 10 percent of their income, and one-quarter have debt equal to 25 percent of their income (all before making mortgage payments, car payments, child support payments, and the like). As I discuss here, repaying that debt typically involves high interest rates and considerable fees. By comparison, among the middle-class borrowers who are so widely bemoaned for their rampant spending and overindebtedness, the median debt share is only 5 percent, and only one-quarter have debt that exceeds 10 percent of their incomes. By any yardstick, credit card use among poor households has created a debt overhang that many households will bear for years, if not decades. Recognizing that the usage pattern relates so closely to the use by LMI households of other financial products, policymakers must consider the possibility that a taste for mainstream financial products is not always necessarily positive for LMI households.

I thank Karen Pence for gracious assistance with programming to interpret data from the Survey of Consumer Finance; James Carlson for assistance with statistical analysis; David Hogan and Adair Morse for useful comments; and Allison Mann for advice of all kinds.

NOTES

1. The statistics reported in this paragraph are compiled from the annual Cards Profitability Survey published by *Cards and Payments* magazine (formerly *Cards Management*). Figure 9.2 presents a detailed time series of the relevant information. Other sources suggest higher borrowing rates at the early end of this period, but I use the *Cards and*

Payments data because of its consistency and availability over the entire period covered by this discussion.

2. There was a sharp fall shortly after the implementation of the Bankruptcy Abuse Prevention and Consumer Protection Act (BAPCPA) of 2005, to 3.9 percent for 2006, but the rate trended steadily upward throughout 2007. It remains unclear whether the decline will be permanent.

3. The most detailed evidence of that trend comes from Black and Morgan's (1999) comparison of the characteristics of credit card holders in the 1989 and 1995 cross-sectional SCF studies.

4. Premium cards typically bear higher interchange rates than subprime and prime cards, even though premium cardholders present lower risk to the issuer and their transactions involve no offsetting benefit for the merchant.

5. The information in this paragraph is based on strategy analysis in the annual reports of large credit card issuers.

6. This is not because subprime products are designed for LMI households. Product design depends much more on stability of income and on past repayment patterns than on the amount of current income. Subprime products are more likely to appear in LMI households because those are the households that will have the unstable incomes and poor or spotty repayment histories that make them poor customers for prime or superprime card products. Conversely, those with relatively high incomes are more likely to have relatively stable income profiles and better repayment histories. There are exceptions, of course, but the pattern is useful as a generalization. For analysis of the relation between social status and consumer debt, see McCloud (2007).

7. Carddata.com reports that the average late fee among large issuers currently is about $35.

8. This paragraph describes two cards featured at a leading card comparison website as among the most attractive subprime cards in the fall of 2007.

9. This fact seems surprising given the logistical difficulties of making payments on a credit card account without a checking account.

10. The maintenance of a continuing sense of participation in the larger economy has substantial positive spillover effects (see Phelps 1997).

11. The SCF uses a dual sampling technique that includes a probability sample collected in specified geographic regions and a sample from the tax list provided by the Internal Revenue Service. The resulting sample oversamples higher wealth groups, but weighting of the data can be used to obtain estimates applicable to the U.S. population as a whole (see Kennickell 2006b).

12. Of course, the measures of credit card debt have other problems, particularly the difficulty of identifying outstanding credit card debt at the time of the interview and the fact that the outstanding debt at any particular point in time might not be representative of a person's average credit card debt. It is plausible to believe, however, that those problems produce random errors.

13. The SCF attempts to ascertain the amount that went unpaid on the last statement. As of 2004, the relevant question (X413) asked: "After the last payments were made on these accounts, roughly what was the balance still owed on these accounts? WE WANT THE TOTAL AMOUNT OWED, NOT THE MINIMUM PAYMENT."

14. The descriptive statistics in this section reflect weighting of the data to compensate for the oversampling of high-income households, as well as averaging of the five implicates for each household.
15. As discussed earlier, the SCF collects data only on the outstanding balance at any given time. Although this obviously is not a perfect measure of credit card debt, it is the best that the SCF has to offer, and for simplicity of exposition I refer to it as "credit card debt" throughout this chapter.
16. Like most scholars who write about the SCF, I emphasize the size of balances among those who carry any balance at all (see, for example, Bucks, Kennickell, and Moore 2006).
17. For example, there is reason to believe that differing attitudes about debt explain a great deal of the difference in borrowing by those of different races (McCloud 2007). The effects of education and occupation on borrowing also are likely to differ for those of different races, at least in part because of differing levels of wealth (Conley 1999; McCloud 2007).
18. Credit card lenders rely heavily, for example, on information about past spending and repayment patterns, much of which is far more detailed than the information available from credit reporting agencies. The information is proprietary in part because of its competitive value. The issuer familiar with years of a cardholder's spending, borrowing, and repayment history has a considerable advantage in designing and pricing products over an issuer that has never had a relationship with the cardholder. Among other things, consumers face high switching costs when competing issuers are less well placed to extend credit than their existing card issuer. This contributes, in turn, to the ability of issuers to charge higher prices to LMI customers (and other customers in distress).
19. I also estimated tobit and ordinary least squares (OLS) models of credit card balances, using a similar set of variables as explanatory variables. The variables were much less closely related to the dependent variable in those models, presumably because of the substantial measurement error in self-reported survey data about the level of credit card balances.
20. I separately tested first-order interactions among all of the independent variables. Columns 7 and 8 reflect the addition to the model of the interactive variables that were economically and statistically significant in any of the models.
21. The conclusion that education has a different effect on nonwhite households than it does on white households is not a new one. See note 17.

REFERENCES

Bird, Edward J., Paul A. Hagstrom, and Robert Wild. 1999. "Credit Card Debts of the Poor: High and Rising." *Journal of Policy Analysis and Management* 18(1): 125–33.

Black, Sandra E., and Donald P. Morgan. 1999. "Meet the New Borrowers." *Current Issues in Economics and Finance* 5(3): 1–6.

Bucks, Brian K., Arthur B. Kennickell, and Kevin B. Moore. 2006. "Recent Changes in U.S. Family Finances: Evidence from the 2001 and 2004 Survey of Consumer Finances." *Federal Reserve Bulletin* 92 (Mar.): A1–38.

Cards Profitability Survey. 1990–2007. *Cards and Payments*. Source Media, Inc.

Caskey, John P. 1996. *Fringe Banking: Check-Cashing Outlets, Pawnshops, and the Poor*. New York: Russell Sage Foundation.

Conley, Dalton. 1999. *Being Black, Living in the Red: Race, Wealth, and Social Policy in America*. Berkeley: University of California Press.

Cross, Gary. 2000. *An All-Consuming Century: Why Commercialism Won in Modern America*. New York: Columbia University Press.

Frank, Robert H. 1999. *Luxury Fever: Money and Happiness in an Era of Excess*. New York: Free Press.

Furletti, Mark, and Christopher Ody. 2006. "Measuring U.S. Credit Card Borrowing: An Analysis of the G.19's Estimate of Consumer Revolving Credit." Payment Cards Center discussion paper 06-03. Philadelphia: Federal Reserve Bank of Philadelphia.

Hacker, Jacob S. 2002. *The Divided Welfare State: The Battle over Public and Private Social Benefits in the United States*. Cambridge: Cambridge University Press.

Hogarth, Jeanne M., Christoslav Anguelov, and Jinkook Lee. 2004. "Why Don't Households Have a Checking Account?" *Journal of Consumer Affairs* 38(1): 1–34.

Hogarth, Jeanne M., and Kevin H. O'Donnell. 1999. "Banking Relationships of Lower-Income Families and the Governmental Trend Toward Electronic Payment." *Federal Reserve Bulletin* 85(July): 459–73.

Howard, Christopher. 2007. *The Welfare State Nobody Knows: Debunking Myths About U.S. Social Policy*. Princeton, N.J.: Princeton University Press.

Johnson, Kathleen W. 2005. "Recent Developments in the Credit Card Market and the Financial Obligations Ratio." *Federal Reserve Bulletin* 89(Aug.): 473–86.

Kennickell, Arthur B. 2006a. *Codebook for 2004 Survey of Consumer Finances*. Washington: Board of Governors of the Federal Reserve System (February 9). Available at: http://www.federalreserve.gov/PUBS/oss/oss2/2004/codebk2004.txt (accessed January 22, 2009).

———. 2006b. "How Do We Know if We Aren't Looking? An Investigation of Data Quality in the 2004 SCF." Paper presented to the annual meetings of the American Statistical Association. Seattle (August 7–10).

Lindamood, Suzanne, Sherman D. Hanna, Lan Bi, Jeanne M. Hogarth, Darryl E. Getter, and Sandra J. Huston. 2007. "Using the Survey of Consumer Finances: Some Methodological Considerations and Issues." *Journal of Consumer Affairs* 41(2): 195–222.

Littwin, Angela. 2008a. "Beyond Usury: A Study of Credit Card Use and Preference Among Low-Income Consumers." *Texas Law Review* 86(3): 451–506.

———. 2008b. "Testing the Substitution Hypothesis: Would Credit Card Regulation Force Low-Income Borrowers Into Less Desirable Lending Alternatives?" Working paper. Available at: http://bdp.law.harvard.edu/pdfs/papers/Littwin/Testing-Substitution.pdf (accessed January 22, 2009).

Mann, Ronald J. 2006. *Charging Ahead: The Growth and Regulation of Payment Card Markets Around the World*. Cambridge: Cambridge University Press.

———. 2007. "Bankruptcy Reform and the 'Sweat Box' of Credit Card Debt." *Illinois Law Review* 2007(1): 375–404.

Mann, Ronald J., and Jim Hawkins. 2007. "Just Until Payday." *UCLA Law Review* 54(4): 855–912.

McCloud, Laura. 2007. "Charging into Hardship: The Effect of Social Location, Permanent Income, and Status Inconsistency on Consumer Debt." Paper presented to the annual meeting of the American Sociological Association. New York (August 11–14). Available at: http://www.allacademic.com/meta/p_mla_apa_research_citation/1/8/4/6/5/ p184657_index.html (accessed January 22, 2009).

Nilson Report. 1990–2007. Carpinteria, California: The Nilson Report.

Phelps, Edmund S. 1997. *Rewarding Work: How to Restore Participation and Self-Support to Free Enterprise.* Cambridge, Mass.: Harvard University Press.

Schor, Juliet B. 1999. *The Overspent American: Why We Want What We Don't Need.* New York: HarperCollins.

Warren, Elizabeth. 2007. "Unsafe at Any Rate." *Democracy: A Journal of Ideas* 5(Summer): 8–19.

Yoo, Peter S. 1997. "Charging up a Mountain of Debt: Accounting for the Growth of Credit Card Debt." *Federal Reserve Bank of St. Louis Review* 79(2): 3–14.

———. 1998. "Still Charging: The Growth of Credit Card Debt Between 1992 and 1995." *Federal Reserve Bank of St. Louis Review* 80(1): 19–28.

Zinman, Jonathan. 2007. "Where Is the Missing Credit Card Debt? Clues and Implications." Federal Reserve Bank of Philla Payment Cards Center Discussion Paper No. 07–11. Available at: http://www.dartmouth.edu/~jzinman/Papers/Zinman_MissingCardDebt_ sep07.pdf (accessed January 22, 2009).

Chapter 10

Immigrants' Access to Financial Services and Asset Accumulation

Una Okonkwo Osili and Anna L. Paulson

More than 191 million people live outside their country of birth, and about 20 percent of these emigrants live in the United States (United Nations 2005). Today at least one in nine U.S. residents, or 35 million people, were born abroad, and nearly one in five U.S. schoolchildren have an immigrant parent (Capps et al. 2004). Immigrants make up a disproportionate share of low- and moderate-income U.S. residents. Among individuals with below-median income, one in six were born abroad.

Since 1990, the growth in the immigrant population has been fastest outside of traditional immigrant-receiving regions (Singer 2004). As a result, immigrants are now an important component of the population of virtually every U.S. community. One characteristic of healthy communities is broad participation in financial markets. Immigrants, however, are much less likely than the native-born to participate in a wide variety of financial markets (see figure 10.1 and table 10.1).

Not unrelated to this is the substantial wealth gap between immigrants and the native-born. The median immigrant family has wealth (real and financial) of $8,300 per person, just 23 percent that of the median family born in the United States (see table 10.1). Immigrants are much more likely to have zero wealth and are also less likely to have accumulated higher levels of wealth. The gap in financial wealth is even more striking. The median immigrant family has just 17 percent of the financial wealth of the median native-born family.

In the tradition of Melvin Oliver and Thomas Shapiro (1995), we can think of wealth as a summary of past experiences that translate into today's economic opportunity. Together with their labor market experiences and family background, immigrants bring perspectives acquired in their country of origin to the United States. In addition to offering a summary of the past, wealth is an important measure of the economic prospects of future generations. By studying the wealth of U.S. immigrants, we can gain insights into how past experiences have shaped their current circumstances, and we can also gauge whether the economic adaptation of current immigrants and their children will keep pace with their demographic growth.

FIGURE 10.1 / Lowess Estimates of the Probability of Ownership of Assets Versus Age

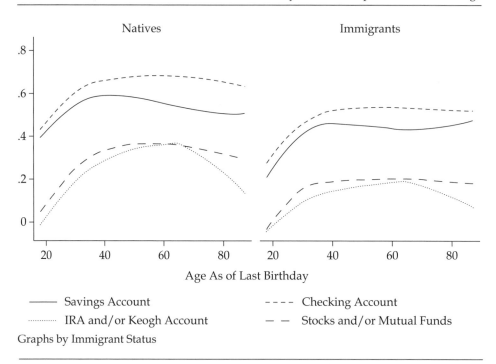

Age As of Last Birthday

———— Savings Account   - - - - Checking Account
·········· IRA and/or Keogh Account   — — Stocks and/or Mutual Funds

Graphs by Immigrant Status

Source: Authors' calculations based on Survey of Income and Program Participation.
Notes: For each observation in the figure, a weighted regression is performed using 80 percent (bandwidth = 0.8) of the data around that point. The data are weighted using a tri-cube weighting procedure that puts more weight on the points closest to the observation in question. The weighted regression results are used to produce a predicted value for each observation.

    This chapter explores two broad areas that influence immigrants' wealth accumulation and particularly their decisions to participate in various financial markets: characteristics that influence the behavior of both immigrants and the native-born, like education and marital status, and characteristics that are unique to immigrants, such as legal status and time in the United States. In addition, we discuss potential explanations for the persistently low financial market participation of immigrants, including the desire to purchase a home, country-of-origin experiences, remittances, wealth held abroad, return migration intentions, and supply-side factors, like the location of financial institutions and the characteristics of financial products. The analysis relies primarily on data from the 2001 Survey of Income and Program Participation (SIPP).
    Consistent with many models of savings behavior, we find that socioeconomic and demographic characteristics like age, education, family structure, ethnicity, and income play an important role in immigrant as well as native-born choices regarding financial services. These characteristics, however, are only part of the

TABLE 10.1 / Income and Wealth of Immigrant and Native-Born Households

	All		Income Below 40th Percentile		Whites		Blacks		Hispanics		Asians	
	Native	Immigrant	Native	Immigrant	Native	Immigrant	Native	Immigrant	Native	Immigrant	Native	Immigrant
Income and wealth (in thousands of dollars)												
Median monthly household income	$1.59	$1.10	$0.82	$0.56	$1.75	$1.59	$1.06	$1.05	$1.02	$0.78	$2.00	$1.49
Median household wealth	36.10	8.30	15.68	2.22	51.53	34.10	4.60	3.84	4.40	2.17	31.60	19.50
Median financial wealth	2.20	0.37	0.40	0.02	4.57	2.50	0.05	0.22	0.18	0.01	4.00	1.52
Mean monthly household income	2.15	1.71	0.94	0.68	2.34	2.22	1.45	1.31	1.43	1.10	2.38	2.24
	(2.31)	(2.37)	(0.96)	(1.00)	(2.45)	(3.10)	(1.43)	(1.05)	(1.37)	(1.22)	(2.94)	(2.78)
Mean household wealth	109.89	57.09	93.74	39.34	131.60	101.48	31.22	18.33	35.07	23.29	86.44	68.41
	(791.1)	(144.7)	(1223)	(107.7)	(897.8)	(183.2)	(77.9)	(44.5)	(104.1)	(77.2)	(147.7)	(176.6)
Percentage who own:												
Any asset	90%	78%	81%	67%	95%	90%	72%	68%	77%	66%	94%	88%
Savings and/or checking account	80	67	68	55	86	80	59	61	65	52	88	80
Interest-earning assets at banks	71	55	56	41	77	69	47	50	52	38	80	67
Savings account	58	46	43	33	63	55	41	45	45	32	66	57
Interest-bearing checking account	41	27	29	19	46	38	20	23	24	15	51	35

(Table continues on p. 288.)

TABLE 10.1 / *Continued*

	All		Income Below 40th Percentile		Whites		Blacks		Hispanics		Asians	
	Native	Immigrant	Native	Immigrant	Native	Immigrant	Native	Immigrant	Native	Immigrant	Native	Immigrant
Non-interest-bearing checking account	33	30	29	25	35	33	25	25	28	25	28	37
Any checking account	67	52	55	41	74	64	43	44	48	37	74	66
IRA or KEOGH account	30	16	18	9	36	25	8	8	11	6	30	22
Stock and/or mutual funds	36	21	21	10	42	36	14	14	14	5	33	33
Home	69	50	54	37	75	60	48	38	46	42	57	54
Median wealth, conditional on ownership (in thousands of dollars)												
All assets	$33.25	$13.60	$27.60	$5.83	$40.90	$32.50	$9.75	$3.25	$6.05	$5.20	$23.86	$18.00
Interest-earning assets at banks	2.00	1.25	1.50	1.00	2.50	2.50	0.47	0.52	0.60	0.35	2.27	2.00
Non-interest-bearing checking account	0.33	0.30	0.25	0.20	0.40	0.38	0.17	0.30	0.29	0.20	0.27	0.33
IRA or KEOGH account	8.50	5.33	9.50	7.69	9.00	8.25	4.00	3.00	3.40	3.25	8.00	4.50
Stock and/or mutual funds	5.00	3.33	5.00	5.50	5.26	4.00	3.00	2.33	2.50	3.75	6.00	3.00
Home equity	35.00	27.50	45.00	31.00	40.00	41.25	20.00	16.00	17.00	13.60	29.17	32.50
Number of observations	13,330	2,508	5,366	1,151	10,124	764	1,980	181	973	1,030	174	522

Source: Authors' calculations based on Survey of Income and Program Participation.
Notes: Sample is restricted to wave 3 of the 2001 to 2003 SIPP households with a reference person who was at least eighteen years old, lived in an MSA, and had a non-missing value for immigrant status. Standard errors are in parentheses. Data are weighted to reflect the U.S. population. All income and wealth figures are household per-capita figures and reported in thousands of dollars.

story. Immigrants are less likely to participate in a broad array of financial markets compared with the native-born, even after taking into account differences in socioeconomic and demographic factors.

Although there is some evidence that immigrants are as likely as otherwise similar native-born individuals to hold a checking account if they have spent enough time in the United States, adaptation is less complete for financial products that look to the future: savings accounts, IRA-Keogh accounts, and stock and mutual funds.

The findings suggest that immigrants' desire to purchase a home may lead them to make financial decisions that account for some of the differences in their financial market participation relative to the native-born. Exposure to a weak institutional environment and banking crises in the country of origin is associated with lower financial market participation in the United States as well. This factor is reinforced for immigrants who live in neighborhoods with many other immigrants from the same country of origin. It is likely that one role of these ethnic networks is to provide informal substitutes for formal financial products (see Barr, this volume; Bond and Townsend 1996). Data limitations prevent us from examining this hypothesis directly.

It is also important to recognize that immigrants' financial choices are influenced by how the features of products and services offered by banks compare with those offered by the alternative financial services sector. These include cost, anonymity, documentation requirements, minimum balance requirements, and convenience—both in the United States and, in the case of remittances, in the country of origin. Less tangible, but enormously important, an institution's "culture" determines how welcoming and familiar it feels to a potential immigrant customer. Many of these factors also influence the financial decisions of low- and moderate-income individuals who were born in the United States. Peter Tufano (this volume) has some suggestions about how financial service providers could make their products more attractive to many individuals, including immigrants.

The rest of the chapter is organized as follows. In the next section, we describe the data used in the study, compare the wealth and financial market participation of immigrants and the native-born for various racial and ethnic groups, and describe the estimation procedures we use in the analysis. We then discuss regression estimates of the probability of owning a checking account, a savings account, an IRA-Keogh account, and stock or mutual funds. This analysis allows us to quantify the effects of characteristics on financial market participation and estimate the gap in participation between immigrants and the native-born after controlling for these characteristics. In the next section, we examine how various measures of adaptation to the United States affect the financial behavior of immigrants relative to the native-born. In the following section, we consider potential explanations for the persistence of the gap in financial market participation between immigrants and the native-born, including housing, country-of-origin factors, ethnic concentration, remittances, wealth held abroad, return migration intentions, and supply-side factors. Finally, we offer conclusions and a discussion of policy priorities based on our findings.

DATA, SUMMARY STATISTICS, AND EMPIRICAL SPECIFICATION

Data

We rely primarily on data from the 2001 Survey of Income and Program Participation (SIPP). The 2001 SIPP is a nationally representative, random sample of U.S. households that is unique in providing detailed information about both the immigration experience and wealth and financial market holdings. Data were collected in nine quarterly waves from 2001 to 2003. We use immigration information that was collected during a topical module in wave 2, together with socioeconomic and demographic information from the core module in wave 3 and wealth and financial market participation information from the first assets and liabilities topical module in wave 3 to create a single cross-section of the data for analysis. We restrict the sample to households with a reference person who was at least eighteen years old and lived in a metropolitan statistical area (MSA), for a total sample of 15,838, of whom 16 percent (2,508) were born abroad. All of the analysis makes use of sampling weights to ensure that the data are representative of the U.S. population.

The SIPP data include an unknown number of undocumented immigrants. Although the survey procedures themselves do not deliberately screen out undocumented immigrants, it is likely that these individuals are less willing to participate in the survey. As a potentially useful benchmark, the U.S. Census Bureau estimates that it undercounts the illegal immigrant population by 15 percent in the decennial census (Costanzo et al. 2001).

Summary Statistics

WEALTH AND FINANCIAL MARKET PARTICIPATION   We begin with an overview of some stylized facts. The median family with a U.S.-born head has more than four times the total wealth and nearly six times the financial wealth of the median immigrant-headed family (see table 10.1). When we examine the components of financial wealth separately, however, a different picture of the immigrant-native wealth gap emerges. If we restrict our attention to immigrants and natives who own a particular asset, the difference in the amount of wealth held in that asset is much smaller than the difference in total wealth. For example, among households that have an interest-bearing account at a bank, immigrants have a median balance of $1,250—roughly 60 percent of that of the median family born in the United States (see table 10.1). The value of median non-interest-bearing accounts for immigrants is 90 percent that of the native-born, the figure for IRA-Keogh accounts is 63 percent, and for stock and mutual funds it is 67 percent. These findings are consistent with recent studies that document that immigrants have substantially lower wealth levels than the native-born; conditional on holding a given asset, however, immigrant-native wealth differences are relatively small

(Amuedo-Dorantes and Pozo 2002; Cobb-Clark and Hildebrand 2006; Hao 2004; Krivo and Kaufman 2004).

Why is the gap between immigrants and the native-born so much larger when we look at total wealth versus its components? Although there is a large literature that examines sources of immigrant-native differences in labor market, health, and educational outcomes, relatively little is known about the determinants of wealth differences between immigrants and the native-born. One important answer seems to lie in financial market participation. Figure 10.1 presents nonparametric regressions of the likelihood of owning various financial assets for immigrants and the native-born as a function of age.[1] These estimates show that immigrants of all ages are less likely to participate in a wide range of financial markets compared to the native-born.

This pattern is reinforced by examining the data on financial market participation presented in table 10.1. While 58 percent of native-born households have a savings account, only 46 percent of immigrant households do. Sixty-seven percent of native-born households have a checking account compared with 52 percent of immigrant households. Overall, 80 percent of native-born households have either a savings or a checking account compared with just 67 percent of immigrant households.[2] When we turn our attention away from these very safe and liquid assets and look at higher-return, higher-risk assets, the difference is larger. For example, twice as many (30 percent) native-born households as immigrant households have an IRA or Keogh account. Similarly, while 36 percent of native-born households own stock or a mutual fund, the figure for immigrant households is just 21 percent.

The comparison of all immigrants with all of the native-born obscures a diversity of experience across racial, ethnic, and income subgroups. In table 10.1, when we divide the sample into groups based on income and ethnicity, we observe that financial market participation varies substantially depending on the subgroup. White and Asian immigrants and natives of European or Asian descent have relatively high rates of asset ownership, while Hispanic immigrants and natives of Hispanic descent have low rates of ownership. However, the gap in financial market participation between the native-born and immigrant households is generally fairly similar.

One notable exception to this pattern is found among black households. Black immigrant households are *slightly* more likely to participate in many financial markets than native-born black households. Sixty-one percent of black immigrant households have a savings or checking account compared with 59 percent of black native-born households. This appears to be due mostly to low financial market participation among native-born black households rather than particularly high asset ownership among black immigrants. However, it is important to note that black immigrants also differ significantly from native-born blacks in educational attainment, labor market experience, and family structure (see table 10.2).[3]

DIFFERENCES IN CHARACTERISTICS   Disparities in wealth and financial market participation between immigrant and native-born households are likely to be

TABLE 10.2 / Summary Statistics, Immigrants Versus Natives

	All		Income Below 40th Percentile		Whites		Blacks		Hispanics		Asians	
	Native	Immigrant	Native	Immigrant	Native	Immigrant	Native	Immigrant	Native	Immigrant	Native	Immigrant
Married	51.15%	59.88%	28.46%	48.87%	54.74%	56.29%	31.59%	46.91%	49.15%	60.07%	57.30%	68.92%
Male	51.09	57.66	40.24	50.03	53.47	55.34	36.70	50.96	51.78	59.14	59.01	60.61
Household size	2.46	3.15	1.94	2.68	2.38	2.60	2.61	2.88	3.05	3.66	2.75	3.10
	(1.42)	(1.81)	(1.26)	(1.71)	(1.33)	(1.53)	(1.59)	(1.69)	(1.72)	(2.02)	(1.48)	(1.57)
Education												
Less than high school	12.27%	28.24%	22.16%	39.59%	9.20%	14.39%	20.15%	21.50%	30.90%	49.94%	8.85%	10.41%
High school graduate	26.67	22.02	32.73	26.24	25.91	24.06	30.18	22.36	29.42	23.47	20.83	16.06
More than high school	61.06	49.73	45.11	34.17	64.89	61.55	49.68	56.14	39.68	26.59	70.33	73.53
Number of observations	13,330	2,508	5,366	1,151	10,124	764	1,980	181	973	1,030	174	522

Source: Authors' calculations based on Survey of Income and Program Participation.
Notes: Sample is restricted to wave 3 of the 2001 to 2003 SIPP households with a reference person who was at least eighteen years old, lived in an MSA, and had a non-missing value for immigrant status. Standard errors are in parentheses. Data are weighted to reflect the U.S. population.

driven (at least in part) by differences in household income, age, education, and family structure as well as other characteristics. Monthly per capita income is significantly lower for immigrants than for the native-born. In particular, median monthly per capita household income for immigrant households is $1,103 compared with $1,593 for native-born households (see table 10.1).

Note that the income gap, while substantial, is much smaller than the wealth gap: the median income of immigrant households is 69 percent that of native-born households, while the median wealth of immigrant households is just 23 percent. This is consistent with other studies that document that differences in wealth exceed the income gaps for various racial and ethnic groups. The large body of empirical studies on wealth (for example, Altonji and Doraszelski 2005; Blau and Graham 1990; Hurst, Luoh, and Stafford 1998; Menchik and Jianakoplos 1997; Wolff 1998, 2000) show that white households have at least five times the wealth of nonwhite households, yet earn, on average, just twice as much as nonwhite households.

Like other studies, we find that the gap, both in income and in wealth, depends very much on the comparison group. For example, the median black immigrant household has nearly the same income as the median black native-born household, but the median income of native-born black households is just 67 percent that of the median native-born white household.

Table 10.2 provides a detailed comparison of other characteristics of immigrants and the native-born. Compared to the native-born, immigrants are more likely to be married, to have children, and to have a male household head. Immigrants also tend to have strikingly less education than the native-born. Nearly 28 percent of immigrants in the sample have not completed high school compared with only 12 percent of the native-born sample. White and Asian immigrants are more likely to have completed education beyond high school, as are white and Asian natives. Hispanic immigrants have notably low levels of education, with nearly half never having completed high school. Hispanic natives are also relatively less educated, with about one-third not having completed high school.

Table 10.3 summarizes some important characteristics of the SIPP immigrant population. Just over one-half of the sample immigrants have become naturalized U.S. citizens. Sixty-one percent of the immigrant sample reports speaking English either well or very well. The vast majority of these immigrants arrived in the United States as adults, and about half have lived in the United States for sixteen or more years. The Americas (Central, North, and South, plus the Caribbean) account for nearly 40 percent of the immigrant sample, with almost one-third coming from Mexico alone.

Estimating Financial Market Participation

The fact that the wealth gap between immigrants and the native-born manifests itself, at least partly, in financial market participation can provide insights into reasons for limited participation in financial markets. Some research on low rates of financial market participation emphasizes the presence of market frictions,

TABLE 10.3 / Immigrant Characteristics

	All	Income Below 40th Percentile	Race-Ethnicity			
			White	Black	Hispanic	Asian
Citizen	51.77%	46.99%	63.93%	55.94%	37.89%	58.31%
Speaks English well	60.74	50.16	81.22	86.15	38.35	61.80
Arrived before age eighteen	18.62	14.21	20.29	0.11	19.91	16.50
Arrived age eighteen or later	81.38	85.79	79.71	88.59	80.09	83.50
In United States for five years or less	15.73	16.05	15.50	22.73	14.16	16.77
In United States for six to fifteen years	31.96	32.22	21.23	32.34	36.68	37.30
In United States for sixteen years or more	52.31	51.72	63.27	44.93	49.16	45.93
Region of origin						
The Americas	39.70	55.26	16.34	46.90	98.56	1.54
Asia and Australasia	25.03	19.11	10.71	11.93	0.44	95.17
Europe	19.40	18.78	58.88	7.19	0.56	0.87
Middle East	3.19	2.49	9.19	1.26	0.00	1.09
Africa	3.92	3.80	3.98	31.52	0.23	0.92
Other	0.57	0.57	0.90	1.20	0.21	0.41
Number of observations	2,508	1,151	764	181	1,030	522

Source: Authors' calculations based on Survey of Income and Program Participation.
Notes: Sample is restricted to wave 3 of the 2001 to 2003 SIPP households with a reference person who was at least eighteen years old, lived in an MSA, and had a nonmissing value for immigrant status. Standard errors are in parentheses. Data are weighted to represent the U.S. population. The Americas include Central, North, and South America, as well as the Caribbean.

mostly in the form of high fixed entry or transaction costs (Bertaut and Starr-McCluer 2000; Vissing-Jorgensen 2002) and the role of information networks (Hong, Kubik, and Stein 2004). The large gap in financial market participation that we observe between immigrants and the native-born suggests that these factors are important for understanding these differences.

In addition to the substantive reasons outlined earlier, focusing on financial market participation rather than on levels of wealth has some empirical advantages. Researchers have noted concerns with measurement error and nonresponse in reported wealth holdings (see, for example, Smith 1995). Survey respondents are more likely to refuse to answer questions about levels of financial wealth than questions about financial market participation. Estimates of financial market participation using the SIPP data rely much less on imputed responses relative to information on levels of financial asset holdings.[4] By focusing on financial market participation as the key outcome of interest, we avoid some of these issues.

All of these characteristics (and others) are likely to affect the decision to participate in various financial markets. To control for the effect of characteristics on the financial market participation of immigrants and the native-born more generally, we estimate the decision to participate in a particular financial market using the following linear probability model:

$$S_{isj} = \alpha + \beta_1 I_i + \beta_2 X_i + \delta_s + \varepsilon_{isj}$$

where S_{isj} is the decision to own asset j for household i living in metropolitan statistical area s. Individual controls are incorporated in X_i and include education, income quintiles, wealth quintiles, marital status, sex, age, whether the household is headed by a single parent, and controls for the number of adult males, females, and children of various ages living in the household. The estimates also include controls for black, Hispanic, Asian, and "other" (except when we look only at households belonging to a specific racial or ethnic group). A full set of MSA controls are included in δ_s. Finally, the regression includes the key variable of interest: I or "immigrant," which is equal to one if the household reference person was born abroad. The estimate of the coefficient β_1 indicates the remaining gap in financial market participation between immigrants and the native-born holding characteristics fixed.

All of the reported standard errors are corrected to account for the heteroskedasticity that is implicit in the linear probability model.[5] One additional econometric concern is the potential endogeneity of wealth and income: owning stocks leads to higher wealth rather than the other way around, for example. We follow the literature in this area and include wealth and income controls and take a number of steps to address this issue. First, the nature of the dependent variable and the way we measure the independent variables in question minimize the potential for reverse causality. By focusing on financial market participation, using a zero/one variable, and including wealth and income as quintiles rather than levels, we eliminate the sort of automatic feedback we would be worried about if we included the wealth levels (including stock holdings) in a regression where, for example, the dependent variable was equal to the level of stock holdings.

The literature on portfolio choice emphasizes the importance of fixed transaction costs and risk aversion in explaining financial choices, and we prefer specifications that include their likely correlates, income and wealth quintiles. We have also estimated all of the models in the chapter without these variables, and the general patterns remain consistent, although the estimated size of the coefficient on being an immigrant is, as we would expect, larger when income and wealth are not included in the analysis.

CHARACTERISTICS, IMMIGRANT STATUS, AND FINANCIAL MARKET PARTICIPATION

Regression estimates of whether or not a household owns various financial assets for the whole sample and for various subgroups are found in table 10.4. Table 10.4 reports the estimates of the coefficient on the immigrant variable (β_1) for checking

TABLE 10.4 / Estimates of Account Ownership for Socioeconomic and Demographic Groups

	All (1)	Income Below 40th Percentile (2)	Whites (3)	Blacks (4)	Hispanics (5)	Asians (6)
Checking account ownership						
Immigrant	-0.058***	-0.058***	-0.061***	-0.030	-0.089***	-0.001
	(0.012)	(0.019)	(0.018)	(0.038)	(0.023)	(0.043)
Native ownership rate	67.47%	55.13%	73.51%	43.20%	48.32%	73.52%
Immigrant ownership rate	52.19	40.64	64.46	43.67	36.57	66.02
Adjusted R-squared	0.2135	0.2214	0.1332	0.2459	0.2509	0.2242
Savings account ownership						
Immigrant	-0.047***	-0.046**	-0.048**	0.007	-0.066***	-0.028
	(0.013)	(0.019)	(0.019)	(0.039)	(0.023)	(0.049)
Native ownership rate	58.36%	43.07%	62.54%	41.34%	44.72%	65.74%
Immigrant ownership rate	45.88	32.52	55.00	45.36	32.44	57.35
Adjusted R-squared	0.1737	0.1474	0.1276	0.2489	0.2324	0.1868
IRA-Keogh ownership						
Immigrant	-0.054***	-0.035***	-0.074***	-0.011	-0.023*	-0.074*
	(0.010)	(0.012)	(0.016)	(0.023)	(0.013)	(0.038)

Native ownership rate	30.36%	17.51%	36.14%	8.44%	11.33%	29.98%
Immigrant ownership rate	15.50	8.71	25.47	8.31	5.76	21.71
Adjusted R-squared	0.3020	0.2679	0.2706	0.2105	0.2569	0.2927
Stock–mutual fund ownership						
Immigrant	−0.030***	−0.022*	−0.029*	−0.032	−0.062***	0.027
	(0.010)	(0.013)	(0.016)	(0.027)	(0.012)	(0.045)
Native ownership rate	36.17%	20.82%	42.25%	14.42%	14.38%	33.16%
Immigrant ownership rate	21.39	10.15	35.64	14.47	5.09	33.50
Adjusted R-squared	0.3251	0.2827	0.282	0.282	0.3148	0.3357
Number of observations	15,838	6,517	10,888	2,161	2,003	696

Source: Authors' calculations based on Survey of Income and Program Participation.

Notes: The sample consists of all 2001 to 2003 SIPP wave 3 households with a reference person at least eighteen years of age with a populated immigrant status who resided in an MSA. The dependent variable is equal to one if the household reference person and/or his or her spouse owned the relevant asset, and zero otherwise. Linear models with MSA fixed effects are used, and the results are adjusted to take into account sampling weights. Standard errors, in parentheses, are corrected for heteroskedasticity. Data are weighted to represent the U.S. population. In addition to immigrant status, each regression controls for: income and wealth quintiles, education categories, age, age-squared, marital status, sex, the number of adult males, adult females, children age zero to five, children age six to twelve, and children age thirteen to seventeen in the household. Columns 1 and 2 also include controls for black, Hispanic, Asian, and "other."

***significant at at least the 1 percent level; **significant at at least the 5 percent level; *significant at at least the 10 percent level.

account ownership, savings account ownership, IRA-Keogh account ownership, and stock or mutual funds ownership for the whole sample, for those with income below the fortieth percentile, and for whites, blacks, Hispanics, and Asians. In addition to controlling for immigrant status, the regressions include controls for the complete set of individual and geographic characteristics described earlier.

Estimates of the Impact of Characteristics on Financial Market Participation

Before turning our attention to the role of being an immigrant, we highlight some of the key relationships between education, income, wealth, race and ethnicity, and financial market participation that are shared by immigrants and the native-born.[6] In general, the qualitative effect of education, wealth, and income is similar for checking accounts, savings accounts, IRA-Keogh accounts, and stock and mutual funds, so we focus our discussion on checking accounts, the most commonly held financial asset.

Income has a strong positive correlation with checking account ownership. For the whole sample, relative to the lowest income quintile, households with per capita monthly income in the second quintile are 9.1 percentage points more likely to have a checking account. Households with incomes in the third, fourth, and fifth quintiles are 11.0 to 13.5 percentage points more likely to have a checking account compared with households in the lowest income quintile.

Wealthier households are also more likely to have checking accounts according to these estimates. Households in the second wealth quintile are 12.9 percentage points more likely to have a checking account than households in the lowest wealth quintile. The effect of wealth on the ownership of IRA-Keogh accounts and stock and mutual funds is even stronger.

Some studies focus on the importance of education in lowering the information costs of participating in various financial markets (see, for example, Bernheim, Garrett, and Maki 2001). Our results are consistent with these theories. We find that checking account ownership increases significantly with education. Households headed by someone with a high school degree are 10 percentage points more likely to have a checking account than households whose head has not completed high school. Additional schooling raises the likelihood of having a checking account: households whose head has completed some college are 16.9 percentage points more likely to have a checking account; those with a bachelor's or an advanced degree are more than 20 percentage points more likely to have a checking account than households whose heads have not completed high school. The impact of education is similar across the different types of financial assets.

Households headed by Hispanic or black individuals are less likely to own various financial products. In contrast, households headed by Asians are as likely to have a savings or checking account as households headed by whites. Asian-headed households, however, are less likely to have IRA-Keogh accounts and to own stock or mutual funds. This is consistent with recent empirical studies of house-

TABLE 10.5 / Differences in Checking Account Ownership Before and After Controlling for Characteristics

	Difference Before Controlling for Characteristics (1)	Difference After Controlling for Characteristics (2)	Percentage of Difference Accounted for by Characteristics (3)
All	15.0%	5.8%	61.3%
Income below 40th percentile	14.0	5.8	58.6
White	10.0	6.1	39.0
Black	−1.0	3.0	400.0
Hispanic	11.0	8.9	19.1
Asian	8.0	0.1	98.8

Source: Authors' calculations based on Survey of Income and Program Participation.
Notes: Column 1 is equal to the difference in the percentage of native-born- and immigrant-headed households that own any type of checking account from table 10.1. Column 2 is equal to the absolute value of the estimated coefficient, β_1, on the immigrant variable for the checking account ownership regressions displayed in table 10.4. Column 3 is equal to (column 1–column 2)/ column 1.

hold financial behavior that document significant differences in the use of financial services by race, even after controlling for income and education (Altonji and Doraszelski 2005; Blau and Graham 1990; Chiteji and Stafford 1999; Smith 1995).

Estimates of the Impact of Being an Immigrant on Financial Market Participation

Even after controlling for characteristics, we find that immigrants are generally significantly less likely to have a checking account, a savings account, or an IRA or Keogh account or to own stock or mutual funds (table 10.4). The gap in financial market participation ranges from 3 percentage points (for stock and mutual funds) to 5.8 percentage points (for checking) for the whole sample after controlling for wealth, income, education, age, marital status, being a single parent, family structure, and MSA fixed effects.

Table 10.5 compares checking account ownership for immigrants and natives before and after controlling for characteristics. For the whole sample, the raw gap in checking account ownership is 15 percentage points (see table 10.1). After controlling for characteristics, the gap is predicted to be 5.8 percentage points (the estimated coefficient β_1 from table 10.4). This implies that differences in characteristics account for about 9 percentage points, or 61 percent, of the difference in checking account ownership between immigrants and the native-born. The remaining 39 percent is not explained by differences in characteristics and has something to do with being an immigrant.

When we do the same comparison of white immigrants with native-born whites and Hispanic immigrants with native-born Hispanics, we find that more of the difference in checking account ownership is related to being an immigrant. For example, among whites, 39 percent of the difference in checking account ownership can be explained by differences in characteristics, and 61 percent has to do with being an immigrant. Among Hispanics, 81 percent of the gap in checking account ownership between native-born Hispanics and Hispanics who were born abroad has to do with immigrant status (table 10.5).

When we restrict the sample to households headed by blacks, we find no statistically significant difference in checking account ownership, savings account ownership, IRA-Keogh ownership, and stock and mutual fund ownership between immigrants and the native-born once we have controlled for differences in characteristics (table 10.4). Recall that black immigrants have similar ownership rates of the various financial assets to native-born blacks (table 10.1).

The main source of this pattern seems to be that blacks who were born in the United States have lower than expected (given their characteristics) financial market participation, not that black immigrants have particularly high rates of financial market participation. This is generally consistent with the research of Francine Blau and John Graham (1990), who analyze data from the National Longitudinal Study of Youth (NLSY) and find that almost three-quarters of the black-white wealth gap cannot be explained by measured characteristics.

In addition, we find no significant difference in checking account, savings account, and stock and mutual fund ownership for immigrant and native-born Asians after controlling for characteristics. However, Asian immigrants are less likely to have an IRA-Keogh account than otherwise similar natives of Asian descent.

IMMIGRANT ADAPTATION

The previous section shows that characteristics are only part of the story and that simply being an immigrant seems to lead to lower financial market participation. In this section, we discuss the effect of various aspects of the immigrant experience that may affect the likelihood of owning financial assets.

Table 10.6 repeats the regressions presented in table 10.4 for different subsamples of immigrants who vary in how adapted (or adaptable) they are to the United States. Specifically, we run financial market participation regressions for various financial products with groups of immigrants who vary along the characteristics described earlier. For example, in one regression, we restrict the immigrant sample to immigrants who have become naturalized citizens. In another, we look only at immigrants who have *not* become naturalized citizens. By comparing the coefficient on the immigrant variable in these two regressions, we gain insights into how legal status affects the likelihood that immigrants will participate in various financial markets, holding other characteristics fixed. The native-born sample remains the same for each of the regressions.

TABLE 10.6 / Estimates of Account Ownership for Immigrant Groups Compared to the Native-Born

	All (1)	In United States Five Years or Less, Adult at Arrival (2)	In United States Six to Fifteen Years, Adult at Arrival (3)	In United States Sixteen Years or More, Adult at Arrival (4)	Noncitizen (5)	Citizen (6)
Checking account ownership						
Immigrant	-0.058***	-0.075***	-0.112***	-0.018	-0.085***	-0.032**
	(0.012)	(0.027)	(0.021)	(0.020)	(0.016)	(0.016)
Native ownership rate	67.47%	67.47%	67.47%	67.47%	67.47%	67.47%
Immigrant ownership rate	52.19	46.33	43.63	57.74	42.57	61.15
Adjusted R-squared	0.2135	0.2052	0.2119	0.2000	0.2195	0.1964
Savings account ownership						
Immigrant	-0.047***	-0.073**	-0.054**	-0.049**	-0.064***	-0.034**
	(0.013)	(0.029)	(0.022)	(0.021)	(0.017)	(0.016)
Native ownership rate	58.36%	58.36%	58.36%	58.36%	58.36%	58.36%
Immigrant ownership rate	45.88	40.11	42.83	46.29	38.70	52.56
Adjusted R-squared	0.1737	0.1693	0.1716	0.1654	0.1763	0.164
IRA-Keogh ownership						
Immigrant	-0.054***	-0.106***	-0.055***	-0.054***	-0.060***	-0.047***
	(0.010)	(0.017)	(0.015)	(0.016)	(0.012)	(0.012)
Native ownership rate	30.36%	30.36%	30.36%	30.36%	30.36%	30.36%
Immigrant ownership rate	15.50	3.39	11.98	19.60	7.81	22.67
Adjusted R-squared	0.3020	0.3025	0.3009	0.3022	0.3056	0.2981

(Table continues on p. 302.)

TABLE 10.6 / *Continued*

	All (1)	In United States Five Years or Less, Adult at Arrival (2)	In United States Six to Fifteen Years, Adult at Arrival (3)	In United States Sixteen Years or More, Adult at Arrival (4)	Noncitizen (5)	Citizen (6)
Stock–mutual funds ownership						
Immigrant	−0.030***	−0.083***	−0.013	−0.035**	−0.044***	−0.017
	(0.010)	(0.020)	(0.016)	(0.017)	(0.012)	(0.013)
Native ownership rate	36.17%	36.17%	36.17%	36.17%	36.17%	36.17%
Immigrant ownership rate	21.39	9.81	18.75	23.39	12.50	29.67
Adjusted R-squared	0.3251	0.3153	0.3180	0.3147	0.3248	0.3142
Number of observations	15,838	13,654	13,945	14,050	14,556	14,612

Source: Authors' calculations based on Survey of Income and Program Participation.

Notes: The sample consists of all 2001 to 2003 SIPP wave 3 households with a reference person at least eighteen years of age with a populated immigrant status who resided in an MSA. The dependent variable is equal to one if the household reference person and/or his or her spouse owned the relevant asset, and zero otherwise. Linear models with MSA fixed effects are used, and the results are adjusted to take into account sampling weights. Standard errors, in parentheses, are corrected for heteroskedasticity. Data are weighted to represent the U.S. population. In addition to immigrant status, each regression controls for: income and wealth quintiles, education categories, age, age-squared, marital status, sex, the number of adult males, adult females, children age zero to five, children age six to twelve, and children age thirteen to seventeen in the household, black, Hispanic, Asian, and "other."

***significant at at least the 1 percent level; **significant at at least the 5 percent level; *significant at at least the 10 percent level.

For comparison purposes, the first column of table 10.6 presents the estimates for the whole sample from table 10.4. In columns 2 through 4, we examine the effect of time in the United States by dividing the immigrant sample into three groups: those who have been in the United States for less than five years, for six to fifteen years, and for sixteen or more years. These estimates also restrict the sample to immigrants who arrived in the United States as adults.[7] The negative association between being an immigrant and checking account ownership appears to dissipate with time in the United States. For investments that look to the future, however, even immigrants who have been in the United States for sixteen or more years and who arrived as adults are less likely than otherwise similar native-born households to own a savings account, to have an IRA or Keogh account, or to own stock.

Legal Status

A number of studies have emphasized the effect of legal status on wages and occupation choice. For example, Deborah Cobb-Clark and Sherrie Kossoudji (2002) find that the 1986 Immigration Reform and Control Act (IRCA), which granted amnesty to previously undocumented workers, significantly improved wages and labor market opportunities for this group of workers. Legal status can be a barrier to financial market participation both in perception and in reality.[8] Many U.S. banks now accept identification issued by foreign governments to comply with the 2001 USA Patriot Act "know your customer" provisions, and the Internal Revenue Service (IRS) issues individual taxpayer identification numbers (ITINs) to individuals who do not qualify for Social Security numbers (SSNs) but have taxable income. Some financial institutions, however, have chosen not to do so. In addition, financial institutions have been criticized for making account ownership too easy for undocumented immigrants. Anecdotal accounts suggest that many immigrants remain concerned that financial institutions will share their identity and financial information with immigration authorities.[9]

The SIPP data contain information on whether immigrants have become naturalized U.S. citizens. Comparing households headed by naturalized-citizen immigrants with native-born households, we continue to find significant, although smaller, differences in financial asset ownership between immigrants and the native-born once other characteristics have been controlled for (columns 5 and 6). For example, immigrants who are naturalized citizens are 3 percentage points less likely to have a checking account than the native-born, while immigrants who are not citizens are nearly 8.5 percentage points less likely to have a checking account. We see a similar pattern for savings accounts and IRA and Keogh account ownership. Interestingly, there is no statistically significant difference in stock and mutual fund ownership between naturalized citizens and the native-born, holding characteristics fixed. These findings (and others) are broadly consistent with the work of Amuedo-Dorantes and Bansak (2006), who find that undocumented immigrants are significantly less likely to have a bank account, while immigrants who speak English, who earn more, who stay for longer periods of time in the United States, and who bring their spouses along with them to the United States are significantly more likely to have bank accounts.

POTENTIAL EXPLANATIONS

In this section, we examine a number of potential explanations for the persistent gap in financial market participation between immigrants and the native-born. We consider the possibility that prioritizing the accumulation of real assets, specifically housing, slows down the accumulation of financial assets like retirement accounts and stock and mutual funds for immigrants relative to the native-born. We also consider how country-of-origin characteristics and the tendency of immigrants to cluster in neighborhoods with other immigrants from the same country shape financial choices, drawing on our previous work (Osili and Paulson 2004, 2008a, 2008b). We supplement this analysis with information from the New Immigrant Survey (NIS) to examine the role of return migration intentions, remittances, and the possibility of owning assets abroad. In addition, we draw on the existing literature to consider the role of supply-side factors like the location of financial institutions and the characteristics of the products and services they offer.

Housing and Financial Market Participation

Sixty-nine percent of native-born households and 50 percent of immigrant households own a home (table 10.1). Among homeowners, median home equity is $35,000 for native-born households and $27,500 for immigrant households. These figures are roughly consistent with previous research. For example, George Borjas (2002) and Sherrie Kossoudji and Stanley Sedo (2004) find that while immigrants are less likely to own homes than similar native-born individuals, conditional on homeownership, the difference in home equity between immigrants and the native-born is smaller than the gap in homeownership.

This comparison of homeownership rates and home equity accumulation among immigrants follows the same pattern that we have seen for financial market participation for immigrants versus the native-born: large gaps in the percentage of families who own the asset and smaller gaps in the value of the asset conditional on ownership. However, along other dimensions, homeownership diverges from the patterns we see for financial asset holdings.

In table 10.7, we present regression estimates of the probability of homeownership for various groups of immigrants and natives, controlling for the set of characteristics that we discussed earlier. Overall, immigrants are 4.5 percentage points less likely to own a home than otherwise similar native-born households. The gap is smaller for immigrants who are citizens (column 6) and for immigrants who have lived in the United States for a longer period (column 4). In contrast to the patterns for financial asset ownership, adaptation appears to be complete for immigrants who have lived in the United States for sixteen years or more, despite having arrived in

TABLE 10.7 / Estimates of Homeownership for Immigrant Subgroups Compared to the Native-Born

	All (1)	In United States Five Years or Less, Adult at Arrival (2)	In United States Six to Fifteen Years, Adult at Arrival (3)	In United States Sixteen Years or More, Adult at Arrival (4)	Noncitizen (5)	Citizen (6)
Immigrant	−0.045***	−0.110***	−0.057***	−0.011	−0.067***	−0.022*
	(0.009)	(0.020)	(0.017)	(0.014)	(0.012)	(0.012)
Native ownership rate	68.78%	68.78%	68.78%	68.78%	68.78%	68.78%
Immigrant ownership rate	49.98	22.52	41.93	64.63	35.45	63.51
Adjusted R-squared	0.5529	0.5511	0.5476	0.5454	0.5572	0.5413
Number of observations	15,838	13,654	13,945	14,050	14,556	14,612

Source: Authors' calculations based on Survey of Income and Program Participation.
Notes: The sample consists of all 2001 to 2003 SIPP wave 3 households with a reference person at least eighteen years of age with a populated immigrant status who resided in an MSA. The dependent variable is equal to one if the household reference person and/or his or her spouse owned the relevant asset, and zero otherwise. Linear models with MSA fixed effects are used, and the results are adjusted to take into account sampling weights. Standard errors, in parentheses, are corrected for heteroskedasticity. Data are weighted to represent the U.S. population. In addition to immigrant status, each regression controls for: income and wealth quintiles, education categories, age, age-squared, marital status, sex, the number of adult males, adult females, children age zero to five, children age six to twelve, and children age thirteen to seventeen in the household, black, Hispanic, Asian, and "other."
***significant at at least the 1 percent level; **significant at at least the 5 percent level; *significant at at least the 10 percent level.

the country as adults. There is no statistically significant gap in homeownership between this group of immigrants and otherwise similar native-born households.[10] Changes in the effect of being an immigrant on homeownership with time in the U.S. most closely resemble those for checking accounts and hint that the goal of buying a home in the U.S. may take precedence over accumulating other financial assets.

Country-of-Origin Characteristics

Experience with banks prior to migration is likely to affect financial choices in the United States as well. Although even in developed countries there is significant variation in the fraction of individuals who use financial services, in some developing countries the norm is to be without a bank account. Approximately 75 percent of households in Mexico lack an account, for example, as do 90 percent of Kenyans (Beck, Demirgüç-Kunt, and Martinez Peria 2007). Recent survey evidence from the United States suggests that a significant fraction of households choose not to hold bank accounts because they "often are imbued with a cultural distrust of banks, and they may be concerned with privacy" (Federal Deposit Insurance Corporation 2003).

In some countries, banks are not a safe place to put money, especially for relatively poor people. Growing up in a place where financial crises, lack of transparency, fraud, inflation, and theft erode account values leads immigrants from some countries to distrust banks. For example, the banking crisis that crippled Mexico in the mid-1990s heightened suspicions that banks were unreliable (Hernandez-Coss 2005).

Not all immigrants, however, come to the United States with negative perceptions of financial institutions. Immigrants who come from countries that do a better job of protecting private property and providing incentives for investment are more likely to participate in U.S. financial markets (Osili and Paulson 2008a, 2008b). Holding income, education, and wealth (and other factors) constant, we find that immigrants from countries with more effective institutions are more likely to have a relationship with a bank and also are more likely to use formal financial markets more extensively. These findings are summarized in figure 10.2, which shows the predicted relationship between institutional quality and having a bank account for immigrants from various countries. These results are robust to different ways of measuring country-of-origin institutional quality, adding additional country-of-origin controls, and various methods of addressing potential bias due to unobserved individual characteristics, including specifications with country fixed effects. Country-of-origin institutions affect the financial market participation of recent immigrants as well as of those with up to twenty-seven years of U.S. experience. These institutions also influence the behavior not only of immigrants who arrive in the United States as children but of those who arrive as adults. Institutional quality appears to shape preferences and beliefs in a way that influences financial behavior.[11]

FIGURE 10.2 / Financial Market Participation and Institutional Quality

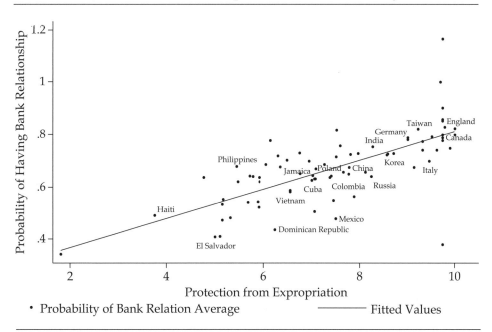

Source: Authors' calculations based on Survey of Income and Program Participation.

Ethnic Concentration

In addition to studying the effects of country-of-origin characteristics, researchers have tried to understand how immigrant outcomes vary with the characteristics of their destination communities. One aspect of the destination community that has received close attention is ethnic concentration: the tendency for immigrants to cluster together in cities or neighborhoods with other immigrants from the same country. Not all immigrants settle in the same way. For example, as we calculated from census data, the median Cuban immigrant in 1990 lived in an area where 17 percent of the population was also from Cuba, and the median Mexican immigrant lived in an area where 9 percent of the population was also from Mexico. By contrast, immigrants from Vietnam and India were much less likely to cluster: the former accounted for only 0.7 percent of their typical neighborhood, the latter just 0.3 percent. In addition to variation by country, there is also variation in the tendency to cluster for immigrants from a particular country: for example, Mexican immigrants in Chicago accounted for 4.2 percent of the population, but Mexicans in Milwaukee accounted for only 0.5 percent of the population.

The geographic concentration of immigrants has been shown to have important consequences for the pace of economic and social adaptation. For example, several studies have found that immigrant networks influence employment probabilities (Munshi 2003), wage growth, and human capital accumulation (Borjas 1985, 2000), as well as language proficiency (Chiswick and Miller 1996).

Residential settlement may have an adverse impact on financial market decisions if immigrants who reside in ethnically concentrated communities are isolated from mainstream society and lack information and knowledge about U.S. financial institutions. Thus, ethnic concentration may have a *direct* effect on financial market outcomes by limiting or even curtailing the flow of information about mainstream financial services—thus reinforcing low rates of financial asset ownership.

Social interactions and peer effects have been shown to affect portfolio selection and financial market decisions in other contexts (see, for example, Duflo and Saez 2003; Hong, Kubik, and Stein 2004).[12] Ethnic concentration may also have an *indirect* effect on financial market outcomes if immigrants who reside in ethnically concentrated communities also face less favorable labor market prospects.

In Osili and Paulson (2004), we show that immigrants who live in ethnically concentrated metropolitan areas are less likely to participate in U.S. financial markets. Our results imply, for example, that if an immigrant from Chicago were to move to Milwaukee, the likelihood that he would have a checking account would increase by five percentage points, and the likelihood that he would have a savings account would go up by two percentage points. Recall that Mexican immigrants account for 4.2 percent of the population of Chicago, but that Mexicans in Milwaukee account for only 0.5 percent of that metropolitan area's population. These findings rely on estimates that include MSA fixed effects to address the concern that immigrants choose where to live.

Ethnic concentration may also reinforce the effect of country-of-origin characteristics. We find that the effect of home country institutions is stronger for immigrants who live in neighborhoods with other immigrants from the same country (Osili and Paulson 2008a, 2008b). For these immigrants, attitudes toward institutions that were forged in the country of origin are likely to be reinforced through interactions with other immigrants from the same country who share exposure to that country's institutions.

Remittances, Return Migration Intentions, and Wealth Held Abroad

One potential explanation for why immigrant financial market participation lags behind that of otherwise similar native-born households could be the fact that immigrants often support family members living in the country of origin through remittances. This financial responsibility could delay or substitute for the accumulation of financial assets in the United States. However, the relationship between financial market participation and remittances may be complicated. Sending remittances is often cheaper for people with bank accounts, for

TABLE 10.8 / Financial Market Participation, Remittances, Return Migration
Intentions, and Wealth Held Abroad

	Have Savings, Checking, or Money Market Account	Own Stock
Remit	73.20%	17.25%
Do not remit	50.50	11.05
Plan to stay in United States	50.19	8.16
Plan to leave United States	56.41	20.66
Own wealth abroad	73.40	21.16
Do not own wealth abroad	47.46	8.51

Source: Authors' calculations based on New Immigrant Survey data.

example. To explore this issue, we tabulated information from the New Immigrant Survey (NIS) on financial market participation and remittances (see table 10.8). At first glance, these data suggest that remittances do not substitute for owning accounts in the United States: remitters are more likely to have a savings, checking, or money market account and to own stock in the United States than are nonremitters.[13]

Another potential influence on immigrant participation in U.S. financial markets is return migration intentions. Christian Dustmann (1997) and Oded Galor and Oded Stark (1990) argue that immigrants who have a higher probability of returning to a lower-wage country should save more while they are in the United States. High fixed costs might also discourage immigrants who plan to leave the United States soon from participating in U.S. financial markets. NIS tabulations of financial market participation as a function of return migration intentions suggest that the Dustmann (1997) and Galor and Stark (1990) view has validity, as those who plan to leave the United States have higher rates of account ownership than those who plan to stay in the United States (table 10.8).

Finally, data from the NIS allows us to examine the role of wealth held abroad. One possibility is that immigrants hold financial assets abroad, possibly in their countries of origin, instead of in the United States. Our tabulations (see table 10.8) suggest that this is not a likely explanation for the lower financial market participation of immigrants in the United States. Immigrants who own assets abroad are also more likely to own financial assets in the United States.

Though suggestive, these inferences based on tabulations from the NIS should be viewed as preliminary. The NIS focuses on recent immigrants, all of whom are legal, permanent residents. Their experiences may not translate to immigrants more generally. In addition, the figures in table 10.8 are raw tabulations and do not account for any differences in characteristics that might be correlated with both financial market participation and remittances, wealth held abroad, or return migration intentions.

Supply-Side Factors: Location and the Design of Financial Institution and Products

Our analysis emphasizes demand-side explanations for explaining financial market participation.[14] To some extent, the regression analysis controls for many supply-side factors as well. For example, the inclusion of MSA fixed effects controls for variation in the supply of financial services at the MSA level. Of course, much of the meaningful variation in the location and distance to financial service providers may occur at the neighborhood level within an MSA. To the extent that financial institutions—both mainstream institutions like banks and credit unions and alternative financial services providers like check-cashers and currency exchanges—rely on potential customer characteristics in deciding where to open branches, these supply-side factors are controlled for in the analysis by the inclusion of household characteristics like income, wealth, education, and immigrant status. The potential correlation of the availability of financial services and products with household characteristics should be taken into account in interpreting the estimated coefficients on these characteristics.

In addition to decisions about where to locate, financial institutions may have other practices that make them more or less attractive to potential immigrant clients. Banks often face stiff competition for the financial business of immigrants. One source of competition comes from the alternative financial services sector. The number of check-cashing outlets, pawnbrokers, and rent-to-own businesses increased from twenty-five thousand to thirty-five thousand between 1995 and 1999 (Temkin and Sawyer 2004). Meanwhile, the number of payday lenders grew nationwide from virtually no establishments in 1994 to nine thousand in 2000. The growth of these and other kinds of alternative financial services demonstrates the high demand for financial services outside of the mainstream banking sector.

In a direct cost comparison, banks often charge less for similar services. For example, a bank may charge no fees for an account holder to cash a check. But check-cashers provide this service only for a fee. In practice, however, bank accounts are often very expensive for low-income immigrants. Capturing the savings associated with having a bank account requires careful management of the account in order to avoid high overdraft or other fees (Dunham 2001).

Minimum balance requirements discourage immigrants from owning bank accounts. For every increase of $100 in the initial minimum balance, the probability of owning an account (among lower-income households) decreases by as much as 2.5 percentage points depending on the type of account (Washington 2006). Survey responses among Latin American immigrants show that negative views about banks are related to perceptions of high minimum balance requirements (Suro et al. 2002).

The procedures that banks use to screen potential clients may be an additional barrier. Conventional methods to measure income and creditworthiness may not accurately reflect an immigrant's economic status. Immigrants may not have the pay stubs or other proof of income often required by banks to confirm income. They are often deemed ineligible to open an account when their conventionally measured assets and income are screened by standardized automated processes. For example, the Chex Systems database, which is used by approximately 80 percent of U.S. bank branches to determine whether a prospective banking customer can be permitted to open an account, is accessed with a Social Security number.

SUMMARY OF FINDINGS AND POLICY PRIORITIES

Key Findings

Native-born households have four times the total wealth and nearly six times the financial wealth of immigrant households. Some of this difference in wealth manifests itself in financial market participation. We find that immigrant households are less likely than otherwise similar households headed by native-born individuals to own a wide variety of financial assets: checking accounts, savings accounts, IRA-Keogh accounts, and stock and mutual funds.

For checking accounts, immigrants "catch up" with native-born households as they spend more time in the United States. This adaptation occurs at a fairly measured pace, playing out over the first sixteen years of U.S. residence. Checking accounts are a tool for managing current income and expenditures. For financial assets that represent the future—saving to retire, to purchase a home, or to start a business, or saving for future generations—only the small minority of immigrants who arrived before the age of eighteen catch up with otherwise similar native-born. The vast majority of immigrants who arrived in the United States as adults are less likely than the native-born to have savings accounts, IRA-Keogh accounts, and stock and mutual funds even after sixteen years or more in the United States. These patterns suggest that wealth differences between immigrants and the native-born may persist across generations.

Among immigrant subgroups, we find evidence that black and Asian immigrants are as likely to participate in various financial markets as otherwise similar native-born of black and Hispanic ethnicity. This raises an important policy question about whether the appropriate benchmark for immigrant financial access should be behavior that is similar to that of the majority or that of the minority group to which they belong.

Leading explanations for the lower financial market participation of immigrants include a desire to prioritize the accumulation of real assets, particularly housing, over financial assets; the tendency to locate in ethnic enclaves; and country-of-origin characteristics, including institutional quality. Supply-side explanations are likely to be important as well. Much of the literature focuses on understanding supply-side issues related to savings and checking accounts. Although this orientation is undoubtedly important, a more complete analysis would include analysis of supply-side issues as they relate to IRA and Keogh account ownership and stock and mutual fund ownership as well.

Policy Priorities

Our results, together with recent demographic trends, suggest that, in addition to policy interventions that focus specifically on homeownership and country-of-origin experiences, one important priority is to reach out to the children of immigrants. Persistently lower ownership of savings accounts, IRA-Keogh accounts, and stock and mutual funds among immigrant families means that the children of immigrants may face important milestones, like the decision to pursue higher education, at a financial disadvantage relative to children whose parents were born in the United States. The next wave of immigrant growth will come not from new arrivals but from the children of immigrants already here. In some states with large immigrant populations—Arizona, Illinois, and Massachusetts, for example—the second generation is already larger than the first. By 2020, second-generation Latinos are projected to outnumber their immigrant parents throughout the country (Suro and Passel 2003). Currently, the children of immigrants account for 19 percent of school-age children in the United States (Capps et al. 2004).

For children and youth, early exposure to financial literacy either in the home or at school can have an important impact on their financial decisions as adults. Using data from the PSID, Ngina Chiteji and Frank Stafford (1999) find that financial asset ownership among parents influences the portfolio decisions of their adult children. By exposing their children to financial decisionmaking early in life, parents may lower the information costs associated with learning about financial markets. In addition, schools can play an important role in lowering information costs. Douglas Bernheim, Daniel Garrett, and Dean Maki (2001) find that adults who took a high school course in money management had significantly higher savings rates than those who were not exposed to these courses in their youth.

Immigrant enclaves are another area where connections to the financial mainstream are fragile and efforts to connect immigrants (and other low-income residents) could yield dividends. In an area where ethnic concentration is very high, getting just one immigrant to open a new bank account might lead many others to do the same as they learn about the process and the benefits of account ownership from an individual who shares their country of origin and language.

A key measure of success for the millions of immigrants who come to the United States seeking economic prosperity is the extent to which they participate in the financial mainstream. By analyzing the wealth and financial decisions of immigrants relative to the native-born, we assess both their current economic position and the prospects for future generations. This analysis reveals important gaps in financial market participation that are likely to persist across generations. Policy interventions that help immigrants achieve their financial goals are likely to have broad payoffs for society as a whole, enabling us to profit more fully from the ambitions and hopes that bring many immigrants to the United States.

We are grateful for research support from the Russell Sage Foundation and to Daniel DiFranco and Shirley Chiu for excellent research assistance. We appreciate comments from Michael Barr, Rebecca Blank, Catalina Amuedo-Dorantes, Helen Koshy, and other participants at the "Access, Assets, and Poverty" conference. The views presented here are our own and are not necessarily those of the Federal Reserve Bank of Chicago.

NOTES

1. For each observation in figure 10.1, a weighted regression is performed using 80 percent (bandwidth = 0.8) of the data around that point. The data are weighted using a tri-cube weighting procedure that puts more weight on the points closest to the observation in question. The weighted regression results are used to produce a predicted value for each observation.

2. These figures are lower than similar figures from the 2001 Survey of Consumer Finances (SCF), which reports that 91 percent of all households have a transaction account. There are two main differences between the SCF and the SIPP data that are likely to account for this discrepancy. First, the SCF oversamples wealthy households, and second, the SCF includes accounts that are likely to be held by wealthy individuals in its definition of transaction accounts (money market mutual funds and call accounts at brokerage firms, for example). In addition, even when sampling weights are used, the SIPP underrepresents high-income families. For more details, see *Social Security Bulletin* 65(1):63–69 (executive summary, May 1, 2004).

3. Several authors find higher employment rates and income levels for some black immigrants relative to their native-born counterparts (see, for example, Butcher 1994; Foner 2001; Waters 1999).

4. James Smith (1995) documents item nonresponse rates for financial market participation of less than 2 percent in the SIPP. Nonresponse rates for levels of financial asset holdings are much higher, ranging from 13.3 percent for checking accounts to 41.5 percent for stock.

5. We use a linear probability model because it is computationally attractive given the large number of fixed effects, it is consistent under weak assumptions, and the coefficient estimates are easy to interpret. In particular, the coefficients on interaction terms are straightforward to interpret (see Ai and Norton 2003). Nonlinear estimation methods, such as probit or logit, generate similar results.

6. These estimated coefficients are not reported in the tables to conserve on space. They are available upon request from the authors.

7. In estimates that are not reported here, we have also examined the role of age at migration directly. Consistent with other studies that show that immigrants who arrived at younger ages have higher levels of language proficiency and higher earnings compared with immigrants who arrived as adults (see, for example, Bleakley and Chin 2004), we find relatively complete financial adaptation for immigrants who arrived in the United States as children for all of the financial assets that we consider.

8. Catalina Amuedo-Dorantes and Cynthia Bansak (2006) find that only 9 percent of the Mexican migrants surveyed by the Mexican Migration Project had a bank account in the United States. Approximately 60 percent of that sample is undocumented.

9. For some immigrants, concerns about proper documentation contribute to a more general distrust of banks. Many people fear that the failure to produce valid immigration papers at a bank will jeopardize their ability to stay in the United States (Suro et al. 2002). A nationwide survey of Latin American immigrants living in the United States found that 25 percent believed that to open an account they needed a Social Security number or a driver's license. Other common misconceptions held by immigrants are that they will lose access to the funds in their account when the documentation they used to open an account expires, or that the funds in their accounts will be liquidated if they are deported (Hogarth, Anguelov, and Lee 2005).

10. In estimates not reported here, we find patterns in the difference between immigrant and native homeownership that are similar to those we find for other financial assets when we run separate regressions for immigrants and natives with incomes below the fortieth percentile who are white, black, Hispanic, or Asian.

11. In addition to general country-of-origin characteristics like institutional quality, experiencing adverse financial outcomes may have an important impact on future behavior. In ongoing work (Osili and Paulson 2007), we find that living through a bank crisis before migrating to the United States significantly lowers the likelihood of having a bank account in the United States, even controlling for institutional quality in the country of origin.

12. Esther Duflo and Emmanuel Saez (2003) find that an employee's decision to enroll in a 401(k) plan and contribution amounts to a retirement plan in a large university are influenced by the decisions of other employees. Similarly, Harrison Hong and his colleagues (2004) argue that social interactions matter for stock market participation because individuals may learn about the benefits and costs from their friends and neighbors.

13. Of course, one reason to open a bank account is to lower the cost of remitting and to increase access to savings vehicles. Interestingly, Amuedo-Dorantes and Bansak (2006) find that the Mexican immigrants who have a bank account bring larger amounts back to Mexico with them when they return.

14. For a more complete discussion of financial institution practices as they relate to immigrants, see Paulson et al. (2006), especially chapter 3.

REFERENCES

Ai, Chunrong, and Edward C. Norton. 2003. "Interaction Terms in Logit and Probit Models." *Economic Letters* 80(1): 123–29.

Altonji, Joseph A., and Ulrich Doraszelski. 2005. "The Role of Permanent Income and Demographics in Black-White Differences in Wealth." *Journal of Human Resources* 40(1): 1–30.

Amuedo-Dorantes, Catalina, and Cynthia Bansak. 2006. "Money Transfers Among Banked and Unbanked Mexican Immigrants." *Southern Economic Journal* 73(2): 374–401.

Amuedo-Dorantes, Catalina, and Susan Pozo. 2002. "Precautionary Saving by Young Immigrants and Young Natives." *Southern Economic Journal* 69(1): 48–71.

Beck, Thorsten, Asli Demirgüç-Kunt, and Maria Soledad Martinez Peria. 2007. "Reaching Out: Access to and Use of Banking Services Across Countries." *Journal of Financial Economics* 85(1): 234–66.

Bernheim, B. Douglas, Daniel M. Garrett, and Dean M. Maki. 2001. "Education and Saving: The Long-Term Effects of High School Financial Curriculum Mandates." *Journal of Public Economics* 80(3): 435–65.

Bertaut, Carol, and Martha Starr-McCluer. 2000. "Household Portfolios in the United States." Finance and Economics Discussion Series working paper 2000-26. Washington: Board of Governors of the Federal Reserve System.

Blau, Francine D., and John Graham. 1990. "Black-White Differences in Wealth and Asset Composition." *Quarterly Journal of Economics* 105(2): 321–39.

Bleakley, Hoyt, and Aimee Chin. 2004. "Language Skills and Earnings: Evidence from Childhood Migrants." *Review of Economics and Statistics* 86(2): 481–96.

Bond, Philip, and Robert Townsend. 1996. "Formal and Informal Financing in a Chicago Ethnic Neighborhood." *Economic Perspectives* 20(4): 1–27.

Borjas, George J. 1985. "Assimilation, Changes in Cohort Quality, and the Earnings of Immigrants." *Journal of Labor Economics* 3(4): 463–89.

———. 2000. "Ethnic Enclaves and Assimilation." *Swedish Economic Policy Review* 7(2): 89–122.

———. 2002. "Homeownership in the Immigrant Population." *Journal of Urban Economics* 52(3): 448–76.

Butcher, Kristin F. 1994. "Immigrants in the United States: A Comparison with Native Blacks and Other Immigrants." *Industrial and Labor Relations Review* 47(2): 265–84.

Capps, Randolph, Michael E. Fix, Jason Ost, Jane Reardon-Anderson, and Jeffrey S. Passel. 2004. "The Health and Well-Being of Young Children of Immigrants." Research report. Washington, D.C.: Urban Institute.

Chiswick, Barry R., and Paul W. Miller. 1996. "Ethnic Networks and Language Proficiency Among Immigrants in the United States." *Journal of Population Economics* 9(1): 19–35.

Chiteji, Ngina S., and Frank P. Stafford. 1999. "Portfolio Choices of Parents and Their Children as Young Adults: Asset Accumulation by African-American Families." *American Economic Review* 89(2): 377–80.

Cobb-Clark, Deborah, and Vincent Hildebrand. 2006. "The Wealth and Asset Holdings of U.S. and Foreign-Born Households: Evidence from SIPP Data." *Review of Income and Wealth* 52(1): 17–42.

Cobb-Clark, Deborah, and Sherrie Kossoudji. 2002. "Coming Out of the Shadows: Learning About Legal Status and Wages from the Legalized Population." *Journal of Labor Economics* 20(3): 598–628.

Costanzo, Joe, Cynthia Davis, Caribert Irazi, Daniel Goodkind, and Roberto Ramirez. 2001. "Evaluating Components of International Migration: The Residual Foreign-Born Population." Population Division working paper 61. Washington: U.S. Census Bureau.

Czajka, John L., Jonathan E. Jacobson, and Scott Cody. 2004. "Survey Estimates of Wealth: A Comparative Analysis and Review of the Survey of Income and Program Participation." *Social Security Bulletin* 65(1): 63–69. Available at: http://www.ssa.gov/policy/docs/ssb/v65n1/v65n1p63.html (accessed September 15, 2008).

Duflo, Esther, and Emmanuel Saez. 2003. "The Role of Information and Social Interactions in Retirement Plan Decisions: Evidence from a Randomized Experiment." *Quarterly Journal of Economics* 118(3): 815–42.

Dunham, Constance. 2001. "The Role of Banks and Nonbanks in Serving Low- and Moderate-Income Communities." Paper presented to the Federal Reserve System Community Affairs Research Conference, "Changing Financial Markets and Community Development." Washington (April 5–6).

Dustmann, Christian. 1997. "Return Migration, Savings, and Uncertainty." *Journal of Development Economics* 52(2): 295–316.

Federal Deposit Insurance Corporation (FDIC). 2003. "Financial Education in a Dynamic Banking Environment." Washington: FDIC (November 5). Available at: http://www.fdic.gov/bank/analytical/fyi/2003/110503fyi.html (accessed October 1, 2007).

Foner, Nancy. 2001. *Islands in the City: West Indian Migration to New York.* New York: Columbia University Press.

Galor, Oded, and Oded Stark. 1990. "Migrants' Savings, the Probability of Return Migration, and Migrants' Performance." *International Economic Review* 31(2): 463–67.

Hao, Lingxin. 2004. "Wealth of Immigrant and Native-born Americans." *International Migration Review* 38(2): 518–46.

Hernandez-Coss, Raul. 2005. "The U.S.-Mexico Remittance Corridor: Lessons on Shifting from Informal to Formal Transfer Systems." Working paper 47. Washington, D.C.: World Bank and International Bank for Reconstruction and Development.

Hogarth, Jeanne M., Christoslav E. Anguelov, and Jinhook Lee. 2005. "Who Has a Bank Account? Exploring Changes over Time, 1989–2001." *Journal of Family and Economic Issues* 26(1): 7–30.

Hong, Harrison, Jeffrey D. Kubik, and Jeremy C. Stein. 2004. "Social Interaction and Stock-Market Participation." *Journal of Finance* 59(1): 137–63.

Hurst, Erik, Ming Ching Luoh, and Frank P. Stafford. 1998. "The Wealth Dynamics of American Families, 1984–1994." In *Brookings Papers on Economic Activity 1998,* vol. 1, *Macroeconomics,* edited by George L. Perry and William C. Brainard. Washington, D.C.: Brookings Institution Press.

Kossoudji, Sherrie, and Stanley A. Sedo. 2004. "Rooms of One's Own: Gender, Race, and Home Ownership as Wealth Accumulation in the United States." Discussion paper 1397. Bonn: Institute for the Study of Labor.

Krivo, Lauren J., and Robert L. Kaufman. 2004. "Housing and Wealth Inequality: Racial-Ethnic Differences in Home Equity in the United States." *Demography* 41(3): 585–605.

Menchik, Paul L., and Nancy Ammon Jianakoplos. 1997. "Black-White Wealth Inequality: Is Inheritance the Reason?" *Economic Inquiry* 35(2): 428–42.

Munshi, Kaivan. 2003. "Networks in the Modern Economy: Mexican Migrants in the U.S. Labor Market." *Quarterly Journal of Economics* 118(2): 549–99.

Oliver, Melvin L., and Thomas M. Shapiro. 1995. *Black Wealth/White Wealth: A New Perspective on Racial Inequality.* New York: Routledge.

Osili, Una Okonkwo, and Anna Paulson. 2004. "Immigrant-Native Differences in Financial Market Participation." Working paper WP-04-18. Chicago: Federal Reserve Bank of Chicago.

———. 2007. "Bank Crises and Investor Confidence: Learning from the Experience of U.S. Immigrants." Unpublished paper. Chicago: Federal Reserve Bank of Chicago.

————. 2008a. "Institutions and Financial Development: Evidence from International Migrants in the U.S." *Review of Economics and Statistics* 90(3): 498–517.

————. 2008b. "What Can We Learn about Financial Access from U.S. Immigrants? The Role of Country of Origin Institutions and Immigrant Beliefs." *World Bank Economic Review* Available at: doi:10.1093/wber/lhn019 (accessed November 21, 2008).

Paulson, Anna, Audrey Singer, Robin Newberger, and Jeremy Smith. 2006. "Financial Access for Immigrants: Lessons from Diverse Perspectives." Chicago and Washington, D.C.: Federal Reserve Bank of Chicago and Brookings Institution.

Singer, Audrey. 2004. "The Rise of New Immigrant Gateways." Living Cities Census Series. Washington: Brookings Institution, Center on Urban and Metropolitan Policy.

Smith, James P. 1995. "Racial and Ethnic Differences in Wealth." *Journal of Human Resources* 30(supp.): S158–83.

Suro, Roberto, Sergio Bendixen, B. Lindsay Lowell, and Dulce C. Benavides. 2002. "Billions in Motion: Latino Immigrants, Remittances, and Banking." Washington, D.C.: Pew Hispanic Center and Multilateral Investment Fund.

Suro, Roberto, and Jeffrey Passel. 2003. "The Rise of the Second Generation: Changing Patterns of Hispanic Population Growth." Washington, D.C.: Pew Hispanic Center.

Temkin, Kenneth, and Noah Sawyer. 2004. "Alternative Financial Service Providers." Washington: Fannie Mae Foundation and Urban Institute.

United Nations. 2005. *Costs and Benefits of International Migration.* Geneva, Switzerland: International Organization for Migration.

Vissing-Jorgensen, Annette. 2002. "Towards an Explanation of Household Portfolio Choice Heterogeneity: Nonfinancial Income and Participation Cost Structures." Working paper 8884. Cambridge, Mass.: National Bureau of Economic Research.

Washington, Ebonya. 2006. "The Impact of Banking and Fringe Banking Regulation on the Number of Unbanked Americans." *Journal of Human Resources* 41(1): 106–37.

Waters, Mary 1999. *Black Identities: West Indian Immigrant Dreams and American Realities.* Cambridge, Mass.: Harvard University Press.

Wolff, Edward N. 1998. "Recent Trends in the Size Distribution of Household Wealth." *Journal of Economic Perspectives* 12(3): 131–50.

————. 2000. "Recent Trends in Wealth Ownership, 1983–1989." Working paper 300. Annandale-on-Hudson, N.Y.: Bard College, Jerome Levy Economics Institute.

Index